Welcome to Gr...

Boasting the best mass transit in America, one of the largest green spaces in a major city, and an ambitious Million Trees initiative to green its streets and clean its air, New York City is, truly, the Big Green Apple. The city is flush with earth-friendly retailers, restaurants, and services. But in a city this size, *where* do you find them?

Right here! The definitive local source for green living, *Greenopia* brings you more than thirteen hundred of the greenest New York businesses in categories that echo your lifestyle: food, home, travel, pets, beauty, and more!

Designed to help you lead a healthier life while leaving a lighter footprint on the planet, I created Greenopia for people like me who want to be green but don't have time to research where to go for every purchase they make. As a life-long asthmatic, and after having a child who was diagnosed with autism-related learning disabilities, I was determined to reduce the toxins in our lives. In 1994, my husband and I set out to build a green home from the ground up, but finding resources was challenging. So, with the help of a great research team, I developed *Greenopia* as the go-to guide for everything green in your city.

Whether you're looking for a nontoxic dry cleaner or organic coffee shop, dye-free sheets, or all-natural pet shampoo, you'll find it in our user-friendly book. Our researchers combed the five boroughs on foot to uncover the eco-secrets of each neighborhood. Companies cannot pay to be listed and must meet several standards to be included. Each business is rated using our Green-Leaf Award system to show you its eco-commitment level at a glance.

Visit greenopia.com for updates on New York's latest offerings. Tell us what you think of the listings you find here—and let us know if there are any that we missed. We'd love to hear from you.

Gay Browne
Founder

Acknowledgments

Greenopia is a group of dedicated professionals from diverse backgrounds who have come together with a common goal. We are looking to do our part to create a better world for ourselves and to leave a lighter footprint on the one we leave behind for our families and future generations. We hope that dedication is reflected in the pages that follow and that this guide becomes a resource you use every day.

The work of our research and publishing teams was extensive, and we gratefully acknowledge their unceasing commitment. Greenopia gives special thanks to Ferris Kawar, who assembled our esteemed group of local advisors and trained our researchers; Ron Durgin, who uprooted his life to manage our research efforts; to our New York City "borough chiefs"—Victoria Foraker, Veronika Forero, Siobhan Kelly, and Sarah Woutat—who directed our teams on the ground; and all of our researchers: Elizabeth Barry, Kristy Bredin, Antuan Cannon, Joy Cernac, Darvia Douglass, Emily Erickson, Timothy Ettus, Kelsey Gerry, Christopher John, Elizabeth Kersey, Jake Kersey, Phoebe Lipkis, Katie McGlynn, Max Mecklenburg, Janna Olson, Katrin Redfern, Stan Teplitz, Tiffany Threadgould, and Arina Vikdorchik.

We also thank our editor and writer, Nancy Arbuckle, writer Jacob Gordon, and indexer Seth Maislin, as well as all those who supported our publishing efforts: Elizabeth Barry, Joy Cernac, Hannah Davey, Anna Davison, Robert Eidson, Janna Olson, and Rebecca Zendt. Our thanks also goes to all the other incredible staff members who had a hand in making this guide and Greenopia what it is: Ryan Andersen, Stephanie Hanford, Elizabeth Harrington, Craig Henderson, Doug Mazeffa, and I-Chung Wang.

A special note of gratitude is extended to everyone at Chronicle Books and Public for their creativity and support in introducing our all-new *Greenopia* series design, a design that will go with us to each new city as we grow.

And from the Greenopia team, many thanks to all of our families and loved ones for their support and understanding throughout the long hours we were absent from their lives during the creation of this guide.

Use the
off switch.

Bring
your own
mug.

Our NYC Advisors

We would like to recognize and thank our New York City Advisory Council and the experts who contributed their knowledge to each section of the guide. We are indebted to this stellar group of individuals who gave us their time and shared their expertise to help us ensure the accuracy and quality of our listings and to give us input on the guide content and criteria overall. Their collaboration and guidance were invaluable. We are enormously grateful for their input, advice, experience, and enthusiasm.

Yael Alkalay, CEO/founder, Red Flower

Chris Benedict, R.A., founder, Architecture and Energy, Ltd.

David Bergman, principal, David Bergman Architect/Fire & Water Lighting

Wendy E. Brawer, founding director, Green Map

John Calvelli, senior vice president for public affairs, Wildlife Conservation Society

Mary R. Cleaver, president, The Cleaver Co., Inc.

Paulette Cole, CEO and creative director, ABC Carpet & Home

Jill Danyelle, creative ecologist, danyelle.org

Josh Dorfman, founder and CEO, Vivavi

Emma Hamilton, agent, EcoBroker®, The Corcoran Group

Deirdre Imus, president/founder, Deirdre Imus Environmental Center for Pediatric Oncology at Hackensack University Medical Center; cofounder/codirector, Imus Cattle Ranch for Kids with Cancer; and author

Bruce M. Kahn, Ph.D., 2nd vice president, Wealth Management, Citi/Smith Barney

Dave Kirstner, CEO and founder, and **Chris Skelley**, president, Green Apple Cleaners

Phil and Randy Klein, co-owners, Whiskers Holistic Petcare

Bob Muldoon, associate regional representative, Sierra Club

Joy Pierson, president, and **Bart Potenza**, vice president and founder, Candle Cafe

Beth Karen Rehman, marketing associate, Zen Home Cleaning

Paul Steely White, executive director, Transportation Alternatives

Ellen Zachos, owner, Acme Plant Stuff

We would also like to express our appreciation to **Just Food** for creating our Eating in Season charts, to the **Monterey Bay Aquarium Foundation** for the use of their Northeast Seafood Watch Guide, to **NYC & Company** and the **City of New York** for their invaluable contributions to this guide and for embracing Greenopia and our mission, and to **Opportunity Green** and **Brand Neutral** for their contributions to our work and for helping to build sustainable enterprises.

Contents

About This Guide

This first edition of **Greenopia New York City** features more than thirteen hundred of the most eco-friendly businesses, services, and organizations in the city. **We personally surveyed every corner of the five-borough area** to uncover, identify, and evaluate green businesses.

Greenopia is not a paid directory, so companies cannot pay to be included. Instead, **the businesses listed must meet our guidelines and qualifications.**

In each section we provide an introduction that outlines **why sustainability is particularly important in that category.** We also share what **criteria we use in our evaluation and a description of how the ratings are applied for each category.** In addition, we look at what the business is doing in its day-to-day operations to demonstrate its commitment to environmentally friendly practices.

Every listed business and organization **must meet our minimum-qualifying standard** to be included in the guide and recognized as a "Greenopia Distinguished Business." In many categories we use our **own Green-Leaf Award system** to identify relative performance among listed businesses on key measures of their eco-friendly services and products. Businesses can earn from one to four leaves. Those that earn four leaves meet our highest standards.

We invite your comments about the businesses and services featured in the guide. You can play an active role in identifying and supporting the green merchants in your area and encourage businesses to become a part of the Greenopia community. If you discover a business that we have not included, or if you are a business owner yourself and we missed you, please let us know. You will find us at **greenopia.com.**

As more businesses adopt green practices, we as consumers have increased opportunities to make ecologically smart choices. **Together we will have a positive and powerful environmental impact.**

How to Use Your Greenopia Guide

Each of the twelve chapters in this guide is introduced by a local expert, many of whom served on our local Advisory Council (see page vii). Within each chapter, we've broken out the various retailers, services, and organizations by category—fifty-three in all. Browse the Contents pages for all categories, or turn to the index to find specific businesses alphabetically, or by region and category.

Scattered throughout the guide are relevant highlighted terms, which are defined in our Greenopia Glossary located in the "References" section. We have also included in each chapter a number of useful charts and practical tips for greener living.

The green businesses and resources you'll find here are the core of Greenopia. Below is a sample listing and key with a brief explanation:

1 **Candle 79** **2** 🍃🍃🍃🍃 **3** **$$$**   L D BR C
4 154 E. 79th St. **5** (Lexington Ave.), **6** Upper East Side (Man), 212-537-7179
Mon–Sat 12pm–3:30pm 5:30pm–10:30pm Sun 12pm–4pm 5pm–10pm **candlecafe.com**
7 Upscale vegan menu featuring cuisine made with local, seasonal, organic ingredients fresh from farm to table. Participates in composting program.

1 Businesses are listed in alphabetical order within the category.

2 The number of leaves awarded is based on the criteria stated at the beginning of the category. Some categories are not leaf awarded, so a leaf rating will not always appear in the listing.

3 In some listings, look for other relevant information in the category's criteria statement. For example, in "Restaurants and Cafés," one to four $ denotes the average price of an entrée, while a **B L D BR N** designation indicates if breakfast, lunch, dinner, brunch, or a late-night menu is served; a **C** means that catering services are provided.

Each entry highlights everything you need to locate or contact the business: street address and **4** cross street, **5** borough or city, **6** neighborhood, phone or other information, hours, and web address. Note that some addresses are not published by request, and if there is more than one location, all locations are listed under the business name.

Boroughs are abbreviated as follows: Bronx (Brx), Brooklyn (Bkn), Manhattan (Man), Queens (Qns), Staten Island (S.I.).

7 A description of the eco-friendly products or services offered by the business.

We encourage you to comment on the businesses, services, and resources you find in *Greenopia*. Visit **greenopia.com** to write a review and share your experiences with others.

PLANYC:
A Greener, Greater New York

In December 2006, Mayor Michael R. Bloomberg challenged New Yorkers to generate ideas for achieving a more sustainable future. New Yorkers in all five boroughs responded. The result is the most sweeping plan to enhance New York's urban environment in the city's modern history. Its impact will not only help ensure a higher quality of life for generations of New Yorkers to come; it will also contribute to a 30 percent reduction in global warming emissions.

This plan began as a means to manage New York City's growing needs within the city's limited land. It quickly grew to a more encompassing process and a more holistic approach embracing economic opportunity and growth; the preservation of diversity of all kinds; and the right to a healthy environment for all New Yorkers. The goal is a convenient and enjoyable city full of excitement and energy that is, at the same time, fair, healthy, and sustainable.

The plan focuses on five key components—land, air, water, energy, and transportation—all of them interdependent. Ultimately, the objective is for every New Yorker to breathe the cleanest air of any big city in America, to drink the purest water, to use energy in the most efficient way possible, and to fund and expand the city's transportation network on an unprecedented scale. All of these choices have lead to one ultimate impact: a reduction in global warming emissions.

Meeting these sweeping goals will require a great deal of commitment on the part of every New Yorker. Collaboration at all levels is necessary, as is the political will to make them happen. And the realities of financing cannot be ignored. This is a long-overdue investment in a better future for those who live in this amazing city and those who visit.

Here, in more detail, are some of the key components of PLANYC:

Land

- Create homes for a growing population while making housing more affordable and sustainable.

- Ensure that all New Yorkers live within a ten-minute walk of a park.

- Clean up all contaminated land in New York City.

Water

- Open 90 percent of waterways for recreation by reducing water pollution and preserving natural areas.

- Ensure drinking water is pure and reliable.

Transportation

- Add transit capacity for millions more residents, visitors, and workers to improve travel times.
- Reach a full "state of good repair" on New York City's roads, subways, and rails, for the first time in history.

Energy

- Provide cleaner, more reliable power for every New Yorker by upgrading energy infrastructure.

Air Quality

- Achieve the cleanest air quality of any city in America.

Climate Change

- Reduce global-warming emissions by 30 percent.

Together, all of these goals address the most significant issue of all: global warming. Unless greenhouse gases are reduced substantially within the next several decades, the impacts of climate change will be irreversible.

Every aspect of PLANYC targets climate change—reducing the number of cars on the road by implementing congestion pricing, upgrading existing power plants to produce cleaner power, making the city's buildings more energy efficient, greening city building codes, planting a million more trees by 2017, conserving water, improving and expanding transit systems, and greening the city's streets. The goal is to prevent an additional 15.6 million metric tons of greenhouse gases from being released in the atmosphere as the city continues to grow. New York will take the lead in meeting this challenge, and, in so doing, inspire action around the world.

But Mayor Bloomberg can't reach the target of reducing carbon emissions by 30 percent by 2030 without you. You can make a difference. We all can. Each New Yorker's small steps will add up to big strides to make New York City a healthier place to live.

Find out more about PLANYC and how you can help meet the challenges it sets forth at **nyc.gov/planyc2030.**

Eating Out

Sharing the Passion Daily

By Bart Potenza and Joy Pierson

Here in the heart of New York City, there is a beautiful green community and it's growing strong! We are thrilled to be part of that community. Our passion is compassion and sustainability. We share our passion with our guests through our vegan, organic, seasonal, delicious, and balanced cuisine, and through our "green" philosophy. We were the first certified-green restaurant in New York City, and we help other restaurants embrace green habits. We are careful to compost, our cleaning products are natural, and our energy and water systems are as efficient as they can be. Even our wholesale pastries are delivered in trucks powered by "veggie fuel." Our daily goal is to nourish the body, the mind, and the spirit of everyone who steps inside Candle Café and Candle 79.

But still at the heart of all this is our food, fresh from farm to table. Our chefs maintain wonderful relationships with a group of local farmers, each with his or her own specialty. One might produce the best mushrooms, another tomatoes, still another greens. We count on each other! Our relationships are based on mutual need and respect, and are personal statements that address, on a grassroots level, the troubling issues of the industrialization and centralization of our nation's food supply, the destruction of our environment, and the health of our children.

We believe that eating a plant-based diet and choosing local organic foods is one of the best and simplest ways to create a more peaceful, sustainable world. Taste the beauty in food fresh from farm to table. It will change your life—we know—it changed ours. As we say at the Candles, "All's well that eats well."

Bart Potenza is the founder of Candle Café and Candle 79. Joy Pierson is Bart's business partner and the coordinator of marketing for Candle Café and Candle 79. Bart and Joy coauthored *The Candle Café Cookbook: More Than 150 Enlightened Recipes from New York's Renowned Vege-tarian Restaurant.*

Restaurants and Cafés

One of the most intimate moments we share with our planet is when we're holding a fork. The food we eat comes from the earth and turns into the stuff we're made of. Every day, more restaurants and cafés are recognizing that a healthy planet yields healthy food, which ends up making healthy people. That sounds tasty to us. But not every establishment offering green eats makes a big deal out of it, so we looked below the surface to find healthy and natural fare from across the cuisine spectrum suitable for any type of budget. We encourage you to do the same. Dig a little deeper—ask your server what organic and/or locally grown items the restaurant is serving that day so you can make your selections wisely. Oftentimes, establishments don't identify on their menus all the organic and locally grown ingredients they use.

Eating green is not just about personal health and nutrition. Selecting sustainably produced or raised food means understanding the complexities of its life cycle—from production through distribution. It also means you support local farmers and are more in tune with the eco-systems around you—that you know what foods are grown locally, what's in season, and you opt for those choices. Restaurant owners, chefs, distributors, farmers, and all those linked to the "sustainable food chain" face a number of difficult choices as they strive to provide the healthiest options for their customers, the community, and the planet. We encourage you to support them in their efforts at every opportunity.

Although we looked at all sorts of ways a restaurant or café might demonstrate its commitment to sustainability, our primary focus was on the food, as we expect yours is. However, we also looked at other green aspects of the business—its composting, recycling, and energy efficiency programs—and whether or not available carryout containers were biodegradable, compostable, and/or were made with recycled, recyclable, and/or chlorine free materials.

The restaurants and cafés in our guide have demonstrated an ongoing and concerted effort toward balancing the issues outlined above. Given this commitment, our leaf awards are based on the following:

- the percentage of produce purchased that is either certified organic and/or locally grown without pesticides and chemical fertilizers;

- the percentage of poultry and eggs that are certified organic and free-range/cage-free, and/or locally raised and free-range/cage-free without the use of hormones and/or antibiotics;

- the percentage of dairy products and grains that are certified organic;

- the source of the seafood—whether it was wild-caught or farm-raised, and, if farm-raised, the composition of its diet;

- the percentage of meat (or meat substitutes such as soy) that is certified organic and/or grass fed and produced without the use of hormones and antibiotics; and

- the percentage of certified organic coffee, tea, juice, alcohol, and other nondairy beverages.

(Read more about organic standards for food at the end of this chapter.)

Of the food and/or beverages served during any given one-week period:

at least 25% meet the above criteria.

at least 50% meet the above criteria.

at least 75% meet the above criteria.

at least 90% meet the above criteria.

Average price of an entrée:

$	$10 or less	$$$	$21–$30
$$	$11–$20	$$$$	$31 and up

Meals and services provided:

B	Breakfast	BR	Brunch
L	Lunch	N	Late-night menu
D	Dinner	C	Catering

American
(Contemporary)

Applewood 🍃🍃🍃🍃 **$$$ D BR C**
501 11th St. (7th Ave.), Park Slope (Bkn), 718-768-2044
Tue–Sat 5pm–11pm Sun 10am–3pm **applewoodny.com**
American cuisine made with ingredients from local farms, hormone- and antibiotic-free meats and poultry, wild-caught fish. Outdoor dining.

A'shay 🍃 **$$ D C**
229 S. 4th St. (bet. Roebling & Havemeyer Sts.), Williamsburg (Bkn), 718-384-8014
Tue–Sat 5pm–11pm Sun 5pm–10pm **ashayrestaurant.com**
Fusion of American comfort food, Caribbean, and other international flavors with seasonal menu using some local ingredients.

Back Forty ▰▰▰▰ $$ D BR C

190 Ave. B (E. 12th St.), East Village (Man), 212-388-1990
Mon–Thu 6pm–11pm Fri–Sat 6pm–12am Sun 12pm–3:30pm 6pm–10pm
backfortynyc.com
Seasonal, locally sourced cuisine served at large farm tables. Features
bar constructed with reclaimed wood. Participates in biodiesel recycling
program. Outdoor dining available.

Blue Hill ▰▰▰▰ $$$$ D

75 Washington Pl. (bet. 6th Ave. & Washington Sq. W.), Greenwich Village
(Man), 212-539-1776
Mon–Sat 5:30pm–11pm Sun 5:30pm–10pm **bluehillnyc.com**
Seasonal American cuisine celebrating ingredients from Blue Hill at Stone
Barns farm, as well as other local Hudson Valley farms. Participates in
biodiesel recycling and composting programs. Housed in landmark New
York City speakeasy.

Broadway East ▰▰▰ $$$ B L D BR C

171 E. Broadway (bet. Rutgers & Jefferson Sts.), Lower East Side (Man),
212-228-3100
Tue–Sat 5:30pm–11pm Sun 5:30pm–10:30pm **broadwayeast.com**
Menu celebrates seasonal, organic, locally sourced ingredients. Reclaimed
wood tabletops. Participates in composting and biodiesel recycling programs.

Brooklyn Label ▰▰▰ $ B L D BR N C

180 Franklin St. (Java St.), Greenpoint (Bkn), 718-389-2806
Mon–Thu 7am–10pm Fri 7am–11pm Sat 9am–11pm Sun 9am–4pm
brooklynlabel.com
Neighborhood eatery and coffee shop with menu featuring many organic
ingredients, fair trade coffee and tea. Outdoor dining.

Brown Betty Cafe ▰▰▰ $$ B L D C

446 Grand Ave. (Fulton St.), Clinton Hill (Bkn), 718-398-8800
Mon–Thu 8am–5pm Fri–Sat 8am–10pm Sun 8am–5pm
brownbettycafe.com
Cafe serving New American cuisine using some organic ingredients.
Outdoor seating available.

Cafe Fresh ▰▰▰ $ B L D BR C

1241 Amsterdam Ave. (121st St.), Morningside Heights (Man), 212-222-6340
Daily 7:30am–8pm
Classic sidewalk cafe serving sandwiches and pastries made with organic,
seasonal ingredients; organic coffee and tea.

Chestnut ▰▰▰ $$$ D BR C

271 Smith St. (Degraw St.), Carroll Gardens (Bkn), 718-243-0049
Tue–Sat 5:30pm–11pm Sun 11:30am–3pm 5:30pm–10pm
chestnutonsmith.com
New American cuisine highlighting seasonal dishes made with locally
sourced ingredients.

City Bakery, The ▰▰▰▰ $$ B L D BR

3 W. 18th St. (5th Ave.), Union Square (Man), 212-366-1414
Mon–Fri 7:30am–7pm Sat 7:30am–6:30pm Sun 9am–6pm
thecitybakery.com
Seasonal American cuisine and fresh, house-made baked goods made with
organic and locally sourced ingredients. Participates in composting program.

Community Food & Juice 🍃🍃🍃🍃 $$$ B L D BR
2893 Broadway (bet. 112th & 113th Sts.), Morningside Heights (Man), 212-665-2800
Mon–Fri 8am–3:30pm 6pm–11pm Sat 9am–4pm 6pm–11pm Sun 9am–4pm 6pm–10pm **communityrestaurant.com**
Restaurant and cafe serving seasonal cuisine prepared with organic ingredients from local farms and Greenmarkets. Fair trade coffee, organic juice bar. Dining tables made from reclaimed wood.

Cookshop 🍃🍃🍃 $$$ L D BR
156 10th Ave. (20th St.), Chelsea (Man), 212-924-4440
Mon–Fri 11:30am–3pm 5:30pm–11:30pm Sat 11am–3pm 5:30pm–11:30pm Sun 11am–3pm 5:30pm–10pm **cookshopny.com**
Seasonal American cuisine made with ingredients from city's Greenmarkets, sustainably raised meats. Participates in biodiesel recycling and composting programs. Outdoor dining.

Corner Shop Cafe 🍃🍃🍃 $$ B L D BR
643 Broadway (Bleecker St.), NoHo (Man), 212-253-7467
Mon–Fri 9am–11pm Sat–Sun 10am–11pm **cornershopcafe.com**
American cuisine made with mostly organic ingredients; organic coffee; biodynamic wines. Participates in biodiesel recycling program. Promotes awareness of sustainable, organic eating.

Craft Restaurant 🍃🍃🍃 $$$$ L D
43 E. 19th St. (bet. Park Ave. S. & Broadway), Gramercy Park (Man), 212-780-0880
Mon–Thu 12pm–2pm 5:30pm–10pm Fri 12pm–2:15pm 5:30pm–11pm Sat 5:30pm–11pm Sun 5pm–9pm **craftrestaurant.com**
Contemporary American haute cuisine featuring seasonal, organic, locally sourced ingredients. Dishes served family style; menu changes daily.

Craftbar Restaurant 🍃🍃🍃 $$$ L D BR
900 Broadway (bet. 19th & 20th Sts.), Gramercy Park (Man), 212-461-4300
Mon–Wed 12pm–10pm Thu–Fri 12pm–11pm Sat 10am–11pm Sun 10am–5:30pm **craftrestaurant.com/craftbar.html**
Mediterranean-inspired American menu with emphasis on seasonal, locally sourced organic ingredients.

Craftsteak New York 🍃🍃🍃 $$$$ D
85 10th Ave. (15th St.), Chelsea (Man), 212-400-6699
Mon–Thu 5:30pm–10pm Fri–Sat 5:30pm–11pm Sun 5pm–9pm
craftrestaurant.com/craftsteak_newyork.html
Menu offers seasonal, locally sourced ingredients. Steak dry-aged in-house. Participates in biodiesel recycling and composting programs.

Diner 🍃🍃🍃🍃 $$ B L D BR
85 Broadway (Berry St.), Williamsburg (Bkn), 718-486-3077
Daily 11am–2am **dinernyc.com**
Menu featuring rotating seasonal specialties made with locally sourced and some organic ingredients. Participates in composting and biodiesel recycling programs.

E.A.T. 🍃 $$ B L D BR
1064 Madison Ave. (bet. E. 80th & E. 81st Sts.), Upper East Side (Man), 212-772-0022
Daily 7am–10pm **elismanhattan.com/eat.html**
Luncheonette menu offers dishes made with some organic ingredients. Prepared foods, market items.

Eat Records 🍃🍃 $ B L D BR C
124 Meserole Ave. (Leonard St.), Greenpoint (Bkn),
Mon–Fri 9am–10pm Sat–Sun 10am–8pm
Casual cafe and used-record shop serving sandwiches and light menu
prepared with ingredients from local and organic farms. Outdoor dining.
Live music every Friday.

Elettaria 🍃🍃🍃 $$$ L D C
33 W. 8th St. (MacDougal St.), Greenwich Village (Man), 212-677-3833
Daily 5pm–12am **elettarianyc.com**
Named for "green cardamom," with cuisine combining American and Indian
flavors. Seasonal ingredients from local, organic purveyors. Participates in
composting program.

Ella Cafe 🍃🍃 $$ B L D BR C
177 Bedford Ave. (bet. N. 7th & N. 8th Sts.), Williamsburg (Bkn), 718-218-8079
Mon–Fri 8am–10pm Sat 9am–10pm Sun 10am–10pm **ellacafe.com**
Cafe serving cuisine made with locally sourced organic ingredients,
organic coffee and tea. Participates in composting program.

Farm on Adderley, The 🍃🍃🍃🍃 $$ L D BR C
1108 Cortelyou Rd. (Stratford Rd.), Ditmas Park/Flatbush (Bkn), 718-287-3101
Mon 5:30pm–11pm Tue–Fri 11am–2:30pm 5:30–11pm
Sat–Sun 11am–3:30pm 5:30–11pm **thefarmonadderley.com**
American menu focused on ingredients from local farms. Compostable
take-out containers. Participates in biodiesel recycling program.

Fette Sau 🍃 $$ D N
354 Metropolitan Ave. (Havemeyer St.), Williamsburg (Bkn), 718-963-3404
Daily 5pm–11pm
Certified organic beef and pork barbecue smoked in-house. Outdoor seating
available; reclaimed wood picnic tables.

Flatbush Farm 🍃🍃 $$ D BR
76 St. Marks Ave. (bet. 6th & Flatbush Aves.), Park Slope (Bkn), 718-622-3276
Mon–Thu 5:30pm–11pm Fri–Sat 5:30pm–12am Sat–Sun 10:30am–3pm
flatbushfarm.com
Restaurant and bar committed to relationships with local farmers and
purveyors, featuring seasonal produce, locally wild-caught seafood,
hormone- and antibiotic-free meats. Outdoor dining.

Free Foods 🍃🍃🍃 $$ B L D C
18 W. 45th St. (bet. 5th & 6th Aves.), Midtown (Man), 212-302-7195
Mon–Thu 7am–8pm Fri 7am–5pm **freefoodsnyc.com**
American cuisine prepared with many organic, locally sourced ingredients.
Available to eat in, take out, or for corporate catering.

Friend of a Farmer 🍃🍃 $$ B L D BR
77 Irving Pl. (bet. E. 18th & E. 19th Sts.), Gramercy Park (Man), 212-477-2188
Mon–Thu 8am–10pm Fri 8am–11pm Sat 9:30am–11pm Sun 9:30am–10pm
friendofafarmernyc.com
Restaurant serving home-style cuisine made with seasonal ingredients,
specializing in handmade breads, muffins, pastries, and pies.

Garden Cafe, The 🍃🍃🍃 $$$ D
620 Vanderbilt Ave. (Prospect Pl.), Prospect Heights (Bkn), 718-857-8863
Tue–Sat 6pm–close
Neighborhood cafe serving American cuisine prepared with locally sourced
organic ingredients, free-range poultry and eggs. Participates in biodiesel
recycling program.

Gizzi's Coffee 🍃🍃 $ B L D BR
16 W. 8th St. (bet. MacDougal St. & 5th Ave.), Greenwich Village (Man), 212-260-9700
Mon–Fri 8am–9pm Sat 9am–10pm Sun 9am–8pm **gizzisny.com**
Organic fair trade coffee and tea shop serving sandwiches, salads, and bakery items made with mostly organic ingredients. Some vegetarian and vegan options. Live music Friday, Saturday nights.

Good Fork, The 🍃🍃🍃 $$ D
391 Van Brunt St. (Coffey St.), Red Hook (Bkn), 718-643-6636
Tue–Sat 5:30pm–10:30pm Sun 5:30pm–10pm **goodfork.com**
New American menu featuring produce from Red Hook's own neighborhood Added Value farm. Participates in composting and biodiesel recycling programs. Outdoor dining available.

Gotham Bar and Grill 🍃🍃 $$$ L D
12 E. 12th St. (University Pl.), Greenwich Village (Man), 212-620-4020
Mon–Thu 12pm–2:15pm 5:30pm–10pm Fri 12pm–2:15pm 5:30pm–11pm
Sat 5pm–11pm Sun 5pm–10pm **gothambarandgrill.com**
Contemporary American cuisine prepared with seasonal ingredients since 1984. Many organic ingredients, wild-caught seafood. Participates in biodiesel recycling and composting programs.

Gramercy Tavern 🍃🍃🍃🍃 $$$$ L D
42 E. 20th St. (bet. Broadway and Park Ave.), Gramercy Park (Man), 212-477-0777
Main Dining Room: Mon–Thu 12pm–2pm 5:30pm–10pm Fri 12pm–2pm 5:30pm–11pm Sat 5:30pm–11pm Sun 5:30pm–11pm
Tavern: Mon–Thu 12pm–11pm Fri–Sat 12pm–12am Sun 12pm–11pm
gramercytavern.com
Menu reflects blend of fresh Greenmarket ingredients and dedication to seasonal cooking. Local and artisinal cheeses, seasonal desserts.

Green Table, The 🍃🍃🍃🍃 $$ L D BR C
75 9th Ave. (15th St.), Chelsea (Man), 212-741-6623
Seasonal hours **cleaverco.com**
Seasonal cuisine featuring organic and locally sourced ingredients; organic wines and beers. Menu changes daily. Bar made from reclaimed wood. Participates in composting program.

Grocery, The 🍃🍃 $$$ D
288 Smith St. (bet. Union & Sackett Sts.), Carroll Gardens (Bkn), 718-596-3335
Tue–Thu 5:30pm–10pm Fri–Sat 5:30pm–11pm **thegroceryrestaurant.com**
Market-driven menu featuring mostly vegetarian, organic, seasonal dishes. Garden seating available summer.

Gusto Grilled Organics 🍃🍃🍃🍃 $$ B L D BR N
519 Ave. of the Americas (14th St.), Union Square (Man), 212-242-5800
Mon–Thu 8am–12am Fri–Sat 8am–2am Sun 8am–12am **gustorganics.com**
Cuisine prepared entirely with certified organic ingredients. Participates in composting program. Uses wind power.

Huckleberry Bar 🍃🍃 $ L D BR N
588 Grand St. (Lorimer St.), Williamsburg (Bkn), 718-218-8555
Mon–Sun 4pm–4am **huckleberrybar.com**
Restaurant and bar offering seasonal menu featuring cuisine and cocktails made with organic local ingredients. Nightly live entertainment.

Irving Mill 🍃🍃🍃 $$$ L D BR

116 E. 16th St. (bet. Irving Pl. & Union Square E.), Gramercy Park (Man),
212-254-1600
Mon–Tue 12pm–2:30pm 5:30pm–10pm Wed–Fri 12pm–2:30pm
5:30 pm–11pm Sat 11:30am–2:30pm 5pm–11pm Sun 11:30am–2:30pm
5pm–10pm **irvingmill.com**
Seasonal French- and Italian-influenced American fare made with locally
sourced ingredients. Most produce from Union Square Greenmarket.

Jessie's Brooklyn Kitchen 🍃🍃🍃 $$ B L D BR C

200 Smith St. (Baltic St.), Cobble Hill (Bkn), 718-858-8807
Tue–Fri 9am–6pm Sat 11am–4pm Sun 11am–3pm
jessiesbrooklynkitchen.com
Comfort food specializing in seasonal, organic ingredients. Home-delivery
community dinner plan available; organic lunch boxes for children and adults.

Josie's Kitchen 🍃🍃🍃🍃 $$ L D C

1614 2nd Ave. (E. 84th St.), Upper East Side (Man), 212-734-6644
Mon–Thu 5:30pm–10:30pm Fri 5:30pm–11pm Sat 5pm–11pm Sun 5pm–10pm
josiesnyc.com
Creative American menu specializing in organic and all-natural dishes; locally
sourced ingredients; healthy cuisine preparation.

Josie's Restaurant East 🍃🍃🍃🍃 $$ L D BR C

565 3rd Ave. (37th St.), Clinton (Man), 212-490-1558
Mon–Thu 12pm–10:30pm Fri 12pm–12am Sat 11:30am–11pm
Sun 11am–10pm **josiesnyc.com**
Eclectic menu specializing in organic and all-natural ingredients; wild-caught
seafood and sushi dishes, locally grown produce, organic and free-range
meat and poultry.

Josie's Restaurant West 🍃🍃🍃🍃 $$ L D BR C

300 Amsterdam Ave. (74th St.), Upper West Side (Man), 212-769-1212
Mon–Thu 12pm–11pm Fri 12pm–12am Sat 11am–12am
Sun 10:30am–10:30pm **josiesnyc.com**
New American cuisine featuring organic ingredients prepared healthfully;
dishes made with wild-caught seafood, free-range poultry, organic meat
and produce.

Le Pain Quotidien 🍃🍃🍃🍃 $$ B L D BR C

70 W. 40th St. (bet. 5th & 6th Aves.), Bryant Park (Man), 212-354-5224
124 7th Ave. (bet. 17th & 18th Sts.), Chelsea (Man), 212-255-2777
922 7th Ave. (58th St.), Columbus Cir. (Man), 212-757-0775
10 5th Ave. (8th St.), Greenwich Village (Man), 212-253-2324
100 Grand St. (bet. Green & Mercer Sts.), SoHo (Man), 212-625-9009
38 E. 19th St. (bet. Broadway & Park Ave.), Union Square (Man),
212-673-7900
801 Broadway (11th St.), Union Square (Man), 212-677-5277
1131 Madison Ave. (bet. 84th & 85th Sts.), Upper East Side (Man),
212-327-4900
1270 1st Ave. (bet. 68th & 69th Sts.), Upper East Side (Man), 212-988-5001
252 E. 77th St. (bet. 2nd & 3rd Aves.), Upper East Side (Man), 212-249-8600
833 Lexington Ave. (bet. 63rd & 64th Sts.), Upper East Side (Man),
212-755-5810
2463 Broadway (91st St.), Upper West Side (Man); opening April '08
494 Amsterdam Ave. (84th St.), Upper West Side (Man), 212-877-1200
50 W. 72nd St. (bet. CPW & Columbus Ave.), Upper West Side (Man),
212-712-9700
60 W. 65th St. (bet. CPW & Columbus Ave.), Upper West Side (Man),
212-721-4001

550 Hudson St. (Perry St.), West Village (Man), 212-255-2275
Hours vary by location lepainquotidien.com
Cafe and bakery serving organic breads and pastries. Light menu featuring many organic ingredients; organic coffee.

Lenora's Way 🌿🌿 $ L D BR N

303 Bedford Ave. (bet. S. 1st and S. 2nd Sts.), Williamsburg (Bkn), 718-963-3435
Seasonal hours lenorasway.com
Restaurant and bar serving American cuisine with some organic ingredients. Outdoor patio open during summer.

Little D Eatery 🌿🌿 $$ D BR

434 7th Ave. (bet. 14th & 15th Sts.), Park Slope (Bkn), 718-369-3144
Tue–Fri 6pm–11pm Sat 11am–3pm 6pm–11pm Sun 11am–3pm 6pm–10pm
littled-eatery.com
American meze-inspired cuisine prepared with some organic and locally sourced ingredients. Outdoor dining.

Lodge 🌿 $$ L D BR

318 Grand St. (Havemeyer St.), Williamsburg (Bkn), 718-486-9400
Mon–Fri 11am–11pm Sat–Sun 11am–12am lodgenyc.com
American comfort food featuring some organic ingredients, grass-fed beef, organic beers and wines. Outdoor dining.

Mae Mae 🌿🌿 $$ L D

68 Vandam St. (bet. Hudson & Varick Sts.), West Village (Man), 212-924-5109
Mon–Tue 11:30am–4pm Wed 11:30am–9pm Thu–Fri 11:30am–4pm
greatperformances.com
Seasonal menu featuring organic ingredients from own Katchkie Farm and other local farms. Extensive wine selection.

Marlow & Sons 🌿🌿🌿🌿 $$ B L D BR

81 Broadway (Berry St.), Williamsburg (Bkn), 718-384-1441
Daily 8am–12am marlowandsons.com
Neighborhood restaurant featuring raw bar and general store. Menu changes daily to reflect seasonal specialties; ingredients sourced from local artisan producers. Participates in biodiesel recycling and composting programs.

Organique 🌿🌿🌿 $ B L D C

110 E. 23rd St. (Park Ave.), Flatiron (Man), 212-674-2229
Mon–Fri 7am–10pm Sat 8am–8pm Sun 10am–8pm organiqueonline.com
Cafe serving prepared and create-your-own sandwiches, salads, hamburgers, and desserts made with organic ingredients; organic coffee and tea. Participates in composting program.

Paloma 🌿🌿🌿 $$ D BR C

60 Greenpoint Ave. (bet. Franklin & West Sts.), Greenpoint (Bkn),
718-349-2400
Tue–Thu 6pm–11pm Fri 6pm–12am Sat 11am–3:30pm 6pm–12am
Sun 11am–3:30pm 5:30pm–11:30pm palomanyc.com
Neighborhood restaurant serving locally grown produce and grass-fed, hormone-free meat dishes. Many cocktails made with house-infused organic vodka. Local artwork on display, film screenings.

Papa Lima 🌿🌿 $ B L D C

362 Bedford Ave. (bet. S. 3rd & S. 4th Sts.), Williamsburg (Bkn), 718-218-7720
Daily 9am–11pm papalimasandwich.com
Neighborhood sandwich shop using some organic and seasonal ingredients. Wi-Fi available. BYOB.

Pret A Manger 🍃🍃🍃🍃 $ B L C

60 Broad St. (bet. Beaver & Exchange Pls.), Financial District (Man),
212-825-8825
530 7th Ave. (bet. 38th & 39th Sts.), Herald Square (Man), 646-728-0750
1200 6th Ave. (bet. 47th & 48th Sts.), Midtown (Man), 646-537-0030
135 W. 50th St. (bet. 6th & 7th Aves.), Midtown (Man), 212-489-6458
1350 6th Ave. (55th St.), Midtown (Man), 212-307-6100
30 Rockefeller Ctr. Concourse Level (bet. 49th & 50th Sts.), Midtown (Man),
212-246-6944
425 Madison Ave. (bet. 48th & 49th Sts.), Midtown (Man), 646-537-0020
11 W. 42nd St. (bet. 5th & 6th Aves.), Midtown South (Man), 212-997-5520
287 Madison Ave. (bet. 40th & 41st Sts.), Midtown South (Man),
212-867-0400
1410 Broadway (39th St.), Times Square (Man), 646-572-0490
205 E. 42nd St. (bet. 2nd & 3rd Aves.), Tudor City (Man), 212-867-1905
380 Lexington Ave. (41st St.), Tudor City (Man), 212-871-6274
400 Park Ave. (bet. 54th & 55th Sts.), Tudor City (Man), 212-207-4101
630 Lexington Ave. (54th St.), Tudor City (Man), 646-497-0510
Hours vary by location **pret.com**
Cafe serving only organic foods and drinks, prepared fresh daily. Recycled
packaging.

Riverdale Garden, The 🍃🍃 $$$ D

4576 Manhattan College Pkwy. (bet. Broadway & Irwin Aves.), Riverdale
(Brx), 718-884-5232
Tue–Sat 6pm–10pm **riverdalegarden.com**
Seasonal, local American cuisine featuring wild-caught fish and some organic
poultry, produce, dairy. Cozy atmosphere, indoor fireplace, outdoor dining.
Full bar; personal wines welcome on Tue (corking fee). Banquets and private
rooms. Free valet parking.

Roebling Tea Room 🍃🍃 $ B L D BR N

143 Roebling St. (Metropolitan Ave.), Williamsburg (Bkn), 718-963-0760
Seasonal hours **roeblingtearoom.com**
Teahouse offering large selection of organic tea, full food menu featuring
organic and locally sourced ingredients. Outdoor dining.

Rose Water 🍃🍃🍃🍃 $$$ D BR

787 Union St. (bet. 5th & 6th Aves.), Park Slope (Bkn), 718-783-3800
Mon–Tue 5:30pm–10pm Wed–Thu 5:30pm–10:30pm Fri 5:30pm–11pm
Sat 10am–3pm 5:30pm–11pm Sun 10am–3pm 5:30pm–10pm
rosewaterrestaurant.com
Seasonal menu using many locally sourced ingredients. Participates in
biodiesel recycling program. Outdoor dining available.

Saul Restaurant 🍃🍃🍃🍃 $$$ D

140 Smith St. (bet. Bergen & Dean Sts.), Boerum Hill (Bkn), 718-935-9844
Mon–Thu 5:30pm–10:30pm Fri–Sat 5:30pm–11pm Sun 5:30pm–10:30pm
saulrestaurant.com
French-influenced cuisine with a seasonal menu. Ingredients sourced locally
from sustainable farms.

Savoy 🍃🍃🍃🍃 $$$ L D

70 Prince St. (Crosby St.), SoHo (Man), 212-219-8570
Mon–Thu 12pm–10:30pm Fri–Sat 12pm–11pm Sun 4pm–10pm
savoynyc.com
Contemporary, eclectic American cuisine made with locally sourced organic
ingredients, wild-caught seafood. Participates in biodiesel recycling program.

Smooch Cafe 🍃🍃🍃🍃 $ B L D BR N C
264 Carlton Ave. (Dekalb Ave.), Fort Greene (Bkn), 718-624-4075
Mon–Sat 8am–12am Sun 8am–11pm **smoochcafe.com**
Organic American cuisine. Organic desserts, selection of organic beer and
wine. Take-out containers made from biodegradable materials. Participates
in biodiesel recycling program.

Sputnik 🍃🍃🍃 $ L D N C
262 Taaffe Pl. (Dekalb Ave.), Fort Greene (Bkn), 718-398-6666
Mon–Fri 5pm–2am Sat–Sun 5pm–4am **barsputnik.com**
Bar and restaurant specializing in organic bison and ostrich burgers and
many other organic menu choices. Participates in composting and biodiesel
recycling programs. Live music.

Taste Restaurant 🍃 $$$$ B L D BR N
1413 3rd Ave. (80th St.), Upper East Side (Man), 212-717-9798
Mon–Fri 6am–10pm Sat–Sun 8am–3:30pm 6am–10pm **elizabar.com**
Seasonal dishes made with some organic ingredients; menu changes nightly.
Greenhouse on roof.

Tasting Room, The 🍃🍃🍃🍃 $$$ D BR C
264 Elizabeth St. (bet. Houston & Prince Sts.), SoHo (Man), 212-358-7831
Seasonal hours **thetastingroomnyc.com**
Casual fine dining featuring cuisine made with ingredients from local organic
vendors. Menu changes daily, reflecting market offerings.

Telepan 🍃🍃🍃🍃 $$$$ L D BR
72 W. 69th St. (Columbus Ave.), West Side (Man), 212-580-4300
Mon–Tue 5pm–11pm Wed–Thu 11:30am–2:30pm 5pm–11pm
Fri 11:30am–2:30pm 5pm–11:30pm Sat 11am–2:30pm 5pm–11:30pm
Sun 11am–2:30pm 5pm–10:30pm **telepan-ny.com**
Seasonal menu featuring organic ingredients from the city's Greenmarkets
and from local farms. Organic biodynamic wines.

Tini Wine Bar 🍃🍃🍃 $ D BR C
414 Van Brunt St. (bet. Van Dyke & Coffey Sts.), Red Hook (Bkn),
718-855-4206
Tue–Thu 5pm–11pm Fri 5pm–12am Sat 11am–12am Sun 11am–11pm
tiniwinebar.com
Wine bar and cafe serving cuisine made with artisanal, locally
sourced organic ingredients in a space furnished with reclaimed
and handmade materials.

Wave Hill Cafe 🍃🍃 $$ L D
675 W. 252nd St. (Independence Ave.), Bronx (Brx), 718-549-3200
Seasonal hours **wavehill.org/visit/cafe.html**
Cafe offering seasonal menu featuring fresh produce from Katchkie Farm
and other local producers. Participates in composting and biodiesel recycling
programs. Outdoor dining.

WD-50 🍃 $$$ D
50 Clinton St. (bet. Stanton & Rivington Sts.), Lower East Side (Man),
212-477-2900
Mon–Sat 6pm–11:30pm Sun 6pm–10:30pm **wd-50.com**
Modern American fare, using seasonal ingredients from local purveyors and
city's Greenmarkets.

`wichcraft 🍃 🍃 $ B L D BR

269 11th Ave. (27th St.), Chelsea (Man), 212-780-0577
11 E. 20th St. (Broadway), Flatiron (Man), 212-780-0577
60 E. 8th St. (Broadway), Greenwich Village (Man), 212-780-0577
1 Rockefeller Plz. (50th St.), Midtown (Man), 212-780-0577
11 W. 40th St. (6th Ave.), Midtown (Man), 212-780-0577
245 Park Ave. (47th St.), Midtown (Man), 212-780-0577
555 5th Ave. (46th St.), Midtown (Man), 212-780-0577
1 Park Ave. (33rd St.), Murray Hill (Man), 212-780-0577
568 Broadway (bet. Prince & Spring Sts.), SoHo (Man), 212-780-0577
397 Greenwich St. (Beach St.), Tribeca (Man), 212-780-0577
Hours vary by location **wichcraftnyc.com**
Handmade gourmet sandwiches and sweets prepared with all-natural ingredients, mostly locally sourced. Participates in biodiesel recycling program. Free Wi-Fi.

American
(including Southern/Cajun)

Brook's Valley 🍃 🍃 $$ D BR

415 Tompkins Ave. (Hancock St.), Bedford-Stuyvesant (Bkn), 718-443-1121
Wed–Fri 5pm–10pm Sat 12pm–10pm Sun 12pm–7pm **brooksvalley.com**
Menu offers variety of soul food, Caribbean, and vegetarian dishes. Features wild-caught seafood, locally sourced ingredients.

Egg 🍃 🍃 🍃 $$ B L D

135A N. 5th St. (Bedford Ave.), Williamsburg (Bkn), 718-302-5151
Mon–Wed 7am–3pm Thu–Fri 7am–3pm 6pm–10pm Sat 8am–2pm
6pm–10pm Sun 8am–2pm **pigandegg.com**
American, Southern-influenced cuisine made with many locally sourced and organic ingredients.

Queen's Hideaway, The 🍃 🍃 $$$ D

222 Franklin St. (Green St.), Greenpoint (Bkn), 718-383-2355
Seasonal hours **thequeenshideaway.com**
Cuisine from the American South prepared with seasonal ingredients. Participates in biodiesel recycling program. Outdoor dining available.

Ronnybrook Milk Bar 🍃 🍃 🍃 $ B L BR

75 9th Ave. (15th St.), Chelsea (Man), 212-741-6455
Mon–Fri 8:30am–7pm Sat–Sun 10am–6pm **ronnybrookmilkbar.com**
American country kitchen and classic malt shoppe featuring Ronnybrook Farm's organic dairy products and seasonal, local menu ingredients.

Asian

Hangawi 🍃 🍃 $$ L D

12 E. 32nd St. (bet. 5th & Madison Aves.), Murray Hill (Man), 212-213-0077
Mon–Thu 12pm–3pm 5pm–10:30pm Fri 12pm–3pm 5pm–11pm
Sat 12pm–11pm Sun 12pm–10pm **hangawirestaurant.com**
Korean cuisine specializing in vegan dishes made with organic ingredients.

Silent H 🍃 $$ L D C

79 Berry St. (N. 9th St.), Williamsburg (Bkn), 718-218-7063
Seasonal hours **silenthbrooklyn.com**
Vietnamese home-style cooking using sustainably raised meats and some organic ingredients.

Asian Fusion

Village Natural 🍃🍃 $$ L D BR
46 Greenwich Ave. (bet. 6th & 7th Aves.), Greenwich Village (Man),
212-727-0968
Mon–Fri 11am–11pm Sat 10am–11pm Sun 10am–10pm
Asian-inspired cuisine made with many organic ingredients, prepared
healthfully. Participates in biodiesel recycling program.

Burgers

Better Burger 🍃🍃🍃🍃 $ L D C
178 8th Ave. (W. 19th St.), Chelsea (Man), 212-989-6688
587 9th Ave. (42nd St.), Midtown West (Man), 212-629-6622
561 3rd Ave. (E. 37th St.), Murray Hill (Man), 212-949-7528
Hours vary by location **betterburgernyc.com**
Menu featuring burgers and other fast food–type cuisine prepared
healthfully. All-natural and organic locally sourced ingredients.

Black Iron Burger Shop 🍃🍃🍃🍃 $$ L D BR N C
540 E. 5th St. (Ave. A), East Village (Man), 212-677-6067
Seasonal hours **blackironburger.com**
Classic burger joint and pub serving cuisine prepared with ingredients from
local organic farms.

Zaitzeff 🍃🍃 $$ B D
72 Nassau St. (John St.), Civic Center (Man), 212-571-7272
18 Ave. B (bet. 2nd & 3rd Sts.), East Village (Man), 212-477-7137
Hours vary by location **zaitzeff.com**
Burgers made with all-natural organic beef; organic free-range chicken.

Zen Burger 🍃🍃 $ B L D
465 Lexington Ave. (bet. 45th & 46th Sts.), Midtown East (Man),
212-661-6080
Mon–Fri 8am–10pm Sat 10am–9pm Sun 10am–8pm **zenburger.com**
Healthfully prepared, fast food–style cuisine using many all-natural and
organic ingredients.

Californian

Second Helpings 🍃🍃🍃 $ B L D C
448 9th St. (7th Ave.), Park Slope (Bkn), 718-965-1925
Mon–Fri 8am–8:30pm Sat–Sun 10:30am–8pm **secondhelpings.com**
California cuisine prepared with organic locally sourced ingredients.
Free-range poultry, organic meats and produce. Outdoor dining.

Spring Street Natural Restaurant 🍃🍃🍃 $$ B L D BR
62 Spring St. (Lafayette St.), SoHo (Man), 212-966-0290
Mon–Thu 9am–11:30pm Fri 9am–12:30am Sat 10:30am–12:30am
Sun 10:30am–11:30pm **springstreetnatural.com**
Menu offers wide selection of seasonal dishes, vegetarian and macrobiotic
choices. Features organic produce, flour, and grains, free-range poultry,
wild-caught seafood.

202 ✐ $$ B L D BR
75 9th Ave. (bet. 15th & 16th Sts.), Chelsea (Man), 646-638-1173
Mon–Fri 8:30am–4:30pm 5:30pm–10pm Sat–Sun 10am–11pm
nicolefarhi.com
Cafe housed in Nicole Fahri lifestyle store serving California cuisine prepared
with organic ingredients and locally grown produce.

Wildgreen Cafe ✐ $ B L D BR
1555 3rd Ave. (88th St.), Yorkville (Man), 212-828-7656
Mon–Fri 6am–11pm Sat–Sun 7am–10:30pm
Cuisine to go, prepared at the cafe with all-natural and some
organic ingredients.

Ethiopian/African

Joloff Restaurant ✐ $ L D
930 Fulton St. (St. James), Clinton Hill (Bkn), 718-636-4011
Mon–Sat 12pm–11pm Sun 12pm–10pm
Mostly vegan West African and Senegalese food made with locally
grown produce.

French

Cafe ✐✐✐✐ $$ D
973 Columbus Ave. (108th St.), Upper West Side (Man), 212-222-2033
Tue–Sat 6pm–11pm **marcandblue.com**
Family-owned restaurant serving French-Caribbean cuisine made with
organic, seasonal ingredients.

Café Cluny ✐ $$$$ B L D BR
284 W. 12th St. (W. 4th St.), West Village (Man), 212-255-6900
Mon–Fri 8am–12am Sat–Sun 9am–4pm 5:30pm–12am **cafecluny.com**
Neighborhood restaurant applying French twist to traditional American
cuisine, using some seasonal, organic ingredients.

Cafe Lalo ✐✐✐ $ B L D BR N
201 W. 83rd St. (Amsterdam Ave.), Upper West Side (Man), 212-496-6031
Mon–Thu 8am–2am Fri 8am–4am Sat 9am–4am Sun 9am–2am **cafelalo.com**
French cafe serving organic menu items, organic pastries and desserts, fair
trade and organic coffee and tea. Participates in composting program.

Chanterelle ✐✐ $$$ L D
2 Harrison St. (Hudson St.), Tribeca (Man), 212-966-6960
Mon–Wed 5:30pm–11pm Thu–Sat 12pm–2:30pm 5:30pm–11pm
Sun 5pm–10:30pm **chanterellenyc.com**
Traditional French cuisine featuring organic meat and seafood dishes, other
organic ingredients. Participates in biodiesel recycling program.

Cosmo Crepérie ✐ $ B L C
875 3rd Ave. (E. 53rd St.), Turtle Bay (Man), 212-223-3930
Mon–Fri 7am–6pm **cosmocreperie.com**
Family-run business serving traditional French crepes made with some organic ingredients, organic coffee and tea. Participates in composting program.

Fada Restaurant *$$ L D BR*

530 Driggs Ave. (N. 8th St.), Williamsburg (Bkn), 718-388-6607
Mon–Thu 4pm–12am Fri–Sat 10am–1am Sun 10am–12am **fadany.com**
French bistro offering some dishes made with organic meats, free-range poultry, and wild-caught fish. Outdoor seating available.

Ici *$$$ B L D BR C*

246 Dekalb Ave. (Vanderbilt Ave.), Fort Greene (Bkn), 718-789-2778
Tue–Thu 8am–10pm Fri–Sat 8am–11pm Sun 8am–10pm **icirestaurant.com**
Seasonal French cuisine promoting locally grown produce, wild-caught fish, all-natural and organic meats. Patio seating available.

Jules Bistro *$$ B L D BR*

65 St. Marks Pl. (bet. 1st & 2nd Aves.), East Village (Man), 212-477-5560
Mon–Fri 11am–11pm Sat–Sun 9:30am–12am **julesbistro.com**
Traditional French bistro serving cuisine made with many organic locally sourced ingredients; wild-caught fish and seafood. Live jazz.

Mas (Farmhouse) *$$$$ D*

39 Downing St. (Bedford St.), West Village (Man), 212-255-1790
Daily 6pm–11:30pm **masfarmhouse.com**
French-inspired cuisine, with seasonal menu featuring local market ingredients, wild-caught fish and seafood, organic meats.

Payard Bistro *$$$ B L D C*

1032 Lexington Ave. (74th St.), Upper East Side (Man), 212-717-5252
Mon–Thu 12pm–10:30pm Fri–Sat 12pm–11pm **payard.com**
Seasonal menus offer French cuisine inspired by locally produced ingredients found at Union Square Greenmarket.

Provence *$$$ L D BR*

38 MacDougal St. (Prince St.), SoHo (Man), 212-475-7500
Mon–Fri 5:30pm–close Sat–Sun 11:30am–3pm 5:30pm–close
provencenyc.com
Provençal cuisine made with organic locally sourced ingredients.

Simple Cafe *$ B L D BR C*

346 Bedford Ave. (S. 3rd St.), Williamsburg (Bkn), 718-218-7067
Tue–Sun 9am–11pm **simplecafenyc.com**
Neighborhood bistro serving French-inspired food prepared with some locally grown and organic ingredients. Outdoor seating available.

Tocqueville *$$$$ L D C*

1 E. 15th St. (5th Ave.), Union Square (Man), 212-647-1515
Mon–Sat 11:45am–2:30pm 5:30pm–10:30pm **tocquevillerestaurant.com**
Seasonal French-American cuisine made with fresh ingredients from local Union Square Greenmarket.

Italian

Aurora *$$$ L D BR*

510 Broome St. (Watts St.), SoHo (Man), 212-334-9020
70 Grand St. (Wythe Ave.), Williamsburg (Bkn), 718-388-5100
Mon–Wed 12pm–3:30pm Thu 12pm–3:30pm 6pm–11pm
Fri 12pm–3:30pm 6pm–12am Sat–Sun 11am–4pm 6pm–12am
auroraristorante.com
Regional Italian cuisine, with fresh pasta, breads, and desserts made on premises using local and some organic ingredients. Participates in biodiesel recycling program.

Del Posto 🍃🍃 $$$$ L D

85 10th Ave. (bet. 15th &16th Sts.), Chelsea (Man), 212-497-8090
Mon–Tue 5pm–11pm Wed–Fri 12pm–2pm 5pm–11pm Sat 4:30pm–11pm
Sun 4:30pm–10pm **delposto.com**
Italian menu featuring local, seasonal fare prepared with some organic
ingredients. Participates in composting and biodiesel recycling programs.
Live music some evenings.

Esca 🍃🍃🍃🍃 $$$ B L D

402 W. 43rd St. (bet. 9th & 10th Aves.), Clinton (Man), 212-564-7272
Mon 12pm–2:30pm 5pm–10:30pm Tue–Sat 12pm–2:30pm 5pm–11:30pm
Sun 4:30pm–10:30pm **esca-nyc.com**
Southern Italian cuisine featuring fresh wild-caught fish and seafood; largely
organic menu changes daily. Outdoor dining.

Franny's 🍃🍃🍃🍃 $$ L D

295 Flatbush Ave. (St. Marks Ave.), Prospect Heights (Bkn), 718-230-0221
Tue–Thu 5:30pm–11pm Fri 5:30pm–11:30pm Sat 12pm–11:30pm
Sun 12pm–10pm **frannysbrooklyn.com**
Family-owned restaurant featuring Italian cuisine made with organic locally
grown ingredients. Menus printed on recycled paper; biodegradable to-go
containers; participates in composting program.

Hearth 🍃🍃🍃 $$$$ D

403 E. 12th St. (1st Ave.), East Village (Man), 646-602-1300
Mon–Thu 6pm–10pm Fri–Sat 6pm–11pm Sun 6pm–10pm
restauranthearth.com
Italian home-style cuisine prepared with organic ingredients from local
markets and farms. Participates in composting program.

Locanda Vini e Olli 🍃🍃 $$$ D

129 Gates Ave. (Cambridge St.), Clinton Hill (Bkn), 718-622-9202
Tue–Thu 6pm–10:30pm Fri–Sat 6pm–11:30pm Sun 6pm–10pm
locandany.com
Tuscan menu offering home-style cooking; handmade pasta, some locally
grown organic ingredients. Outdoor dining.

NorthWest Bistro 🍃🍃🍃 $$$ L D BR N

392 Columbus Ave. (bet. W. 78th & W. 79th Sts.), Upper West Side (Man),
212-799-4530
Mon 11:30am–12am Tue–Thu 11:30am–1am Fri–Sat 11:30am–3am
Sun 11:30am–12am
Bistro serving American-Italian cuisine made with organic and locally grown
ingredients. Patio seating available in summer.

Scottadito Osteria Toscana 🍃🍃🍃 $$ L D BR C

788A Union St. (bet. 6th & 7th Aves.), Park Slope (Bkn), 718-636-4800
Daily 11am–11pm **scottadito.com**
Traditional Tuscan cuisine committed to serving dishes made with ingredi-
ents sustainably grown, harvested, and sourced. Outdoor dining.

Latin American
(including Caribbean/Cuban)

Cafe Habana 🌿🌿 $ L D BR C
17 Prince St. (Elizabeth St.), SoHo (Man), 212-625-2001
Daily 9am–12am **ecoeatery.com**
Central Mexican- and Cuban-influenced Latin cuisine made with many locally
sourced, sustainably grown ingredients. To-go cafe next door.

Empanadas del Parque Cafe 🌿 $ B L D C
56-27 Van Doren St. (108th St.), Corona (Qns), 718-592-7288
Tue–Sun 7am–9pm **empanadascafe.com**
Family-run cafe offering handmade empanadas prepared to order using
organic whole grain flour.

H.I.M. Ital Restaurant & Juice Bar 🌿🌿 $ L D C
754 Burke Ave. (White Plains Rd.), Williamsbridge (Brx), 718-653-9627
Mon–Sat 10:30am–9:30pm
Organic, vegan, salt-free Caribbean cuisine; fresh organic juice bar.

Habana Outpost 🌿🌿🌿 $ L D BR
757 Fulton St. (S. Portland Ave.), Fort Greene (Bkn), 718-858-9500
Seasonal hours **ecoeatery.com**
Cuban- and Central Mexican–influenced Latin cuisine prepared with sustain-
able ingredients. Housed in solar-powered building; compostable packaging.
Outdoor dining. Live entertainment some evenings.

Palo Santo 🌿🌿🌿 $$ L D BR
652 Union St. (4th Ave.), Park Slope (Bkn), 718-636-6311
Seasonal hours **palosanto.us**
Menu featuring locally sourced organic ingredients; rooftop garden provides
some fresh produce and herbs. Interior constructed with salvaged architectural elements. Participates in composting program.

Mediterranean
(including Greek)

Cafe Bar 🌿🌿 $ B L D BR N
32-90 36th St. (34th Ave.), Astoria (Qns), 718-204-5273
Mon–Fri 11am–2am Sat–Sun 11am–4am **cafebarastoria.com**
Cafe and bar offering light fare made with some organic ingredients;
organic wines; fresh juices.

Cavo Cafe Lounge & Garden 🌿 $$$ L D N
42-18 31st Ave. (42nd St.), Astoria (Qns), 718-721-1001
Daily 5pm–4am **cavocafelounge.com**
Modern Greek cuisine featuring organic poultry, wild-caught fish, and
some local organic meats and produce. Live entertainment; outdoor garden
seating available.

DUMBO General Store 🌿🌿 $ B L BR C
111 Front St. (bet. Washington & Adams Sts.), DUMBO (Bkn), 718-855-5288
Mon–Fri 7:30am–4pm Sat 8am–4pm Sun 8:30am–4pm
dumbogeneralstore.com
Cafe featuring salads, panini, and breakfast dishes made with many organic
ingredients; organic fair trade coffee and tea.

E.U., The $$ L D BR C
235 E. 4th St. (Ave. A), East Village (Man), 212-254-2900
Mon–Fri 5:30pm–11:30pm Sat 11:30am–3pm 5:30pm–11:30pm
Sun 11:30am–3pm 5:30pm–10pm **theeunyc.com**
Pan-European menu featuring classic national dishes prepared with organic
and locally sourced meats, produce, and other ingredients.

Five Points $$$ L D BR
31 Great Jones St. (Lafayette St.), NoHo (Man), 212-253-5700
Mon–Fri 12pm–3pm 5:30pm–11:30pm Sat 11:30am–3pm 5:30pm–11:30pm
Sun 11:30am–3pm 5:30pm–10:00pm **fivepointsrestaurant.com**
Rustic Mediterranean-influenced cuisine featuring seasonal, locally sourced,
mostly organic ingredients. Participates in composting and biodiesel recycling programs. Outdoor dining.

Il Buco $$$ L D
47 Bond St. (bet. Bowery & Lafayette Sts.), NoHo (Man), 212-533-1932
Mon 6pm–12am Tue–Thu 12pm–3:30pm 6pm–12am
Fri–Sat 12pm–3:30pm 6pm–1am Sun 5pm–12am **ilbuco.com**
Mediterranean cuisine made with ingredients sourced from local farms
and producers. Participates in biodiesel recycling program. Antique
interior decor.

Little Owl, The $$$ L D BR
90 Bedford St. (Grove St.), Greenwich Village (Man), 212-741-4695
Mon–Fri 5pm–11pm Sat 11am–2pm 5pm–11pm Sun 11am–2pm 5pm–10pm
thelittleowlnyc.com
Small restaurant with Mediterranean-influenced seasonal menu committed
to local, fresh ingredients. Participates in biodiesel recycling program.

Siggy's Good Food $$ B L D C
76 Henry St. (Clark St.), Brooklyn Heights (Bkn), 718-237-3199
Mon–Fri 11am–10:30pm Sat 9am–10:30pm Sun 9am–9:30pm
siggysgoodfood.com
Traditional and original Mediterranean recipes, including many vegetarian
options, made with organic ingredients. Selection of organic wine and beer,
organic juice bar. Outdoor dining available.

Superfine $$ L D BR
126 Front St. (Pearl St.), DUMBO (Bkn), 718-243-9005
Tue–Sat 11am–3pm 6pm–11pm Sun 11am–3pm 4pm–10pm
Mediterranean cuisine featuring organic ingredients, many locally sourced.
Live entertainment some evenings.

Thalassa $$$$ L D BR C
179 Franklin St. (Hudson St.), Tribeca (Man), 212-941-7661
Seasonal hours **thalassanyc.com**
Fine Greek cuisine featuring wild-caught fish, raw bar, organic and
free-range chicken, organic produce, and artisanal cheeses. Participates
in biodiesel recycling program. Live entertainment some evenings.

Mexican

Bonita 🌿🌿🌿 $$ L D BR C
243 Dekalb Ave. (bet. Vanderbilt & Claremont Aves.), Fort Greene (Bkn), 718-622-5300
338 Bedford Ave. (bet. S. 2nd & S. 3rd Sts.), Williamsburg (Bkn), 718-384-9500
Mon–Thu 11am–11pm Fri–Sat 11am–12am Sun 11am–11pm **bonitanyc.com**
Mexican cuisine featuring seasonal and organic ingredients; organic meats and poultry, organic and wild-caught seafood.

Cosmic Cantina 🌿🌿🌿 $ L D N
101 3rd Ave. (13th St.), East Village (Man), 212-420-0975
Daily 11am–5am
Burritos, tacos, quesadillas, and other Mexican fare featuring organic ingredients. Vegetarian and vegan choices.

Hecho en DUMBO 🌿🌿 $$ D
111 Front St. (bet. Washington & Adams Sts.), DUMBO (Bkn), 718-855-5288
Mon–Wed 6pm–10:30pm Thu–Sat 6pm–12am **hechoendumbo.com**
Traditional Mexican dishes made with local organic ingredients. Live music some evenings.

Taco Chulo 🌿🌿 $ L D BR
318 Grand St. (bet. Havemeyer St. & Marcy Ave.), Williamsburg (Bkn), 718-302-2485
Mon–Fri 12pm–11pm Sat–Sun 11am–11pm **tacochulo.com**
Taco bar and margarita lounge featuring organic ingredients, many vegetarian options. Participates in biodiesel recycling program. Live entertainment some evenings.

Middle Eastern

Nanoosh 🌿🌿 $ L D
2012 Broadway (bet. 68th & 69th Sts.), Lincoln Square (Man), 212-362-7922
Mon–Tue 11am–10pm Thu–Sat 11am–11pm Sun 11am–10pm **nanoosh.com**
Organic hummus bar serving fresh Mediterranean foods. Live entertainment some evenings.

Pizza

Cafe Viva 🌿🌿 $ L D
2578 Broadway (bet. 97th & 98th Sts.), Upper West Side (Man), 212-663-8482
Daily 11:30am–11:30pm
Cafe serving gourmet pizzas and pastas made with many organic ingredients.

Fornino: The Art and Science of Pizza 🌿🌿 $$ L D
187 Bedford Ave. (N. 7th St.), Williamsburg (Bkn), 718-384-6004
Mon–Thu 12pm–11pm Fri–Sat 12pm–12am Sun 12pm–11pm
Artisanal pizzas baked in wood-burning ovens, prepared with organic flour, produce, and meats. On-site greenhouse provides fresh vegetable and herb ingredients.

Pintaile's Pizza 🌿 $ L D

26 E. 91st St. (Madison Ave.), Upper East Side (Man), 212-722-1967
1573 York Ave. (E. 84th St.), Yorkville (Man), 212-396-3479
Daily 11am–9:30pm
Thin-crust pizza made with organic flour and wheat germ; varied choices
of toppings.

Slice, the Perfect Food 🌿🌿🌿🌿 $ L D N C

1413 2nd Ave. (bet. 73rd & 74th Sts.), Upper East Side (Man), 212-249-4353
Mon–Thu 11am–11pm Fri–Sat 11am–1am Sun 11am–11pm **sliceperfect.com**
Pizza made with all-natural organic ingredients. Some vegan and
gluten-free choices.

Seafood

A Salt & Battery 🌿🌿🌿 $$ L D

112 Greenwich Ave. (bet. 12th & 13th Sts.), West Village (Man),
212-691-2713
Daily 11:30am–10:00pm **asaltandbattery.com**
Classic fish-and-chip shop serving wild-caught fish and Long Island–grown
potatoes.

Vegetarian/Vegan/Raw

Angelica Kitchen 🌿🌿🌿🌿 $$ L D

300 E. 12th St. (2nd Ave.), East Village (Man), 212-473-0305
Daily 11:30am–10:30pm **angelicakitchen.com**
Organic vegan cuisine made with ingredients from local farms and
producers. Participates in composting program.

Bliss Bakery & Cafe 🌿🌿🌿 $$ B L D BR

191 Bedford Ave. (N. 7th St.), Williamsburg (Bkn), 718-599-2547
Mon–Fri 9am–11pm Sat–Sun 10am–11pm
Cafe serving vegan and vegetarian dishes prepared with organic, locally
sourced ingredients.

Blossom 🌿🌿🌿 $$ L D BR C

187 9th Ave. (bet. 21st & 22nd Sts.), Chelsea (Man), 212-627-1144
466 Columbus Ave. (bet. 82nd & 83rd Sts.), West Side (Man), 212-875-2600
Mon–Fri 11am–10pm Sat 11am–10:30pm Sun 11am–9:30pm
blossomnyc.com
Vegan cuisine featuring gourmet recipes prepared with organic, locally
grown ingredients.

Bonobo's Vegetarian 🌿🌿🌿 $ L D BR

18 E. 23rd St. (bet. Madison & Park Aves.), Gramercy Park (Man),
212-505-1200
Daily 11am–8pm **bonobosrestaurant.com**
Vegan, raw cuisine using organic ingredients. Participates in
composting program.

Bread.A Bakery 🌿🌿🌿 $ B L D C
41-46 College Point Blvd. (bet. 41st & Sanford Aves.), Flushing (Qns),
718-886-1888
Mon 8am–8pm Tue–Wed 8am–7:30pm Thu 8am–7pm Fri–Sat 8am–8pm Sun
8:30am–7:30pm **breadaorganic.com**
Bakery and cafe serving Asian-influenced vegan and vegetarian cuisine,
sandwiches, soups, salads. Bakery prepares fresh, handmade vegan and
vegetarian breads, cookies, and cakes prepared with natural and organic
ingredients. Organic coffee, tea, and beverages.

BushBaby 🌿 $ B L D BR C
1197 Fulton St. (Bedford Ave.), Bedford-Stuyvesant (Bkn), 718-636-5336
Tue–Fri 10am–9pm Sat 9am–9pm Sun 9am–5pm
Neighborhood cafe serving light vegetarian and vegan-friendly cuisine using
some organic ingredients.

Candle 79 🌿🌿🌿🌿🌿 $$$ L D BR C
154 E. 79th St. (Lexington Ave.), Upper East Side (Man), 212-537-7179
Mon–Sat 12pm–3:30pm 5:30pm–10:30pm Sun 12pm–4pm 5pm–10pm
candlecafe.com
Upscale vegan menu featuring cuisine made with local, seasonal organic
ingredients fresh from farm to table. Participates in composting program.

Candle Cafe 🌿🌿🌿🌿 $$ L D BR C
1307 3rd Ave. (E. 75th St.), Upper East Side (Man), 212-472-0970
Mon–Sat 11:30am–10:30pm Sun 11:30am–9:30pm **candlecafe.com**
Vegetarian and vegan cuisine prepared with seasonal organic ingredients
sourced mostly from local farms. Participates in composting program and
delivers wholesale pastries in veggie-fueled trucks.

Caravan of Dreams 🌿🌿🌿🌿 $$ B L D BR C
405 E. 6th St. (1st Ave.), East Village (Man), 212-254-1613
Mon–Fri 11am–11pm Sat 11am–12am Sun 11am–11pm
caravanofdreams.net
Neighborhood restaurant serving vegan cuisine made with organic ingredients. Outdoor dining. Participates in composting and biodiesel recycling
programs. Live entertainment some evenings.

Counter 🌿🌿🌿🌿 $$ L D BR N C
105 1st Ave. (6th St.), East Village (Man), 212-982-5870
Mon–Thu 5pm–12am Fri 5pm–1am Sat 11am–1am Sun 11am–12am
counternyc.com
French-Mediterranean bistro and wine and martini bar dedicated to serving
organic vegetarian and vegan cuisine. Menu features ingredients from local
organic farmers, artisans, winemakers. Over 300 organic and biodynamic wines.

Earth Matters 🌿🌿🌿 $ B L D BR
177 Ludlow St. (bet. Houston & Stanton Sts.), Lower East Side (Man),
212-475-4180
Daily 8am–11pm **earthmatters.com**
Market serving prepared dishes made with organic ingredients; many
vegetarian choices. Fair trade coffee, organic juice, and smoothies.
Organic grocery items.

Earth Tonez 🌿🌿🌿🌿 $ L D C
349 5th Ave. (5th St.), Park Slope (Bkn), 718-395-1516
Mon–Thu 11am–9pm Fri 11am–5pm Sat 5pm–11pm Sun 11am–9pm
Vegetarian and vegan cafe serving soups, sandwiches, wraps, salads, and
desserts made with organic ingredients. Biodegradable to-go containers.

Green Bean Cafe, The 🍃🍃🍃🍃 $ B L D C
1431 York Ave. (E. 75th St.), Yorkville (Man), 212-861-8060
Seasonal hours **beangonegreen.com**
Neighborhood cafe featuring vegetarian and vegan dishes made with organic ingredients; fair trade, organic coffee and tea.

Happy Buddha 🍃🍃🍃 $$ L D
135–37 37th Ave. (bet. Main & Prince Sts.), Flushing (Qns), 718-358-0079
Daily 11am–10pm **happybuddha.com**
Vegetarian, Buddhist-inspired cuisine; organic teas, smoothies, and some entrees.

Imhotep 🍃🍃🍃🍃 $ B L C
734 Nostrand Ave. (Park Pl.), Crown Heights (Bkn), 718-493-2395
Daily 8am–2pm
Cafe and natural foods market serving vegan cuisine made with organic, locally grown ingredients; organic juices.

Jill's 🍃🍃🍃🍃 $$ L D C
231 Court St. (bet. Baltic & Warren Sts.), Cobble Hill (Bkn), 718-797-0330
Mon–Sat 11am–9pm Sun 11am–8pm **jillpettijohn.com**
Organic, vegan cafe offering a fusion of raw and cooked food. Also offers nutritional cleanse. Outdoor dining.

Jubbs Longevity 🍃🍃🍃🍃 $$ L D
508 E. 12th St. (bet. Aves. A & B), East Village (Man), 212-353-5000
Daily 11am–9pm **jubbslongevity.com**
Deli and patisserie serving organic, vegan meals, desserts, drinks, snacks. Organic "LifeFood" and chef classes available. Participates in composting program.

Lucky Cat, The 🍃🍃🍃 $ L D BR N C
245 Grand St. (bet. Driggs Ave. & Roebling St.), Williamsburg (Bkn), 718-782-0437
Mon–Fri 12pm–late Sat–Sun 10am–close **theluckycat.com**
Vegetarian cuisine using only organic, locally grown ingredients. Features live performances some evenings. Outdoor dining.

Mamalu Cafe 🍃🍃🍃🍃 $$ B L D BR C
232 N. 12th St. (bet. Union & Driggs Aves.), Williamsburg (Bkn), 718-486-6312
Tue–Fri 9am–7pm Sat 10am–7pm Sun 10am–6pm **mamalunyc.com**
Vegetarian cafe serving gourmet organic cuisine and snacks. Designed specially for children, featuring large indoor play space.

Mana 🍃🍃🍃 $$ L D
646 Amsterdam Ave. (bet. 91st & 92nd Sts.), Upper West Side (Man), 212-787-1110
Daily 11:30am–10:30pm **manaorganiccafe.com**
Vegetarian, Asian-inspired cuisine prepared healthfully with organic ingredients, cooked with filtered water. Participates in biodiesel recycling program.

Mighty Diamond 🍃🍃 $ L D N
347 Graham Ave. (bet. Metropolitan Ave. & Conselyea St.), Williamsburg (Bkn), 718-384-7778
Daily 12pm–11pm
Vegetarian restaurant serving Caribbean cuisine made with many organic ingredients. Outdoor dining.

Organic Grill, The 🌿🌿🌿🌿 $ B L D BR

123 1st Ave. (E. 7th St.), East Village (Man), 212-477-7177
Mon–Thu 12pm–10pm Fri 12pm–11pm Sat 10am–11pm Sun 10am–10pm
theorganicgrill.com
Cuisine prepared with organic ingredients from local and artisanal producers; mostly vegetarian dishes, some wild-caught seafood.

Organic Soul Cafe 🌿🌿🌿 $$ B L D BR N

638 E. 6th St., 1st Flr. (bet. Aves. B & C), East Village (Man), 212-677-1863
Seasonal hours **sixthstreetcenter.org/cafe_index.html**
Vegetarian and vegan cafe offering raw options, some fish dishes.
Outdoor dining.

Phoebe's Cafe 🌿 $ B L BR

323 Graham Ave. (Metropolitan Ave.), Williamsburg (Bkn), 718-599-3218
Seasonal hours **phoebescafe.com**
Cafe serving vegetarian and seafood dishes using some locally produced
and organic ingredients. Garden seating available.

Pure Food and Wine 🌿🌿🌿🌿 $$$ D

54 Irving Pl. (bet. 17th & 18th Sts.), Gramercy Park (Man), 212-477-1010
Daily 5:30pm–10:30pm **purefoodandwine.com**
Raw organic cuisine featuring local, seasonal ingredients. Large selection of
organic and biodynamic wines. Organic herb garden services kitchen. Participates in composting and biodiesel recycling programs; compostable to-go
containers. Garden-style dining.

Quantum Leap 🌿🌿🌿 $$ L D BR

203 1st Ave. (bet. 12th & 13th Sts.), East Village (Man), 212-673-9848
226 Thompson St. (bet. Bleecker & W. 3rd Sts.), West Village (Man),
212-677-8050
Hours vary by location
Vegan and vegetarian cuisine made with organic ingredients since 1974.
Participates in biodiesel recycling program.

Quintessence 🌿🌿🌿🌿 $$ L D BR

263 E. 10th St. (bet. 1st Ave. & Ave. A), East Village (Man), 646-654-1823
Seasonal hours **raw-q.com**
Raw organic menu featuring international influences in a spa-like atmosphere. Participates in biodiesel recycling program. Raw food classes and
other events.

Reboot 🌿🌿🌿🌿 $$ D C

37 Ave. A (bet. E. 2nd & E. 3rd Sts.), East Village (Man), 212-748-9797
Wed–Sun 5pm–12am **rebootnyc.com**
Vegetarian pizzas and entrees made with organic, locally sourced ingredients. Incorporates macrobiotic, vegan, ayurvedic, and raw foods principles
into its menu. Participates in biodiesel recycling and composting programs.
Open audio/visual jam Sunday nights

Sacred Chow 🌿🌿🌿🌿 $ L D BR C

277 Sullivan St. (bet. Bleecker and 3rd Sts.), Greenwich Village (Man),
212-337-0863
Mon–Thu 11am–10pm Fri–Sat 11am–11pm Sun 11am–10pm
sacredchow.com
Vegan bistro serving all-organic cuisine, with most ingredients locally
sourced. Organic beer, wine, and herbal elixirs.

Souen $$$ L D
210 6th Ave. (Prince St.), SoHo (Man), 212-807-7421
28 E. 13th St. (bet. University Pl. & 5th Ave.), Union Square (Man),
212-627-7150
Hours vary by location **souen.net**
Macrobiotic restaurant serving some organic, unrefined and unprocessed,
vegan and vegetarian cuisine.

Strictly Roots 🍃🍃🍃🍃 $ L D
2058 Adam Clayton Powell Blvd. (bet. 122nd & 123rd Sts.), Central Harlem
(Man), 212-864-8699
Mon–Fri 8am–10pm Sat 11am–10pm Sun 12pm–8pm
West Indian and Caribbean vegan cuisine using all-organic ingredients.
Menu changes daily.

Teany 🍃🍃🍃🍃 $ B L D BR
90 Rivington St. (bet. Orchard & Ludlow Sts.), Lower East Side (Man),
212-475-9190
Mon–Thu 10am–11pm Fri–Sat 10am–1am Sun 10am–11pm **teany.com**
Cafe serving organic vegetarian and vegan cuisine. More than 95 tea varieties, many organic and fair trade. Participates in composting and biodiesel
recycling programs.

Uncle Marky's Organics 🍃🍃 $$ L D
235 E. 53rd St. (bet. 2nd & 3rd Aves.), Midtown East (Man), 212-421-6444
Mon–Fri 11am–9:30pm Sat 12pm–7:30pm Sun 12pm–8:30pm
Take-out eatery, serving cuisine made with many certified organic ingredients. Vegan options.

Uptown Juice Bar 🍃🍃🍃 $ B L D BR
54 W. 125th St. (bet. 5th Ave. & Malcolm X Blvd.), Central Harlem (Man),
212-987-2660
Daily 8am–10pm **uptownjuicebar.com**
Cafe serving eclectic cuisine made with mostly organic ingredients. Prepared
foods, vegetarian menu, nondairy desserts and bakery items. Organic juice bar.

Urban Spring 🍃🍃🍃🍃 $ B L D
185 Dekalb Ave. (Carlton St.), Fort Greene (Bkn), 718-237-0797
Mon–Sat 8am–7pm Sun 9am–6pm **urbanspring.net**
Vegan and vegetarian cuisine made with organic, locally grown ingredients;
organic juices, fruit smoothies, snacks. Biodegradable packaging. Participates in biodiesel recycling and composting programs. Built with reclaimed
materials from Washington Square's Peace Church.

did you know?

If every U.S. citizen ate just one meal a week composed of locally and organically raised meats and
produce, we'd reduce our country's oil consumption
by over 1.1 million barrels of oil every week.

Organic agriculture has the potential to mitigate
nearly 30 percent of global greenhouse gas emissions
and save one-sixth of global energy use, according to
Britain's Institute of Science in Society.

Wine Bars and Breweries

Your favorite restaurant serves organic food. The specialty market around the corner has organic and hormone-free artisan cheeses. That loaf of bread you just bought is made from sustainably harvested wheat. Just thinking about it makes you want to celebrate with a nice glass of wine . . . or maybe a bottle of brew!

Well, shouldn't that refreshment be sustainably produced? We think so. In fact, conventional wine-grape growing is responsible for a whole bunch of environmental ills: depletion of soil fertility (a critical factor in wine quality), groundwater pollution, and destruction of beneficial insects and birds. What's more, vineyard workers are exposed to toxic chemicals, as are nearby communities. So, when it comes to wine, also ask for ones made from grapes that have been sustainably grown.

The same is true for the barley and hops that are used to make beer. Hops are particularly prone to fungus damage, so those produced conventionally rely heavily on the use of fungicides. Similarly, herbicides, insecticides, and fossil fuel fertilizers are used on conventionally grown beer-making grains.

Throw in the fossil fuel used to transport the heavy glass bottles and the refrigeration required, and you've got a recipe for resource depletion. That means it's time to check out your local microbrewery. Beer can be produced in small vats and thus lends itself to urban production. So by supporting your local brewpub, you'll be building the local economy and saving a boatload of fossil fuel.

Because this is an emerging field requiring strict adherence to USDA guidelines (see page 44 for more information), and since both supply and customer demand fluctuate, we have reduced our minimum threshold for inclusion in the guide. To be listed, at least 15 percent of the wines, beers, and/or spirits served by an establishment must be organic and/or biodynamic. We also looked at whether the business demonstrates a commitment to sustainability by actively promoting organic selections to its patrons.

at least 15% meet the above criteria.

at least 25% meet the above criteria.

at least 50% meet the above criteria.

at least 75% meet the above criteria.

Blind Tiger Ale House 🍃

281 Bleecker St. (Jones St.), West Village (Man), 212-462-4682
Daily 11:30am–4am **blindtigeralehouse.com**
Bar featuring rotating selection of organic and seasonal specialty
draughts from local and regional brewers. Interior space constructed
with reclaimed wood.

Bridge Vineyards: Urban Winery 🍃🍃

20 Broadway St. (Kent Ave.), Williamsburg (Bkn), 718-384-2800
Wed–Sun 2pm–12am **bridgevineyards.com**
Tasting room and wine shop serving and selling sustainable North Fork
wines and offering local artisanal cheese pairings.

Counter 🍃🍃🍃🍃

105 1st Ave. (6th St.), East Village (Man), 212-982-5870
Mon–Thu 5pm–12am Fri 5pm–1am Sat 11am–1am Sun 11am–12am
counternyc.com
Wine and martini bar serving over 300 organic and biodynamic wines;
full organic beer and liquor menu.

Crescent and Vine 🍃

25-03 Ditmars Blvd. (Crescent St.), Astoria (Qns), 718-240-4774
Daily 5pm–4am
Wine bar featuring a small selection of organic and biodynamic wines.

DBA 🍃

41 1st Ave. (bet. 2nd & 3rd Sts.), East Village (Man), 212-475-5097
Daily 1pm–4am **drinkgoodstuff.com**
Bar offering small selection of organic red wines and beers. Draught beer
served on seasonal availability.

Gusto Grilled Organics 🍃🍃🍃🍃

519 Avenue of the Americas (14th St.), Union Square (Man), 212-242-5800
Daily 8am–12am **gustorganics.com**
Cafe serving organic and biodynamic wines and organic beer. Food menu
features organic, locally sourced ingredients.

Jimmy's No. 43 🍃

43 E. 7th St. (bet. 2nd & 3rd Aves.), East Village (Man), 212-982-3006
Mon–Thu 3pm–2am Fri–Sat 3pm–4am Sun 3pm–2am **jimmysno43.com**
Bar offering rotating draught list with handcrafted offerings from local
brewers. Wines from Long Island vineyards.

Rebar at Retreat 🍃

147 Front St., Mezzanine (bet. Jay & Pearl Sts.), DUMBO (Bkn), 718- 285-6457
Mon–Wed 4pm–2am Thu–Sat 4pm–4am Sun 4pm–2am **rebarnyc.com**
Extensive organic and biodynamic wine list; some organic beers rotate on tap.

Sixpoint Craft Ales 🍃🍃

40 Van Dyke St. (Dwight St.), Red Hook (Bkn), 646-924-9365
Mon–Fri 8am–5pm **sixpointcraftales.com**
Brewery crafting and serving beer made with organic hops and barley in an
energy- and water-efficient process. Packaging made with 100% recycled
materials. Tours available.

Smooch Cafe 🍃🍃🍃

264 Carlton Ave. (DeKalb Ave.), Fort Greene (Bkn), 718-624-4075
Mon–Sat 8am–12am Sun 8am–11pm **smoochcafe.com**
Wine bar and cafe with varied selection of biodynamic and organic wine,
organic beer.

Tini Wine Bar 🍃🍃

414 Van Brunt St. (Coffey St.), Red Hook (Bkn), 718-855-4206
Tue–Thu 5pm–11pm Fri 5pm–12am Sat 11am–12am Sun 11am–11pm
tiniwinebar.com
Wine bar serving organic and biodynamic wine. Food menu features many locally sourced organic ingredients.

Village Pourhouse 🍃🍃

64 3rd Ave. (E. 11th St.), East Village (Man), 212-979-2337
Mon–Thu 11am–2am Fri-Sat 11am–4am Sun 11am–2am   **pourhousenyc.com**
Tavern featuring line of all-organic beers. Occasionally hosts green events.

Green Tip

Support your local microbrewery and seek out organic beers and other spirits. Herbicides, insecticides, and fossil fuel fertilizers are used on conventionally grown beer-making grains, and you can avoid ingesting traces of these chemicals if you select brands that use only organically grown hops and barley. Choose vodka made from organic potatoes to avoid exposure to herbicides, insecticides, and the use of fossil fuel fertilizers.

Green Tip

When ordering wine in a restaurant, select organic choices from the wine list or ask the sommelier or waiter to choose one for you. Even if they do not have offerings, keep in mind that consumer demand guides a business, so if customers are interested in organic options, the business might try to satisfy that demand. Most conventionally grown wine contains 240 types of chemicals. If you're giving a gift or enjoying it yourself, look for libations that haven't been made with ingredients grown with the use of herbicides or pesticides. Look for wines that are free of added sulfites and were made with organic grapes. Also, ask about "unlabeled or uncertified" organic wines from regions around the world that never started using chemical pesticides in the first place but do not label their wines as "organic" even though they meet the standards.

Coffeehouses and Teahouses

Coffee and tea are the most commonly consumed beverages in the world after water. And coffeehouses and tea shops have played a major role in human civilization ever since people got the hankering for something hot to drink (and maybe a little something to eat on the side).

Coffee and tea also have huge ecological and social impacts. Much of today's coffee crop is grown in technified "sun farms" rather than in the shady rainforest understory. Coffee "sun farms" rely heavily on chemical fertilizers and pesticides and harbor 90 percent fewer bird species than do shade plantations. In fact, shade-grown-coffee farms play a key role in the conservation of migratory birds.

Keep in mind that not all shade-grown coffee is organic and not all organic coffee is shade-grown. We hope you will do your best to find an ecologically friendly product that you like. Growing coffee and tea in a sustainable fashion preserves healthy ecosystems and protects wildlife. And while you're reading those labels, check for **fair trade certification** (see page 43 for more information). This indicates that growers are getting a living wage for their harvest.

In short, there's a long story behind that little latte and a quite a tale behind that pot of tea. It's one we're sure you'll be happy to get to know. *(Oh, and don't forget to bring your own mug or cup if that coffee or tea is to go!)*

We have determined leaf awards based primarily on the percentage of certified organic coffees and teas that are served and available for purchase. However, because many of these establishments also use a wide range of milk products and offer prepared food items, we have factored in whether or not there are certified organic options in these areas as well. We also evaluated the percentage of fresh or bottled juices, soft drinks, and smoothie ingredients that are certified organic. We also looked at whether or not the disposable cups and other available carry-out containers were biodegradable, compostable, and/or made with recycled, recyclable, and/or chlorine-free materials.

Of all the products served and available for sale:

🍃 at least 25% meet the above criteria.

🍃🍃 at least 50% meet the above criteria.

🍃🍃🍃 at least 75% meet the above criteria.

🍃🍃🍃🍃 at least 90% meet the above criteria.

Amai Tea & Bake House 🍃

171 3rd Ave. (bet.16th & 17th Sts.), Gramercy Park (Man), 212-863-9630
Mon–Sat 8am–10pm Sun 10am–5pm **amainyc.com**
Cafe offering variety of tea and fair trade coffee. Handmade desserts and
baked goods using all-natural ingredients, including own "Botanical Brownies."

Atlas 🍃🍃

116 Havemeyer St. (Grand St.), Williamsburg (Bkn), 718-782-7470
Daily 7am–10pm
Cafe serving organic, fair trade coffee and tea.

Bidonville Coffee & Tea 🍃🍃

47 Willoughby Ave. (Adelphi St.), Fort Greene (Bkn), 718-855-4515
Mon–Fri 7am–6pm Sat–Sun 8am–6pm
Coffeehouse serving organic and fair trade coffee, teas, and baked goods.

Bluestockings 🍃🍃🍃

172 Allen St. (bet. Stanton & Rivington Sts.), Lower East Side (Man),
212-777-6028
Daily 11am–11pm **bluestockings.com**
Bookstore, activist center, and cafe serving organic and fair trade coffee and
tea; vegan organic baked goods. Readings, workshops, performances, open
discussions, and films featured nightly.

Brooklyn's Brown 🍃🍃

Weekdays: 7th Ave. & 7th St. Weekends: Union St. & Prospect Park West,
Park Slope (Bkn),
Seasonal hours **brooklynsbrown.com**
Coffee truck serving only organic, fair trade blends; organic baked goods.

Cafe Grumpy 🍃🍃

224 W. 20th St. (bet. 7th & 8th Aves.), Chelsea (Man), 212-255-5511
193 Meserole Ave. (Diamond St.), Greenpoint (Bkn), 718-349-7623
Hours vary by location **cafegrumpy.com**
Coffee shop serving Intelligentsia direct trade coffee and local Ronnybrook
Farms dairy products.

Champion Coffee 🍃🍃

1108 Manhattan Ave. (bet. Clay & Dupont Sts.), Greenpoint (Bkn), 718-383-5195
Daily 7am–7pm **championcoffee.net**
Coffee shop serving Caffe Vito organic espresso and organic coffee and tea.
Patio seating available. Wi-Fi.

Coffee Den, The 🍃

144 Union St. (Hicks St.), Carroll Gardens (Bkn), 718-875-8720
Mon–Fri 7am–8pm Sat–Sun 8am–8pm **coffeedenbrooklyn.com**
Cafe serving organic coffee; baked goods and prepared food selection.
Features sing-and-dance-along for kids every Tuesday.

El Beit 🍃🍃

158 Bedford Ave. (bet. N. 8th & N. 9th Sts.), Williamsburg (Bkn), 718-302-1810
Daily 7am–11pm
Coffee shop serving direct trade coffee and organic tea. Free Wi-Fi.

Ella Cafe 🍃🍃🍃🍃

177 Bedford Ave. (bet. N. 7th & N. 8th Sts.), Williamsburg (Bkn),
718-218-8079
Mon–Fri 8am–10pm Sat 9am–10pm Sun 10am–10pm **ellacafe.com**
Cafe serving organic, fair trade coffee and tea; food menu featuring locally
grown organic ingredients.

Flying Saucer Cafe 🍃🍃

494 Atlantic Ave. (bet. Nevins St. & 3rd Ave.), Boerum Hill (Bkn), 718-624-0139
Seasonal hours
Organic and fair trade coffee and tea, baked goods from local bakeries.
Garden seating available summer.

Forest Natural 🍃🍃🍃

120 Norman Ave. (Eckford St.), Greenpoint (Bkn), 718-383-7417
Mon–Fri 7am–10pm Sat–Sun 9am–10pm **forestnatural.com**
Neighborhood coffee shop and juice bar featuring organic coffee, tea, juice,
and smoothies.

Frank White 🍃🍃

936 Atlantic Ave. (St. James Pl.), Prospect Heights (Bkn), 718-622-0840
Mon–Fri 8am–4pm Sat–Sun 9am–5pm **frankwhitenyc.com**
Small cafe and art gallery serving fair trade and organic coffee, organic tea,
some food items. House specialty waffles served weekends.

Freeze Peach Cafe 🍃🍃

22-00 29th St. (Ditmars Blvd.), Astoria (Qns), 718-877-6545
Mon–Fri 7am–11pm Sat–Sun 10am–11pm **freezepeach.org**
Cafe featuring organic, fair trade coffee and some organic loose tea.
Wi-Fi available.

Gimme Coffee 🍃

228 Mott St. (bet. Prince & Spring Sts.), SoHo (Man), 212-226-4011
495 Lorimer St. (bet. Powers & Grand Sts.), Williamsburg (Bkn), 718-388-7771
Hours vary by location **gimmecoffee.com**
Neighborhood coffee shop carrying selection of organic and fair trade coffee.

Gizzi's Coffee 🍃🍃

16 W. 8th St. (bet. MacDougal St. & 5th Ave.), Greenwich Village (Man),
212-260-9700
Mon–Fri 8am–9pm Sat 9am–10pm Sun 9am–8pm **gizzisny.com**
Organic, fair trade coffee and tea shop. Menu offers sandwiches, salads,
and bakery items made with some organic ingredients.

Gorilla Coffee 🍃🍃🍃

97 5th Ave. (Park Pl.), Park Slope (Bkn), 718-230-3243
Mon–Sat 7am–9pm Sun 8am–9pm **gorillacoffee.com**
Coffee shop and in-house roaster serving only certified organic and fair
trade coffee.

Gramstand 🍃

214 Ave. A (bet. 13th & 14th Sts.), East Village (Man), 212-533-1934
Mon–Fri 7:30am–11pm Sat–Sun 9am–11pm **gramstand.com**
Tea shop offering over 500 types of tea including some organic and fair
trade options. Readings, live music, exhibitions.

Grounded 🍃🍃🍃

28 Jane St. (bet. W. 4th St. & Greenwich Ave.), West Village (Man),
212-647-0943
Mon–Fri 7am–8pm Sat–Sun 7:30am–8pm **groundedcoffee.com**
Neighborhood coffeehouse serving all-organic, fair trade coffee and loose
tea; locally sourced organic dairy products and baked goods. Free Wi-Fi.

Has Beans 🍃

620 5th Ave. (17th St.), Red Hook (Bkn), 718-499-3828
Mon–Fri 6:30am–9pm Sat 7:30–9pm Sun 7:30am–6pm **hasbeansbrooklyn.com**
Coffeehouse offering selection of organic and fair trade coffee and tea.
Wi-Fi available.

Himalaya Teahouse 🍃🍃🍃

33-17 31st Ave. (33rd St.), Astoria (Qns), 718-777-7450
Mon, Wed–Fri 5pm–11pm Sat–Sun 12pm–11pm **himalayateahouse.com**
Teahouse serving large variety of organic and fair trade tea. Himalayan
cuisine made with some organic ingredients.

Homage 🍃🍃🍃🍃

151 Smith St. (Bergen St.), Boerum Hill (Bkn), 718-596-8151
Mon–Fri 8am–8pm Sat 10am–9pm Sun 11am–7pm **homagebrooklyn.com**
Small coffee shop attached to skateboard and snowboard store serving
organic coffee and tea. Organic dairy products and house-made organic
baked goods.

Hop Scotch Cafe 🍃🍃🍃

139 Ave. A (8th St.), East Village (Man), 212-529-2233
Mon–Fri 8am–1am Sat–Sun 9am–1am
Cafe serving organic coffee, tea, juices. Vegan, organic baked goods and
treats. Kid-friendly.

Irving Farm Coffee Company 🍃

56 7th Ave. (14th St.), West Village (Man), 212-475-5200
Hours vary by location **irvingfarm.com**
Neighborhood coffee shop offering some fair trade and organic coffee and tea.

Jack's Coffee 🍃🍃🍃

138 W. 10th St. (bet. Greenwich Ave. & Waverly Pl.), Greenwich Village
(Man), 212-929-0821
222 Front St. (Beekman St.), South St. Seaport (Man), 212-227-7631
Hours vary by location **jacksstirbrew.com**
Coffee shop offering good selection of fair trade, organic, shade-grown
coffee, with dairy products from local Hudson Valley cooperative; locally
made baked goods.

Joe, the art of coffee 🍃🍃

141 Waverly Pl. (6th Ave.), Greenwich Village (Man), 212-924-6750
130 Greene St. (bet. Prince & Houston Sts.), SoHo (Man), 212-941-7330
9 E. 13th St. (bet. 5th Ave. & University Pl.), Union Square (Man),
212-924-7400
Hours vary by location **joetheartofcoffee.com**
Family-owned coffee shop serving locally made food items and fair trade,
organic coffee and tea. Offers classes on barista techniques.

Kiva Cafe 🍃🍃🍃

139 Reade St. (bet. Greenwich & Hudson Sts.), Tribeca (Man), 212-587-1198
Mon–Fri 8am–8pm Sat 9am–6pm **kivacafe.com**
Cafe serving fair trade and organic teas, organic dairy products, selection
of pastries and sandwiches.

Local 🍃🍃🍃

144 Sullivan St. (bet. Prince & Houston Sts.), SoHo (Man), 212-253-2601
Mon–Fri 8am–7pm Sat 9am–7pm Sun 9am–6pm
Organic, fair trade coffee and tea; baked goods, soups, and sandwiches
made with organic ingredients from local purveyors and farmers' markets.

Mamalu Cafe 🍃🍃🍃

232 N. 12th St. (bet. Union & Driggs Aves.), Williamsburg (Bkn), 718-486-6312
Tue–Fri 9am–7pm Sat 10am–7pm Sun 10am–6pm **mamalunyc.com**
Cafe serving some organic coffee, organic and fair trade tea. Food menu
offers variety of organic choices. Features large indoor play space for kids.

Mojo Coffee 🍃🍃🍃🍃

128 Charles St. (bet. Washington & Greenwich Sts.), West Village (Man),
212-691-6656
Mon–Fri 6:30am–8pm Sat–Sun 7:30am–8pm
Neighborhood organic, fair trade coffee and sandwich shop. Recycled
wood tables.

Ninth Street Espresso 🍃🍃🍃🍃

75 9th Ave. (bet. 15th & 16th Sts.), Chelsea (Man), 212-228-2930
700 E. 9th St. (bet. Aves. C & D), East Village (Man), 212-358-9225
Daily 7am–8pm **ninthstreetespresso.com**
Coffee bar serving artisanal, organic, shade-grown, and fair trade coffee
and espresso.

Oslo Coffee Company 🍃

133 Roebling St. (bet. N. 3rd & N. 4th Sts.), Williamsburg (Bkn), 718-782-0332
328 Bedford Ave. (bet. S. 2nd & S. 3rd Sts.), Williamsburg (Bkn), 718-782-0332
Mon–Fri 7am–6pm Sat–Sun 9am–6pm **oslocoffee.com**
Neighborhood coffee shop serving some direct trade coffee and baked
goods from local Blue Sky Bakery.

Outpost Lounge 🍃🍃🍃

1014 Fulton St. (Classon St.), Clinton Hill (Bkn), 718-636-1260
Mon–Fri 8am–11pm Sat–Sun 9am–11pm **outpostlounge.com**
Cafe and bar serving organic, fair trade coffee and tea, organic food and
juice menu. Patio seating available. Space built using reclaimed materials.

Ozzie's Coffee & Tea 🍃

249 5th Ave. (Carroll St.), Park Slope (Bkn), 718-768-6868
57 7th Ave. (Lincoln Pl.), Park Slope (Bkn), 718-398-6695
Hours vary by location **ozziescoffee.com**
Coffee shop and roaster featuring some organic and fair trade coffee.
Wi-Fi available.

Potion Cafe 🍃

248 McKibbin St. (bet. Bushwick Ave. & White St.), Williamsburg (Bkn),
718-628-5470
Mon 8am–3pm Tue–Fri 8am–10pm Sat–Sun 9am–10pm
Neighborhood coffee shop serving some organic, fair trade coffee and
chocolate. Sandwiches, bagels, pastries, beer, and wine available. Local
art on display.

Prospect Perk Café 🍃🍃

183 Sterling Pl. (Flatbush Ave.), Prospect Heights (Bkn), 718-783-7375
Mon–Fri 6am–7pm Sat–Sun 6am–8pm **prospectperk.com**
Cafe serving organic, fair trade coffee and tea. Organic juice bar, light
food menu.

Red Horse Café 🍃

497 6th Ave. (13th St.), Park Slope (Bkn), 718-499-4973
Mon–Thu 7am–10pm Fri 7am–12am Sat 8am–12am Sun 8am–10pm
redhorsecafe.com
Coffee shop serving organic coffee, preservative-free baked goods, beer, wine.

Roebling Tea Room 🍃
143 Roebling St. (Metropolitan Ave.), Williamsburg (Bkn), 718-963-0760
Seasonal hours   **roeblingtearoom.com**
Some organic and fair trade options among extensive tea selection. Also
offers full menu focused on sustainable ingredients.

71 Irving Place 🍃
71 Irving Pl. (bet. 18th & 19th Sts.), Gramercy Park (Man), 212-995-5252
Hours vary by location   **irvingfarm.com**
Neighborhood coffee shop offering some fair trade and organic coffee
and tea.

Spot's Cafe 🍃🍃🍃
18 Saint Marks Pl. (3rd Ave.), East Village (Man), 212-260-1430
Mon–Sat 7am–1am Sun 9am–9pm
Coffee shop serving fair trade, organic coffee and tea.

Sympathy for the Kettle 🍃🍃🍃
109 St. Marks Pl. (bet. 1st Ave. & Ave. A), East Village (Man), 212-979-1650
Tue–Sun 12pm–10pm   **sympathyforthekettle.com**
Neighborhood teahouse serving organic, fair trade tea. Focus on educating
clients and the community on the health benefits of tea.

T Salon 🍃🍃
75 9th Ave. (W. 15th St.), Chelsea (Man), 212-243-0432
Mon–Sat 9am–8pm Sun 10am–6pm   **tsalon.com**
Cafe serving 100% fair trade tea, raw food items, organic ice cream. Uses
corn-based cups and compostable packaging.

Tavalon Tea Bar 🍃🍃🍃
22 E. 14th St. (bet. University Pl. & 5th Ave.), Union Square (Man),
212-807-7027
Daily 8:30am–9:30pm   **tavalon.com**
Teahouse offering a selection of infusions steeped with organic and
all-natural loose tea.

Think Coffee 🍃🍃🍃
248 Mercer St. (bet. 3rd & 4th Sts.), East Village (Man), 212-228-6226
Mon–Fri 7am–12am Sat–Sun 8am–12am   **thinkcoffeenyc.com**
Cafe serving fair trade coffee and teas; many shade-grown and
organic choices.

Tillie's of Brooklyn 🍃🍃
248 Dekalb Ave. (Vanderbilt Ave.), Fort Greene (Bkn), 718-783-6140
Mon–Fri 7:30am–10pm Sat–Sun 8:30am–10pm   **tilliesofbrooklyn.com**
Organic and fair trade coffee and tea; some organic fruit drinks; vegan
baked goods. Free Wi-Fi. Open mic night showcasing local musicians and
spoken word artists.

Tiny Cup 🍃
279 Nostrand Ave. (Clifton Pl.), Bedford-Stuyvesant (Bkn), 718-399-9200
Mon–Fri 7:30am–8pm Sat–Sun 9am–8pm
Neighborhood cafe offering some direct trade coffee, organic tea, and a
variety of vegetarian and vegan dishes and pastries made in-house.

Urban Rustic 🌿🌿🌿

236 N. 12th St. (Union Ave.), Williamsburg (Bkn), 718-388-9444
Daily 7am–10pm **urbanrusticnyc.com**
Cafe featuring all-organic coffee on tap. Full menu highlights organic, seasonal ingredients. Juice bar and grocery store.

Uro Cafe 🌿

277 Driggs Ave. (bet. Leonard & Eckford Sts.), Greenpoint (Bkn), 718-599-1230
Mon–Fri 7am–6pm Sat 8am–6pm Sun 9am–4:30pm
Coffee shop offering some organic coffee choices, organic juices.

Vox Pop 🌿🌿🌿

1022 Cortelyou Rd. (Coney Island Ave.), Ditmas Park (Bkn), 718-940-2084
308 Bowery (Bleecker St.), East Village (Man); opens April '08
Mon–Tue 7am–9pm Wed–Thu 7am–10pm Fri 7am–12am Sat 8am–12am Sun 8am–11pm **voxpopnet.net**
Fair trade and organic coffee and tea. Also features organic, vegetarian food items, organic wine.

Wyckoff Starr 🌿

30 Wyckoff Ave. (Starr St.), Bushwick (Bkn), 718-484-9766
Mon–Fri 7am–7pm Sat–Sun 9am–7pm
Small neighborhood coffee shop offering organic coffee and goods from local artisan bakers.

Juice Bars

The advent of juice bars and smoothie shops has been a real boon to those of us who like our fruit in a cup and our vitamins on the go. Keeping our immune systems healthy has gotten easier, and if we choose organic options, we can keep our planetary system healthy as well. And when you sidle up to that juice bar, don't forget to have a reusable cup in hand to avoid using throwaway polystyrene or plastic!

We have determined leaf awards based primarily on the percentage of certified organic fresh juices, smoothie ingredients, and dairy products used. We have also factored in the percentage of available coffee and teas that are certified organic and/or fair trade, as well as the percentage of bottled juices, soft drinks, and prepared food items that are certified organic. We also looked at whether or not the disposable cups and available carry-out containers were biodegradable, compostable, and/or made with recycled, recyclable, and/or chlorine-free materials.

Of all the products served or available for sale, and the ingredients used:

🌿 at least 25% meet the above criteria.

🌿🌿 at least 50% meet the above criteria.

🌿🌿🌿 at least 75% meet the above criteria.

🌿🌿🌿🌿 at least 90% meet the above criteria.

Back to the Land 🌿🌿🌿🌿
142 7th Ave. (Carroll St.), Park Slope (Bkn), 718-768-5654
Daily 9am–7pm backtothelandnaturalfoods.com
Neighborhood juice bar and grocery store offering organic and sustainable products for more than 35 years.

Balance Life, Inc. 🌿🌿🌿🌿
624 5th Ave. (17th St.), Red Hook (Bkn), 718-768-1091
Daily 9am–9pm
Organic juice prepared to go; natural grocer. Participates in composting program.

Broadway Natural 🌿🌿🌿
30-11 Broadway (31st St.), Astoria (Qns), 718-545-1100
Mon–Fri 8am–10pm Sat–Sun 9am–9pm
Organic vegetable and fruit juices, with vitamin and protein supplements available.

Columbus Natural Food 🌿🌿🌿
725 Columbus Ave. (W. 95th St.), Upper West Side (Man), 212-663-0345
Daily 8am–9:30pm
Neighborhood grocer with fresh organic juice bar.

Downtown Natural Market 🌿🌿🌿🌿
51 Willoughby St. (Jay St.), Downtown Brooklyn (Bkn), 718-834-1215
Mon–Fri 8:30am–7pm Sat 10pm–6pm Sun 12pm–6pm
Fresh organic juices and smoothies. Some organic prepared foods available. Also features natural grocery section.

Elaa Juice Bar 🌿🌿🌿
711 Fulton St. (Fort Greene Pl.), Fort Greene (Bkn), 718-858-3522
Seasonal hours
Juice bar offering organic juices; salads and sandwiches made with some organic ingredients.

Elm Health 🌿🌿🌿🌿
1695 1st Ave. (E. 88th St.), Yorkville (Man), 212-348-8500
Mon–Fri 8:30am–9pm Sat–Sun 9am–9pm
Fresh juice bar serving organic juice and smoothies, fair trade coffee, and organic prepared foods.

Exotic Superfoods 🌿🌿🌿🌿
185-02 Horace Harding Expy. (Utopia Pkwy.), Fresh Meadows (Qns), 718-353-4807
Mon–Sat 10:30am–10pm exoticsuperfoods.com
Juice bar serving organic, raw vegetable, fruit, and wheatgrass ingredients. Selection of raw, organic prepared salads.

Food Liberation 🌿🌿🌿🌿
1349 Lexington Ave. (bet. 89th & 90th Sts.), Yorkville (Man), 212-348-2286
Mon–Fri 8:30am–7pm Sat 10am–6pm
Organic juice bar and natural market. Offers step-by-step nutritional program for healthier eating.

Forest Natural 🌿🌿🌿
120 Norman St. (Eckford St.), Greenpoint (Bkn), 718-383-7417
Mon–Fri 7am–10pm Sat–Sun 9am–10pm forestnatural.com
Neighborhood juice bar and coffee shop featuring organic juice, smoothies, coffee, and tea.

Fresh Juice Bar Health Eatery 🍃🍃

38-01 30th Ave. (Steinway St.), Astoria (Qns), 718-626-FRESH
Mon–Fri 6am–11pm Sat–Sun 7am–10pm **freshnyjuicebar.com**
Fresh juice bar and cafe featuring selection of organic juices, coffee, tea, and prepared food items.

Fresh Start Healthy Food Market & Organic Eatery 🍃🍃🍃🍃

29-13 23rd Ave. (bet. 31st St. & Ditmars Blvd.), Astoria (Qns), 718-204-7868
Mon–Fri 8am–9pm Sat 9am–9pm Sun 11am–7pm
freshstartorganicmarket.com
Juice bar and natural grocer featuring fresh juices prepared with organic wheatgrass, fruits, and vegetables. Powdered supplements added upon request. Also serves sandwiches, salads.

Gary Null's Uptown Whole Foods 🍃🍃🍃🍃

2421 Broadway (89th St.), Upper West Side (Man), 212-874-4000
Daily 8am–11pm **garysmarketplace.com**
Entirely organic juice bar; vegan, organic prepared foods. Grocery section.

General Store 🍃🍃🍃🍃

318 Grand St. (Havemeyer St.), Williamsburg (Bkn), 718-486-9400
Daily 8am–11pm **lodgenyc.com**
Juices made with organic vegetables and fruits. Features full menu with many all-natural and organic choices.

Govinda's Organic Market 🍃🍃🍃🍃

387 Atlantic Ave. (bet. Bond & Hoyt Sts.), Boerum Hill (Bkn), 718-834-7672
Mon–Sat 8am–9pm Sun 10am–9pm **govindaorganicmarket.com**
Neighborhood organic juice bar and natural grocer offering fresh juices made with organic ingredients, fair trade and organic tea and coffee, market items.

H.I.M. Ital Restaurant & Juice Bar 🍃🍃

754 Burke Ave. (White Plains Rd.), Williamsbridge (Brx), 718-653-9627
Mon–Sat 10:30am–9:30pm
Cafe offering fresh organic fruit and vegetable juices.

Health 4-U: Nature's Market 🍃🍃🍃🍃

432 Park Ave. S (bet. 29th & 30th Sts.), Murray Hill (Man), 212-532-2644
Mon–Fri 8am–8pm Sat 10am–7pm
Juice bar and health food store providing organic produce and wide variety of vegetarian, organic, and all-natural products.

Health Bay Natural Foods Inc. 🍃🍃🍃

161-30 Crossbay Blvd. (161st Ave.), Howard Beach (Qns), 718-845-0517
Mon–Sat 10am–7pm Sun 11am–5pm
Juice bar and natural market serving organic juices, wheat- and gluten-free foods, supplements, and other grocery items.

Health Conscious Natural Food 🍃🍃🍃

231-22 Merrick Blvd. (231st St.), Springfield Gardens (Qns), 718-712-7740
Mon–Thu 9:30am–7pm Fri–Sat 9:30am–8pm
Organic juice bar. Also offers vegetarian food, organic produce and natural market items, African and Jamaican products.

Health Nuts, The 🍃🍃🍃🍃

211-35 26th Ave. (154th St.), Bayside (Qns), 718-225-8164
1208 2nd Ave. (63rd St.), Sutton Place (Man), 212-593-0116
835 2nd Ave. (45th St.), Tudor City (Man), 212-490-2979
2611 Broadway (98th St.), Upper West Side (Man), 212-678-0054
Hours vary by location
All-organic juice bar, selection of organic prepared food items, organic and
fair trade coffee and tea. Also features grocery store.

Healthfully Organic Market 🍃🍃🍃🍃

98 E. 4th St. (bet. 1st & 2nd Aves.), East Village (Man), 212-598-0777
Mon–Fri 9am–10pm Sat 10am–9pm Sun 10am–8pm **healthfully.com**
Organic juice bar located inside natural grocery. Also serves organic coffee.

Healthy Life 🍃🍃🍃🍃

169-28 Hillside Ave. (169th St.), Jamaica (Qns), 718-206-3356
Mon–Fri 7am–9pm Sat–Sun 9am–9pm
Juice bar and market serving organic juices, coffee, and tea.

Healthy Nibbles 🍃🍃🍃🍃

305 Flatbush Ave. (Prospect Pl.), Prospect Heights (Bkn), 718-636-5835
Mon–Sat 10am–8pm Sun 10am–7pm **healthynibbles.com**
Small cafe serving juices, smoothies, wraps, and burgers prepared with
organic and locally grown ingredients.

House of Health 🍃🍃🍃

1014 Lexington Ave. (bet. 72nd & 73rd Sts.), Upper East Side (Man),
212-772-8422
Mon–Fri 8am–9:30pm Sat 10am–9pm Sun 10am–8pm
Organic juice and smoothie bar in all-natural health food store.

Linda's Natural Market 🍃🍃🍃🍃

81-22 Lefferts Blvd. (Grenfell St.), Kew Gardens (Qns), 718-847-2233
Mon–Tue 10am–7pm Wed 10am–8pm Thu–Fri 10am–7pm Sat 10am–6pm
Sun 11am–5:30pm **lindasorganic.com**
Juice bar and market featuring organic vegetables, fruit, and wheatgrass.
Organic deli and grocery items.

Matter of Health, A 🍃🍃🍃🍃

1478 1st Ave. (E. 77th St.), Upper East Side (Man), 212-288-8280
Mon–Fri 8am–8:30pm Sat 9am–7:30pm Sun 10am–7pm
Organic juice bar featuring macrobiotic vegan and vegetarian food.
Grocery section.

Millennium Health 🍃🍃

241 Bedford Ave., Ste. A (bet. Metropolitan Ave. & N. 4th St.),
Williamsburg (Bkn), 718-599-3081
Daily 9am–12am
Juice bar and market carrying mostly organic and natural products.

Natural Frontier Market 🍃🍃🍃

266 3rd Ave. (bet. 21st & 22nd Sts.), Gramercy Park (Man), 212-228-9133
1104 Cortelyou Rd. (Stratford Rd.), Kensington (Bkn), 718-284-3593
1424 3rd Ave. (E. 81st St.), Upper East Side (Man), 212-794-0922
Hours vary by location **naturalfrontiermarket.net**
Health store and juice bar offering variety of organic options and
natural supplements.

New York Naturals 🍐🍐🍐🍐

253 Flatbush Ave. (6th Ave.), Prospect Heights (Bkn), 718-230-7094
Mon–Fri 8am–10pm Sat 9am–10pm Sun 10am–10pm **nynaturals.com**
Organic juice and smoothie bar housed in natural grocery store.

Nourish NYC 🍐🍐🍐🍐

43-15 Queens Blvd. (43rd St.), Sunnyside (Qns), 718-433-4443
Daily 10am–7pm **nourishnyc.com**
Organic juice bar serving fresh fruit and vegetable ingredients, soy-
and fruit-based smoothies. Also features natural grocery store.

Organic Soul Cafe 🍐🍐🍐🍐

638 E. 6th St., 1st Flr., Sixth St. Community Center (bet. Aves. B & C), Lower
East Side (Man), 212-677-1863
Seasonal hours **sixthstreetcenter.org/cafe**
Juice bar and cafe offering all-organic juices. Menu features mostly vegetar-
ian and vegan cuisine, with some seafood options. Outdoor seating.

Park Natural & Organic 🍐🍐🍐🍐

350 Court St. (Union St.), Carroll Gardens (Bkn), 718-802-1652
Mon–Sat 8am–8pm Sun 9am–7pm **parknatural.com**
Organic juice bar, with deli serving organic prepared foods, and
natural market.

Perelandra 🍐🍐🍐🍐

175 Remsen St. (bet. Clinton & Court Sts.), Brooklyn Heights (Bkn),
718-855-6068
Mon–Fri 8:30am–7pm Sat 9:30am–7pm **perelandranatural.com**
Organic juice bar and cafe housed in natural foods store. Menu changes
daily, reflecting seasonal, locally sourced ingredients.

Probiotics 🍐🍐🍐

5666 Broadway (bet. W. 233rd & David Michael Ruddle Sts.), Riverdale (Brx),
718-432-7200
Mon–Fri 7am–7pm Sat 8am–6pm
Grocery store offering natural and organic products, organic prepared foods
and juices. Pharmacy section offers wide range of natural vitamins, herbal
tinctures, and homeopathic remedies.

Pure Juice and Takeaway 🍐🍐🍐🍐

126 E. 17th St. (Irving Pl.), Gramercy Park (Man), 212-477-7151
Mon 10am–10pm Tue–Sat 10am–11pm Sun 10am–10pm
purefoodandwine.com/purejuice.html
Organic juices and smoothies; take-out raw food, wraps, salads,
and desserts.

SAI Organics 🍐🍐🍐🍐

30-21 30th Ave. (31st St.), Astoria (Qns), 718-278-1726
36-07 30th Ave. (36th St.), Astoria (Qns), 718-956-1793
Mon–Sat 8am–9pm Sun 8am–6:30pm **saiorganics.com**
Organic juice bar featuring fresh health foods and organic vegetables.

24 Carrots 🍐🍐🍐🍐

244 W. 72nd St. (bet. West End Ave. & Broadway), West Side (Man),
212-595-2550
Daily 9am–10pm **24carrotsnyc.com**
Organic juice bar with vegan and gluten-free prepared food items, vitamins.

Uptown Juice Bar 🍃🍃🍃

54 W. 125th St. (bet. 5th Ave. & Malcom X Blvd.), Central Harlem (Man),
212-987-2660
Daily 8am–10pm **uptownjuicebar.com**
Cafe serving fresh organic juices; nondairy desserts, baked goods, and full
food menu featuring organic ingredients.

Urban Roots 🍃🍃🍃

51 Ave. A (3rd St.), East Village (Man), 212-780-0288
Daily 10am–9:30pm
All-organic juice bar, market. Also serves organic and fair trade coffee, some
organic food items.

Vital Health Foods 🍃🍃🍃🍃

196-14 Linden Blvd. (197th St.), St. Albans (Qns), 718-525-0992
Mon–Thu 9:30am–7pm Fri–Sat 9am–7pm
Organic juice bar and natural market with selection of organic
smoothies, tea.

Vitality & Health Organic Market 🍃🍃🍃

46-03 Broadway (46th St.), Astoria (Qns), 718-274-1591
Mon–Fri 7am–10pm Sat–Sun 8am–10pm **vitalityandhealth.org**
Health food store and juice bar offering fresh juices made with organic
ingredients; fair trade coffee, some organic prepared foods.

Vitality Health 🍃🍃🍃🍃

1412 1st Ave. (E. 75th St.), Upper East Side (Man), 212-472-7700
Mon 8:30am–7:30pm Tue–Fri 8:30am–8pm Sat 8:30am–6pm Sun 11:30am–6pm
Market and juice bar using all-organic ingredients, many from local farmers.

Vitamin Depot Nutrition Center 🍃🍃🍃🍃

7721 5th Ave. (77th St.), Bay Ridge (Bkn), 718-238-0676
Mon–Sat 8am–6:30pm
All-organic juice bar inside neighborhood natural grocery store and
nutrition center.

did you know?

Among conventionally raised produce, apples, bell
peppers, celery, cherries, grapes (imported), lettuce,
nectarines, peaches, pears, potatoes, spinach, and
strawberries are the HIGHEST in pesticides. The list
of conventionally raised fruits and vegetables that are
LOWEST in pesticides includes asparagus, avocados,
bananas, broccoli, cabbage, eggplant, kiwi, mangos,
onions, pineapples, sweet corn (frozen), and sweet
peas (frozen).

If you can't find organic options, you can lower your
pesticide exposure by almost 90 percent by avoiding
the twelve most contaminated fruits and vegetables
above. Visit **foodsnews.org** to get a complete ranking
of fruits and veggies developed by the Environmental
Working Group (**ewg.org**).

Chocolatiers and Dessert Shops

A masterfully made dessert rich in organic ingredients, a chocolate torte made from cacao grown without harm to the planet, ice cream made from milk free of hormones and other additives—these are not only delicious and pleasurable treats for you, they also treat the planet well. Maybe your diet is at odds with your dessert, but there's no need to go off your green values when it's time to indulge.

The chocolatiers and dessert purveyors included here were given leaf awards based on the percentage of certified organic ingredients used in their menu items and/or prepared food items. To determine this, we looked into the percentage of chocolate and dairy products they used that are certified organic, as well as the percentage of eggs that are either certified organic and free-range/cage-free, and/or locally raised and free-range/cage-free without the use of hormones and/or antibiotics. We also took a look at all the prepared chocolate and non-chocolate food items and determined what percentage is certified organic. In addition, we factored in whether or not the chocolate used qualified for fair trade certification and whether or not the available bags and carry-out containers were biodegradable, compostable, and/or made with recycled, recyclable, and/or chlorine-free materials.

Of all the goods offered:

- at least 25% meet the above criteria.
- at least 50% meet the above criteria.
- at least 75% meet the above criteria.
- at least 90% meet the above criteria.

Blue Marble Ice Cream

420 Atlantic Ave. (bet. Bond & Nevins Sts.), Boerum Hill (Bkn), 718-858-1100
Seasonal hours **bluemarbleicecream.com**
Organic ice cream, fair trade and organic coffee, handcrafted tea, locally baked goods. Space constructed using sustainable materials.

Grom

2165 Broadway (bet. 76th & 77th Sts.), West Side (Man), 646-290-7233
Daily 11am–11pm **grom.it**
Gelato, sorbet, and slushes made fresh daily with organic eggs, chocolate, and fruit. Offerings change monthly according to ingredient seasonality.

Oko

152 5th Ave. (Douglass St.), Park Slope (Bkn), 718-398-3671
Seasonal hours **okoyogurt.com**
All-natural frozen yogurt made with fruit-sweetened Greek yogurt base. Also sells fair trade, organic coffee and tea.

Vere 🍃🍃🍃🍃

12 W. 27th St., 6th Flr. (bet. Broadway & 6th Ave.), Midtown (Man),
866-410-8373
Hours and factory tours Fri 12pm–6pm **veregoods.com**
Handmade organic and vegan chocolate confections low in sugar and
gluten-free, made with shade-grown, pesticide-free, sustainably grown and
harvested cocoa beans.

Yogurberry 🍃

80-49 37th Ave. (80th St.), Jackson Heights (Qns),
Daily 11am–9:30pm **yogurberry.com**
All-natural, low-fat frozen yogurt made with Stonyfield Farms organic
dairy products.

Bakeries

Enter a bakery that serves up organic treats and you've entered a
world where good taste and good health join in perfect combination. And they do so in a sustainable way.

A loaf of whole grain bread, a pie plump with organic apples, some
wholesome breakfast muffins—look for food that is both delicious
and environmentally friendly. It's out there waiting for you.

**Our leaf awards for the bakeries included here were based on
the following:**

• the percentage of grains and dairy products used that are certified organic;

• the percentage of eggs that are either certified organic and
  free-range/cage-free, and/or locally raised and free-range/
  cage-free without the use of hormones and/or antibiotics;

• the percentage of produce used that is certified organic and/or
  locally grown without pesticides and chemical fertilizers; and

• the percentage of stocked prepared foods and beverages that
  are certified organic.

We also looked at whether or not the available bags and carry-out
containers were biodegradable, compostable, and/or made with
recycled, recyclable, and/or chlorine-free materials.

🍃   at least 25% meets the above criteria.

🍃🍃   at least 50% meets the above criteria.

🍃🍃🍃   at least 75% meets the above criteria.

🍃🍃🍃🍃   at least 90% meets the above criteria.

Babycakes 🍥🍥🍥🍥

248 Broome St. (Ludlow St.), Lower East Side (Man), 212-677-5047
Mon 10am–8pm Tue–Thu 10am–10pm Fri–Sat 10am–11pm Sun 10am–8pm
babycakesnyc.com
All-natural, organic baked goods free from wheat, gluten, dairy, casein, eggs.

Birdbath 🍥🍥🍥🍥

223 1st Ave. (E. 13th St.), East Village (Man), 646-722-6565
145 7th Ave. S. (Charles St.), West Village (Man), 646-722-6570
Mon–Thu 8am–8pm Fri–Sat 8am–10pm Sun 9am–9pm
buildagreenbakery.com
Neighborhood green bakery offering wide variety of goods prepared with organic, seasonal ingredients. Uses corn-based biodegradable cups and no-wax containers. Interior built with sustainable and salvaged materials; uses wind-powered energy; composting program. Offers discount if you arrive by bicycle or skateboard.

Bread.A Bakery 🍥🍥🍥🍥

41-46 College Point Blvd. (41st Ave.), Flushing (Qns), 718-886-1888 x 14
Mon 8am–8pm Tue–Wed 8am–7:30pm Thu 8am–7pm Fri–Sat 8am–8pm
Sun 8:30am–7:30pm **breadaorganic.com**
Bakery and cafe serving handmade breads, cookies, and cakes prepared with natural and organic grains, dairy, and other ingredients. Cakes made to order. Vegan and vegetarian food menu available.

City Bakery, The 🍥🍥🍥🍥

3 W. 18th St. (5th Ave.), Union Square (Man), 212-366-1414
Mon–Fri 7:30am–7pm Sat 7:30am–6:30pm Sun 9am–6pm
thecitybakery.com
Bakery featuring organic, seasonal, fair trade ingredients. Participates in composting program. Kids' birthday parties.

Grandaisy Bakery 🍥🍥

73 Sullivan St. (Spring St.), SoHo (Man), 212-334-9435
Daily 7am–7pm **grandaisybakery.com**
Artisan bakery using some locally sourced ingredients. Greenware cups. Staff wears organic cotton T-shirts.

Silver Moon Bakery 🍥🍥

2740 Broadway (105th St.), Upper West Side (Man), 212-866-4717
Mon–Fri 7:30am–8pm Sat–Sun 8:30am–7pm **silvermoonbakery.com**
French bakery serving fresh breads and pastries made with organic milk and eggs. Biodegradable utensils, recycled cups and bowls.

Whole Earth Bakery and Kitchen 🍥🍥🍥🍥

130 St. Marks Pl. (bet. 1st Ave. & Ave. A), East Village (Man), 212-677-7597
Daily 9am–11:30pm
Vegan bakery using organic grains, flour, and natural sweeteners.

WRITE A REVIEW

We've done our best to find the greenest places to eat out in NYC. Now, tell us what you think: How was the food? The service? What was your experience overall? Visit **greenopia.com** to post your review or tell us about a favorite place we might have missed.

Fair Trade Certification

Fair trade certification strives to ensure that farmers in the developing world get a fair price for their crops and have good conditions under which to work. Fair trade helps guarantee freedom of association, prohibits forced child labor, and preserves agricultural traditions by keeping farming profitable, especially for small-scale and family farmers. Developing-world farmers often lack market access and pay high premiums to dealers. By forming cooperatives, cutting out intermediaries, guaranteeing a set floor price for crops (including a bonus for organics), and setting labor and environmental standards, it is the goal of the fair trade model to create market opportunities for disadvantaged producers.

TransFair, a leading fair trade certifier, currently offers certification in the United States for coffee, tea and herbs, cocoa and chocolate, fresh fruit, sugar, rice, and vanilla.

Although it is not widely recognized, fair trade certification also has strong ecological benefits. TransFair enforces strict environmental guidelines created by Fairtrade Labelling Organizations International (FLO), the world's main association of fair trade groups based in Bonn, Germany. Through detailed integrated farm-management practices, these standards serve to protect watersheds, virgin forests, and wildlife; prevent erosion; promote natural soil fertility; conserve water; and prohibit the use of genetically modified organisms.

TransFair's long list of prohibited agrochemicals also helps protect workers and reduce fossil fuel dependence. TransFair claims that its environmental standards are the most stringent in the industry, second only to the USDA's organic label. Since TransFair guarantees growers a premium for organic crops, this also creates an incentive to go organic and helps pay for ongoing certification fees.

The Rainforest Alliance is another third-party certifier of sustainable agricultural products and also has programs for sustainable forestry and tourism. Through their labeling program, a product can be certified if it meets their high standards of land conservation, integrated farm management practices, and fair labor conditions. The Rainforest Alliance's agricultural program currently covers bananas, citrus, cocoa, coffee, and flowers.

For more information, visit **transfairusa.org** and **rainforest-alliance.org.**

Organic Standards for Food

In the words of the U.S. Department of Agriculture, "Organic food is produced by farmers who emphasize the use of renewable resources and the conservation of soil and water to enhance environmental quality for future generations." Thus, "organic" refers to a specific set of standards used throughout the entire process of food production. Food that is certified organic comes from farms (in the United States or in other countries) that have been inspected and approved under the USDA's guidelines by a government-approved certifier. Organic certification prohibits the use of most conventional pesticides, synthetic fertilizers, sewage sludge, bioengineering, and irradiation (also called "ionizing radiation" or "cold pasteurization"). Organic meat, eggs, poultry, and dairy come from animals not treated with antibiotics or growth hormones. Certified organic food is, by definition, free from genetically modified organisms, or GMOs. Also, any handling or processing of organic food must be done by certified companies.

Organic Content—Single-Ingredient Foods

Check package labeling carefully and look for signs at the supermarket to guide you to organic foods. The USDA's strict labeling rules help you know the exact organic content of the food you buy. The USDA Organic seal also tells you that a product is at least 95 percent organic. Look for the word *organic* and a small sticker version of the USDA Organic seal on vegetables or pieces of fruit. The word *organic* and the seal may also appear on packages of meat, cartons of milk or eggs, cheese, and other single-ingredient foods.

Organic Labeling—Multi-Ingredient Foods

Federal organic legislation allows four labeling categories for the wide variety of products that use organic ingredients. Products made entirely with certified organic ingredients and methods can be labeled "100 percent organic." Products with 95 percent to 100 percent organic ingredients can use the word *organic* on packaging, advertising, etc. Both may also display the USDA organic seal. A third category, containing a minimum of 70 percent organic ingredients, can be labeled "made with organic ingredients." In addition, products can also display the logo of the individual certification body that approved them. Products made with less than 70 percent organic ingredients cannot advertise this information to consumers and can only mention this fact in the product's ingredient statement, not on the front of the package. Similar percentages and labels apply in the European Union.

Small and Transitional Farmers

Although organic certification is an excellent way to ensure the quality and eco-friendliness of the food you buy, not all farmers and food producers are officially certified. The organic certification process is rigorous and often expensive. Small farms in particular may not be certified, or may be "transitional," meaning they are on their way to certification. If you go to Greenmarkets or farmers' markets, the best way to understand what you're buying and how it is grown is to talk to the farmer or vendor. Local farmers may be happy to show you around their farms so you can see for yourself as well.

Green Tip

Buy organic food. Organic food is grown without the use of pesticides and other harmful chemicals, which can have adverse effects on farmworkers, the environment, and those who eat the tainted foods. The National Academy of Sciences researchers determined that 80 percent of commonly used pesticides are carcinogenic. (Source: NRDC) Organic certification also prohibits the use of most conventional pesticides, synthetic fertilizers, sewage sludge, bioengineering, and irradiation. New studies show you can get more nutrients from organic foods, too.

Top 10 Reasons to Buy Organic

1. Protect the health of future generations.
2. Protect water quality.
3. Nurture soil quality and prevent erosion.
4. Save energy.
5. Keep poisons off your plate.
6. Protect farmworker health.
7. Help small farmers.
8. Promote biodiversity.
9. Expose the hidden environmental and social costs of conventional foods.
10. Enjoy better flavor and greater nourishment.

Seafood Guide

How to Use This Guide

The seafood in this guide may occur in more than one column based on how it is caught, where it is from, etc. Please read all columns and be sure to check labels or ask questions when shopping or eating out.

- Where is the seafood from?
- Is it farmed or wild-caught?
- How was it caught?

If you're not sure, choose something else from the green or yellow columns.

Best Choices are abundant, well managed, and caught or farmed in environmentally friendly ways.

Good Alternatives are an option, but there are concerns with how they're caught or farmed—or with the health of their habitat due to other human impacts.

Avoid for now, as these items are caught or farmed in ways that harm other marine life or the environment.

Key

Northeast = Connecticut to Maine

Mid-Atlantic = North Carolina to New York

Southeast = Texas to South Carolina

* Limit consumption due to concerns about mercury or other contaminants. Visit **oceansalive.org/eat.cfm.**

\+ Some or all of this fishery is certified as sustainable to the Marine Stewardship Council standard. Visit **msc.org.**

Make Choices for Healthy Oceans

You Have the Power

Your consumer choices make a difference. Buy seafood from the green or yellow columns to support those fisheries and fish farms that are healthier for ocean wildlife and the environment.

Visit seafoodwatch.org for:

- More detailed information about these recommendations
- Recommendations for seafood not on this list
- The latest version of this and other regional guides
- Information on seafood and your health and much more.

Best Choices

Arctic Char (farmed)
Barramundi (US farmed)
Catfish (US farmed)
Clams, Mussels, Oysters (farmed)
Clams: Softshell/Steamers (wild)
Crab: Dungeness
Croaker: Atlantic*
Halibut: Pacific+
Herring: Atlantic/Sardines
Lobster: Spiny (US)
Pollock (Alaska wild)+
Salmon (Alaska wild)+

Scallops: Bay (farmed)
Squid: Longfin (US)
Striped Bass (farmed or wild*)
Sturgeon, Caviar (farmed)
Swordfish (Canada, US harpoon, handline)*
Tilapia (US farmed)
Trout: Rainbow (farmed)
Tuna: Albacore (US+, British Columbia troll/pole)
Tuna: Skipjack (troll/pole)

Good Alternatives

Basa, Swai (farmed)
Black Sea Bass
Bluefish*
Clams: Atlantic Surf, Hard, Ocean Quahog (wild)
Crab: Blue*, Jonah, King (US), Snow
Crab: Imitation/Surimi
Haddock (hook & line)
Hake: Silver, Red and Offshore
Lobster: American/Maine
Mahimahi/Dolphinfish (US)
Oysters (wild)*

Scallops: Sea (Canada and Northeast)
Scup/Porgy
Shrimp: Northern
Shrimp (US farmed or wild)
Squid
Swordfish (US longline)*
Tilefish (Mid-Atlantic)
Tuna: Bigeye, Yellowfin (troll/pole)
Tuna: canned light, canned white/Albacore*

Avoid

Chilean Seabass/Toothfish*
Cod: Atlantic
Crab: King (imported)
Dogfish (Atlantic)*
Flounders, Soles (Atlantic)
Haddock (trawled)
Hake: White
Halibut: Atlantic
Mahimahi/Dolphinfish (imported)
Monkfish
Orange Roughy*
Salmon (farmed, including Atlantic)*

Scallops: Sea (Mid-Atlantic)
Sharks* and Skates
Shrimp (imported farmed or wild)
Snapper: Red
Sturgeon*, Caviar (imported wild)
Swordfish (imported)*
Tilefish (Southeast)*
Tuna: Albacore, Bigeye, Yellowfin (longline)*
Tuna: Bluefin*

 The Seafood Watch Guide has been reprinted with the permission of the Monterey Bay Aquarium Foundation. Visit seafoodwatch.org for more seafood recommendations and the latest updated information.

Eating
In

The Return of the Russets

By Mary Cleaver

These days I am encouraged by the greenish glow that is washing over the Big Apple. Not that long ago, it was nearly impossible to find a locally grown tomato for sale in New York City in August, when they ought to have been plentiful. Now, you can find more than two hundred delicious varieties, as well as a myriad of other fruits and vegetables available year-round. This February, I was able to grace the tables at a dinner for two hundred people with golden russets, an heirloom variety of apples being grown once again in the Hudson Valley.

In the past fifty years, America has lost more than 60 percent of its family farms to industrial agriculture, and, with it, more than 30 percent of its topsoil. Industrial agriculture, in hand with government-subsidized farm policies, makes food seem cheap, but the cost to our environment, our health, and future generations is massive.

You can be a positive contributor to the food supply by making it your priority to cook from scratch or to work with those who do. Take the time to learn where your food comes from and how it was grown. Look for food that is raised as close to home as possible, preferably by growers practicing sustainable, organic, or biodynamic farming.

As urban dwellers, it is fair to say that most of us are not growing our own food, but we can do the next best thing and get to know those who are. Cook whenever you can and teach your children to cook. In taking these actions, you too can be part of the greening of the Big Apple.

Mary Cleaver runs a catering and event planning business that celebrates sustainable agriculture with haute green cuisine. Her restaurant, The Green Table, is adjacent to the catering kitchen in the Chelsea Market (**cleaverco.com**).

Grocery Stores

Most of us spend a significant portion of our food budget every week at our local grocery store. We recommend spending that all-important grocery money on products that are healthier for you and the planet.

A good way to start is by buying organic and/or locally grown products. Organic products are better for your health, and organic agriculture is better for the environment. And food that's locally grown tends to be picked at its freshest and tastiest. Its purchase directly supports nearby farms and helps sustain local communities, while at the same time reducing the amount of fuel consumed and pollution created by transporting the products to market. Some grocery store chains and local markets have begun to mark their produce as "locally grown" to demonstrate this commitment as well, making it easier to choose wisely.

Conscious shopping also demands that we purchase nonfood items (personal care products, cleaning supplies, paper products) that are also environmentally friendly. Look for shampoos and toothpastes that are organic or all natural. Household cleaners can be full of toxins, and many paper products are whitened with chlorine. Look for alternatives. Read the labels carefully on everything you buy.

We have evaluated our grocery stores in the fifteen product areas described below. In addition, we looked at whether or not the stores offered reusable bags to their customers, or if their bags and any available carry-out containers were biodegradable or compostable and/or made with recycled, recyclable, and/or chlorine-free materials.

- For produce, we checked the percentage purchased that is certified organic and/or locally grown without pesticides and chemical fertilizers.

- For meat and meat alternatives, we determined the percentage that is certified organic and/or grass-fed and produced without the use of hormones and antibiotics.

- For poultry and eggs, we evaluated the percentage purchased that is certified organic and free-range/cage-free, and/or locally raised and free-range/cage-free without the use of hormones and antibiotics.

- With seafood, we checked into whether it was wild-caught or sustainably farm-raised and processed without chemical treatment.

- For dairy products, we checked the percentage of certified organic options or ones that were locally produced without hormones and antibiotics.

- We looked into the percentage of certified organic canned and dry goods, nondairy beverages, and frozen foods.

- For prepared foods, we determined the percentage made with certified organic ingredients and/or locally grown ingredients without pesticides and chemical fertilizers.

- For personal care products, we looked into the percentage that is organic or all natural.

- For personal care tools and household cleaning tools, we determined the percentage made with environmentally friendly materials.

- We checked the percentage of available household cleansers, soaps, and detergents that are nontoxic.

- For household paper products, we looked at the percentage made from recycled content and whitened without chlorine.

> 🍃 at least 25% of the products meet the above criteria.
> 🍃🍃 at least 50% of the products meet the above criteria.
> 🍃🍃🍃 at least 75% of the products meet the above criteria.
> 🍃🍃🍃🍃 at least 90% of the products meet the above criteria.

Amish Market 🍃

17 Battery Pl. (bet. West & Washington Sts.), Battery Park City (Man), 212-871-6300
731 9th Ave. (bet. 49th & 50th Sts.), Midtown West (Man), 212-245-2360
240 E. 45th St. (bet. 2nd & 3rd Aves.), Murray Hill (Man), 212-370-1761
8000 Cooper Ave. (80th St.), Ridgewood (Qns), 718-894-1199
53 Park Pl. (W. Broadway), Tribeca (Man), 212-608-3863
Hours vary by location **amishfinefood.com**
Natural and organic dry goods, produce, chocolate, gluten-free products, and beverages. Good selection of biodegradable household cleansers and recycled-content household paper products.

Apple Drugs 🍃

376 Kingston Ave. (Crown St.), Crown Heights (Bkn), 718-467-6700
Mon–Sat 9:30am–8pm Sun 10am–6pm
Combination grocery store and pharmacy. Organic canned and dry goods, frozen foods, cereals, honey, nut butters, free-range eggs. Pharmacy includes all-natural personal care products, homeopathic drugs, and herbal tinctures.

Astoria Natural Center 🍃🍃🍃

41-03 31st Ave. (41st St.), Astoria (Qns), 718-204-1151
Mon–Sat 10am–7:30pm Sun 11am–6pm
Natural and organic supplements, dry goods, frozen foods, and soy products; vegan and vegetarian foods; natural body care products.

Back to the Land ✍ ✍ ✍

142 7th Ave. (Carroll St.), Park Slope (Bkn), 718-768-5654
Daily 9am–9pm **backtothelandnaturalfoods.com**
Neighborhood natural foods grocery store and juice bar committed to sustainability for over 35 years. Offers fresh, natural, organic and whole foods, nutritional products, body care products, and health information.

Balance Life, Inc. ✍ ✍ ✍ ✍

624 5th Ave. (17th St.), Red Hook (Bkn), 718-768-1091
Daily 9am–9pm
Organic food items; vitamins and supplements; juice bar. Gives juice compost to local gardens.

Bay Ridge Health Food ✍ ✍ ✍ ✍

9220 3rd Ave. (93rd St.), Bay Ridge (Bkn), 718-491-4075
Mon–Sat 10am–8pm
Neighborhood natural foods grocery store selling all natural and certified organic dry, canned, and frozen foods and nondairy products; all-natural personal care products, supplements; nontoxic household cleaning supplies.

Broadway Natural ✍ ✍ ✍

30-11 Broadway (31st St.), Astoria (Qns), 718-545-1100
Mon–Fri 8am–10pm Sat–Sun 9am–9pm
Health food store with organic herbicide- and pesticide-free produce, antibiotic- and hormone-free dairy goods; organic dry goods, vitamins, natural herbs, and health care products. Organic juice bar.

Brooklyn Natural ✍

49 Bogart St. (Grattan St.), Bushwick (Bkn), 718-381-0650
Daily 7am–1:30am
Small grocery store offering some natural and organic food items, including organic eggs, dairy products, and frozen foods; some all-natural personal care products and nontoxic cleaning products and tools.

Columbus Natural Food ✍ ✍ ✍

725 Columbus Ave. (W. 95th St.), Upper West Side (Man), 212-663-0345
Daily 8am–9:30pm
Neighborhood grocer carrying wide selection of organic produce, fair trade coffee and teas, prepared foods, personal care products, and herbal remedies. Participates in composting program.

Commodities Natural Market ✍ ✍ ✍ ✍

165 1st Ave. (E. 10th St.), East Village (Man), 212-260-2600
Seasonal Hours **commoditiesnaturalmarket.com**
Family-owned grocery store offering wide selection of organic and locally sourced produce; organic dairy, eggs, meats, poultry, wild-caught fish; and other all-natural or nontoxic personal care and grocery items. Alternative fuel delivery vehicles. Participates in composting and biodiesel recycling programs.

Danny & Veer Health Food ✍ ✍

1827A Flatbush Ave. (Ave. K), Flatlands (Bkn), 718-676-0034
Mon–Sat 9am–7pm
Market carrying all-natural foods, supplements, and bodybuilding products.

DNY Natural Land ✍ ✍

322 Flatbush Ave. (bet. Park & Sterling Pls.), Prospect Heights (Bkn), 718-783-0038
Daily 24 hrs.
Neighborhood market carrying a good selection of certified organic and all-natural products, including meats, poultry, and eggs.

Downtown Natural Market 🌿🌿🌿

51 Willoughby St. (Jay St.), Downtown Brooklyn (Bkn), 718-834-1215
Mon–Fri 8:30am–7pm Sat 10pm–6pm Sun 12pm–6pm
Natural grocery store carrying wide selection of organic and all-natural
products; prepared organic vegetarian foods; juice bar.

Earth Matters 🌿🌿🌿

177 Ludlow St. (bet. Houston & Stanton Sts.), Lower East Side (Man),
212-475-4180
Daily 8am–11pm   **earthmatters.com**
Fresh organic produce, kosher chicken, bulk grains, cereals, granola, natural
vitamins, and beauty products. Indoor internet cafe serving vegetarian
options, organic menu, and fair trade coffee.

East New York Food Co-op 🌿🌿

419 New Lots Ave. (bet. Vermont St. & New Jersey Ave.), East New York
(Bkn), 718-676-2721
Wed–Sat 11am–7pm
Grocery co-op working closely with East NY Farms. Offers weekly health
screenings and biweekly nutritional cooking classes that are open to the public.

Eli's Manhattan 🌿

1411 3rd Ave. (bet. 80th & 81st Sts.), Upper East Side (Man), 212-717-8100
Daily 7am–9pm   **elizabar.com**
Large gourmet grocery store offering fresh, local, and some organic foods,
cheeses, baked goods, fair trade coffee, deli meats, and prepared foods.
Provides catering. In-store cafe.

Elm Health 🌿🌿🌿

1695 1st Ave. (E. 88th St.), Yorkville (Man), 212-348-8500
Mon–Fri 8:30am–9pm Sat–Sun 9am–9pm
Organic produce; frozen, refrigerated, and prepared foods; natural beauty
products and cruelty-free cosmetics. Expert nutritionist on staff to assist and
answer questions.

Eric's Health Food Shoppe 🌿🌿🌿

508 Brighton Beach Ave. (Brighton 5th St.), Brighton Beach (Bkn),
718-615-4040
Mon–Fri 8am–8pm Sat 9am–7pm Sun 9am–6pm   **ericshealthfood.com**
Grocer offering a full line of organic and all-natural items, including bulk
products, vitamins, and supplements.

Exotic Superfoods 🌿🌿🌿🌿

185-02 Horace Harding Expwy (Utopia Pkwy.), Fresh Meadows (Qns),
718-353-4807
Mon–Sat 10:30am–10pm   **exoticsuperfoods.com**
Natural foods market carrying raw food items; selection of prepared salads;
juice bar.

Fairway Market 🌿

2328 12th Ave. (bet. W. 132nd & W. 133rd Sts.), Harlem (Man), 212-234-3883
480-500 Van-Brunt St. (Reed St.), Red Hook (Bkn), 718-694-6868
2127 Broadway (74th St.), Upper West Side (Man), 212-595-1888
Hours vary by location   **fairwaymarket.com**
Supermarket featuring a variety of organic goods. Delivery and catering
services available.

Family Health Foods 🍃🍃🍃🍃

1789 Victory Blvd. (Manor Rd.), Castleton Corners (S.I.), 718-442-0357
177 New Dorp Ln. (9th St.), New Dorp (S.I.), 718-351-7004
7001 Amboy Rd. (Page Ave.), Richmond Valley (S.I.), 718-967-9674
604 Forest Ave. (Pelton Ave.), West Brighton (S.I.), 718-442-4022
Mon–Sat 9am–7pm Sun 10am–5pm **familyhealthfoods.com**
Natural foods supermarket serving the area for over 35 years. Large selection of natural and organic groceries, organic produce, frozen foods, bulk nuts and dried fruits. Specializes in wheat-free, gluten-free, and dairy-free diets. Deli and juice bar with natural and organic ingredients.

Flatbush Food Coop 🍃🍃🍃

1318 Cortelyou Rd. (bet. Argyle & Rugby Rds.), Flatbush (Bkn), 718-284-9717
Daily 7am–9pm **flatbushfoodcoop.com**
Full-service natural foods co-op specializing in organic products, including organic and locally grown produce, organic cage-free eggs and dairy, organic bulk foods, and other natural grocery items. Open to the public.

Food For Health 🍃🍃🍃🍃

1653 3rd Ave. (bet. 92nd & 93rd Sts.), Yorkville (Man), 212-369-9202
Mon–Thu 9am–8:30pm Fri 9am–8pm Sat 10am–7:30pm Sun 11am–7pm
Health food store with organic produce, extensive natural supplements, beauty products, organic bulk section, juice bar, and gluten-free products.

Food Liberation 🍃🍃🍃🍃

1349 Lexington Ave. (bet. 89th & 90th Sts.), Yorkville (Man), 212-348-2286
Mon–Fri 8:30am–7pm Sat 10am–6pm
Neighborhood grocery offering organic, natural grocery items, prepared foods, personal care products, and household cleansers. Offers consulting services on nutrition.

Forager's Market 🍃🍃

56 Adams St. (Front St.), DUMBO (Bkn), 718-801-8400
Mon–Sat 8:30am–9pm Sun 9am–8pm **foragersmarket.com**
Full-service grocer offering grass-fed beef, local poultry, seasonal local produce, and biodegradable packaging. Serves lunch. Catering services and gift baskets available.

Forces of Nature 🍃🍃🍃🍃

1608 Sheepshead Bay Road (E. 16th St.), Sheepshead Bay (Bkn), 718-616-9000
Mon–Sat 9am–9pm Sun 10am–7pm
Wide selection of organic grocery items, including produce, meats, poultry, eggs, dairy and nondairy beverages, frozen foods, and personal care products.

4th St. Food Co-op 🍃🍃🍃🍃

58 E. 4th St. (bet. Bowery & 2nd Aves.), East Village (Man), 212-674-3623
Mon–Wed 11am–9pm Thu 9am–9pm Fri 1pm–9pm Sat–Sun 11am–9pm
4thstreetfoodcoop.org
Local, vegetarian, fair trade, and organic products at a reasonable price. The co-op is run 100% on wind power and is involved in local green community groups and events.

Fresh Farm 🍃

282 Broadway (Marcy Ave.), Williamsburg (Bkn), 718-486-7747
Mon–Sat 7:30am–9:30pm Sun 8:30am–8:30pm
Neighborhood market dedicated to organic dried goods and personal care products.

Fresh Start Health Food Market & Organic Eatery 🌿🌿🌿🌿

29-13 23rd Ave. (bet. 31st St. & Ditmars Blvd.), Astoria (Qns), 718-204-7868
Mon–Fri 8am–9pm Sat 9am–9pm Sun 11am–7pm
freshstartorganicmarket.com
Vegan, vegetarian, and organic food; nutritional supplements; gluten- and
allergen-free foods; personal and household care products. Indoor and
outdoor cafe and juice bar.

Garden, The 🌿🌿🌿

921 Manhattan Ave. (bet. Greenpoint Ave. & Kent St.), Greenpoint (Bkn),
718-389-6448
Mon–Sat 8am–8pm Sun 9am–7pm
Full-service grocery store offering many organic food items, natural meats,
and natural personal care products.

Gary Null's Uptown Whole Foods 🌿🌿🌿🌿

2421 Broadway (89th St.), Upper West Side (Man), 212-874-4000
Daily 8am–11pm **garysmarketplace.com**
Wide variety of organic produce, gluten-free food, natural products,
kosher food and natural supplements; organic bulk section; vegan bakery
and raw-food cakes.

Go Natural 🌿🌿🌿

45-03 Queens Blvd. (45th St.), Sunnyside (Qns), 718-482-0008
Mon–Fri 10am–8pm Sat 10am–7pm Sun 11am–6pm
Organic homemade soups, juices, organic produce, grass-fed beef, and or-
ganic chicken. Participates in composting and biodiesel recycling programs.

Good 'N Natural 🌿🌿🌿

2173 White Plains Rd. (Lydig Ave.), Pelham (Brx), 718-931-4335
Mon–Fri 9:30am–8pm Sat 10:30am–7pm Sun 11am–6pm
Natural foods market featuring organic produce, poultry, seafood, eggs,
nontoxic household cleaners, and other organic foods.

Govinda's Organic Market 🌿🌿🌿🌿

387 Atlantic Ave. (bet. Bond & Hoyt Sts.), Boerum Hill (Bkn), 718-834-7672
Mon–Sat 8am–9pm Sun 10am–9pm **govindaorganicmarket.com**
Wide variety of fresh, natural, organic and whole foods, nutritional products,
body care products, and health information. Organic juice bar. Free neighborhood delivery.

Greene Grape Provisions, The 🌿🌿🌿

753 Fulton St. (S. Portland Ave.), Fort Greene (Bkn), 718-233-2700
Daily 8am–9pm
Gourmet and organic grocer with fresh fish, meat, and prepared foods.

Guru Health Foods 🌿🌿🌿

86-18 Parsons Blvd. (86th Ave.), Jamaica Center (Qns), 718-291-7406
Mon–Tue 10am–8pm Wed 10am–7pm Thu–Sat 10am–8pm Sun 10am–6pm
Organic produce and dried herbs in bulk. Vitamins and herbal supplements;
dry, canned, and frozen organic food; natural and organic personal care
products. Educational books.

Health & Harmony 🌿🌿🌿🌿

470 Hudson St. (bet. Grove & Barrow Sts.), West Village (Man), 212-691-3036
Mon–Fri 8am–8:30pm Sat 9am–7:30pm Sun 9am–7pm
Natural grocer carrying organic produce and all-natural foods.

Health 4-U: Nature's Market 🍃🍃🍃

432 Park Ave. S (bet. 29th & 30th Sts.), Murray Hill (Man), 212-532-2644
Mon–Fri 8am–8pm Sat 10am–7pm
Health food store and juice bar. Organic locally grown produce; variety of fresh and frozen vegetarian, organic, and all-natural foods; organic and all-natural personal care products; nontoxic household cleaning products.

Health Bay Natural Foods Inc. 🍃🍃🍃

161-30 Crossbay Blvd. (161st Ave.), Howard Beach (Qns), 718-845-0517
Mon–Sat 10am–7pm Sun 11am–5pm
Organic produce, dairy products, and dry goods; organic and all-natural personal care products; environmentally friendly personal care tools.

Health Conscious Natural Food 🍃🍃🍃

231-22 Merrick Blvd. (231st St.), Springfield Gardens (Qns), 718-712-7740
Mon–Thu 9:30am–7pm Fri–Sat 9:30am–8pm
Vegetarian food; 100% organic juice bar and produce; bulk herbs; vitamins and personal products.

Health Nuts, The 🍃🍃🍃🍃

211-35 26th Ave. (154th St.), Bayside (Qns), 718-225-8164
1208 2nd Ave. (64th St.), Lenox Hill (Man), 212-593-0116
2141 Broadway (75th St.), Lincoln Square (Man), 212-724-1972
835 2nd Ave. (45th St.), Midtown East (Man), 212-490-2979
2611 Broadway (99th St.), Upper West Side (Man), 212-678-0054
Hours vary by location
Health food store with wide selection of organic produce and foods; natural body care products; organic dairy. All-organic juice bar.

Healthfully Organic Market 🍃🍃🍃🍃

98 E. 4th St. (bet. 1st & 2nd Aves.), East Village (Man), 212-598-0777
Mon–Fri 9am–10pm Sat 10am–9pm Sun 10am–8pm **healthfully.com**
Market provides organic produce, bulk foods, vitamins, organic coffee, and juice bar.

Healthy Life Nutritional Center 🍃🍃🍃🍃

271 W. 231st St. (bet. Corlear & Kingsbridge Aves.), Riverdale (Brx), 718-884-8884
Mon–Sat 10am–7pm
Market offering organic eggs, dairy, soy milk, bread, granola, canned and dry goods, frozen foods, and nondairy beverages; eco-friendly personal care products, all-natural vitamins, and diet and nutritional support.

House of Health 🍃🍃🍃🍃

1014 Lexington Ave. (bet. 72nd & 73rd Sts.), Upper East Side (Man), 212-772-8422
Mon–Fri 8am–9:30pm Sat 10am–9pm Sun 10am–8pm
Health store and juice bar carrying all-natural organic groceries and produce.

Imhotep 🍃🍃🍃🍃

734 Nostrand Ave. (Park Pl.), Crown Heights (Bkn), 718-493-2395
Daily 8am–10:30pm
Vegan restaurant and grocery store carrying organic and natural products including vitamins, herbs, and teas.

Integral Yoga Natural Foods 🌿🌿🌿🌿

229 W. 13th St. (7th Ave.), Greenwich Village (Man), 212-243-2642
Mon–Fri 8am–9:30pm Sat 8am–8:30pm Sun 9am–8:30pm
integralyoganaturalfoods.com
One of NYC's oldest vegetarian markets, providing organic produce, personal and household products, beverages, and dry goods.

Jackson Heights Health Foods 🌿🌿🌿

83-10 37th Ave. (83rd St.), Jackson Heights (Qns), 718-429-9511
Mon–Sat 9:30am–8pm Sun 10am–6pm
Organic produce, dry goods, dairy, and bulk herbs; natural and organic tinctures, supplements, homeopathic remedies, cleaning and beauty products.

Jin's Big Apple 🌿

60-07 Roosevelt Ave. (61st St.), Woodside (Qns), 718-779-4281
Daily 24 hrs.
Organic produce, dry goods, poultry, dairy, frozen foods, and bulk nuts and grains; vegetarian and vegan foods.

Karrot Health Food Store 🌿🌿🌿

304 W. 117th St. (bet. Frederick Douglass & Manhattan Aves.),
Central Harlem (Man), 212-870-0290
431 Myrtle Ave. (bet. Clinton & Waverly Aves.), Clinton Hill (Bkn),
718-522-9753
Hours vary by location
Selection of organic and natural foods, supplements, personal care products, prepared foods, and gluten-free groceries.

Khim's Millenium Market 🌿🌿

260 Bushwick Ave. (bet. Montrose & Johnson Sts.), Williamsburg (Bkn),
718-497-4650
265 Bedford Ave. (bet. Grand & N. 1st Sts.), Williamsburg (Bkn),
718-218-7540
280 Bedford Ave. (S. 1st St.), Williamsburg (Bkn), 718-387-0063
324 Graham Ave. (Devoe St.), Williamsburg (Bkn), 718-302-4152
Daily 24 hrs.
Grocery store offering a wide variety of organic food items, including frozen foods and dairy products.

Kidfresh 🌿🌿🌿🌿

1628 2nd Ave. (84th St.), Yorkville (Man), 800-365-4337
Mon–Fri 9am–7:30pm Sat 9am–7pm Sun 10am–6pm **kidfresh.com**
Grocery store focused on educating kids about healthy organic food and lifestyles. Offers children's cooking classes, and sponsors nutrition and healthy eating classes in schools.

Lifethyme Natural Market 🌿🌿🌿🌿

410 6th Ave. (W. 9th St.), Greenwich Village (Man), 212-420-9099
Mon–Fri 8am–10pm Sat–Sun 9am–10pm **lifethymemarket.com**
Complete natural market supporting local Tri-State farmers and providing unique, select imported produce. Provides prepared vegetarian, vegan, and gourmet dishes.

Linda's Natural Market ✍ ✍ ✍ ✍

81-22 Lefferts Blvd. (Grenfell St.), Kew Gardens (Qns), 718-847-2233
Mon–Tue 10am–7pm Wed 10am–8pm Thu–Fri 10am–7pm Sat 10am–6pm
Sun 11am–5:30pm **lindasorganic.com**
Neighborhood natural foods grocery store providing organic and sustainable
products from prepared foods to cosmetics; organic juice bar; organic and
vegan-centered cooking classes.

M&B Organics ✍ ✍ ✍

6331 Ave. N (Ralph Ave.), Mill Basin (Bkn), 718-251-2511
Mon–Fri 9am–7pm Sat 9am–5pm Sun 10am–5pm
Health food shop carrying organic grocery items, vitamins, and supplements.

Makal ✍ ✍ ✍

2008 65th St. (bet. 20th & 21st Aves.), Bensonhurst (Bkn), 718-259-2371
Mon–Sat 11am–7pm
Organic grocery store specializing in Amish-produced meat, produce, honey,
eggs, and dairy.

Manhattan Fruit Exchange ✍ ✍

75 9th Ave. (bet. 15th & 16th Sts.), Chelsea (Man), 212-989-2444
Mon–Sat 8am–8pm Sun 10am–7pm **manhattanfruitexchange.com**
Located in the Chelsea Market. Large organic section of fruits and vegetables from garden variety to exotic. Fresh-squeezed juices; organic dairy
products; dried fruits.

Mani Market Place ✍ ✍

697 Columbus Ave. (94th St.), Upper West Side (Man), 212-662-4392
Daily 6am–11pm
Neighborhood market with a variety of local and organic groceries, including
meat, fish, poultry, eggs, dairy, and frozen foods.

Matany Health Food Store ✍ ✍ ✍ ✍

154 Bedford Ave. (bet. N. 8th & N. 9th Sts.), Williamsburg (Bkn),
718-218-7980
Daily 7am–12am
Neighborhood health food store offering natural and organic products,
including bulk items.

Matter of Health, A ✍ ✍ ✍ ✍

1478 1st Ave. (E. 77th St.), Upper East Side (Man), 212-288-8280
Mon–Fri 8am–8:30pm Sat 9am–7:30pm Sun 10am–7pm
Long-standing health food store with wide selection of organic natural food.
Popular juice bar and fresh food counter that features vegan, macrobiotic,
and vegetarian food.

Millennium Health ✍ ✍ ✍

241 Bedford Ave., Ste. A (bet. Metropolitan Ave. & N. 4th St.), Williamsburg
(Bkn), 718-599-3081
Daily 9am–12am
Market and juice bar carrying organic and natural products.

Mr. G White Point Health Food ✍ ✍

132-25A 14th Ave. (132nd St.), College Point (Qns), 718-747-6262
Daily 9:30am–7:30pm
Organic fresh juices, dry goods, natural vitamins, remedies, herbal supple-
ments; natural and organic body care products.

Natural 🍃🍃🍃

72-56 Austin St. (Ascan Ave.), Forest Hills (Qns), 718-268-4477
336A Graham Ave. (Metropolitan Ave.), Williamsburg (Bkn), 718-486-2838
Mon–Sat 10am–8pm Sun 10am–7pm
Natural and organic products including vitamins, food, and paper products.

Natural Frontier Market 🍃🍃🍃

266 3rd Ave. (bet. 21st & 22nd Sts.), Gramercy Park (Man), 212-228-9133
1104 Cortelyou Rd. (Stratford Rd.), Kensington (Bkn), 718-284-3593
1424 3rd Ave. (E. 81st St.), Upper East Side (Man), 212-794-0922
Hours vary by location **naturalfrontiermarket.net**
Health store and juice bar with a variety of organic options and natural
supplements.

Natural Green Market 🍃🍃🍃🍃

162 3rd Ave. (E. 16th St.), Gramercy (Man), 212-780-0263
Mon–Fri 8am–11pm Sat–Sun 9am–10pm
Gourmet health food store with organic fresh produce, bulk granola; vegan
snacks and cookies.

Natural Market 🍃

98-88 Queens Blvd. (66th Ave.), Rego Park (Qns), 718-459-6010
Daily 6am–12am
Market with a selection of organic dry goods, meat, poultry, beauty prod-
ucts, and tea.

Nature's Pantry 🍃🍃🍃

263-15 Hillside Ave. (264th St.), Floral Park (Qns), 718-347-3037
Mon–Sat 9:30am–6pm
Vitamins and herbal supplements; organic dry, canned, and frozen food;
natural and organic personal care products.

Neil's Natural Market 🍃🍃🍃

46-10 Hollis Ct. (Utopia Pkwy.), Fresh Meadows (Qns), 718-321-2088
Mon–Sat 10am–9pm Sun 10am–7pm
Organic and all-natural foods and health care products.

New York Naturals 🍃🍃🍃

253 Flatbush Ave. (6th Ave.), Prospect Heights (Bkn), 718-230-7094
Mon–Fri 8am–10pm Sat 9am–10pm Sun 10am–10pm **nynaturals.com**
Grocery store with dried goods, organic produce, herbs, and alternative
medication. Customers can order meat from a farmer online each week and
pick up at store.

Northside Health Food 🍃🍃🍃

169 Bedford Ave. (N. 8th St.), Williamsburg (Bkn), 718-387-1078
Daily 8:30am–11:30pm
Organic food, bulk items, beauty supplies, and health supplements.

Nourish NYC 🍃🍃🍃

43-15 Queens Blvd. (43rd St.), Sunnyside (Qns), 718-433-4443
Daily 10am–7pm **nourishnyc.com**
Natural and organic supplements, vitamins, dry goods, frozen food; sports/
fitness products; eco-friendly gifts and candles; essential oils; mother and
baby products; body care. Organic juice bar.

Nutrisserie 🌿🌿🌿

142 W. 72nd St. (bet. Amsterdam & Columbus Aves.), Upper West Side (Man), 212-799-2454
Mon–Sat 9am–8pm Sun 10am–7pm
Natural and organic groceries, organic produce, discounted supplements; natural deli and juice bar.

Organic Forever 🌿🌿🌿🌿

2053 8th Ave. (bet. 111th & 112th Sts.), Central Harlem (Man), 212-666-3012
69-12 Austin St. (Yellowstone Blvd.), Forest Hills (Qns), 718-263-5430
Hours vary by location **organicforever.com**
Health food grocer providing a broad selection of organic produce, raw food selection, gluten-free options; natural living products and forum offering education, support, and information.

Park Natural & Organic 🌿🌿🌿

350 Court St. (Union St.), Carroll Gardens (Bkn), 718-802-1652
Mon–Sat 8am–8pm Sun 9am–7pm **parknatural.com**
Organic grocer committed to sustainable products. Carries essential oils, vitamins, and supplements. Deli and juice bar.

Park Slope Food Coop 🌿🌿🌿

782 Union St. (bet. 6th & 7th Aves.), Park Slope (Bkn), 718-622-0560
Mon–Fri 8am–10pm Sat 6am–10pm Sun 6am–7:30pm **foodcoop.com**
Wide variety of local and organic produce, dairy, meats, poultry, and wild-caught fish, as well as conventional grocery items. Membership open to the public.

Peas & Pickles 🌿

79 Henry St. (Orange St.), Brooklyn Heights (Bkn), 718-596-8219
45-55 Washington St. (Front St.), DUMBO (Bkn), 718-488-8336
Daily 24 hrs.
Grocery store carrying some organic essentials.

Perelandra 🌿🌿🌿🌿

175 Remsen St. (bet. Clinton & Court Sts.), Brooklyn Heights (Bkn), 718-855-6068
Mon–Fri 8:30am–8:30pm Sat 9:30am–8:30pm Sun 11am–7pm
perelandranatural.com
Natural and organic foods; certified organic produce; environmentally friendly body care; healthy, homemade vegetarian foods; dietary supplements; juice bar.

Pole Vision Life Strength 🌿🌿🌿

189-07 Union Tpke. (73rd St.), Fresh Meadows (Qns), 718-454-3663
Mon–Fri 9:30am–7:30pm Sat 10am–7:30pm Sun 10am–6pm
Organic produce and dry goods market; health and beauty products; educational materials.

Probiotics 🌿🌿🌿🌿

5666 Broadway (bet. W. 233rd & David Michael Ruddle Sts.), Riverdale (Brx), 718-432-7200
Mon–Fri 7am–7pm, Sat 8am–6pm, Sun 8am–4pm
Grocery store offering natural and organic products and 100% organic prepared foods and juices. Pharmacy section offering a wide range of natural vitamins, herbal tinctures, and homeopathic remedies.

Quantum Leap Natural Food Market 🍴🍴

65-60 Fresh Meadow Ln. (67th Ave.), Fresh Meadows (Qns), 718-762-3572
Mon–Thu 10am–10pm Fri–Sat 10am–11pm Sun 10am–10pm
Neighborhood market offering organic produce, herbs, and supplements;
homeopathic medicines available.

Queens Health Emporium 🍴🍴🍴

159-01 Horace Harding Expy. (159th St.), Fresh Meadows (Qns),
718-358-6500
Mon–Sat 9:30am–8pm Sun 10am–6pm **queenshealthemporium.com**
Fresh, natural, organic, macrobiotic, and whole foods; body care products;
educational health information; juice bar and deli.

Riverdale Health Food Store 🍴🍴🍴

5910 Riverdale Ave. (W. 259th St.), Riverdale (Brx), 718-601-1650
Mon–Sat 9am–7pm
Health food market featuring organic dry goods, produce, supplements, and
personal care products.

S.Y. Organic Farm, Inc. 🍴🍴🍴

724 Broadway (Flushing Ave.), Williamsburg (Bkn), 718-486-0400
Mon–Sat 10am–7pm Sun 11am–6pm
Health food store offering organic vitamins, beauty supplies, bulk food,
dairy, and dry foods. Wide range of vegetarian items.

SAI Organics 🍴🍴🍴

30-21 30th Ave. (31st St.), Astoria (Qns), 718-278-1726
36-07 30th Ave. (36th St.), Astoria (Qns), 718-956-1793
Mon–Sat 8am–9pm Sun 8am–6:30pm **saiorganics.com**
Health food store featuring a selection of organic vegetables, dairy, grains,
frozen food, coffee, tea; natural and organic beauty and cleaning products;
organic juice bar.

7 Grains Health Foods 🍴

2259 Adam Clayton Powell Blvd. (133rd St.), Central Harlem (Man),
212-862-3760
Mon–Sat 10am–6pm Sun 10am–5pm
Neighborhood health food store providing natural organic groceries and
healthy options.

Smith Organic Market 🍴🍴🍴

149 Smith St. (Bergen St.), Boerum Hill (Bkn), 718-625-5251
Daily 6am–11:30pm
Vegetarian neighborhood grocer carrying all organic essentials.

South Bronx Food Cooperative 🍴🍴🍴

754 Melrose Ave. (bet. 156th & 157th Sts.), Melrose (Brx), 646-226-0758
Sat 11am–5pm **sbxfc.org**
Organic grocery operated by members and open to the public. Membership includes free cooking classes, health/nutrition workshops, composting
classes, health screenings, and other events.

Sunac Natural 🍴🍴🍴

150 N. 7th St. (Bedford Ave.), Williamsburg (Bkn), 718-218-9451
440 Union Ave. (Metropolitan Ave.), Williamsburg (Bkn), 718-643-0508
Daily 24 hrs.
Grocery store offering organic, natural, fresh, and prepared foods; natural
beauty, cleaning, and paper supplies.

Sundial 🍃🍃🍃🍃

3609 Boston Rd. (bet. E. 222nd & E. 223rd Sts.), Wakefield (Brx),
718-798-3962
Mon–Sat 10am–6pm **sundialherbs.com**
Market specializing in traditional Ethiopian herbal remedies and provisions.
Other organic Caribbean and African groceries available.

Supreme Health Food Center 🍃🍃🍃

4624 16th Ave. (45th St.), Borough Park (Bkn), 718-853-3090
Mon–Wed 10am–7pm Thu 10am–8pm Fri 10am–1:30pm Sun 10:30am–6pm
Small grocer carrying organic produce, dry goods, vitamins, and supplements.

Tastebud's Natural Foods 🍃

1807 Hylan Blvd. (Buel Ave.), Dongan Hills (S.I.), 718-351-8693
Mon–Sat 9am–8pm Sun 10am–7pm
Organic and natural foods and produce. Organic juice bar.

Tony's Health Food 🍃🍃

2923 Glenwood Rd. (Nostrand Ave.), Flatbush (Bkn), 718-859-1138
Mon–Sat 9:30am–7:30pm Sun 9:30–4pm
Market carrying natural foods, supplements, and body building products.

Trader Joe's 🍃🍃

90-30 Metropolitan Ave. (Woodhaven Blvd.), Rego Park (Qns), 718-275-1791
142 E. 14th St. (bet. Irving Pl. & 3rd Ave.), Union Square (Man), 212-529-4612
Hours vary by location **traderjoes.com**
Organic and natural foods; nontoxic cleaning products; unbleached and
recycled paper products; some organic wine.

12th St. Market 🍃🍃

1201 8th Ave. (12th St.), Park Slope (Bkn), 718-832-7796
Daily 7am–11pm
Neighborhood grocer and deli carrying organic produce, sustainably raised
meats, and other organic and all-natural groceries.

Ujamma Health Food 🍃🍃🍃

398 Utica Ave. (bet. Crown & Montgomery Sts.), Crown Heights (Bkn),
718-771-8478
Mon–Sat 10am–8pm Sun 11am–5pm
Small, long-standing neighborhood grocery carrying organic cooking oils,
grains, flour, bulk items, nondairy milk and ice cream, frozen and other
foods; personal care products and household cleansers. Organic juice bar
open during summer months.

Union Market 🍃🍃🍃

402-404 7th Ave. (bet. 12th & 13th Sts.), Park Slope (Bkn), 718-499-4026
754-756 Union St. (6th Ave.), Park Slope (Bkn), 718-230-5152
Daily 7am–9pm **unionmarket.com**
Neighborhood gourmet grocer with selection of organic products, including
grass-fed and sustainably raised meats and poultry.

Urban Rustic 🍃🍃🍃🍃

236 N. 12th St. (Union Ave.), Williamsburg (Bkn), 718-388-9444
Daily 7am–10pm **urbanrusticnyc.com**
All-organic selection of local in-season produce, meat, dairy, and bread.
Juice bar, self-serve salad bar, and grocery store.

Vegan's Delight, LLC 🌿🌿🌿

3565C Boston Rd. (bet. Tiemann & Kingsland Aves.), Wakefield (Brx), 718-653-4140
Mon–Sat 7:30am–7pm **vegansdelight.com**
Vegan take-out meals, juice bar, and grocery. Meals prepared by micro-cosmic science principles and only in spring water. Pastries and salads also available.

Vital Health Foods 🌿🌿

196-14 Linden Blvd. (197th St.), St. Albans (Qns), 718-525-0992
Mon–Thu 9:30am–7pm Fri–Sat 9am–7pm
Vegetarian food, organic juice bar, bulk herbs, vitamins, and personal products.

Vitality & Health Organic Market 🌿🌿🌿🌿

46-03 Broadway (46th St.), Astoria (Qns), 718-274-1591
Mon–Fri 7am–10pm Sat–Sun 8am–10pm **vitalityandhealth.org**
Health food store and café with organic produce; organic and natural dairy, meats, organic salad bar, supplements, sandwiches, juice bar, and household products. Wi-Fi available.

Vitality Health 🌿🌿🌿🌿

1412 1st Ave. (E. 75th St.), Upper East Side (Man), 212-472-7700
Mon 8:30am–7:30pm Tue–Fri 8:30am–8pm Sat 8:30am–6pm Sun 11:30am–6pm
Family-oriented market with a focus on organic and all-natural food for children and babies.

Vitamin Depot Nutrition Center 🌿🌿🌿

7721 5th Ave. (77th St.), Bay Ridge (Bkn), 718-238-0676
Mon–Sat 8am–6:30pm
Neighborhood grocer carrying mostly organic items and a large selction of vitamins and supplements. Organic juice bar.

Watkins Health Food 🌿🌿

54 W. 125th St. (bet. 5th & Lenox Aves.), Central Harlem (Man), 212-831-2955
Daily 9am–8pm
Health food store providing sugar-free snacks, dry goods, organic produce, and vegetarian groceries.

Westerly Natural Market 🌿🌿🌿

913 8th Ave. (W. 54th St.), Midtown West (Man), 212-586-5262
Mon–Fri 7am–12am Sat 8am–12am Sun 9am–12am
westerlynaturalmarket.com
Natural grocery offering all-organic produce and a variety of natural and organic foods such as meat, poultry, eggs, and dairy products.

Whole Foods Market 🌿🌿🌿🌿

250 7th Ave. (24th St.), Chelsea (Man), 212-924-5969
10 Columbus Cir., Ste. SC101 (58th St.), Columbus Circle (Man), 212-823-9600
95 E. Houston St. (bet. Bowery & Chrystie Sts.), Lower East Side (Man), 212-420-1320
40 E. 14th St. (Union Sq. West), Union Square (Man), 212-673-5388
Mon–Sun 8am–11pm **wholefoodsmarket.com**
Full-service grocery store offering many organic and fair trade products. Bulk selection; natural body care products. In-store bakery, deli, and fresh meat and seafood counters. Some stores provide catering and delivery. Offsets 100% of the electricity the stores use with clean, sustainable wind energy.

Specialty Markets

Businesses in this category vary widely, due to the many different product areas they focus on. The stores listed here are not just specialists in their niche but also offer food and/or beverages that are organic and healthy as well as tasty.

Where there is one primary product area at a given market, we focused on that in awarding our leaves. If a market offers goods in several product categories, we have evaluated all the major ones. Specialty markets can be rated in all food areas, depending on what they offer. In addition, we looked at whether or not the stores offered reusable bags to their customers, or if their bags and any available carry-out containers were biodegradable or compostable and/or made with recycled, recyclable, and/or chlorine-free paper.

- For produce, we checked the percentage purchased that is certified organic and/or locally grown without pesticides and chemical fertilizers.

- For meat and meat alternatives, we determined the percentage that is certified organic and/or grass-fed and produced without the use of hormones and antibiotics.

- For poultry and eggs, we evaluated the percentage purchased that is certified organic and free-range/cage-free, and/or locally raised and free-range/cage-free without the use of hormones and antibiotics.

- With seafood, we checked into whether it was wild-caught or sustainably farm-raised and processed without chemical treatment.

- For dairy products, we checked the percentage of certified organic options or ones that were locally produced without hormones and antibiotics.

- We looked into the percentage of certified organic canned and dry goods and nondairy beverages.

- For prepared foods, we determined the percentage made with certified organic ingredients and/or locally grown ingredients without pesticides and chemical fertilizers.

at least 25% of the products meet the above criteria.

at least 50% of the products meet the above criteria.

at least 75% of the products meet the above criteria.

at least 90% of the products meet the above criteria.

Artisanal Fromagerie 🍃🍃🍃🍃

2 Park Ave. (32nd St.), Murray Hill (Man), 212-725-8585
Daily 11am–7pm **artisanalbistro.com**
Selection of 250 artisanal, handcrafted cheeses from small,
sustainable farms.

Bedford Cheese Shop 🍃

229 Bedford Ave. (N. 4th St.), Williamsburg (Bkn), 718-599-7588
Mon–Fri 11am–9pm Sat 10am–9pm Sun 10am–8pm
bedfordcheeseshop.com
Cheese shop carrying selection from small, artisanal producers.

Carroll Gardens Fish Market 🍃

359 Court St. (Carroll St.), Carroll Gardens (Bkn), 718-797-4884
Mon–Sat 8am–7pm
Seafood market regularly carrying some wild-caught fish.

Cosmic Enterprise 🍃

147 Rockaway Ave. (bet. Atlantic Ave. & Fulton St.), Bronxville/Bedford-
Stuyvesant (Bkn), 718-342-6257
Mon–Thu 12pm–8pm Fri–Sat 1pm–9pm
Herbal health food store carrying organic foods, herbs, spices, tonics,
candles, incense, and natural soaps.

David's Health Foods 🍃🍃

2211 Ave. U (E. 22nd St.), Gravesend (Bkn), 718-934-2980
Mon–Thu 9am–7pm Fri 9am–5:30pm Sun 10am–6pm
Health food shop carrying a variety of natural vitamins, herbs, and some
organic groceries.

Dorian's Seafood Market 🍃

1580 York Ave. (E. 83rd St.), Yorkville (Man), 212-535-2256
Mon–Fri 8:30am–7pm Sat 9am–6pm
Seafood market offering some wild-caught seafood.

Garden of Eden Gourmet 🍃🍃

180 Montague St. (bet. Court & Clinton Sts.), Brooklyn Heights (Bkn),
718-222-1515
162 W. 23rd St. (7th Ave.), Chelsea (Man), 212-675-6300
7 E. 14th St. (5th Ave.), Union Square (Man), 212-255-4200
2780 Broadway (bet. 107th & 108th Sts.), Upper West Side (Man),
212-222-7300
Hours vary by location **edengourmet.com**
Gourmet food market specializing in organic poultry, fresh meats, ecologically safe caviar and seafood, eggs and dairy items; variety of homemade
sauces, soups, salads, desserts. Provides delivery and catering services.

Get Fresh 🍃🍃

370 5th Ave. (5th St.), Park Slope (Bkn), 718-360-8469
Mon–Fri 11am–9pm Sat–Sun 11am–7pm **getfreshnyc.com**
"Ready-to-cook" foods made with local and organic ingredients and packaged in recycled, compostable containers. Also sells locally crafted food
products, books on sustainable eating.

Gramercy Meat Market 🍃🍃🍃🍃

383 2nd Ave. (23rd St.), Gramercy Park (Man), 212-481-1114
Daily 9am–7:30pm **gramercymeat.com**
Butcher shop selling complete line of organic and kosher meats.

Health Hut 🍃🍃🍃
117 Lee Ave. (Hooper St.), Williamsburg (Bkn), 718-388-0493
Daily 10am–7pm
Community health food store offering organic dry goods and all-natural vitamins and supplements.

Healthy Choice 🍃🍃
49A Division Ave. (Driggs Ave.), Williamsburg (Bkn), 718-218-7151
Mon–Thu 10am–7pm Fri 10am–2pm Sun 11am–7pm
Health food store carrying a wide variety of kosher and organic dry goods, nondairy cheeses, and all-natural vitamins and supplements. Delivers within 25-block radius.

Healthy Garden 🍃🍃
459 Wilson Ave. (Cornelia St.), Bushwick (Bkn), 718-919-5700
Mon–Sat 10am–6pm
Organic dry goods, meats, and dairy products. Participates in biodiesel recycling and composting programs.

Healthy Life 🍃🍃🍃
169-28 Hillside Ave. (169th St.), Jamaica (Qns), 718-206-3356
Mon–Fri 7am–9pm Sat–Sun 9am–9pm
Neighborhood specialty market offering many all-natural Sri Lankan foods with some organic options, organic juice bar, natural beauty and health products.

High Vibe 🍃🍃🍃🍃
138 E. 3rd St. (Ave. A), East Village (Man), 888-554-6645
Mon–Fri 10am–8pm Sat–Sun 12pm–7pm **highvibe.com**
Organic and raw food store carrying prepared foods, organic supplements, natural beauty products, and health books.

HIM Health Food Market 🍃
4374B White Plains Rd. (bet. Nereid Ave. & E. 237th St.), Wakefield (Brx), 718-798-0018
Mon–Sat 10am–7pm
Health food store carrying vegan groceries and herbs, some organic food. Hot vegan meals available Fridays and Saturdays.

Jamal & Prince Organic Food Market 🍃🍃🍃🍃
558 Halsey St. (Stuyvesant Ave.), Bedford-Stuyvesant (Bkn), 718-573-0831
Mon–Sat 8am–8:30pm Sun 1pm–7pm
Seasonal organic produce and dry goods, and other grocery items. Participates in biodiesel recycling and composting programs.

Leaf of Life 🍃🍃🍃
1325 Flatbush Ave. (Foster Ave.), Flatbush (Bkn), 718-826-9020
Mon–Sat 10am–7:30pm **leafoflifevitamins.com**
Small shop with a wide selection of natural vitamins, herbs, organic food products, natural body care products and remedies; organic juice bar.

Mastiha Shop 🍃
145 Orchard St. (Rivington St.), Lower East Side (Man), 212-253-0895
Tue 12pm–7pm Wed–Fri 12pm–8pm Sat 12am–9pm Sun 11am–7pm
mastihashopny.com
Cakes and pastries, dry goods, and cooking oils made with mastiha, a resin from the eastern Mediterranean with antimicrobiological qualities and a healing effect on inflammatory and cardiac conditions.

Nature Division 🌿🌿🌿

186 Division Ave. (Havemeyer St.), Williamsburg (Bkn), 718-387-2785
Mon–Thu 11am–7pm Sun 11am–7pm
Neighborhood health food store offering kosher and organic dry goods, wide selection of vitamins and supplements.

Nature's Organic Natural Foods 🌿🌿🌿

776 Nostrand Ave. (bet. Sterling & St.John's Pls.), Crown Heights (Bkn), 718-773-4649
Mon–Sat 9am–9pm Sun 8am–8pm
Neighborhood health food store carrying organic dry goods, and beverages. Organic juice bar.

Ottomanelli Brothers 🌿🌿

395 Amsterdam Ave. (79th St.), West Side (Man), 212-496-1049
1549 York Ave. (82nd St.), Yorkville (Man), 212-772-7900
Hours vary by location nycotto.com
Neighborhood butcher shop providing 100% grass-fed beef, organic poultry, and other organic meats and game.

Park Slope Seafood 🌿

215 7th Ave. (bet. 3rd & 4th Sts.), Park Slope (Bkn), 718-832-7965
Mon–Sat 10am–7:30pm Sun 10am–6:30pm
Neighborhood seafood market offering some wild-caught fish.

Pumpkin's Organic Market 🌿🌿🌿🌿

1302 8th Ave. (13th St.), Park Slope (Bkn), 718-499-8539
Daily 10am–8pm pumpkinsorganicmarket.com
Small, organic, vegetarian market selling wide variety of organic and locally grown produce, grains, tea, coffee, all-natural cleaning products, and bulk items.

Raskin's Fish Market 🌿🌿

320 Kingston Ave. (bet. President & Union Sts.), Crown Heights (Bkn), 718-756-9521
Mon–Thu 8am–7pm Fri 8am–3pm raskinfish.com
Family-owned kosher fish market offering good selection of wild-caught and organically farm-raised seafood.

Riverdale Fish Co. 🌿

550 W. 235th St. (bet. Johnson & Oxford Aves.), Riverdale (Brx), 718-548-4442
Mon–Fri 9am–7pm Sat 9am–6:30pm
Seafood market carrying some wild-caught fish.

Saxelby Cheesemongers 🌿🌿🌿🌿

120 Essex St. (bet. Rivington & Delancey Sts.), Lower East Side (Man), 212-228-8204
Mon–Sat 9am–7pm saxelbycheese.com
Specialty cheese shop carrying a variety of certified organic and sustainably sourced cheeses, milk, yogurt, and eggs.

Staubitz Market 🌿🌿

222 Court St. (bet. Warren & Baltic Sts.), Cobble Hill (Bkn), 718-624-0014
Mon–Fri 9am–7pm Sat 8am–6pm staubitz.com
Butcher shop and meat market carrying free-range, antibiotic-free poultry and grass-fed beef.

Stingray Fish Market 🌿🌿

375 E. 98th St. (Riverdale Ave.), Brownsville (Bkn),
718-498-2796
Mon–Fri 3pm–8pm Sat 9am–9pm Sun 9am–6pm
Neighborhood fish market carrying almost exclusively wild-caught seafood.

Stinky Bklyn 🌿

261 Smith St. (bet. Douglass & Degraw Sts.), Carroll Gardens (Bkn),
718-522-7425
Mon–Fri 11am–8pm Sat–Sun 10am–8pm   **stinkybklyn.com**
Cheese shop specializing in small, artisanal cheese producers. Charcuterie,
chocolate, and other gourmet foods.

Sunlife Health Food and Juice Bar 🌿

4060 White Plains Rd. (bet. E. 228th & E. 229th Sts.), Wakefield (Brx),
718-547-3760
Mon–Thu 8am–10pm Fri–Sat 8am–12am Sun 10am–10pm
Market carrying vegan products, some organic choices.

Universal Health Food Store & Juice Bar 🌿🌿🌿

4816 White Plains Rd. (bet. E. 242nd & E. 243rd Sts.), Wakefield (Brx),
718-231-3786
Daily 12pm–8pm
Health food store offering organic produce, meat alternatives, all-natural
canned and dry goods, nondairy beverages, and prepared vegan foods.

Urban Roots 🌿🌿🌿

51 Ave. A (3rd St.), East Village (Man), 212-780-0288
Daily 10am–9:30pm
Natural foods store carrying organic produce, dry goods, dairy products,
supplements, and nondairy beverages; organic juice bar.

Wealth of Health Nutrition Center 🌿🌿🌿

1309 Ave. U (E. 13th St.), Gravesend/Sheepshead Bay (Bkn), 718-645-2222
Mon–Thu 9:30am–6pm Fri 9:30am–2pm Sun 10am–6pm
Health and vitamin store selling organic and all-natural dry goods,
herbal supplements.

Wild Edibles Seafood Market 🌿🌿🌿

318 Grand Central Terminal (43rd St.), Midtown (Man), 212-687-4255
535 3rd Ave. (bet. 35th & 36th Sts.), Murray Hill (Man), 212-213-8552
Hours vary by location   **wildedibles.com**
Fish market offering line-caught, hand-picked, and organically farm-raised
seafood. Complies with Blue Ocean Institute sustainability standards.

Zion Organic 🌿🌿🌿🌿

198-07 Hollis Ave. (198th St.), St. Albans (Qns), 718-740-8088
Mon–Sat 8am–5pm   **zionorganic.com**
Herbal beverages made with organic ingredients from Jamaica and the
West Indies.

Grocery and Produce Delivery

These grocery and produce delivery services deliver fresh, healthy food and sustainably made nonfood items to your door. Not only can they save you valuable hours every week, many also offer fast and convenient online ordering capabilities.

We reviewed these delivery services in the following thirteen product areas:

- For produce, we calculated the percentage that is certified organic and/or locally grown without pesticides and chemical fertilizers.

- For meat and meat alternatives, we determined the percentage that is certified organic and/or grass-fed and produced without the use of hormones and antibiotics.

- For poultry and eggs, we evaluated the percentage that is certified organic and free-range/cage-free, and/or locally raised and free-range/cage-free without the use of hormones and antibiotics.

- With seafood, we looked at whether it was wild-caught or sustainably farm-raised without chemical processing.

- For dairy products, we checked the percentage of certified organic options or ones that were locally produced without hormones and antibiotics.

- We looked at the percentage of certified organic canned and dry goods, and nondairy beverages.

- For prepared foods, we determined the percentage made with certified organic ingredients and/or locally grown ingredients without pesticides and chemical fertilizers.

- For personal care products, we looked into the percentage that is organic or all natural.

- For personal care and household cleaning tools, we determined the percentage made with environmentally friendly materials.

- We checked the percentage of household cleansers, soaps, and detergents that are nontoxic.

- For household paper products, we looked at the percentage made from recycled content and whitened without chlorine.

at least 25% of the products meet the above criteria.

at least 50% of the products meet the above criteria.

at least 75% of the products meet the above criteria.

at least 90% of the products meet the above criteria.

Applegate Farms 🌿
750 Rte. 202 S., Ste. 300, Bridgewater NJ 08807, 866-587-5858
Mon–Fri 8am–5pm **applegatefarms.com**
Vegetarian-fed, hormone-free meat products, corn- and soy-fed poultry, organic cheeses. Serves all of New York City.

Bobolink Dairy 🌿🌿🌿🌿
42 Meadowburn Rd., Vernon NJ 07426, 973-764-4888
Wed–Fri 12pm–6pm Sat–Sun 9am–5pm **cowsoutside.com**
Artisanal cheeses made from raw 100% grass-fed cow's milk, pasture-raised seasonal meats, organic wood-fired breads. Sustainable methods practiced in all farm activity. Bread- and cheese-making workshops; tours and tastings available. Ships Mon and Tue via UPS to anywhere in New York area.

Door to Door Organics 🌿🌿🌿🌿
7036D Easton Rd., Pipersville PA 18947, 888-283-4443
Mon–Tue 9am–4pm Wed 6:30am–7pm Thu–Fri 9am–4pm
doortodoororganics.com
Boxes of certified vgetables, fruits, or combinations delivered to homes and businesses via UPS. Serves East Coast and other regions.

8 O'Clock Ranch Meat CSA 🌿🌿🌿🌿
315-347-4352
Online only; year-round **eightoclockranch.com**
Collective of three family-run ranches delivering grass-fed lamb and beef, pasture-raised grain-finished pork, organic goat's milk dairy products, and eggs. Next-day delivery to anywhere in New York area.

Fresh Direct 🌿
718-928-1565
Online only **freshdirect.com**
Organic produce, dairy, eggs, coffee, all-natural baby products, organic wine, and other sustainable grocery items. Minimum order $30 for delivery. Prepaid credit card online orders only. Serves all of New York City.

Get Fresh 🌿🌿🌿🌿
370 5th Ave. (5th St.), Park Slope (Bkn), 718-360-8469
Mon–Fri 11am–9pm Sat–Sun 11am–7pm **getfreshnyc.com**
Healthy, "ready-to-cook" meals prepared with organic, locally sourced ingredients. Serves Brooklyn and Manhattan; pick-up also available.

Manhattan Fruitier 🌿
105 E. 29th St. (bet. Park & Lexington Aves.), Murray Hill (Man), 212-686-0404
Mon–Fri 9am–5pm **manhattanfruitier.com**
Offers some organic, seasonal fruit baskets. Serves all of New York City.

Rawvolution 🌿🌿🌿🌿
800-997-6729
Online only **rawvolution.com**
Prepared organic raw foods. Weekly home delivery Sundays. Online orders only. Serves all of New York City.

Urban Organic 🌿🌿🌿🌿
240 6th St. (4th Ave.), Park Slope (Bkn), 718-499-4321
Mon–Fri 9am–5pm **urbanorganic.com**
Local, organic, seasonal produce delivery. One-time $25 membership fee; free delivery to Brooklyn and Manhattan, $2 to other boroughs.

Greenmarkets, Farmers' Markets, and CSAs

There's no easier way to bring a bit of the farm to the city and to your table than through your local Greenmarkets, farmers' markets, and community-supported agriculture (CSAs). We are getting closer to the source of our food, learning about how it is grown, and meeting the farmers. Kids and adults alike are starting to see where their carrots come from and we are all falling in love again with fresh, tree-ripened peaches.

At a **Greenmarket**, the focus is on local produce, both the quality and freshness of the food and the experience of interacting with the farmer. Although there are a few exceptions (bakers, fishers, people who make preserves), Greenmarket rules require that vendors grow their own products in order to sell them at the market. A farm inspector regularly visits farmers to ensure their compliance with this requirement.

Farmers' markets are also about the food and about the community, although the "grow your own" rule isn't so stringently applied. Here you'll find fresh produce, tasty treats, locally made goods, and many products you can't get at the grocery store. Plus, food items at farmers' markets change naturally with the seasons.

When you buy a share in a local farm operation, you are part of what is called **community-supported agriculture (CSA).** This means you have joined a regional community of growers and consumers and are sharing in both the risks and the benefits of food production. Typically, members, or "shareholders," of the farm pay in advance to cover the costs of the farm. In return, they receive shares of the farm's produce throughout the growing season. By direct sales to community members, growers receive better prices for their crops and gain some financial security.

Farmers follow a range of growing methods: conventional, uncertified organic, certified organic, and **biodynamic.** Most organic farmers advertise their practices, especially certified organic ones. Those farmers that either can't afford organic certification or are using other means deserve your business as well. Supporting regional agriculture and a high-quality food supply is everyone's business.

All Greenmarkets, farmers' markets, and CSAs listed here meet our criteria in that they support regional agriculture and seasonal, quality products. They connect farmers with consumers and strengthen the bond between grower and eater. Considering the variations among vendors within a market or CSA, we have given all equal importance and not awarded leaves to any individual Greenmarket, farmers' market, or CSA.

Greenmarkets

Abingdon Square Greenmarket
W. 12th St. (Hudson St.), West Village (Man), 212-788-7476
Sat 8am–2pm **cenyc.org**

Astoria Greenmarket
14th St. (bet. 31st Ave. & 31st Rd.), Astoria (Qns), 212-788-7476
Wed 8am–5pm **cenyc.org**

Atlas Park Greenmarket
Cooper Ave. (80th St.), Glendale (Qns), 212-788-7476
Sat 8am–4pm **cenyc.org**

Borough Park Greenmarket
14th Ave. (bet. 49th & 50th Sts.), Borough Park (Bkn), 212-788-7476
Thu 8am–3pm **cenyc.org**

Bowling Green Greenmarket
Broadway (Battery Pl.), White Hall (Man), 212-788-7476
Tue, Thu 8am–5pm **cenyc.org**

Bronx Borough Hall Greenmarket
Grand Concourse (bet. E. 156th & E. 158th Sts.), Concourse Village (Brx), 212-788-7476
Tue 8am–6pm **cenyc.org**

Brooklyn Borough Hall Greenmarket
Court St. (Montague St.), Brooklyn Heights (Bkn), 212-788-7476
Tue, Thu, Sat 8am–6pm **cenyc.org**

Carroll Gardens Greenmarket
Carroll St. (bet. Smith & Court Sts.), Carroll Gardens (Bkn), 212-788-7476
Sun 8am–4pm **cenyc.org**

Cedar St. Greenmarket
Cedar St. (bet. Broadway & Church St.), White Hall (Man), 212-788-7476
Tue, Thu 8am–6pm **cenyc.org**

City Hall Park Greenmarket
Chambers St. (Broadway), Tribeca (Man), 212-788-7476
Fri 8am–4pm **cenyc.org**

Columbia Greenmarket
Broadway (bet. W. 114th & W. 115th Sts.), Morningside Heights (Man), 212-788-7476
Thu, Sun 8am–6pm **cenyc.org**

Cortelyou Greenmarket
Cortelyou Rd. (bet. Argyle & Rugby Sts.), Flatbush (Bkn), 212-788-7476
Sun 8am–4pm **cenyc.org**

Dag Hammarskjold Plaza Greenmarket
E. 47th St. (2nd Ave.), Turtle Bay (Man), 212-788-7476
Wed 8am–6pm **cenyc.org**

82nd St./St. Stephens Greenmaket
E. 82nd St. (bet. 1st & York Aves.), Upper East Side (Man), 212-788-7476
Sat 9am–3pm **cenyc.org**

57th St. Greenmarket
9th Ave. (bet. 56th & 57th Sts.), Clinton (Man), 212-788-7476
Wed, Sat 8am–6pm   **cenyc.org**

Fort Greene Park Greenmarket
Washington Park (Dekalb Ave.), Fort Greene (Bkn), 212-788-7476
Sat 8am–5pm   **cenyc.org**

Grand Army Plaza Greenmarket
NW entrance of Prospect Park (Prospect Park West, Eastern Pkwy. &
Flatbush Ave.), Prospect Park (Bkn), 212-788-7476
Sat 8am–4pm   **cenyc.org**

Greenpoint–McCarren Park Greenmarket
Lorimer St. (Driggs Ave.), Greenpoint (Bkn), 212-788-7476
Sat 8am–3pm   **cenyc.org**

Harlem Hospital Greenmarket
Lenox Ave. (bet. W. 136th & W. 137th Sts.), Harlem (Man), 212-788-7476
Thu 8am–5pm   **cenyc.org**

Inwood Greenmarket
Ishman St. (bet. Seaman Ave. & Cooper St.), Inwood (Man), 212-788-7476
Sat 8am–3pm   **cenyc.org**

Jackson Heights Greenmarket
34th Ave. (bet. 77th & 78th Sts.), Jackson Heights (Qns), 212-788-7476
Sun 8am–3pm   **cenyc.org**

LES/Grand St. Greenmarket
Grand St. (Norfolk St.), Lower East Side (Man), 212-788-7476
Sun 8am–4pm   **cenyc.org**

Lincoln Hospital Greenmarket
149th St. (bet. Park & Morris Aves.), Melrose (Brx), 212-788-7476
Tue 8am–3pm   **cenyc.org**

Long Island City Greenmarket
48th Ave. (Vernon Blvd.), Long Island City (Qns), 212-788-7476
Sat 8am–3pm   **cenyc.org**

Mt. Sinai Hospital Greenmarket
E. 99th St. (bet. Madison & Park Aves.), East Harlem (Man), 212-788-7476
Wed 8am–5pm   **cenyc.org**

Murray Hill Greenmarket
2nd Ave. (33rd St.), Murray Hill (Man), 212-788-7476
Sat 8am–3pm   **cenyc.org**

92nd St. Greenmarket
1st Ave. (bet. E. 92nd & E. 93rd Sts.), Upper East Side (Man), 212-788-7476
Sun 9am–5pm   **cenyc.org**

97th St. Greenmarket
W. 97th St. (Columbus Ave.), Upper West Side (Man), 212-788-7476
Fri 8am–2pm   **cenyc.org**

175th St. Greenmarket
175th St. (Broadway), Washington Heights (Man), 212-788-7476
Thu 8am–6pm **cenyc.org**

Poe Park Greenmarket
Grand Concourse (E. 192nd St.), Fordham (Brx), 212-788-7476
Tue 8am–3pm **cenyc.org**

Rockefeller Greenmarket
Rockefeller Plaza (W. 50th St.), Midtown (Man), 212-788-7476
Wed–Fri 8am–6pm **cenyc.org**

St. George Greenmarket
St. Marks St. (Hyatt St.), Tompkinsville (S.I.), 212-788-7476
Sat 8am–2pm **cenyc.org**

St. Marks' Church Greenmarket
E. 10th St. (2nd Ave.), Lower East Side (Man), 212-788-7476
Tue 8am–7pm **cenyc.org**

77th St. Greenmarket
W. 77th St. (inside IS44 schoolyard) (Columbus Ave.), Upper West Side (Man), 212-788-7476
Sun 10am–5pm **cenyc.org**

South Village Greenmarket
6th Ave. (bet. W. Houston & Downing Sts.), SoHo (Man), 212-788-7476
Sun 8am–4pm **cenyc.org**

Staten Island Ferry Whitehall Terminal Greenmarket
4 South St. (inside Ferry Terminal Building) (Whitehall St.), Whitehall (Man), 212-788-7476
Tue 8am–7pm **cenyc.org**

Strangers Gate Greenmarket
Central Park West (106th St.), Upper West Side (Man), 212-788-7476
Sat 8am–3pm **cenyc.org**

Stuyvesant Town Greenmarket
Stuy-Town Oval, 14th St. Loop (Ave. A), Stuyvesant Town (Murray Hill) (Man), 212-788-7476
Sun 9:30am–4pm **cenyc.org**

Sunnyside Greenmarket
Skillman Ave. (bet. 42nd & 43rd Sts.), Sunnyside (Qns), 212-788-7476
Sat 8am–4pm **cenyc.org**

Sunset Park Greenmarket
4th Ave. (bet. 59th & 60th Sts.), Sunset Park (Bkn), 212-788-7476
Sat 8am–3pm **cenyc.org**

Tompkins Square Greenmarket
E. 7th St. (Ave. A), East Village (Man), 212-788-7476
Sun 8am–6pm **cenyc.org**

Tribeca Greenmarket
Greenwich St. (Chambers St.), Tribeca (Man), 212-788-7476
Wed 8am–3pm Sat 8am–3pm **cenyc.org**
Open-air farmers' market with focus on locally grown produce.

Tucker Square Greenmarket

W. 66th St. (Columbus Ave.), Lincoln Sq. (Man), 212-788-7476
Thu Sat 8am–5pm **cenyc.org**

Union Square Greenmarket

E. 17th St. (bet. E. 17th St. & Broadway), Flatiron (Man), 212-788-7476
Mon, Wed, Fri, Sat 8am–6pm **cenyc.org**
Closed day after Thanksgiving.

Williamsburg Greenmarket

Havermeyer St. (Broadway Ave.), Williamsburg (Bkn), 212-788-7476
Thu 8am–4pm **cenyc.org**

Windsor Terrace Greenmarket

Prospect Park West (inside Park entrance) (16th St.), Prospect Park (Bkn),
212-788-7476
Wed 8am–3pm **cenyc.org**

Farmers' Markets

Bissel Gardens Farmers' Market

Baychester Ave. (E. 241st St.), Wakefield (Brx), 718-325-6111
Wed 10am–3pm Sat 9am–3pm Sun 10am–2pm **bisselgardens.org**
Organic vegetables and fruit from Bissel Gardens and local farms.

Coney Island Farmers' Market

W. 16th St. Key Span Park (Surf Ave.), Coney Island (Bkn), 917-873-9261
Sun 8am–3pm
Local, certified organic vegetables and fruit. Juices, preserves, and eight
varieties of organic honey available.

CVC Linden Street/Bushwick Farmers' Market

Knickerbocker Ave., Maria Hernandez Park (Starr St.), Bushwick (Bkn),
718-670-3360
Linden St., Hecture Playground (bet. Central & Wilson Aves.),
Bushwick (Bkn), 718-670-3360
Wed 10am–4pm
Conventionally grown vegetables and fruit, some produce grown locally.
Farmers represent African descendants and farmers from Mexico.

DUMBO Farmers' Market

Main St. Entrance to Brooklyn Bridge Park (Water St.), DUMBO (Bkn),
914-923-4837
Sun 11am–5pm **communitymarkets.biz**
Local conventionally grown produce.

East New York Farmers' Market, The

Scherick Ave. (bet. New Lots & Livonia Aves.), East New York (Bkn),
718-649-7979
Sat 9am–3pm **eastnewyorkfarms.org**
Local organic produce from regional farmers and community gardens.
Flowers, honey, and locally wild-caught fish and crab available. Market also
features handmade foods and crafts.

Flatbush-Caton Merchants Mart Farmers' Market

794-814 Flatbush Ave. (bet. Caton & Lenox Aves.), Flatbush (Bkn),
718-941-1424
Wed 7:30am–5pm
A mix of locally grown and conventionally grown vegetables and fruit.
Honey also available.

Graham Avenue Farmers' Market

Cook St. (Graham Ave.), Williamsburg (Bkn), 718-387-6643
Sat–Sun 8am–5:50pm
Local vegetables and fruit; mix of produce grown conventionally and grown
using organic methods; honey and baked goods.

Grassroots Farmers' Market

W. 145th St. Jackie Robinson Park (Edgecomb Ave.), Harlem (Man),
212-996-1514
Tue Sat 9am–4pm
Local organic vegetables and fruit. Organic herbs and spices grown in local,
New York City community gardens.

Hamer-Campos Farmers' Market & Crafts Fair

430 Beach 66th St., P.S. 42 (Beach Channel Dr.), Far Rockaway (Qns)
Sat 8am–3pm
Farmers' market serving Far Rockaway, sponsored by People United for
Local Leadership.

Harlem Harvest Farmers' Market #1

E. 112th St. (Madison Ave.), Morningside Heights (Man), 212-348-2733
Sat 9am–5pm
Conventionally grown fruit and vegetables, some locally grown. Flowers,
herbs, and baked goods available. Locally produced arts and crafts also
featured.

Harlem Harvest Farmers' Market #2

163 W. 125th St., The Plaza at Adam Clayton Powell State Office Bldg. (7th
Ave.), Central Harlem (Man), 212-348-2733
Tue 8am–5pm
Conventionally grown fruit and vegetables, some locally grown. Flowers,
herbs, and baked goods available. Locally produced arts and crafts.

Harvest Home Forest Avenue Market

Forest Ave. (bet. 156th St. & Westchester Ave.), Melrose (Brx), 212-828-3361
Wed 8am–4pm   **harvesthomefm.org**
Locally grown fruits and vegetables.

Harvest Home Jacobi Market

1400 Pelham Pkwy. (Seymour Ave.), Seymour Ave. (Brx), 212-828-3361
Tue 8am–4pm   **harvesthomefm.org**
Locally grown fruits and vegetables; baked goods and cheeses.

Harvest Home Morris Park Market

1734 Williamsbridge Rd., Our Savior Lutheran School (bet. Morris Park & Van
Nest Aves.), Morris Park (Brx), 212-828-3361
Sat 8am–4pm   **harvesthomefm.org**
Locally grown fruits and vegetables.

Harvest Home Mt. Eden Avenue Market

Mt. Eden Ave., Claremont Park/Bronx Lebanon Hospital (Morris Ave.),
Mt. Eden (Brx), 212-828-3361
Tue 8am–4pm **harvesthomefm.org**
Locally grown fruits and vegetables. Specialty items include baked goods
and cheeses.

Harvest Home 106th Street Market

E. 106th St. (bet. Lexington & 3rd Aves.), East Harlem (Man), 212-828-3361
Sat 10am–3pm **harvesthomefm.org**
Locally grown fruits and vegetables.

Harvest Home Sunday Market

E. 165th St., Bronx Museum (Grand Concourse), West Concourse (Brx),
212-828-3361
Sun 8am–4pm **harvesthomefm.org**
Locally grown fruits and vegetables.

Harvest Home Union Settlement Market

E. 104th St. (3rd Ave.), East Harlem (Man), 212-828-3361
Tue 8am–4pm **harvesthomefm.org**
Locally grown fruits and vegetables.

Harvest Home Youth Market

122nd St., Future Leaders Institute (bet. Lenox & 7th Aves.), Central Harlem
(Man), 212-828-3361
70 E. 129th St., The Storefront School (bet. Park & Madison Aves.),
East Harlem (Man), 212-828-3361
Thu 2pm–5:30pm **harvesthomefm.org**
Locally grown fruits and vegetables.

Hunts Point Farmers' Market

Southern Blvd., Msr. Raul del Valle Sq. (E. 163rd St.), Hunts Point (Brx),
914-923-4837
Wed Sat 8:30am–5pm **communitymarkets.biz**
Local conventionally grown produce.

Jamaica Farmers' Market

160th St. (Jamaica Ave.), Jamaica (Qns), 914-923-4837
Fri, Sat 8:30am–4pm **communitymarkets.biz**
Local conventionally grown produce.

La Familia Verde Farmers' Market

E. Tremont Ave., Tremont Park (E. LaFontaine Ave.), Tremont/Crotona (Brx),
917-861-2783
Tue 8am–2pm **lafamiliaverde.org**
Organic vegetables, herbs, and salad greens from five Bronx community
gardens and local New York farmers.

Lower East Side Girls Club Farmers' Market and Festival Center

212-982-1633
Call or see website for days, hours, and location **girlsclub.org**
Local low-spray vegetables and fruit; baked goods and spice mixes. Market
features Mexican and Spanish food items as well as a bicycle-powered
smoothie blender.

Morningside Park Farmers' Market

110th St. (Manhattan Ave.), Morningside (Man), 914-923-4837
Sat 9am–5pm **communitymarkets.biz**
Local conventionally grown produce.

New York Botanical Garden Farmers' Market

200th St., inside Garden at Moshulo Gate (Kazimiroff Blvd.), Bedford Park
(Brx), 914-923-4837
Wed 10am–3pm **communitymarkets.biz**
Local conventionally grown produce.

New York Hall of Science Farmers' Market

111th St. (48th Ave.), Corona (Qns), 914-923-4837
Sun 10am–4pm **communitymarkets.biz**
Local conventionally grown produce.

Northeast Bronx Farmers' Market

Hammersley Ave., outside Haffen Park (The Valley) (Wickham Ave.), Laconia
(Brx), 718-838-4564
Sat 8am–6pm
Local organic vegetables and fruit. Poultry and fish also available.

Park Slope Farmers' Market

5th Ave., JJ Byrne Park (4th St.), Park Slope (Bkn), 914-923-4837
Sun 11am–5pm **communitymarkets.biz**
Local conventionally grown produce. Baked goods, cider, pickles, plants, and
wild-caught fish.

Queens Botanical Garden Farmers' Market

College Point Blvd., Queens Botanical garden parking Lot (Blossom Ave.),
Flushing (Qns), 914-923-4837
Fri 8:30am–4pm **communitymarkets.biz**
Local conventionally grown produce.

Red Hook Farmers' Market

6 Wolcott St., Red Hook Senior Center (Dwight St.), Red Hook (Bkn),
718-855-5531
Red Hook Community Farm at Columbia St. (Beard St.), Red Hook (Bkn),
718-855-5531
Sat 9am–3pm **added-value.org/market.php**
Organic vegetables and salad greens grown at Red Hook Community Farm,
Brooklyn. Regional farmers provide additional produce, as well as milk,
yogurt, ice cream, fruit, eggs, and pasture-raised meats.

South Bronx Community Garden Market, The

E. 138th St., El Girasol Community Garden (bet. St. Ann's & Cypress Aves.),
Mott Haven (Brx), 718-292-4344
Wed 9am–6pm
Local certified organic vegetables, including produce grown in communitity
gardens. Local fruit grown using low-spray practices.

Taqwa Community Farm Stand

Ogden Ave. (W. 164th St.), Highbridge (Brx), 212-645-9880
Sat 9am–4pm
Organic vegetables and fruit grown in community gardens.
Regional farmers supply additional produce grown using low-spray
and conventional practices.

Urban Oasis Farmers' Market

Troy Ave., Market Pavilion (Clarkson Ave.), Crown Heights (Bkn),
646-641-0389
Wed 2pm–6pm **nyfarmersmarket.com**
Local organic produce. Fruit and baked goods also available. Specialty
produce includes bitter melon, callaloo, and malabar spinach.

Weeksville Farmstand (Farmers' Market)

1698 Bergen St., Weeksville Heritage Center (bet. Buffalo & Rochester
Aves.), Crown Heights (Bkn), 718-756-5250
Sat 9am–1pm **weeksvillesociety.org/node/60**
Local organic produce from three New York family-run farms and the
Weeksville Heritage Center's garden. Fruit produced using IPM. Specialty
items include cider, flavored apple juices, berries, and occasionally
baked goods.

West Farmers' Market

East Tremont Ave., Drew Gardens (Boston Rd.), West Farms (Man),
212-645-9880
Wed 10am–3pm **justfood.org**
Local certified organic vegetables and fruit from city gardens and
regional farms.

Wyckoff Farmhouse Farmers' Market

5816 Clarendon Rd. (bet. Ralph Ave. & E. 59th St.), East Flatbush (Bkn),
718-629-5400
Sun 1pm-4pm **wyckoffassociation.org**
Local certified organic vegetables, herbs, and fruit.

Community-Supported Agriculture (CSAs)

Abundant Life Farm

168 Prospect Rd., Middletown NY 10941, 845-692-3550
Online only **abundantlifefarm.com/farmstand**
Local food from natural, organic, and biodynamic farms delivered to neigh-
borhood buying groups. Check website for signup and ordering details.

Astoria CSA

35-30 35th St., Arrow Park and Community Center (bet. 35th & 36th Aves.),
Astoria (Qns), 718-512-5401
Thu 5pm–7:30pm **astoriacsa.com**
Local certified organic vegetables, salad greens, and herbs. Local fruit grown
using low-spray and IPM practices. Grass-fed and pasture-raised meat, poul-
try, and eggs. Cheese, bread, honey, and jams also available.

Bay Ridge CSA

6753 4th Ave. (bet. Senator & 68th St.), Bay Ridge (Bkn), 845-943-8699
Sat 8:30am–11am **heartyroots.com**
Local vegetables grown using organic methods. Low-spray fruit.

Bed-Stuy CSA

677 Lafayette Ave., Magnolia Tree Earth Center (bet. Tompkins & Marcy
Aves.), Bedford-Stuyvesant (Bkn), 718-387-2116 x12
Sat 10am–2pm **bedstuycsa.wetpaint.com**
Certified naturally grown vegetables. Local fruit, eggs, and meat
shares available.

Carnegie Hill/Yorkville CSA

90th St., Church of the Heavenly Rest (5th Ave.), West Side (Man),
212-502-8562
York Ave., Church of the Epiphany (74th St.), West Side (Man), 212-502-8562
Tue 4pm–7pm **chycsa.org**
Local certified organic produce, including fruit produced using IPM or low-
spray practices. Grass-fed meats; pasture-raised pork, poultry, and eggs;
Thanksgiving turkeys, ducks, and geese; locally baked organic breads.

Carroll Gardens CSA

Smith St., The MTA Transit Garden (2nd Pl.), Carroll Gardens (Bkn),
631-523-6608
Sat 10am–12pm **gardenofevefarm.com/csa_carroll.htm**
Local certified organic vegetables and low-spray fruit. Pastured hormone/
antibiotic-free eggs. Organic flowers also available.

Central Harlem CSA

200 W. 135th St., Thurgood Marshall Academy (bet. 7th & 8th Aves.),
Harlem (Man), 212-694-8715
Thu 4pm–7pm **roxburyfarm.com**
Local vegetables grown using organic and biodynamic methods. Fruit is
conventionally grown. Pastured pork and lamb also available.

Chelsea CSA

441 W. 26th St., Hudson Guild Elliot Center (bet. 9th & 10th Aves.),
Chelsea (Man), 212-924-6710 x245
Tue 4pm–7pm **chelseacsa.org**
Local certified organic vegetables and herbs. Fruit share contains fruit grown
using low-spray practices and certified organic berries. Grass-fed
and pasture-raised meat, poultry, and eggs. Maple syrup and honey
also available.

City Harvest CSA

575 8th Ave., 4th Fl. (bet. 38th & 39th Sts.), Midtown West (Man),
Wed 4pm–7pm **gardenofevefarm.com/csa_City_Harvest.htm**
Local certified organic vegetables. Local fruit grown using low-spray
practices. Pasture-raised, hormone- and antibiotic-free eggs. Organic flowers
also available.

City Island CSA

65 Buckley St. (bet. City Island Ave. and Eastchester Bay), City Island (Brx),
718-885-2051
Wed 7pm–9pm
Certified organic vegetables. Fruit grown using low-spray practices.

Clinton Hill CSA

170 Gates Ave., P.S. 56 (bet. Irving Pl. & Downing St.), Clinton Hill (Bkn),
718-907-0616
Thu 5pm–8pm **clintonhillcsa.org**
Local organic vegetables, salad greens, and herbs. Local fruit grown using
low-spray, IPM practices. Grass-fed and pasture-raised meat, poultry, and
eggs. Organic flowers also available.

Cobble Hill CSA

326 Clinton St., Christ Church (Kane St.), Cobble Hill (Bkn), 917-609-9899
Tue 4pm–8pm **cobblehillcsa.org**
Local certified organic vegetables and fruit produced using IPM practices.
All-natural, hormone/antibiotic-free, pasture raised meats also available.

Columbia University CSA

601 W. 114th St., Broadway Presbyterian Church (Broadway), Morningside Heights (Man), 212-678-3001
Thu 3pm–6pm **roxburyfarm.com**
Local biodynamic vegetables. Local fruit grown using low-spray practices.

Columbus Circle CSA

120 W. 58th St., backyard apartment (bet. 6th & 7th Aves.), Columbus Circle (Man), 212-828-8038
Thu 4pm–7pm **columbuscirclecsa.org**
Local certified organic vegetables; fruit produced using IPM practices; nonhomogenized milk, yogurt, cheese, and butter; organic, pasture-raised poultry and eggs; pasture-raised, grass-fed, hormone/antibiotic-free meat and dairy.

Douglaston CSA

22806 Northern Blvd., Alley Pond Environmental Center (Cross Island Pkwy.), Douglaston (Qns), 718-229-4000 ext.212
Tue 5pm–7:30pm **dumbocsa.org**
Local certified organic vegetables, and salad greens. Local fruit grown using low-spray, IPM practices. Organic eggs and honey also available.

DUMBO/Vinegar Hill CSA

50 Jay St. (bet. Plymouth and Water Sts.), DUMBO (Bkn)
Tue 5pm–8pm **dumbocsa.org**
Brand-new CSA offering certified organic produce through Sang Lee Farms on Long Island.

East New York CSA, The

Scherick Ave. (bet. New Lots & Livonia Aves.), East New York (Bkn), 718-649-7979
Sat 9am–3pm **eastnewyorkfarms.org**
Local organic vegetables from regional farm and United Community Centers Youth Farm.

8 O'Clock Ranch Meat CSA

315-347-4352
Online only; year-round **eightoclockranch.com**
Collective of three family-run ranches delivering grass-fed lamb and beef, pasture-raised grain-finished pork, organic goat's milk dairy products, and eggs. Next-day delivery to anywhere in New York area.

Farm Spot CSA

33-50 82nd St., St. Mark's Church (34th Ave.), Jackson Heights (Qns), 718-512-5097
Thu 4pm–8pm **farmspot.org**
Local certified organic vegetables. Local fruit grown using low-spray practices. Grass-fed and pasture-raised meat, poultry, and eggs. Cheese, bread, and baked goods also available.

Forest Hills CSA

50 Ascan Ave., Church in the Gardens (Greenway North), Forest Hills (Qns), 718-459-1037
Tue 4:30pm–8pm **foresthillscsa.com**
Local organic vegetables and fruit; pasture-raised eggs.

Garden City CSA

225 Cambridge Ave., Waldorf School (track) (bet. Auburn & Nina Aves.),
Garden City (S.I.), 518-672-7500 x105
Thu 1pm–5pm **hawthornevalleyfarm.org**
Local organic and biodynamic vegetables and fruit. Biodynamic dairy
products, lacto-fermented vegetables, pastries, and breads.

Greenpoint-Williamsburg CSA

129 Russell St., south side of McGolrick Park (bet. Nassau & Driggs Aves.),
Greenpoint (Bkn), 631-523-6608
N. 12th St., McCarren Park in community garden (Driggs Ave.),
Greenpoint (Bkn), 631-523-6608
Sat 9:30am–12pm **greenpoint-williamsburgcsa.org**
Local certified organic vegetables and low-spray fruit. Pastured, hormone/
antibiotic-free eggs. Organic flowers.

Greenwood Heights CSA

6th Ave. (18th St.), Greenwood Heights (Bkn),
Sat 9am–11:30am **greenwoodheightscsa.org**
Local organic vegetables.

Harlem CSA

252 W. 116th St., FoodChange Community Kitchen (bet. 7th & 8th Aves.),
Harlem (Man), 212-894-8094 x8210
Thu 3pm–6:30pm **roxburyfarm.com**
Local vegetables grown using organic and biodynamic methods. Fruit is
conventionally grown. Pastured pork and lamb.

Healthy Kids CSA

2400 Marion Ave., P.S. 85 (bet. E. 184th & 187th Sts.), Fordham (Brx),
718-584-9615
Tue 2pm–6pm
Local organic vegetables, salad greens, and herbs. Local fruit grown using
low-spray, IPM practices. Cheese, yogurt, and granola occasionally offered.

Hearty Roots CSA

266 Skillman Ave., Red Shed Community Garden (Kingsland Ave.),
East Williamsburg (Bkn), 845-943-8699
Sat 10am–12pm **heartyroots.com**
Local organic vegetables, salad greens, and herbs.

Hellgate CSA

22-00 29th St., Freeze Peach Cafe (Ditmars Blvd.), Astoria (Qns),
Tue 5:30pm–7:30pm **hellgatecsa.com**
Certified organic vegetables, herbs, and salad greens. Local fruit grown
using low-spray, IPM practices. Grass-fed, pasture-raised meat, poultry, and
eggs available.

Hell's Kitchen CSA (Upper Meadows Farm CSA)

W. 43rd St. (bet. 9th & 10th Aves.), Hell's Kitchen (Man), 212-265-5469
Sat 10:30am–12:30pm **uppermeadowsfarm.com**
Local certified organic, fruits, and vegetables. Organic eggs, herb vinegars,
honey, maple syrup, and flowers. Shellfish, finfish, clams, and scallops.
Cooking classes available.

Inwood CSA

Park Terrace East, entrance of Isham Park Isham Park (W. 215th St.), Inwood
(Man), 518 672 7500 x 105

Thu 4:30pm–7pm **inwoodcsa.org**

Local organic and biodynamic vegetables and fruit. Biodynamic dairy
products, lacto-fermented vegetables, pastries, and breads.

Kensington Windsor Terrace CSA

E. 4th St., at community garden (bet. Caton St. & Fort Hamilton Expwy.),
Windsor Terrace (Bkn), 631-523-6608

Sat 10am–12pm

gardenofevefarm.com/csa_Kensington_Prospect_Heights.htm

Local certified organic vegetables and low-spray fruit. Pastured, hormone/
antibiotic-free eggs. Organic flowers.

Norwood CSA

302 E. 206th St., Epiphany Lutheran Church (Bainbridge Ave.), Norwood
(Brx), 718-514-3305

Thu 4pm–7pm **norwoodfoodcoop.org**

Local certified organic vegetables; fruit produced using IPM practices;
nonhomogenized milk, yogurt, cheese, and butter; organic, pasture-raised
poultry and eggs; pasture-raised, grass-fed, hormone- and antibiotic-free
meat and dairy.

Park Slope CSA

Union St. Garden of Union (4th Ave.), Park Slope (Bkn), 718-638-8939

Thu 3:30pm–6:30pm **parkslopecsa.org**

Local organic vegetables, salad greens, and herbs; fruit grown using low-
spray practices; pastured, hormone/antibiotic-free eggs; organic flowers and
cider; grass-fed and pasture-raised meat, poultry, and eggs.

Prince George CSA (Midtown CSA)

14 E. 28th St., The Prince George (bet. 5th & Madison Aves.), Midtown
(Man), 212-471-0858

Thu 4pm–7pm **commonground.org/csa**

Local certified organic vegetables; fruit produced using IPM practices;
nonhomogenized milk, yogurt, cheese, and butter; organic, pasture-raised
poultry and eggs; pasture-raised, grass-fed, hormone- and antibiotic-free
meat and dairy; honey, granola, and maple syrup.

Red Hook CSA

Corner of Centre & Clinton Sts., Red Hook (Bkn), 718-855-5531

Seasonal hrs. **added-value.org**

Produce grown at Added Value Community Farm, Brooklyn, NY.

Riverdale CSA

5521 Mosholu Ave., Riverdale Neighborhood House (W. 254th St.), Riverdale
(Brx), 518-672-7500 x 105

Thu 3:30pm–6:45pm **hawthornevalleyfarm.org**

Local organic and biodynamic vegetables and fruit; biodynamic dairy products, lacto-fermented vegetables, pastries, breads; grass-fed, pasture-raised
meat, poultry, and eggs.

Roxbury CSA

550 W. End Ave., Church of Saint Paul & Andrew (bet. W. 86th & W. 87th
Sts.), Upper West Side (Man), 212-539-3826

Thu 4pm–7pm **roxburyfarm.com**

Local vegetables grown using organic and biodynamic methods. Fruit is
conventionally grown. Pastured pork and lamb also available.

Sister's Hill Farm CSA

6301 Riverdale Ave., Mt. St. Vincent College (W. 263rd St.), Riverdale (Brx), 718-549-9200 x257
Tue 4pm–6pm **sistershillfarm.org**
Local organic vegetables, salad greens, and herbs.

6th St. CSA

638 E. 6th St., Sixth Street Community Center (bet. Ave. B & C),
East Village/Lower East Side (Man), 212-677-1863
Tue 5pm–9pm **sixthstreetcenter.org**
Summer/fall share comprised of local certified organic produce. Spring/winter share includes both fresh and frozen local produce. Wild Alaskan salmon, halibut, cod, rockfish, olive oils, wines, pestos, vinegars, and honey available year-round.

South Bronx CSA

E. 138th St., El Girasol Community Garden (bet. St. Ann's & Cypress Aves.),
Mott Haven (Brx), 718-292-4344
Wed 10am–4pm
Local organic vegetables, salad greens, and herbs; local fruit grown using low-spray practices; eggs and honey.

Stanton Street CSA

Rivington St., M'Finda Kalunga Community Garden (bet. Forsyth & Chrystie Sts.), Lower East Side (Man)
Thu 5:30pm–7:30pm Jun–Nov; 2nd Sat of Dec–Mar 12pm–1pm
stantonstreetcsa.wordpress.com
Local organic vegetables; fruit produced using low-spray, IPM practices; organically grown flowers; organic bread, honey, and wild-caught fish; pastured eggs and meats. Check website to enroll.

Staten Island CSA

76 Franklin Ave., Christ Episcopal Church (rear parking lot) (Fillmore St.),
North Shore (S.I.), 718-727-2941
Tue 5:30pm–7:30pm **statenislandcsa.org**
Local organic vegetables and herbs. Conventionally grown fruit share available.

Sunnyside CSA

43-34 39th St., Sunnyside Community Center (bet. 43rd St. & Rt. 25),
Sunnyside (Qns), 718-670-7354
Thu 5pm–8pm **sunnysidecsa.com**
Local organic vegetables, salad greens, herbs, and fruit.

Sweet Pea CSA

Pierrepont St. (bet. Clinton St. & Monroe Pl.), Brooklyn Heights (Bkn)
Wed 4pm–7pm **sweetpeacsa.org**
Local certified organic vegetables. Local fruit grown using low-spray practices. Pasture-raised, hormone/antibiotic-free eggs. Organic flowers also available. Check website for details on signing up.

Tuv Ha'Aretz CSA

344 E. 14th St., 14th St. YMCA (1st Ave.), Lower East Side (Man),
212-780-0800 x225
251 W. 100th St., Anshe Chesed (bet. West End Ave. & Broadway),
Upper West Side (Man), 212-644-2332
Wed 5:30pm–7pm **hazon.org**
Local certified organic vegetables. Local fruit grown using low-spray practices. Organic flower share and hormone/antibiotic-free eggs available.

United Tremont CSA

1861 Anthony Ave., P.S. 28 (Tremont Ave.), Mount Hope (Brx), 718-696-4055, 718-901-2849
Tue 3pm–6:30pm
Local organic vegetables, salad greens, and herbs. Local fruit grown using low-spray, IPM practices. Cheese, yogurt, and granola occasionally offered.

Upper West Side CSA (Chubby Bunny CSA)

550 West End Ave. (bet. W. 87th & W. 86th Sts.), Upper West Side (Man)
Tue 5pm–7pm **chubbybunnynyc.org**
Local organic vegetables. Grass-fed, hormone- and antibiotic-free beef and pork; raw milk, free-range eggs, and low-spray fruit shares are also available. Check website for details on signing up.

Van Cortlandt Village CSA

105 Old Stone Rd., Van Cortlandt Village (Brx), 607-336-7598
Call for days and hours **norwichmeadowsfarm.com**
All local certified organic vegetables. Fruit grown using IPM practices. Specialty items include nonhomogenized milk, yogurt, cheese, and butter; organic pasture-raised poultry and eggs; pasture-raised, grass-fed, hormone- and antibiotic-free meat and dairy. Also honey, granola and maple syrup.

Washington Heights CSA

1 Margaret Corbin Dr. (Park Dr.), Washington Heights (Man)
729 W. 181st St., (behind Ft. Washington Collegiate Church) (Magaw Pl.), Washington Heights (Man)
Tue 4:30pm–7:15pm **home.earthlink.net/~littleseed**
Local certified organic vegetables and herbs. Specialty items include locally grown fruit produced using IPM or low-spray practices and a selection of organic berries. Organic flower share also available. See website for details on signing up.

Washington Square CSA

35 W. 4th St., 10th Flr. (Greene St.), Greenwich Village (Man), 212-998-5588
Thu 4pm–7pm (summer/fall), Tue 4pm–7pm (winter)
washingtonsquarecsa.org
All local certified organic vegetables; fruit produced using IPM practices. Specialty items include nonhomogenized milk, yogurt, cheese, and butter; organic pasture-raised poultry and eggs; pasture-raised, grass-fed, hormone- and antibiotic-free meat and dairy. Also honey, granola, and maple syrup.

West Harlem CSA

1047 Amsterdam Ave., St. John of the Divine Cathedral (W. 110th St.), West Harlem/Morningside Heights (Man), 212-741-8192
Thu 4pm–7pm **stjohndivine.org/westharlemcsa.html**
Local organic vegetables; grass-fed, pasture-raised meat, poultry, and eggs; honey and syrup.

West Village CSA

125 W. 14th St., McBurney YMCA (bet. 6th & 7th Aves.), West Village (Man), 212-604-7572
Tue 4pm–7pm **westvillagecsa.org**
Local certified organic vegetables, herbs, and salad greens. Local fruit share consists of both organic and low-spray, IPM-grown fruit. Maple syrup and honey.

Catering Services and Personal Chefs

Catering your events with certified organic food or food that is locally grown in a sustainable manner is a great way to be healthy and kind to the planet, and to turn people on to sustainable products. This section contains caterers and personal chefs whose primary focus is just that. Readers should also check the "Restaurants and Cafés" section (starting on page 2) to see if a favorite establishment caters—look for the "C" designation next to the restaurant name.

In this category, we identified those services and chefs whose primary focus is to offer organic food and whose menus feature organic items. We evaluated eight different food areas and also determined whether or not reusable utensils were used.

- For produce, we checked the percentage purchased that is certified organic and/or locally grown without pesticides and chemical fertilizers.

- For meat and meat alternatives, we determined the percentage that is certified organic and/or grass-fed and produced without the use of hormones and antibiotics.

- For poultry and eggs, we evaluated the percentage purchased that is certified organic and free-range/cage-free, and/or locally raised and free-range/cage-free without the use of hormones and antibiotics.

- With seafood, we checked into whether it was wild-caught or sustainably farm-raised and processed without chemical treatment.

- For dairy products, we checked the percentage of certified organic options or ones that were locally produced without hormones and antibiotics.

- We looked into the percentage of certified organic canned and dry goods and nondairy beverages.

- For prepared foods, we determined the percentage made with certified organic ingredients and/or locally grown ingredients without pesticides and chemical fertilizers.

- For utensils, we checked into what percentage is reusable.

To be listed, at least 25 percent of the products used by a given catering service or personal chef must meet the outlined criteria. In addition, the service or chef must promote organic foods and sustainable agriculture to their customers as a regular part of their business.

Full-Service Catering

Cleaver Co., The
75 9th Ave. (15th St.), Chelsea (Man), 212-741-9174
By appt. **cleaverco.com**
Full-service catering company with a commitment to supporting a healthy, sustainable food supply. Food is sourced from local family farms exercising humane and environmentally friendly practices. Serves New York City.

Cooks Venture
187 Chrystie St. (Rivington), NoHo (Man), 212-452-1912
By appt.
Full-service catering service using organic, all-natural, and fair trade ingredients. Kitchen includes all Energy-Star appliances and operates on wind energy; composts and recycles all waste. Serves all of New York City; available for international jobs.

Fancy Girl Catering
718-422-9151
By appt. **fancygirlcatering.com**
Catering and event planning company specializing in low-impact services and local organic foods. Serves all five boroughs.

Free Foods
18 W. 45th St. (bet. 5th & 6th Aves.), Midtown (Man), 212-302-7195
Mon–Thu 7am–8pm Fri 7am–5pm **freefoodsnyc.com**
High-concept organic, sustainable cuisine providing a healthy menu for eat-in, take-out, or corporate catering.

Great Performances
304 Hudson St. (Spring St.), SoHo (Man), 212-727-2424
By appt. **greatperformances.com**
Catering service providing organic produce grown on its own Upstate New York farm. Serves all five boroughs.

Jessie's Brooklyn Kitchen
200 Smith St. (Baltic St.), Cobble Hill (Bkn), 718-858-8807
By appt. **jessiesbrooklynkitchen.com**
Catering and personal chef services using food sourced from local family farms and produced without antibiotics, hormones, pesticides, or nitrates. Serves New York City area.

Local Faire
718-493-5085
By appt. **localfaire.com**
Gourmet caterer for dinner parties and other events using local and organic products. Serves all five boroughs, Hamptons, and Upstate New York.

Lucid Food
212-414-0764
By appt. **lucidfood.com**
Catering company committed to sustainability; buys food from local farmers, composts food waste, and recycles. Promotes no-waste and low-waste event options. Serves all five boroughs.

R Cano Events

718-937-6622
Mon–Fri 9am–5pm **rcanoevents.com**
Full-service catering and event planning company specializing in New American cuisine using seasonally and locally grown foods. Serves all of New York City and surrounding areas.

Relish Caterers

220 E. 22nd St., Ste. 3P (bet. 2nd & 3rd Aves.), Gramercy Park (Man), 212-228-1672
Mon–Fri 9am–7pm **relishcaterers.com**
Full-service catering and event planning company with culinary, décor, and production expertise. Green procedures exercised at every event, including waste oil recycling. Serves New York City area.

Roquette Catering

646-483-2520
By appt. **roquettecatering.com**
Full-service catering company using high-quality local and organic ingredients, including produce and eggs from Red Hook, Brooklyn. Serves all five boroughs.

Sage Events

46-36 11th St. (46th Rd.), Long Island City (Qns), 212-888-2664
By appt. **sageamericankitchen.com**
Local naturally grown produce, meat, and poultry used to create customized seasonal menus. Specialists in outdoor catering, weddings, and events. Supports Amish and other family farms. Serves New York City area.

Second Helpings

448 9th St. (7th Ave.), Park Slope (Bkn), 718-965-1925
By appt. **secondhelpings.com**
Provides full-service and personal chef services. Uses only all-natural or certified organic ingredients for traditional or vegetarian dishes. Serves all five boroughs.

Urban Hearth

7101 Colonial Rd., Apt. L1C (71st St.), Bay Ridge (Bkn), 718-757-1366
By appt. **urbanhearth.net**
Personal chef and catering service sources food for dinner parties and events direct from local sustainable, organic farmers. Private cooking lessons available. Complimentary consultation. Serves all of New York City area.

Vegan Worldwide

718-599-5913
By appt. **veganww.com**
Organic, vegan, local, seasonal, sustainable, and compassionate cuisine. Serves the New York City area.

Personal Chefs

Aja Tahari Marsh

646-596-5013
By appt. **ajataharimarsh.com**
Natural foods chef providing personal cooking and in-home catering services for individuals and families, with a focus on vegetarian and vegan cuisine. Uses all-natural and organic ingredients. Provides flower orders and linen/flatware rentals. Serves all of New York City.

Colombe Dujour

917-349-5516
By appt. **colombedujour.com**
All-organic and fair trade personal chef service specializing in home dinner parties. Offers cooking classes. Serves all of New York City.

Conscious Cuisine Personal Chef

917-312-5914
By appt. **be-conscious.net**
Personal chef and nutritional counseling service providing all-organic in-home meals. Serves all five boroughs.

Cooking for Friends

454 15th St., Apt. 4L , Park Slope (Bkn), 718-788-0399
By appt. **cookingforfriends.com**
Personal chef whose services include preparing in-home organic meals, serving catered events, and providing organic preparation instructions; flexible hours; Park Slope Food Co-op member. Serves all of New York City.

Healthy Chef Alex

917-345-2302
By appt. **healthychefalex.com**
Assessment interview, menu planning, personal shopping, home cooking, catering, and holistic health instruction. Focus on organic. Serves all of New York City.

Healthy Plate

631-873-8329
By appt. **healthyplate.org**
Health-supportive chef assisting families and individuals. Offers all-organic dinner parties and in-home catering; cooking classes and demos; holistic health counseling.

Rebecca Friedman, Your Personal Chef!

973-777-9170
By appt. **rebeccafriedman.com**
Organic and kosher personal chef and catering service with mostly vegan and vegetarian options. All meats are organic and/or grass-fed. Customized catering available for diet types, including South Beach, diabetic, celiac, and wheat-free.

Shilloh Personal Chef Services

516-459-6850
Mon–Fri 10am–6pm Sat–Sun by appt. **shilloh.com**
Personal chef service providing organic in-home meals, dinner parties, dinners for two, baby food, cooking classes and demos.

Tall Order

917-328-6348
By appt. **tallorderonline.com**
Personal chefs and catering service offering meals, dinner parties, and special events using local seasonal and organic foods. Private cooking lessons, healthy living lectures, and holistic health counseling programs available. Serves New York City area.

Wine, Beer, and Spirits

In spite of the trend toward organics in the last decade, growers and producers, as well as consumers, largely ignored organic alcoholic beverages. Many thought organic production methods were incompatible with quality beer, wine, and spirits.

However, an increasing number of growers and producers are rediscovering what many brewers, vintners, and distillers have known for centuries: the joys and challenges of growing and processing beer, wine, and spirits without the use of artificial ingredients, chemical pesticides and fertilizers, or synthetic additives.

The shops listed here have made an extra effort to carry an assortment of organic wines, beers, and spirits. You may also find a selection of biodynamic wines in these stores. (Read more about organic standards for wine, beer, and spirits at the end of this chapter.)

The owners and managers of these stores are enthusiastic about the organic and sustainably produced products they carry and possess a wealth of information they would be happy to share. Ask them about their products and show your support for their organic selections.

All of the stores listed here meet our threshold for entry into the guide because of their commitment to quality organic products. Of all the wine, beer, and spirits they stock, a store must carry a minimum of 15 percent organic and/or biodynamic wines, beers, or spirits and demonstrate its commitment to these items by promoting them in special display areas and to their customers.

at least 15% meets the above criteria.
at least 25% meets the above criteria.
at least 50% meets the above criteria.
at least 75% meets the above criteria.

Adam's Wines & Liquors
620 5th Ave. (17th St.), Red Hook (Bkn), 718-768-1521
Mon 1pm–10pm Tue–Sat 11am–10pm Sun 12pm–6pm
Wine and liquor store offering selection of wine from traditionally organic regions of Europe, South America, and South Africa. Tastings on Saturdays.

Appellation Wine & Spirits
156 10th Ave. (bet. 19th & 20th Sts.), Chelsea (Man), 212-741-9474
Mon 12pm–8pm Tue–Sat 11am–10pm Sun 12pm–8pm appellationnyc.com
By its own account, an unconventional wine store focusing on organic and biodynamic wines and small producers.

Bottlerocket 🍃🍃
5 W. 19th St. (5th Ave.), Union Square (Man), 212-929-2323
Mon–Sat 11am–8pm Sun 12pm–6pm **bottlerocketwine.com**
Wine store with "green" section, carrying an assortment of biodynamic,
sustainable, and organic wines.

Bridge Vineyards: Urban Winery 🍃
20 Broadway St. (Kent Ave.), Williamsburg (Bkn), 718-384-2800
Wed–Sun 2pm–12am **bridgevineyards.com**
Wine shop serving and selling sustainable wines from the North Fork region.

Chambers Street Wines 🍃
160 Chambers St. (bet. W. Broadway & Greenwich Sts.), Tribeca (Man),
212-227-1434
Mon–Sat 10am–9pm Sun 12pm–7pm **chambersstwines.com**
Family-owned wine shop offering selection of natural, biodynamic, and
organic wines. Sustainable bottles indicated by green dot on price marker.

Discovery Wines 🍃🍃
10 Ave. A (Houston St.), Lower East Side (Man), 212-674-7833
Mon–Sat 11am–10pm Sun 2pm–8pm **discoverywines.com**
Wine shop featuring family-run wineries; selection of organic, biodynamic,
and sustainable wines.

Gnarly Vines 🍃🍃
350 Myrtle Ave. (bet. Carlton Ave. & Adelphi St.), Fort Greene (Bkn),
718-797-3183
Mon–Thu 12pm–9pm Fri–Sat 12pm–10pm Sun 12pm–9pm **gnarlyvines.com**
Handcrafted wines from small producers; some organic and
biodynamic choices.

Greene Grape, The 🍃🍃🍃
55 Liberty St. (bet. Nassau St. & Broadway), Financial District (Man),
212-406-9463
765 Fulton St. (bet. S. Portland Ave. & S. Oxford St.), Fort Greene (Bkn),
718-797-9463
Mon–Wed 12pm–9pm Thu–Sat 12pm–10pm Sun 12pm–9pm
greenegrape.com
Wine store working exclusively with small producers. Sells handcrafted
organic and biodynamic wines.

Harlem Vintage 🍃
2235 Frederick Douglass Blvd. (121st St.), Central Harlem (Man),
212-866-9463
Mon–Thu 11am–9pm Fri–Sat 11am–10pm Sun 12pm–6pm
harlemvintage.com
Neighborhood wine and spirits store with some organic and biodynamic
choices. Tastings and events educating the community on wine pairings held
Saturday 4pm–7pm.

Hunter's Point Wine and Spirits 🍃🍃🍃
47-07 Vernon Blvd. (47th Ave.), Long Island City (Qns), 718-472-9463
Mon–Thu 10am–9pm Fri–Sat 10am–10pm Sun 12pm–8pm
hunterspointwines.com
Wine shop featuring hard-to-find, small-estate wines and spirits. Wine
tastings Fridays and Saturdays 6pm–8pm.

Lenell's Ltd. 🍃 🍃

416 Van Brunt St. (bet. Coffey & Van Dyke Sts.), Red Hook (Bkn),
718-360-0838
Mon–Sat 12pm–12am Sun 12pm–9pm   **lenells.com**
Shop featuring small family-owned wineries and distilleries, including organic
and biodynamic labels.

Nancy's Wines for Food 🍃

313 Columbus Ave. (75th St.), West Side (Man), 212-877-4040
Mon–Sat 10am–9pm Sun 12pm–6pm   **nancyswines.com**
Small wine shop featuring an organic and biodynamic section.

Park East Wines & Spirits 🍃 🍃

1657 York Ave. (E. 87th St.), Yorkville (Man), 212-534-2093
Mon–Sat 10am–10pm Sun 12pm–6pm
Wine shop carrying organic domestic and international labels.
In-store tastings.

Prospect Wine Shop 🍃 🍃

322 7th Ave. (bet. 8th & 9th Sts.), Park Slope (Bkn), 718-768-1232
Mon–Wed 10am–9pm Thu–Sat 10am–9:30pm Sun 1pm–7pm
prospectwine.com
Local wine shop carrying organic and biodynamic wines. Delivery to
neighboring areas.

Smith & Vine 🍃 🍃 🍃

268 Smith St. (Degraw St.), Carroll Gardens (Bkn), 718-243-2864
Mon–Thu 11am–9pm Fri–Sat 11am–11pm Sun 12pm–8pm
smithandvine.com
Wine and liquor shop carrying biodynamic wines. Also offers private tasting
room and in-home wine seminars.

Thirst Wine Merchants 🍃 🍃

187 Dekalb Ave. (Carlton Ave.), Fort Greene (Bkn), 718-596-7643
Mon–Thu 12pm–9pm Fri 12pm–10pm Sat 10am–10pm Sun 12pm–9pm
thirstwinemerchants.com
Wine and spirits shop offering selection of sustainably produced wines.

Trader Joe's 🍃

138 E. 14th St. (bet. 3rd Ave. & Irving.), Union Square (Man), 212-529-6326
Mon–Sat 9am–10pm Sun 12pm–9pm   **traderjoes.com**
Large wine shop offering a selection of organic wine.

Union Square Wines & Spirits 🍃

140 4th Ave. (13th St.), Union Square (Man), 212-675-8100
Mon–Sat 9am–10pm Sun 12pm–9pm   **unionsquarewines.com**
Wine shop with a designated organic section; customer service counter provides a list of the certified organic, biodynamic, green-farmed, and organic
wines found throughout the store.

Uva Wines and Spirits 🍃

199 Bedford Ave. (N. 6th St.), Williamsburg (Bkn), 718-963-3939
Mon–Fri 12pm–10pm Sat 12pm–10pm Sun 12pm–9pm   **uvawines.com**
Boutique wine shop focusing on natural, sustainable, organic, and biody-
namic wines from small producers.

Vestry Wines 🍃

65 Vestry St. (Washington St.), Tribeca (Man), 212-810-2899
Mon–Sat 11am–9pm Sun 12pm–6pm **vestrywines.com**
Store specializing in wines from California, France, and Italy, with selection of biodynamic, organic, and sustainably produced wines. Tasting bar offers daily samplings. Biodegradable packaging used for wine shipments.

W.I.N.E. Wine & Spirits 🍃

1415 3rd Ave. (80th St.), Upper East Side (Man), 212-717-1999
Mon–Sat 10am–9pm Sun 12pm–9pm **elizabar.com/taste/wine.html**
Wine shop labeling organic bottles with green stickers; list of certified organic and biodynamic varieties available at counter.

Whole Foods Market Bowery Beer Room 🍃🍃

95 E. Houston St. (bet. Bowery & Chrystie Sts.), Lower East Side (Man), 212-420-1320
Daily 8am–11pm **wholefoodsmarket.com**
Organic and local beer section; six local beers on tap sold in reusable growlers.

Wine Therapy 🍃🍃🍃

171 Elizabeth St. (Spring St.), SoHo (Man), 212-625-2999
Mon–Thu 11am–10pm Fri–Sat 11am–11pm Sun 12pm–9pm
winetherapynyc.com
Neighborhood wine shop specializing in organic and biodynamic wines. Wine tastings on Saturdays from 5pm–8pm.

Winery, The 🍃🍃

2166 Frederick Douglass Blvd. (bet. 116th & 117th Sts.), Central Harlem (Man), 212-222-4866
Daily 1pm–9pm **thewineryonline.com**
Boutique carrying handcrafted, organic, and biodynamic wines.

ZAP Wines & Spirits 🍃🍃🍃

105 Court St. (bet. Schermerhorn & State Sts.), Brooklyn Heights (Bkn), 718-643-3395
Mon–Thu 10am–9:30pm Fri–Sat 10am–10:30pm Sun 1pm–7pm
zapwine.com
Wine and spirits shop specializing in organic and biodynamic wines.

WRITE A REVIEW

We've compiled a list of some really great merchants and service providers who offer local, sustainably grown, and/or organic food and beverages. We'd like for you to tell us about your experiences: How was the variety and quality of the food and goods? Your shopping and service experience? Was the price in line with the product? Go to **greenopia.com** and post your review.

Eating in Season
Vegetables

"Eating in season" means choosing fruits and vegetables that are grown locally. Local foods don't have to travel great distances from the farm to your table, so they're fresher, tastier, and more nutritious. Eating seasonally also conserves energy and fuel, because a local strawberry doesn't need an airplane to arrive ripe and ready at your corner market. In this increasingly global marketplace, eating with the seasons is no longer intuitive, but choosing to rely on local farms is a healthy, environmentally reponsible, and above all, delicious decision to make.

The table below is a guide to finding locally grown produce in the New York region and details the harvest season and availability of 70 locally grown fruits and vegetables.

	Jan	Feb	Mar	Apr	May	Jun	Jul	Aug	Sep	Oct	Nov	Dec
Arugula	■	■			■	■	■	■		■	■	
Artichokes, Jerusalem			■	■	■				■	■	■	
Asparagus				■	■							
Beans, Dried	■	■	■						■	■		■
Beans, Lima								■	■			
Beans, Snap							■	■	■			
Beets	■					■	■	■	■	■		
Beet Greens					■	■	■	■				
Bok Choy									■	■		
Broccoli						■	■		■	■		
Brussels Sprouts									■	■	■	
Cabbage	■	■	■			■	■	■	■	■		■
Carrots	■	■	■	■			■	■	■	■		
Cauliflower								■	■	■		
Celery								■	■	■		
Celery Root (Celeriac)									■	■	■	
Collard Greens						■	■		■	■	■	
Corn							■	■	■			
Cucumbers						■	■	■	■			
Eggplant							■	■	■	■		
Endive					■	■	■					
Escarole					■	■	■					
Fennel						■			■	■		
Garlic						■	■	■				
Herbs, Various	■	■			■	■	■	■	■	■	■	
Kale								■	■	■	■	■

Dark green indicates the months the item is in season and harvested locally and should be available at area Greenmarkets, farmers' markets, CSAs, and co-ops.

Light green indicates the months the item isn't typically harvested locally but may have limited availability through greenhouse or hothouse production and storage crops.

(Note that weather affects the length of a growing season and may extend or shorten product availability by a few weeks.)

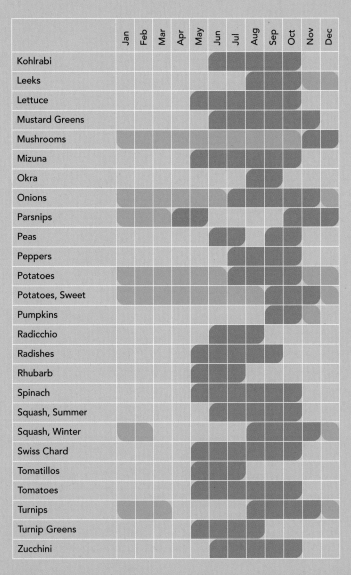

Eating in Season
Fruits

Legend: ● = dark green (in season, harvested locally) ○ = light green (limited availability)

	Jan	Feb	Mar	Apr	May	Jun	Jul	Aug	Sep	Oct	Nov	Dec
Apples	○	○	○	○		●	●	●	●	●	●	○
Apricots						●	●					
Blackberries								●	●			
Blueberries							●	●				
Cantaloupes								●	●			
Cherries, Sweet						●	●					
Cherries, Tart							●					
Currants								●				
Figs								●	●			
Gooseberries					●	●	●					
Grapes								●	●	●		
Nectarines								●	●			
Peaches								●	●			
Pears	○	○						●	●	●	●	○
Plums								●	●			
Raspberries							●		●	●		
Strawberries						●	●					
Watermelon								●	●			

Just Food is a nonprofit organization that works to develop a just and sustainable food system in the New York region. Just Food's efforts help to foster new marketing and food-growing opportunities that address the needs of regional family farms, NYC community gardens, and NYC communities (**justfood.org**).

Organic Standards for Wine, Beer, and Spirits

Wine

Made with Sustainably Grown Grapes—These are wines from vineyards that use environmentally sound methods and seek to maintain the long-term health of the soil and land.

Made with Organic Grapes—Grapes have been grown in accordance with the strict organic rules set by the USDA National Organic Program. In addition, the wine is produced and bottled in a certified organic facility. Low levels of added sulfites are allowed, up to 100 parts per million (ppm). (Sulfites occur naturally during wine fermentation but are also added as preservatives. Conventional wines may contain from 80 to 350 ppm.)

Organic Wine—Grapes have been grown in accordance with the strict organic rules set by the USDA National Organic Program. In addition, the wine is produced and bottled in a certified organic facility. No added sulfites are allowed. Organic wine may carry the USDA ORGANIC green logo.

Vegan Wine—No animal-provided gelatin, egg whites, or milk proteins have been used in the wine-making process. Unlike the many wines that are produced using animal-derived ingredients as part of their filtration process, (to remove impurities and yeast used in fermentation process, and sometimes to adjust tannin levels), vegan wines are free of animal-derived ingredients.

Organic Beer

Organic beer is made from certified organic malted barley, hops, and yeast. Although there are relatively few bottled organic beers on the market, they are clearly labeled. To be labeled "certified organic," the beer must conform to all standards set by the USDA, including the use of organic ingredients. The USDA also specifies which chemicals may be used to clean breweries. If the label reads "made with organic ingredients," the grains used are organic but the beer has not been processed in a certified organic facility. Either way, you are supporting organic farmers and farming methods by purchasing an organic product.

Organic Spirits

Organic spirits are made from organic ingredients such as grains or potatoes. In the United States there are only a few producers and distributors of organic spirits, but these products are available. You can find vodka, rum, grappa, gin, whiskey, and a variety of liqueurs that are organic. Some spirits are made with some organic ingredients but may not qualify for full organic certification.

Beauty

A Daily Ritual

By Yael Alkalay

I feel very fortunate that, like many New Yorkers, I trace my bloodlines all over the world. My grandfather, descended from ten generations of Turkish rabbis, was the first dermatologist in Bulgaria; my mother's family farmed the pampas of Argentina. My heritage bridges numerous cultures, nine languages, and many, many bathing traditions. I have inherited a deep value for ritual and ceremony.

Making a ritual for yourself upon starting the day and upon coming home is a defense against the chaos of the city. Start by treating your skin with certified organic ingredients that can protect and restore your body as you go through the day. Instead of dyes, petrochemicals, and parabens, use unaltered and toxin-free ingredients to naturally replenish.

When you come home, deep and astringent cleansing, a long, hot bath, and intense exfoliation are simple ways of detoxifying the body from exposure to pollution and restoring your state of mind.

Simple habits, too, can become meaningful ceremonies: the temperature of your shower, the soap you use to wash your body, how you sit at the computer, or how you make a cup of tea. How you create your space becomes a more important choice in a place like New York City, where there is so much constantly happening around you.

Protecting yourself does take an added element of knowledge and a degree of thoughtfulness. But luckily, since this is New York, the information is available, rich, and plentiful. That's the beauty of being able to make choices in this city.

Yael Alkalay is the CEO and founder of Red Flower, a line of locally produced eco-luxury beauty and well-being products. The Red Flower shop can be found in the NoLiTa neighborhood of Manhattan (**redflower.com**).

Beauty Products

The cosmetics industry is, in many ways, self-regulating. That means makers of cosmetics do not need approval from the Food and Drug Administration (FDA) for every chemical they use in their products. It's up to us to make sure we're getting products that are natural and nontoxic. That's why it makes sense to shop where you can get help from a knowledgeable staff person.

Organic beauty products, once rare, are now easier to find. Their effectiveness is on par with, and oftentimes superior to, conventional commercial beauty products. If you can't find an organic product that suits you, look for ones that offer organic ingredients combined with all-natural ingredients. Many grocery stores and specialty markets have extensive beauty and personal care sections. Check the "Eating In" section.

We've determined leaf awards based on the percentage of all the beauty product brands sold and/or used by an establishment containing one or more of the following:

- all certified organic ingredients,

- a mix of certified organic ingredients and natural ingredients, and/or

- all-natural ingredients, or mostly natural ingredients, that do not contain any of the following: *mercury, thimerosal, lead acetate, formaldehyde, nickel, toluene, petroleum distillates, acrylonitrile, ethylacrylate, coal tar, dibutyl phthalate, potassium dichromate, methyl cellosolve.*

In addition, we looked at whether or not the products the establishment carried were unpackaged or packaged with eco-friendly materials, and whether or not the store's own carry-out bags or packaging was biodegradable or compostable and/or made with recyclable material, vegetable-based inks, and/or chlorine-free paper.

at least 25% of the products meet the above criteria.

at least 50% of the products meet the above criteria.

at least 75% of the products meet the above criteria.

at least 90% of the products meet the above criteria.

ABC Carpet & Home
888 Broadway (E. 19th St.), Union Square (Man), 212-473-3000
Mon–Fri 10am–8pm Sat 10am–7pm Sun 11am–6:30pm **abchome.com**
Om Apothecary of organic and biodynamic balms and mists drawn from plant and flower essences, extracts, and oils. Nutritional supplements and organic home care products.

Amazon Beauty ⬚⬚⬚⬚

318 E. 70th St. (2nd Ave.), Upper East Side (Man), 646-670-8478
Mon–Sat 11am–8pm **amazonbeautysecret.com**
Beauty products made by women of the Quechua Shuar tribe with
ingredients grown in the rain forest.

Anwaar Co. ⬚⬚⬚⬚

428 Atlantic Ave. (bet. Bond & Nevins Sts.), Boerum Hill (Bkn), 718-875-3791
Daily 8:30am–8pm **anwaarco.com**
Shop carrying hair and skin products made only with all-natural ingredients.

Aphrodisia ⬚⬚⬚⬚

264 Bleecker St. (Cornelia St.), Greenwich Village (Man), 212-989-6440
Mon–Sat 11am–7pm Sun 12pm–5pm **aphrodisiaherbshoppe.com**
Beauty shop open since 1969 selling herbs and spices, products made
with holistic ingredients, culinary and medicinal herbs, curative teas,
and vitamin supplements.

Aveda ⬚⬚

140 5th Ave. (19th St.), Flatiron (Man), 212-645-4797
10 Columbus Cir., Ste. 308 (59th St.), Midtown (Man), 212-823-9714
10 Grand Central, Terminal 87 E (Lexington Ave.), Midtown (Man),
212-682-5397
233 Spring St., Aveda Institute (6th Ave.), SoHo (Man), 212-807-1492
Hours vary by location **aveda.com**
Hair, skin, and body care products; essential oils made from plant-based,
organic, or sustainable ingredients. Uses 100% wind power at
manufacturing facility; uses recycled bottles and packaging, and some
refillable containers.

Aveda Lifestyle Salon ⬚⬚

456 W. Broadway (bet. Prince & Houston Sts.), SoHo (Man), 212-473-0280
Mon–Fri 10am–9pm Sat 8:30am–8pm Sun 12pm–7pm **aveda.com**
Hair, skin, and body care products; essential oils made from plant-based,
organic, or sustainable ingredients. Uses 100% wind power at
manufacturing facility; uses recycled bottles and packaging, and some
refillable containers.

Bare Escentuals ⬚⬚

1140 3rd Ave. (bet. 66th & 67th Sts.), Upper East Side (Man), 646-537-0070
90-15 Queens Blvd. (Woodhaven), Elmhurst (Qns), 718-371-3724
Hours vary by location **bareescentuals.com**
All-natural, mineral-based, allergen-free cosmetics and treatments for
complexion, eyes, lips.

Bathroom, The ⬚

112 Greenwich Ave. (13th St.), West Village (Man), 212-206-1213
94 Charles St. (Bleecker St.), West Village (Man), 212-929-1449
Hours vary by location **inthebathroom.com**
Bath and body product store with a focus on natural products and
beauty treatments.

Body Shop, The ⬚

16 Fulton St. (bet. Water & Front Sts.), Financial District (Man), 212-480-9879
747 Broadway (8th St.), Greenwich Village (Man), 212-979-2944
1270 6th Ave. (bet. 50th & 51st Sts.), Midtown (Man), 212-397-3007
509 Madison Ave. (53rd St.), Midtown (Man), 212-829-8603
714 Lexington Ave. (bet. 56th & 57th Sts.), Midtown (Man), 212-755-7851
901 6th Ave. (bet. 32nd & 33rd Sts.), Midtown South (Man), 212-268-7424
154 Spring St. (bet. W. Broadway & Wooster St.), SoHo (Man), 212-343-7214

Body Shop, The ✎ (cont)

420 Lexington Ave. (44th St.), Tudor City (Man), 212-682-3502
2159 Broadway (76th St.), Upper West Side (Man), 212-721-2947
Hours vary by location   **thebodyshop.com**
Beauty supply, skin care, and aromatherapy shop carrying all-natural items.

Carol's Daughter ✎✎✎

24 W. 125th St. (bet. Lennox & 5th Aves.), Central Harlem (Man),
212-828-6757
1 S. Elliott Pl. (DeKalb Ave.), Fort Greene (Bkn), 718-596-1862
139 Flatbush Ave. (Atlantic Ave.), Fort Greene (Bkn), 718-622-4514
Hours vary by location   **carolsdaughter.com**
Bath and beauty products containing many organic, all-natural ingredients.

CeleBritAy ✎✎✎✎

358 Grand St. (bet. Havemeyer St. & Marcy Ave.), Williamsburg (Bkn),
718-384-0914
Seasonal hours   **celebritayny.com**
Natural health and beauty goods for men and women in an environmentally
friendly fashion; uses recycled glass to bottle products and sterilized yogurt
containers to hold their soy candles.

Dead Sea Beauty Supply ✎✎✎

66-22 99th St. (Queens Blvd.), Rego Park (Qns), 718-838-4000/800-318-1368
Mon–Fri 10am–7pm Sun 10am–7pm
Beauty supply store carrying natural beauty products and cosmetics;
Kamedis hair care products; formaldehyde-, DBP-, toluene-free nail polish.

Erbe ✎✎✎✎

196 Prince St. (bet. McDougal & Sullivan Sts.), SoHo (Man), 212-966-1445
Mon–Sat 11am–7pm Sun 12pm–5pm   **erbespa.com**
Organic botanical products with origins in the work of 16th-century Italian
herbalists and physicians.

Gigi Salon and Spa ✎✎

34-17 30th Ave. (34th St.), Astoria (Qns), 718-777-7755
Mon 12pm–8pm Tue–Fri 10am–8pm Sat 10am–6pm Sun 12pm–6pm
salonspagigi.com
Aveda salon selling all-natural Aveda hair, cosmetic, and beauty supplies.

Healthfully Organic Market ✎✎✎✎

98 E. 4th St. (bet. 1st & 2nd Aves.), East Village (Man), 212-598-0777
Mon–Fri 9am–10pm Sat 10am–9pm Sun 10am–8pm   **healthfully.com**
Natural health and beauty aids; vitamins and sports nutrition.

John Masters Organics ✎✎✎

77 Sullivan St. (bet. Spring & Broome Sts.), SoHo (Man), 212-343-9590
Mon–Fri 11am–7pm Sat 10am–6pm   **johnmasters.com**
One of New York City's only clean-air salons, selling all-organic,
sustainably made products. Ammonia-free, herbal, and clay-based hair
coloring products.

Jurlique Concept Store ✎✎✎✎

477 Madison Ave. (bet. 51st & 52nd Sts.), Midtown (Man), 212-752-1980
436 W. Broadway (bet. Prince & Spring Sts.), SoHo (Man), 212-219-3616
Hours vary by location   **jurlique.com**
Facial and skin care products made from botanicals and herbs sourced from
sustainable, biodynamic farms in S. Australia.

Karen's Body Beautiful 🌿🌿🌿🌿

436 Myrtle Ave. (bet. Clinton & Waverly Aves.), Fort Greene (Bkn),
718-797-4808
Mon–Sat 12pm–8pm Sun 10am–8pm **karensbodybeautiful.com**
Handmade, all-natural personal care products made in a viewable kitchen
on premises.

Kiehl's Since 1851 🌿

109 3rd Ave. (bet. 13th & 14th Sts.), Union Square (Man), 212-677-3171
154 Columbus Ave. (bet. W. 66th & W. 67th Sts.), Upper West Side (Man),
212-799-3438
Hours vary by location **kiehls.com**
Modern apothecary offering skin care, hair care, and beauty products made
with natural ingredients for the entire family.

L' Artisan Parfumeur 🌿🌿🌿

712 5th Ave., 2nd Flr. (53rd St.), Midtown (Man), 212-904-7910
68 Thompson St. (bet. Spring & Broome Sts.), SoHo (Man), 212-334-1500
1100 Madison Ave. (82nd St.), Upper East Side (Man), 212-794-3600
222 Columbus Ave. (70th St.), West Side (Man), 212-787-4400
Hours vary by location **artisan-parfumeur.us**
French beauty and scent shop offering natural perfumes, Ecocert-accredited
Jatamansi organic body line.

Ling Skin Care 🌿🌿🌿

191 Prince St. (Sullivan St.), SoHo (Man), 212-982-8833
12 E. 16th St. (5th Ave.), Union Square (Man), 212-989-8833
105 W. 77th St. (Columbus Ave.), Upper West Side (Man), 212-877-2883
Hours vary by location **lingskincare.com**
Simple, clean skin care products free of chemicals, fragrances, and
artificial colors.

Live Live & Organic 🌿🌿🌿🌿

261 E. 10th St. (bet. 1st Ave. & Ave. A), East Village (Man), 212-505-5504
Daily 11am–10pm **live-live.com**
Organic body care products free of preservatives and solvents; whole-food
vitamins; juicers, water filters, and dehydrators. Also offers lifesyle and
health consultations and classes.

L'Occitane En Provence 🌿

10 Columbus Cir. (8th Ave.), Clinton (Man), 212-333-4880
1598 Broadway (48th St.), Midtown (Man), 646-201-9106
610 5th Ave., Rockefeller Ctr. (49th St.), Midtown (Man), 212-586-1071
92 Prince St. (Mercer St.), SoHo (Man), 212-219-3310
412 Lexington Ave., Passage Ste. MC-66 (E. 43rd St.), Tudor City (Man),
212-557-6754
101 University Pl. (bet. 12th & 13th Sts.), Union Square (Man), 212-673-8630
1046 Madison Ave. (80th St.), Upper East Side (Man), 212-639-9185
1188 3rd Ave. (69th St.), Upper East Side (Man), 212-585-1955
1288 Madison Ave. (bet. 91st & 92nd Sts.), Upper East Side (Man),
212-987-8987
198 Columbus Ave. (69th St.), Upper West Side (Man), 212-874-4326
2303 Broadway (83rd St.), Upper West Side (Man), 212-496-1967
247 Bleecker St. (bet. 6th & 7th Aves.), West Village (Man), 212-367-8428
Hours vary by location **usa.loccitane.com**
Natural bath, body, and hair care products packaged with recycled
materials. Personal skin care consultations.

Lush 🌿

1293 Broadway (34th St.), Herald Sq. (Man), 212-564-9120
531 Broadway (bet. Prince & Spring Sts.), SoHo (Man), 212-925-2323
7 E. 14th St. (bet. 5th Ave. & University Pl.), Union Sq. (Man), 212-255-5133
2165 Broadway (bet. 76th & 77th Sts.), Upper West Side (Man),
212-787-5874
90-15 Queens Blvd., Unit 2028 (90th St.), Woodhaven (Qns), 718-699-8969
Hours vary by location   **lush.com**
Handmade, natural cosmetics and products for the bath, shower, and home.

Malin + Goetz 🌿

177 7th Ave. (bet. 20th & 21st Sts.), Chelsea (Man), 212-727-3777
Mon–Fri 11am–8pm Sat 12pm–8pm Sun 12pm–6pm   **malinandgoetz.com**
Apothecary and perfumery selling products made with natural ingredients.
Appropriate for all skin types.

Mastic Spa 🌿🌿

38-12 30th Ave. (Steinway St.), Astoria (Qns), 718-278-1804
Mon–Fri 11am–8pm Sat 11am–7pm Sun 11am–6pm   **masticspa.com**
All-natural face and body care products for women, men and children.
Offers facials.

Mastiha Shop 🌿🌿🌿

145 Orchard St. (Rivington St.), Lower East Side (Man), 212-253-0895
Tue 12pm–7pm Wed–Fri 12pm–8pm Sat 12pm–9pm Sun 11am–7pm
mastihashopny.com
Essential oils, natural cosmetics, and scented candles made with mastiha, a
resin from the eastern Mediterranean with anti-microbiological qualities and
a healing effect on cardiac and inflammatory conditions.

Mio Mia 🌿

318 Bedford Ave. (bet. S. 1st & 2nd Sts.), Williamsburg (Bkn), 718-388-0149
Mon–Fri 12:30pm–7:30pm Sat 12pm–7pm Sun 12pm–6pm
shopmiomia.com
Beauty supply store carrying selection of natural hair and body products.

Origins 🌿🌿🌿

175 5th Ave. (22nd St.), Flatiron (Man), 212-677-9100
75 Grand Central Station (42nd St.), Grand Central (Man), 212-808-4141
402 W. Broadway (Spring St.), SoHo (Man), 212-219-9764
2327 Broadway (bet. 84th & 85th Sts.), Upper West Side (Man),
212-769-0970
Hours vary by location   **origins.com**
Organic and all-natural beauty, skin care, hair care, and wellness products.

Red Flower 🌿🌿🌿🌿

13 Prince St. (Elizabeth St.), SoHo (Man), 212-966-5301
Daily 12pm–7pm   **redflower.com**
Organic beauty products founded on the principles of world traditions,
sustainable sourcing, ritual, well-being, and aesthetics. Located in Nolita
neighborhood of SoHo.

Sabon 🍃🍃

78 7th Ave. (15th St.), Chelsea (Man), 646-486-1809
1371 6th Ave. (bet. 55th & 56th Sts), Mid-town (Man), 212-974-7352
123 Prince St. (Wooster St.), SoHo (Man), 212-982-0968
93 Spring St. (bet. Mercer St. & Broadway), SoHo (Man), 212-925-0742
782 Lexington Ave. (61st St.), Upper East Side (Man), 212-308-5901
2052 Broadway (bet. 70th & 71st Sts.), Upper West Side (Man), 212-362-0200
434 6th Ave. (10th St.), West Village (Man), 212-473-4346
Hours vary by location **sabonnyc.com**
All-natural soaps, candles, aromatherapy oils, cosmetics, and body care
products made at an agricultural co-op in Israel. Eco-friendly packaging.

Saipua 🍃🍃🍃🍃

392 Van Brunt St. (Dikeman St.), Red Hook (Bkn), 718-624-2929
Thu–Sat 12pm–7pm Sun 12pm–6pm **saipua.com**
Handcrafted, all-natural olive oil soap made in New York. No animal or
petroleum-based ingredients.

Skinny Dip 🍃🍃🍃🍃

540 Driggs Ave. (bet. N. 7th & N. 8th Sts.), Williamsburg (Bkn), 718-599-2616
Seasonal hours **skinnydipnyc.com**
Eco-friendly, nontoxic hair salon and supply store. SLS- and paraben-
free products.

Soapology 🍃🍃

67 8th Ave. (bet. 13th & 14th Sts.), West Village (Man), 212-255-7627
Daily 11am–10pm **soapologynyc.com**
All-natural, organic bath and beauty products, 100% paraben-free.
Recycled and biodegradable packaging.

Space.NK.Apothecary 🍃

99 Greene St. (bet. Prince & Spring Sts.), SoHo (Man), 212-941-4201
Mon–Thu 11am–8pm Fri–Sat 11am–7pm Sun 12pm–6pm **spacenk.com**
Beauty supply store carrying a selection of organic, all-natural, paraben-free,
and nontoxic beauty lines.

Tahitian Noni 🍃

33-14 Queens Blvd. (33rd St.), Long Island City (Qns), 201-537-1061
Mon–Fri 10am–10pm Sat 9am–5pm **tahitiannoni.com**
All-natural beauty products and Noni brand health juices and supplements.

Woodley and Bunny 🍃

490 Driggs Ave. (bet. 9th & 10th Sts.), Williamsburg (Bkn), 718-218-6588
Mon-Fri 10am-9pm Sat 9am-8pm Sun 11am-7pm **woodleyandbunny.com**
Beauty supply shop carrying variety of all-natural hair care, skin care, bath,
body, and fragrance products.

did you know?

The Campaign for Safe Cosmetics estimates that the
average woman will ingest about four pounds of the
lipstick she wears during her life. Most lipsticks are made
from petroleum-based products as well as chemicals
and even coal tar dyes.

Hair and Nail Salons

Anyone who has ever been in, or walked near, a conventional hair and nail salon knows that the chemical vapors coming from within can be overwhelming. And many of the chemicals used in the products are potentially hazardous to the health and safety of the stylists as well as the customers. Improper or poor ventilation can worsen the problems. Environmentally friendly alternatives for toxic ingredients are increasingly available, so it makes sense to choose salons that are healthier for you and the workers inside.

If you already have a favorite salon, ask for the least-toxic treatments and check on the sanitation procedures. (The only way to effectively and naturally clean salon equipment and many tools is by using an FDA-approved autoclave, a device designed to heat solutions and the equipment they contain above their boiling point.) Also, ask your salon to carry beauty products with nontoxic or less-toxic ingredients. Or, don't be shy about asking if you can bring in your own organic shampoo or hair color to be used or applied.

For hair care, we looked at whether the salon used hair coloring that is vegetable-based, low- to ammonia-free, and/or mostly chemical-free. For nail salons, we checked whether or not the nail polishes used are free of the chemicals described below and whether or not the polish remover used is acetone-free. We also asked about proper sanitation procedures and the presence of ventilation systems that allow for outdoor air exchange.

For both hair and nail salons, we reviewed the supplies that are used on customers, as well as the grooming products for sale in the salon. We based our leaf awards on the percentage sold or used that is made with one or more of the following:

- all certified organic ingredients,

- a mix of certified organic ingredients and natural ingredients, and/or

- all-natural ingredients, or mostly natural ingredients, that do not contain *mercury, thimerosal, lead acetate, formaldehyde, nickel, toluene, petroleum distillates, acrylonitrile, ethylacrylate, coal tar, dibutyl phthalate, potassium dichromate, methyl cellosolve.*

Of the salon's practices, supplies used, and products sold:

at least 25% meet the above criteria.

at least 50% meet the above criteria.

at least 75% meet the above criteria.

at least 90% meet the above criteria.

Aria Hair 🍃

553 W. 235th St. (bet. Johnson & Oxford Aves.), Riverdale (Brx), 718-601-2600
Tue–Thu 9am–8pm Fri–Sat 9am–6pm Sun 10am–4pm **ariahair.net**
Salon using and selling Aveda all-natural products. Cosmetic services include vegetable-based lash dye.

Autonomy Salon 🍃🍃🍃

327 Lafayette St. (bet. E. Houston & Bleecker Sts.), NoHo (Man), 212-627-1710
Tue–Sat 11am–7pm **autonomysalon.com**
Hair salon using Davine, an all-natural European line, hair and beauty products.

Aveda Institute 🍃🍃

233 Spring St. (6th Ave.), SoHo (Man), 212-807-1492
Mon–Sat 10am–7pm Sun 12pm–6pm **aveda.com**
Affordable natural beauty treatments provided by students studying Aveda's methods; uses and sells Aveda products.

Aveda Lifestyle Salon—New York 🍃🍃

456 W. Broadway (bet. W. Houston & Prince Sts.), SoHo (Man), 212-473-0280
By appt. **aveda.com**
Salon offering Aveda Signature Services, using and selling all Aveda products.

Belazza 🍃🍃

519 8th Ave. (bet. 35th & 36th Sts.), Clinton (Man), 212-971-6100
Mon–Fri 9am–8pm Sat 10am–8pm **belazza.com**
Salon and spa using wide selection of Aveda and Phyto Organics hair products.

Bella Bella 🍃🍃

35-14 Ditmars Blvd. (35th St.), Astoria (Qns), 718-626-2758
Tue–Sun 9:30am–8pm
Salon using low-ammonia, vegetable-based hair dyes and natural shampoos and conditioners.

Carsten Institute New York 🍃🍃

22 E. 17th St., 2nd Flr. (bet. 5th Ave. & Union Sq. West), SoHo (Man), 212-675-4884
Mon–Sat 8:30am–8pm **carsteninstitute.com**
Beauty school and hair salon working with Aveda products. Holds Earth Day seminars where recyclables are collected from students.

Cocoon Hair Studio 🍃🍃🍃🍃

318 E. 70th St. (2nd Ave.), Upper East Side (Man), 212-879-5630
Mon–Sat 11am–8pm **cocoonhair.com**
Hair products used made with natural ingredients; all-natural and chemical-free processes. Donates portion of profits to help educate Amazon inhabitants to protect and preserve the rain forest.

Gigi Salon and Spa 🍃🍃

34-17 30th Ave. (34th St.), Astoria (Qns), 718-777-7755
Mon 12pm–8pm Tue–Fri 10am–8pm Sat 10am–6pm Sun 12pm–6pm
salonspagigi.com
Aveda-concept salon using full range of Aveda natural hair and cosmetic supplies.

G's Salon 🍃🍃

75 St. Marks Ave. (Flatbush Ave.), Prospect Heights (Bkn), 718-783-4099
Tue–Fri 9am–6:30pm Sat 9am–4pm Sun 11am–4pm
Aveda-concept salon offering natural hair treatments and services.

Iguazu 🍃🍃🍃

350 Hudson St. (King St.), West Village (Man), 212-647-0007
Mon–Sat 11am–8pm **iguazudayspa.com**
Salon offering all-natural hair coloring. Sells natural hair care products.

Il Camelion 🍃🍃

463 4th St. (bet. 7th & 8th Aves.), Park Slope (Bkn), 718-788-1700
By appt.
Aveda-concept hair salon using natural products.

Irene Dinov Salon & Day Spa 🍃

119 Montague St. (bet. Henry & Hicks Sts.), Brooklyn Heights (Bkn),
718-855-5900
Mon–Fri 9am–9pm Sat 9am–6pm Sun 10am–6pm **irenedinov.com**
Aveda-concept salon and day spa offering hair and nail care, body
treatments, laser treatments and hair removal, photofacials.

Jeffrey Stein Salon 🍃🍃

685 3rd Ave. (43rd St.), Murray Hill (Man), 212-557-0005
779 Broadway (9th St.), NoHo (Man), 212-777-7717
1336 3rd Ave. (77th St.), Upper East Side (Man), 212-772-7717
250 Columbus Ave. (72nd St.), Upper West Side (Man), 212-580-6000
495 Columbus Ave. (84th St.), Upper West Side (Man), 212-787-7717
2345 Broadway (86th St.), West Side (Man), 212-595-1177
Hours vary by location
Aveda-concept salon. All-natural and organic hair treatments and services.

Jinsoon Natural Hand & Foot Sspa 🍃🍃

56 E. 4th St. (bet. Bowery & 2nd Ave.), East Village (Man), 212-473-2047
421 E. 73rd St. (bet. 1st & York Aves.), Upper East Side (Man), 212-249-9144
23 Jones St. (bet. W. 4th & Bleeker Sts.), West Village (Man), 212-229-1070
Daily 11am–8pm **jinsoon.com**
Hand and foot spa using essential oils instead of conventional lotions;
toluene-, DBP-, and formaldehyde-free nail polishes.

John Masters Organics 🍃🍃🍃🍃

77 Sullivan St. (bet. Spring & Broome Sts.), SoHo (Man), 212-343-9590
Mon–Fri 11am–7pm Sat 10am–6pm **johnmasters.com**
One of New York City's only clean-air salons, using all organic products.
No chemical services offered. Ammonia-free, herbal, and clay-based hair
color products. Member Global Green's New York Committee.

Joseph Rubin Beauty 🍃🍃

71-33 Kissena Blvd. (71st Ave.), Flushing (Qns), 718-591-5888
Daily 10am–6pm
Salon uses vegetable-based and ammonia-free hair dye; Phyto Organics
products sold.

Locks 'n Lads 🍃🍃🍃🍃

123 E. 7th St. (Ave. A), East Village (Man), 212-677-2262
Mon 12pm–6pm Tue–Wed 12pm–7pm Thu–Sat 11am–7pm Sun 12pm–6pm
locksnlads.com
Hair salon for children and adults using organic and ammonia-free hair
coloring and certified organic products.

Natural Identity 🍃🍃

95-17 63rd Dr. (Queens Blvd.), Rego Park (Qns), 718-896-4852
Daily 10am–7pm
Salon using vegetable-based and ammonia-free hair dyes; Phyto Organics products for sale.

NoLas 🍃🍃

61-10 Woodside Ave. (61st St.), Woodside (Qns), 718-565-1279
Mon–Thu 9am–7pm Fri 9am–8pm Sat 9am–6pm Sun 9am–4pm
Hair salon featuring Aveda products. Also offers skin treatments, waxing, and cosmetics.

Novella Salon 🍃🍃

350 W. 14th St. (bet. 8th & 9th Aves.), West Village (Man), 646-336-6151
Mon–Fri 10am–8pm Sat 10am–7pm Sun 11am–6pm **novellasalon.com**
Aveda-concept salon offering hair cuts, styling, color, and makeup application.

Pamona Beauty Sanctuary 🍃🍃🍃

447 7th Ave. (bet. 15th & 16th Sts.), Park Slope (Bkn), 718-768-1343
By appt.
Hair salon using all-natural product lines, performing some chemical-free coloring.

Parlor 🍃🍃

102 Ave. B (bet. 6th & 7th Sts.), East Village (Man), 212-673-5520
Tue 11am–9pm Wed 10am–9pm Thu–Fri 11am–9pm Sat–Sun 9am–6pm
parlorhairsalon.com
Stylists use Aveda hair care products and treatments. Space is decorated with pieces created by local artists.

Phyto Universe 🍃🍃

715 Lexington Ave. (58th St.), Turtle Bay (Man), 212-308-0270
Mon–Sat 10am–7pm **phytouniverse.com**
Personalized hair analysis and treatments, skin care services. Features 3,000-ft. vertical tropical garden.

Pure Salon 🍃🍃

3262 Johnson Ave. (bet. W. 232nd St. & W. 235th Sts.), Riverdale (Brx), 718-548-4023
Tue–Wed 10am–6pm Thu–Fri 9am–7pm Sat 9am–5pm Sun 10am–4pm
puresalonaveda.com
Aveda-concept salon. Nail service uses toluene- and formaldehyde-free polish and acetone-free polish remover.

Rapunzel Rapunzel 🍃🍃

158 5th Ave. (Douglass St.), Park Slope (Bkn), 718-857-2855
Tue–Sat 10am–7pm Sat 8am–6pm Sun 10am–5pm
Hair salon providing organic and all-natural treatments and coloring.

Salon Above 🍃🍃

2641 Broadway 2nd Flr. (100th St.), Upper West Side (Man), 212-665-7149
By appt. **salonabove.com**
Aveda-concept salon offering hair treatments and coloring, makeup application.

Saloon Highlights 🍃

36-17 30th Ave. (36th St.), Astoria (Qns), 718-956-3366
Mon–Fri 11am–7pm Sat 9am–5pm Sun 10am–3pm **saloonhaircolor.com**
Hair salon offering ammonia-free hair coloring.

Scott J., Aveda SalonSpa 🌿🌿

2929 Broadway (bet. 114th & 115th Sts.), Morningside Heights (Man), 212-496-3902
242 E. 86th St. (bet. 2nd & 3rd Aves.), Upper East Side (Man), 212-496-3901
257 Columbus Ave. (72nd St.), West Side (Man), 212-496-3904
Hours vary by location   scottj.com
Hair salon and spa using Aveda eco-friendly hair and skin products.

Skinny Dip 🌿🌿🌿🌿

540 Driggs Ave. (bet. N. 7th & N. 8th Sts.), Williamsburg (Bkn), 718-599-2616
By appt.   skinnydipnyc.com
Hair salon and supply store using paraben- and SLS-free products. No harsh chemical processes.

Slope Suds 🌿🌿🌿🌿

433 7th Ave. (15th St.), Park Slope (Bkn), 718-788-7837
Tue–Fri 11am–7:30pm Sat 10am–7:30pm Sun 10am–6pm   slopesuds.com
Hair salon and soap bar using only all-natural Davinas hair products.
Sells handmade soaps and scrubs.

Soon Beauty Lab 🌿🌿🌿

318 E. 11th St. (bet. 1st & 2nd Aves.), East Village (Man), 212-260-4423
54 W. 22nd St. (bet. 5th & 6th Aves.), Midtown South (Man), 212-243-0245
Mon–Fri 11am–9pm Sat–Sun 10am–6pm   soonbeautylab.com
Hair salon using organic and all-natural product lines. Specializes in creative, artistic cuts.

Space 🌿

29-09 Ditmars Blvd. (31st St.), Astoria (Qns), 718-726-4477
Mon–Wed 9am–7:30pm Thu–Fri 9am–8pm Sat 8am–7pm Sun 9am–6pm
salonspace.com
Salon and spa offering facials, massages, body scrubs, hand and foot treatments, and waxing using Aveda natural products and low-ammonia hair coloring.

Swing 🌿🌿🌿

280 E. 10th St. (bet. 1st Ave. & Ave. A), East Village (Man), 212-677-2008
Tue–Sun 11am–7pm   swingsalon.com
Hair salon using and selling only Modern Organic Products line.

Tendrils Hair Spa 🌿

87 Fort Greene Pl. (Fulton St.), Fort Greene (Bkn), 718-875-3811
Wed–Sun 10am–6pm   tendrilshairspa.com
Hair and braiding salon using chemical-free products. Sells all-natural hair care products.

Time Salon 🌿

9 Greene Ave. (Fulton St.), Fort Greene (Bkn), 718-522-9030
Tue 9am–4pm Wed–Fri 9am–6pm Sat–Sun 8am–1:00pm
Hair salon using Aveda and Miss Jessie's natural products.

Woodley and Bunny 🌿🌿

490 Driggs Ave. (bet. 9th & 10th Sts.), Williamsburg (Bkn), 718-218-6588
Mon-Fri 10am-9pm Sat 9am-8pm Sun 11am-7pm   woodleyandbunny.com
Hair salon using low-ammonia hair dye, natural product lines. Sells some natural hair care, beauty, and home products.

Day Spas

There is nothing like indulging yourself with a massage, sauna, or special beauty treatment, and the spas listed here can all pamper you. Best of all, you can rest easier knowing that you are nurturing your body in an eco-friendly way.

The day spas we've listed have all created environments that are healthy and restful and have also committed to using and carrying eco-friendly, natural products. We sought out spas that keep their sauna, bath, and Jacuzzi rooms mold-free without using chlorine bleach or chemicals. We determined whether or not the rooms have exhaust fans and/or allow for outdoor air exchange. We also checked into whether or not they are inspected periodically for proper drainage.

If the spa offers hair salon services, we looked into what percentage of the hair coloring used is vegetable-based, low- to ammonia-free, and/or mostly chemical-free. Where nail care is concerned, we asked if the polishes used are phthalate-, toluene-, and formaldehyde-free and if the polish remover used is acetone-free.

We have determined leaf awards based on the criteria outlined above, as well as the percentage of beauty and spa products that the spa sells and uses in-house in its customer treatments that contain one or more of the following:

- all certified organic ingredients,

- a mix of certified organic ingredients and natural ingredients, and/or

- all-natural ingredients, or mostly natural ingredients, that do not contain *mercury, thimerosal, lead acetate, formaldehyde, nickel, toluene, petroleum distillates, acrylonitrile, ethylacrylate, coal tar, dibutyl phthalate, potassium dichromate, methyl cellosolve.*

In addition, we looked at whether or not the products the establishment carries were unpackaged or packaged with eco-friendly materials, and whether or not the spa's own carry-out bags or packaging were biodegradable or compostable and/or made with recyclable material, vegetable-based inks, and/or chlorine-free paper.

Of spa treatments and practices and salon products used and sold:

at least 25% meet the above criteria.

at least 50% meet the above criteria.

at least 75% meet the above criteria.

at least 90% meet the above criteria.

Allediana Skin Care Center ✿✿✿

79-13 37th Ave. (79th St.), Jackson Heights (Qns), 718-651-0805
Mon–Fri 10am–6pm Sat 9am–5pm
Spa offers natural European facials, microdermabrasion, folic acid
treatments, waxing, electrolysis.

Arcadia ✿✿✿✿

228 8th Ave. (bet. 21st & 22nd Sts.), Chelsea (Man), 212-243-5358
Mon–Sat 11am–10pm Sun 11am–9pm arcadianyc.com
Day spa and Zen room providing advanced skin care using Dr. Hauschka
products. Sells locally crafted, artisanal, unique gift items and fine art.

Area Emporium & Spa ✿✿

281 Smith St. (Sackett St.), Carroll Gardens (Bkn), 718-624-3157
By appt. areabrooklyn.com
Spa offering skin care, massage, body treatments, and waxing using
all-natural and organic products.

Bela's Herbal Beauty of New York ✿✿✿

108-09 Liberty Ave. (108th St.), Richmond Hill (Qns), 718-835-8838
119-20 101 Ave. (119th St.), Richmond Hill (Qns), 718-849-8535
Mon–Thu 10am–8pm Fri–Sat 9:30am–8pm
Spa specializing in henna tattoos and hair coloring; threading, natural facials,
and herbal products.

Cynergy Spa ✿

87 Fort Greene Pl. (bet. Fulton & DeKalb Sts.), Fort Greene (Bkn),
718-403-9242
By appt. cynergyspa.com
Facials, massage, body treatments, and spa packages using some
natural ingredients.

Erbe ✿✿✿

196 Prince St. (bet. McDougal & Sullivan Sts.), SoHo (Man), 212-966-1445
Mon–Sat 11am–7pm Sun 12pm–5pm erbespa.com
Spa uses and sells organic botanical products made in the tradition of
16th-century Italian herbalists and physicians.

Essential Therapy ✿✿✿✿

122 E. 25th St. (bet. Park & Lexington Aves.), Gramercy (Man), 212-777-2325
Mon–Fri 10am–10pm Sat–Sun 10am–8pm essentialtherapyny.com
Spa services using organic products; massage incorporates principles
of feng shui.

GB's International Beauty Salon and Spa ✿✿✿

110-08 Liberty Ave. (110th St.), Richmond Hill (Qns), 718-529-5000
Mon–Thu 10am–7pm Fri–Sat 10am–8pm Sun 1pm–4pm
Ayurvedic and natural fruit, clay, and seaweed facials; henna and Herbatint
hair dyes.

Genesis Day Spa ✿✿✿

23-27 Steinway St. (23rd Ave.), Astoria (Qns), 718-545-0449
Mon–Sat 10am–7pm
Organic and natural spa treatments including facials, massage, full-body
exfoliating, manicures, and pedicures.

Glamour Beauty Salon ✿✿

67-14A Roosevelt Ave. (67th St.), Woodside (Qns), 718-639-6110
Mon–Thu 10am–8pm Fri–Sat 10am–9pm Sun 10am–8pm
All-natural facials; honey waxing; henna hair coloring and tattoos.

Great Jones Spa 🌿🌿🌿🌿

29 Great Jones St. (bet. Lafayette St. & Bowery), NoHo (Man), 212-505-3185
Daily 9am–10pm **gjspa.com**
Organic skin care products, nonchlorinated Jacuzzi, organic juice bar. Four-story waterfall recycles its own water.

Greenhouse Holistic 🌿🌿🌿

88 Roebling St. (N. 7th St.), Williamsburg (Bkn), 718-599-3113
By appt. **greenhouseholistic.com**
Hot-stone spa offering massage, facials, and other services using all-natural and organic products.

Hibiscus Day Spa 🌿🌿

558A Halsey St. (Stuyvesant Ave.), Bedford-Stuyvesant (Bkn), 718-573-0831
By appt. **hibiscusdayspa.com**
Holistic spa offering variety of all-natural treatments and therapies: massage, facials, body polishing, waxing, manicures and pedicures.

HomeSpa, The 🌿🌿🌿

300 Court St. (bet. Douglass & Degraw Sts.), Cobble Hill (Bkn), 718-596-8668
By appt. **homespa.com**
Holistic day spa offering massages, facials, and body treatments using organic and all-natural products, including own HomeSpa line.

Iguazu 🌿🌿🌿

350 Hudson St. (King St.), West Village (Man), 212-647-0007
Mon–Sat 11am–8pm **iguazudayspa.com**
Natural and holistic techniques for body treatments, facials, massages, and waxing. Also offers hair and nail services.

Irene Dinov Salon and Day Spa 🌿🌿

119 Montague St. (bet. Henry & Hicks Sts.), Brooklyn Heights (Bkn), 718-855-5900
Mon–Fri 9am–9pm Sat 9am–6pm Sun 10am–6pm **irenedinov.com**
Aveda-concept salon and day spa offering hair and nail care, body treatments, laser treatments and hair removal, photofacials.

La Coupe Spa 🌿🌿

28-14 31st St. (28th Ave.), Astoria (Qns), 718-777-7729
Tue–Sat 10am–8pm Sun 11am–5pm
Spa offering natural facials, ammonia-free hair coloring, and natural mineral-based cosmetics.

Le Cachet Day Spa 🌿🌿🌿🌿

39 E. 30th St. (Madison Ave.), Murray Hill (Man), 212-448-9823
Daily 11am–8pm **lecachetspa.com**
Holistic day spa offering all-natural services and treatments using organic skin and hair care products.

Ling Skin Care 🌿🌿🌿

191 Prince St. (Sullivan St.), SoHo (Man), 212-982-8833
12 E. 16th St. (5th Ave.), Union Square (Man), 212-989-8833
105 W. 77th St. (Columbus Ave.), Upper West Side (Man), 212-877-2883
Hours vary by location **lingskincare.com**
Spa using simple, clean products with no unnecessary chemicals, fragrances, or artificial colors.

Magnolia Beauty Spa 🍃🍃

124 Bedford Ave. (N. 10th St.), Williamsburg (Bkn), 718-599-5780
Mon–Fri 10am–8pm Sat 9am–6pm **magnoliabeautyspa.com**
Spa offering facials and body wraps using organic products.

Mirai Wellness Nail & Spa 🍃🍃🍃🍃

670 Fulton St. (bet. S. Portland & Elliott Sts.), Fort Greene (Bkn),
718-875-0369
Daily 10am–8pm **miraiwellnessspa.com**
Nail and day spa using Jurlique products for facial and massage services.

Phyto Universe 🍃🍃

715 Lexington Ave. (58th St.), Turtle Bay (Man), 212-308-0270
Mon–Sat 10am–7pm **phytouniverse.com**
Day spa offering personalized hair analysis and treatments, skin care ser-
vices. Features a 3,000-ft. vertical tropical garden.

Priti Organic Spa 🍃🍃🍃🍃

35 E. 1st St. (2nd Ave.), East Village (Man), 212-254-3628
Tue–Fri 11am–8pm Sat–Sun 10am–7pm **pritiorganicspa.com**
Natural day spa using organic products. Incorporates fresh flowers, fruits,
herbs, and organic essential oils for their natural healing qualities.

Providence Day Spa 🍃🍃🍃

329 Atlantic Ave. (bet. Smith & Hoyt Sts.), Boerum Hill (Bkn), 718-596-6774
Daily 11am–9pm **providencedayspa.com**
Facials, massage, body treatments, and acupuncture using mostly
organic products.

Pure Spa & Salon 🍃🍃

40-15 Queens Blvd. (40th St.), Sunnyside (Qns), 718-784-6400
Mon–Tue 10am–8pm Wed–Thu 10am–9pm Fri 10am–8pm Sat 10am–7pm
Sun 11am–5pm **purespanyc.com**
All-natural facial and body treatments. Soy candles and aromatherapy
products sold.

Queens Threading and Waxing 🍃🍃🍃

40-14 82nd St. (Roosevelt Ave.), Elmhurst (Qns), 718-505-9730
Mon–Sat 10am–8pm Sun 10am–7:30pm
Salon offering natural facials, eyebrow threading, and waxing.

Rejuvenate Face & Body 🍃🍃🍃🍃

26-17 23rd Ave. (26th St.), Astoria (Qns), 718-626-4434
Mon–Wed 11am–7pm Fri 11am–8pm Sat 10am–6pm **rejuvenatenyc.com**
Holistic face and body spa offering organic and all-natural treatments in a
clean, nontoxic environment. Uses biodegradable cleaning products.

Sage Spa 🍃🍃🍃🍃

405 5th Ave., 2nd Flr. (7th St.), Park Slope (Bkn), 718-832-2030
By appt. **sagebrooklyn.com**
Spa offering massage, aromatherapy, and facials using only Weleda products.

Scott J., Aveda SalonSpa 🌿🌿

2929 Broadway (bet. 114th & 115th Sts.), Morningside Heights (Man), 212-496-3902
242 E. 86th St. (bet. 2nd & 3rd Aves.), Upper East Side (Man), 212-496-3901
257 Columbus Ave. (72nd St.), West Side (Man), 212-496-3904
Hours vary by location **scottj.com**
Aveda-concept salon. Spa services include skin care, botanical skin resurfacing, massage, body wraps and polishes, and custom treatments.

Spa & Wellness Center, The 🌿🌿🌿🌿

8804 3rd Ave. (88th St.), Bay Ridge (Bkn), 718-921-6100
By appt. **thespanewyork.com**
Massage, body treatments, manicures and pedicures, and movement studio. Uses Matisse, Guinot, and own line of natural spa products.

Spa Ja 🌿🌿🌿🌿

300 W. 56th St. (8th Ave.), Midtown West (Man), 212-245-7566
Mon–Sat 9am–9pm Sun 10am–7pm **spaja.com**
Spa and nail salon using organic, all-natural products; noninvasive and chemical-free treatments.

Space 🌿🌿

29-09 Ditmars Blvd. (31st St.), Astoria (Qns), 718-726-4477
Mon–Fri 9am–7:30pm Sat 9am–7pm Sun 9am–6pm **salonspace.com**
Salon and spa offering facials, massage, body scrub, waxing, and hand and foot treatments. Uses Aveda and other natural products, low-ammonia hair coloring.

Spahydra 🌿🌿🌿🌿

35-11 36th St. (35th Ave.), Long Island City (Qns), 718-267-7991
Mon 11am–5pm Wed–Fri 10am–8pm Sat 10am–6pm Sun 11am–5pm
spahydra.com
Natural skin care treatments, massage therapies, vegan manicure and pedicures, organic waxing. Natural tea and tonic offerings, herbal body treatments.

Total Relax Beauty Clinic 🌿🌿🌿

35-65 84th St. (37th Ave.), Jackson Heights (Qns), 718-205-4734
Mon–Sat 11am–7pm
Spa offering natural face and body and treatments; skin detoxing; aromatherapy; homeopathic nutritional supplementation programs for sale.

Tribeca Spa of Tranquility 🌿

462 Greenwich St. (bet. Watts & Desbrosses Sts.), Tribeca (Man), 212-226-4141
By appt. **tribecaspaoftranquility.com**
Natural treatments, including massage, organic body scrubs, aromatherapy, pedicures.

WellSpring Holistic Health Center & Day Spa 🌿🌿🌿🌿

2114 Williamsbridge Rd. (bet. Pelham Pkwy. S & Lydig Ave.), Pelham-Williamsbridge (Brx), 718-239-0505
Mon-Fri 10am-7pm Sat 9am-6pm **wellspringholisticdayspa.com**
Integrated alternative and traditional spa services. Specializing in purification, detoxification, and weight management.

Beauty

The Search for Better Beauty Products

Check the *Skin Deep* Database

Looking for the words *natural* or *safe* won't guarantee that the beauty products you buy really are safe. But some companies are making less harmful products today and are striving to make even safer ones in the future. Choose products that are healthier for you now. Visit the Environmental Working Group's Skin Deep database, **ewg.org/reports/skindeep,** the world's largest searchable database of ingredients in cosmetics. Find out if your favorite products contain hazardous chemicals and find safer alternatives at this site. Also check out **safecosmetics.org** for more information about what's being done to encourage manufacturers to make their products safer.

Tell your cosmetics companies you want safe products. Call them, write them, or e-mail them to let them know where you stand. Look on product packaging for a customer service hotline or check the company's website.

About Fragrance

Look for products that contain natural fragrance rather than synthetic fragrance. The latter is far more common, so you'll have to read labels carefully.

For the past fifty years, 80 to 90 percent of fragrances have been synthesized from petroleum, not from natural sources as advertisers might like us to believe. A few of the commonly found harmful chemicals in fragranced products are *acetone, benzene, phenol, toluene, benzyl acetate,* and *limonene.* Stay away from these!

Harmful health effects of fragrance are caused not only by the chemicals mentioned above and a few thousand other individual chemicals, but each fragrance may well contain hundreds of different chemical combinations.

Since fragrance ingredients are protected under trade secret laws, the consumer is kept in the dark about many of the harmful chemicals that make up synthetic fragrances. When the label says "fragrance," watch out!

Synthetic fragrances are also harmful to marine life and are a source of pollution. One of the EPA's top ten reasons for poor indoor air quality is the presence of artificial fragrances. Fragrance is increasingly cited as a trigger in health conditions such as asthma, allergies, and migraine headaches.

Consume less.

Goods

Adding Sustainability to Your Style

By Jill Danyelle

Whether one eschews fashion or is a slave to it, we all need to get dressed in the morning. While fashion can seem a frivolous manifestation of that need, it is a big business, with billions of dollars of retail trade. Below the surface of an industry that is primarily focused on aesthetics lies a process that is not always pretty. Cotton uses approximately 25 percent of the world's insecticides, which is roughly 84 million pounds a year in the U.S. alone. Additionally, nearly 10 million tons of textiles enter the waste stream annually in the United States and Europe. Add to these impacts manufacturing processes that are often water intensive and lead to toxic effluent, and one can see the need to develop an alternative.

So, what is an eco-conscious consumer to do? Buy some vintage, resale, and thrift pieces. Attend or organize clothing swaps. Utilize a tailor or your sewing machine to modify your existing wardrobe. Donate clothes versus throwing them away. Finally, you may try to shop less, but the fact is everybody will need to purchase something new on occasion. When the time comes, try to focus on quality over quantity by investing in items you will keep for a long time. Read the label. Where is it made? What is it made from? Look for organic wool and cotton, silk, hemp, linen, bamboo, lyocell, recycled fibers, and vegetable-tanned leathers. The simple strategy to a greener wardrobe is a familiar mantra: reuse, reduce, recycle.

Jill Danyelle (**danyelle.org**) created fiftyRX3, a multimedia project on style and sustainability and served as fashion editor for inhabitat.com.

Goods

Clothing and Shoes

A significant percentage of the world's pesticides, herbicides, and water is used in growing and processing the fibers that are made into our clothing. But we are seeing more and more eco-friendly fibers used in some very fashionable ways these days. You will find soy shirts, hemp scarves, recycled cashmere sweaters, and bamboo blouses. Organic wool might make your winter wardrobe, and organic cotton could signal your new summer style. And some of us are even sporting used soda bottles in the form of fleece.

Choosing clothing conscientiously could also mean checking for fair trade certification, whether an item is union made, made by local artisans, or sweatshop-free. Ask about these things so proprietors know you care.

Try to find clothes that are unbleached or bleached with hydrogen peroxide only, and that use natural or low-impact dyes and no wrinkle-free treatments (these can be toxic).

Be sure to also visit vintage clothing stores and resale shops, as they are inherently positive on the reduce/reuse/recycle level.

Sustainable clothing and shoes are areas with still-emerging standards, but at this point, we're evaluating our stores based on the percentage of goods sold that are made with recycled content, organic, natural fibers, or a blend. We also reviewed whether or not the store's carry-out bags or packaging were biodegradable, compostable, and/or made with recycled or recyclable material, vegetable-based inks, and/or chlorine-free paper.

Of the clothing and shoes sold:

at least 25% meet the above criteria.

at least 50% meet the above criteria.

at least 75% meet the above criteria.

at least 90% meet the above criteria.

Type of clothing, shoes and/or gear:

M Men's   C Children's

W Women's   B Baby

Alter M W
109 Franklin St. (Greenpoint Ave.), Greenpoint (Bkn), 718-784-8818
Tue–Fri 1pm–9pm Sat 12pm–9pm Sun 12pm–8pm **alterbrooklyn.com**
Men's and women's clothing, shoes, and accessories made from reconstructed fabrics and natural materials.

Asha Veza 🍃🍃 W

69 5th Ave. (bet. St. Marks & Prospect Pl.), Park Slope (Bkn), 718-783-2742
Seasonal hours **ashaveza.com**
Repurposed and vintage fabrics created by at-risk women as well as lines
created by emerging Bosnian and Indian designers.

AuH₂O 🍃🍃🍃🍃 M W B

84 E. 7th St. (1st Ave.), East Village (Man), 212-466-0844
Tue–Sun 1pm–8pm **auh2odesigns.com**
Shop specializing in unique pieces that are recycled, redesigned, reconstructed, and sewn on-site. Also carries vintage and consignment jewelry,
handbags, and clothing.

Beneath 🍃 W

265 E. 78th St. (2nd Ave.), Upper East Side (Man), 212-288-3800
Tue–Fri 12pm–8pm Sat–Sun 12pm–6pm
Women's boutique with a selection of natural fabrics and comfort wear.

Bird 🍃 W

220 Smith St. (Butler St.), Cobble Hill (Bkn), 718-797-3774
430 7th Ave. (bet. 14th & 15th Sts.), Park Slope (Bkn), 718-768-4940
Mon–Sat 12pm–8pm Sun 12pm–7pm **shopbird.com**
Women's clothing store offering some organic items, including cashmere,
cotton, wool, and other eco-friendly materials.

Camilla Boutique 🍃🍃🍃🍃 M W C B

355 Atlantic Ave. (bet. Hoyt & Bond Sts.), Boerum Hill (Bkn), 718-422-0282
Tue–Sat 12pm–7pm Sun 12pm–6pm **camillaboutique.com**
All eco-friendly clothing for babies, men, and women. Also sells linens, ac-
cessories, jewelry, and craft items in a nontoxic, sustainably designed space.

Candy Plum 🍃🍃🍃 M W C B

30-98 36th St. (31st Ave.), Astoria (Qns), 718-721-2299
Mon–Thu 10am–7pm Fri 12pm–7pm Sat–Sun 12pm–5pm **candyplum.com**
Clothes and jewelry by local artisans using organic or recycled materials.

Cotton Bob's 🍃🍃 C B

123 E. 7th St. (Ave. A), East Village (Man), 212-677-2262
Mon 12pm–6pm Tue–Wed 12pm–7pm Thu–Sat 11am–7pm Sun 12pm–6pm
cottonbobs.com
Children's clothing boutique with organic cotton and locally made items.

Diana Kane 🍃 W

229 5th Ave. (President St.), Park Slope (Bkn), 718-638-6520
78 7th Ave. (Berkeley Pl.), Park Slope (Bkn), 718-638-5674
Hours vary by location **dianakane.com**
Clothing boutique carrying products made from organic and recycled
materials. Lines include Loomstate and Organic.

Ekovaruhuset 🍃🍃🍃🍃 M W

123 Ludlow St. (Rivington St.), Lower East Side (Man), 212-673-1753
Tue–Sun 1pm–8pm **ekovaruhuset.se**
Women's boutique featuring all organic and fair made materials.

Femme Fatale 🍃🍃 W

578 Driggs Ave. (N. 6th St.), Williamsburg (Bkn), 718-497-6055
Mon–Sat 1pm–7:30pm **femmefatalenyc.com**
Boutique supporting local and emerging designers who use recycled
materials and fabrics.

Geminola 🌿🌿🌿🌿 W C B

41 Perry St. (bet. W. 4th St. & 7th Ave.), West Village (Man), 212-675-1994
Mon–Wed 12pm–7pm Thu–Sat 12pm–8pm Sun 12pm–6pm **geminola.com**
Reconstructed clothing made using entirely pre-1950's vintage fabrics. The
store is decorated with recycled and salvaged materials.

Gominyc 🌿🌿🌿🌿 W

443 E. 6th St. (bet. 1st Ave. & Ave. A), East Village (Man), 212-979-0388
Mon–Thu 1pm–8:30pm Fri 1pm–9pm Sat 12pm–9pm Sun 12pm–8:30pm
gominyc.com
Eco-friendly fashion, vegetable-dyed shoes and bags, and eco-friendly
home accessories.

Green Finds/Samples for (eco)mpassion 🌿🌿 M W

2 Great Jones St. (Broadway), NoHo (Man), 212-777-0707
Thu–Sun 12pm–8pm **greenfinds.com**
Carbon-neutral sample sale company featuring eco-designers with 5% of
proceeds going to support different charities.

Green Tree General Store 🌿🌿🌿🌿 M W B

95 Norman Ave. (Manhattan Ave.), Greenpoint (Bkn), 347-422-0565
Wed–Sat 1pm–7pm Sun 12pm–6pm **greentreestore.com**
Sustainably designed shop selling eco-friendly clothing for men, women,
and babies. Gifts, bath supplies, and accessories also available.

Half Pint Citizens 🌿🌿🌿🌿 C B

55 Washington St. (bet. Front & Water Sts.), DUMBO (Bkn), 718-875-4007
Mon–Fri 11am–6pm Sat–Sun 10am–6pm **halfpintcitizens.com**
Carries organic apparel for children and infants; eco-friendly toys and gifts.

Harriet's Alter Ego 🌿🌿 W B

293 Flatbush Ave. (Prospect Pl.), Prospect Heights (Bkn), 718-783-2074
Tue–Sat 12pm–8pm Sun 12pm–5pm **harrietsalteregoonline.com**
Specialty clothing including garments made from recycled fabrics. Also
carries a line of all-natural African skincare products.

Indigo Handloom 🌿🌿 W

68 Jay St., Suite 117 (Water St.), DUMBO (Bkn), 917-779-8420
Seasonal hours **indigohandloom.com**
Women's clothing made with hand-loomed cotton, silks, and other natural
materials. Individual eco-friendly fabric sold wholesale and retail.

Jivamukti Yoga School 🌿🌿🌿🌿 W

841 Broadway, 2nd Flr. (E. 13th St.), Union Square (Man), 212-353-0214
Mon–Fri 8am–9pm Sat 10am–9pm Sun 10am–3pm **jivamuktiyoga.com**
100% vegan and environmentally conscious boutique selling yoga-inspired
apparel; also sells some plant-derived beauty products.

Kaight 🌿🌿🌿🌿 M W

83 Orchard St. (Broome St.), Lower East Side (Man), 212-680-5630
Mon–Sat 12am–8pm Sun 12am–7pm **kaightnyc.com**
An eco-boutique carrying men's and women's clothing made by emerging green designers. Fabrics include organic cotton, bamboo, hemp, silk,
organic wool, and recycled leather.

Lola y Maria 🌿 W

175 Rivington St. (Clinton St.), Lower East Side (Man), 646-602-9556
Tue–Fri 1:30pm–8:30pm Sat 12pm–8:30pm Sun 12pm–8pm **lolaymaria.com**
Boutique featuring emerging independent designers; organic cotton, bam-
boo and collectible vintage fibers available.

Loveday 31 🌿🌿🌿🌿 M W

33-06 31st Ave. (33rd St.), Astoria (Qns), 718-728-4057
Tue–Sun 12pm–7pm **loveday31.com**
Vintage clothing redesigned from the 1960s-1980s. Jewelry by local
designer using recycled beads, leather, and other materials.

Lululemon Athletica 🌿🌿 M W

1928 Broadway (64th St.), Upper West Side (Man), 212-712-1767
Mon–Sat 10am–9pm Sun 11am–7pm **lululemon.com**
Yoga-inspired athletic apparel made from eco-friendly fabrics including
bamboo, soy protein, organic cotton & modal; company-wide goal to be
waste-free by 2012.

Lulu's Kids 🌿 C B

1737 York Ave. (E. 90th St.), Yorkville (Man), 212-289-5383
Daily 10:30am–6pm
Boutique carrying some natural fabric apparel for infants and children.

Moo Shoes 🌿🌿🌿🌿 M W

78 Orchard St. (bet. Grand & Broome Sts.), Lower East Side (Man),
212-254-6512
Mon–Sat 11:30am–7:30pm Sun 12pm–6pm **mooshoes.com**
Vegan business providing cruelty-free shoes, clothing, and accessories.

NY Artificial 🌿🌿 M W

223 W. 10th St (Bleecker St.), West Village (Man), 212-255-0825
Mon–Fri 2pm–8pm Sat 12pm–8pm Sun 12pm–6pm **nyartificial.com**
An alternative, eco-friendly store catering to both vegan and non-vegan
customers using a wide variety of sustainable materials.

NY Design Room 🌿🌿🌿 M W

339 Bedford Ave. (bet. S. 3rd & S. 4th Sts.), Williamsburg (Bkn), 718-302-4981
Tue–Sun 12pm–7pm **nydesignroom.com**
Clothing and gift shop featuring many items made on-site from
repurposed clothing.

NYA 🌿🌿 M W

13 8th Ave. (W. 12th St.), West Village (Man), 212-337-3400
Mon–Sat 12pm–8pm Sun 12pm–6pm **nyartificial.com**
An alternative, eco-friendly store catering to both vegan and non-vegan
customers using a wide variety of sustainable materials.

Om Sweet Home 🌿🌿🌿🌿 M W C B

59 Kent Ave. (N. 11th St.), Williamsburg (Bkn), 718-963-6986
Seasonal hours **omsweethomenyc.com**
Eco-friendly shop offering apparel, housewares, and custom-made
home furnishings.

Omala 🌿 W

400 Atlantic Ave. (Bond St.), Boerum Hill (Bkn), 718-694-9642
Mon–Sat 11am–7pm Sun 12pm–6pm **omala.com**
Yoga-inspired lifestyle store selling bamboo activewear, accessories,
yoga props, and organic body products.

Organic Avenue 🌿🌿🌿🌿 M W C B

101 Stanton St. (Ludlow St.), Lower East Side (Man), 212-334-4593
Daily 10am–10pm **organicavenue.com**
Conscious-lifestyle boutique offering hemp and organic clothing, raw food
staple products, fresh live organic produce, raw food classes, gourmet raw
dinners, conscious events, holistic healing retreats, and more.

Goods

Patagonia 🌿🌿🌿🌿 M W C B

101 Wooster St. (bet. Prince & Spring Sts.), SoHo (Man), 212-343-1776
Mon–Sat 11am–7pm Sun 12pm–6pm **patagonia.com**
Clothing and technical wear made from recycled fibers, organic cotton, hemp, eco-fleece, and chlorine-free wool for everyone in the family.

Showroom 64 🌿🌿 C B

106 Greenwich Ave. (bet. 12th & 13th Sts.), West Village (Man), 212-206-8915
Mon–Sat 11am–7pm Sun 12pm–5pm **showroom64.com**
Offers some unique, eco-friendly designer apparel and accessories for babies, children, and new parents.

Sodafine 🌿🌿🌿🌿 W

119 Grand St. (Berry St.), Williamsburg (Bkn), 718-230-3060
Wed–Sat 12pm–7pm Sun 1pm–6pm **sodafine.com**
Clothing, accessories, and gifts made from organic, natural, and recycled materials; handmade, fair trade, local designers, and vintage finds.

Stella McCartney 🌿 W

429 W. 14th St. (bet. 9th Ave. & Washington St.), Chelsea (Man), 212-255-1556
Mon–Sat 11am–7pm Sun 12:30pm–6pm **stellamccartney.com**
Line of women's organic cotton jeans and 100% organic skin care products.

Terra Plana 🌿🌿🌿🌿 M W

260 Elizabeth St. (bet. Houston & Prince Sts.), SoHo (Man), 212-274-9000
Mon–Sat 11am-7pm Sun 12pm-6pm **terraplana.com**
Eco-conscious shoe company committed to using revolutionary, recycled, and sustainable materials.

TreeHouse 🌿 M W B

430 Graham Ave. (bet. Frost & Wither Sts.), Williamsburg (Bkn), 718-482-8733
Wed–Sun 1pm–8pm **treehousebrooklyn.com**
Small shop featuring products made by local designers and crafters. Offers some clothing, jewelry, accessories, and home furnishings from repurposed or recycled materials.

Tricia's Place 🌿🌿 C

171 Elizabeth St. (Spring St.), SoHo (Man), 212-226-3319
By appt.
Children's clothing boutique carrying organic cotton clothing, both fair trade and sustainably manufactured.

Utowa 🌿 W

17 W. 18th St. (5th Ave.), Flatiron (Man), 212-929-4800
Mon–Sat 11am–7pm Sun 12pm–6pm **utowa.com**
Clothing and accessories made by local designers using natural and recycled fabrics including cashmere, cotton, and bamboo.

Zachary's Smile 🌿🌿🌿 W

317 Lafayette St. (bet. Bleecker & Houston Sts.), NoHo (Man), 212-965-8248
9 Greenwich Ave. (bet. Christopher & W. 10th Sts.), West Village (Man), 212-924-0604
Hours vary by location **zacharyssmile.com**
A collection of redesigned vintage clothing, footwear, and accessories.

Gifts, Accessories, and Baby Products

Before you make your next gift purchase, think about all aspects of the item: where it came from, how it was made, who made it, and its impact on the environment and human health.

The shops listed here, offering items such as toys, candles, crafts, jewelry, fashion accessories, picture frames, baby products, and much more, do take these considerations into account.

We have determined leaf awards based on the percentage of items that are made from or use:

- organic materials,

- natural, renewable, or recycled materials,

- nontoxic or less-toxic glues, paints, and finishes (where applicable), and/or

- fair trade or conflict-free criteria and be certified as such.

Although it's a bonus if the items are also made by local artisans, this was not part of our criteria. As we did with all product retailers, we also looked at whether or not the products the establishment carried were unpackaged or packaged with eco-friendly materials, and whether or not the store's own carry-out bags, boxes, or other packaging was biodegradable, compostable, and/or made with recycled or recyclable material, vegetable-based inks, and/or chlorine-free paper.

- at least 25% of items for sale meet the above criteria.
- at least 50% of items for sale meet the above criteria.
- at least 75% of items for sale meet the above criteria.
- at least 90% of items for sale meet the above criteria.

ABC Carpet & Home

888 Broadway (E. 19th St.), Union Square (Man), 212-473-3000
Mon–Fri 10am–8pm Sat 10am–7pm Sun 11am–6:30pm   abchome.com
Artisan, indigenous, environmentally conscious handcrafted gifts and accessories. "Grounded" jewelry line from recycled gold and responsibly mined diamonds. Baby-sized goodwood furniture, organic crib mattresses, bedding; children's clothing and air purifiers.

Acorn, A Brooklyn Toy Shop

323 Atlantic Ave. (bet. Smith & Hoyt Sts.), Boerum Hill (Bkn), 718-522-3760
Tue–Sat 11am–6pm Sun 12pm–6pm   acorntoyshop.com
Beautifully designed and crafted toys from around the world; unique clothing and artwork by New York designers and artists.

Arcadia 🌿🌿

228 8th Ave. (bet. 21st & 22nd Sts.), Chelsea (Man), 212-243-5358
Mon–Sat 11am–10pm Sun 11am–9pm **arcadianyc.com**
Locally crafted, artisanal, and unique gift items and fine art. There is
also a Zen room and a day spa that offers advanced skincare using
Dr. Hauschka products.

AuH₂O 🌿🌿🌿🌿

84 E. 7th St. (1st Ave.), East Village (Man), 212-466-0844
Seasonal hrs. **auh2odesigns.com**
Shop carries vintage and consignment jewelry, handbags, and clothing.
Also specializes in recycled, redesigned, and reconstructed unique pieces
sewn on-site.

Belle & Maxie 🌿🌿🌿

1209 Cortelyou Rd. (Westminster Rd.), Ditmas Park (Bkn), 718-484-3302
Tue–Sat 11am–6pm **belleandmaxie.com**
Wide selection of wooden nontoxic toys and organic clothing for kids
and babies.

Boing Boing 🌿

204 6th Ave. (Union St.), Park Slope (Bkn), 718-398-0251
Mon–Fri 11am–7pm Sat–Sun 11am–6pm
Shop carrying gear and accessories for expectant mothers and babies using
organic or nontoxic materials.

Brooklyn Collective 🌿

198 Columbia St. (bet. Sackett & Degraw Sts.), Waterfront (Bkn),
718-596-6231
Thu–Sun 1pm–9pm **brooklyncollective.com**
Design collective featuring local designers using repurposed materials for
clothing, body products, jewelry, art, and decor.

Brooklynski 🌿🌿

145 Driggs Ave. (Russell St.), Greenpoint (Bkn), 718-389-0901
Tue–Fri 4pm–8pm Sat 12pm–8pm Sun 12pm–6pm **brooklynski.com**
Eco-friendly gifts and accessories. Many items created by local artisans
and made from repurposed materials.

Bump-to-Baby 🌿🌿

715 9th Ave. (bet. 48th & 49th Sts.), Clinton (Man), 212-245-0796
Mon–Thu 10am–8pm Fri 10am–7pm Sat–Sun 12pm–6pm **realbirth.com**
Shop featuring eco-friendly, organic, and unique products for mom and
baby. Also provides information, classes, and activities for parents-to-be.

Camilla Boutique 🌿🌿🌿🌿

355 Atlantic Ave. (bet. Hoyt & Bond Sts.), Boerum Hill (Bkn), 718-422-0282
Tue–Sat 12pm–7pm Sun 12pm–6pm **camillaboutique.com**
Sustainably designed shop sells eco-friendly linens, accessories, jewelry, craft
items and clothing for babies, men, and women.

Cog & Pearl 🌿🌿🌿

190 5th Ave. (Sackett St.), Park Slope (Bkn), 718-623-8200
Tue–Sat 12pm–8pm Sun 12pm–6pm **cogandpearl.com**
An eclectic mix of handmade jewelry, household items, accessories, apparel,
and gift items made with organic materials.

Corduroy Kid 🍃🍃

613 Vanderbilt Ave. (St. Marks Ave.), Prospect Heights (Bkn), 718-622-4145
Tue–Fri 11am–7pm Sat–Sun 11am–6pm **corduroykid.com**
Children's clothing, toys, and accessories made to fit green and fair
trade standards.

Dinosaur Hill 🍃🍃

306 E. 9th St. (2nd Ave.), East Village (Man), 212-473-5850
Daily 11am–7pm **dinosaurhill.com**
Children's toy and gift shop with a wide variety of natural wooden toys and
American-made items.

Earthly Additions 🍃🍃🍃🍃

169 5th Ave. (Degraw St.), Park Slope (Bkn), 718-622-1060
Daily 11am–7pm **earthlyadditions.com**
Shop carrying all eco-friendly homemade items imported through fair trade
and made from recycled, renewable materials.

Enchanted 🍃🍃🍃

1179 Lexington Ave. (E. 80th St.), Upper East Side (Man), 212-288-3383
Mon–Sat 10am–6pm Sun 12pm–5pm **enchanted-toys.com**
Nonprofit store operated by volunteers and offering natural, handmade
toys. Proceeds benefit the tuition assistance program at the Waldorf School
in Manhattan.

Fragrance Shop New York, The 🍃

21 E. 7th St. (bet. 2nd and 3rd Aves.), East Village (Man), 212-254-8950
Mon–Sat 12pm–8pm Sun 1pm–7pm **fragranceshopnewyork.com**
Fragrance shop with organic and natural lotions and potions; vegetable wax
candles; massage and aromatherapy oils.

Fuego 718 🍃🍃

249 Grand St. (Roebling St.), Williamsburg (Bkn), 718-302-2913
Mon–Sat 1pm–8pm Sun 1pm–6pm
Gift shop with some handmade, recycled, and repurposed items, including
metal art made from petrol barrels, handbags and accessories made from
water bottles, and bags made from rice sacks.

Funkinfunction Longboards 🍃🍃🍃🍃

221 McKibben St., GMDC #16 (bet. Bushwick Ave. & White St.),
Bushwick (Bkn), 971-301-2551
By appt. **funkinfunction.com**
Handmade longboards and skateboards made from repurposed hardwood
scraps. Limited productions designed by Daniel Moyer Designs; signed and
archived.

Giggle 🍃🍃🍃

120 Wooster St. (bet. Prince & Spring St.), SoHo (Man), 212-334-5817
1033 Lexington Ave. (74th St.), Upper East Side (Man), 212-249-4249
Mon–Sat 10am–7pm Sun 11am–6pm **giggle.com**
Collection of responsible apparel, toys, and accessories including healthy,
environmentally conscious, and innovative products.

Golden Calf 🍃

86 N. 6th St. (Wythe Ave.), WIlliamsburg (Bkn), 718-302-8800
Tue–Sat 12pm–7pm **goldencalf.net**
Shop carrying some gifts and furniture made from natural, reclaimed,
and sustainably dyed materials. Also sells restored antique furniture.

Gominyc 🌿🌿🌿🌿

443 E. 6th St. (bet. 1st Ave. and Ave. A), East Village (Man), 212-979-0388
Mon–Thu 1pm–8:30pm Fri 1pm–9pm Sat 12pm–9pm Sun 12pm–8:30pm
gominyc.com
Eco-friendly fashion, vegetable-dyed shoes and bags, and eco-friendly
home accessories.

Green Tree General Store 🌿🌿🌿🌿

95 Norman Ave. (Manhattan Ave.), Greenpoint (Bkn), 347-422-0565
Wed–Sat 1pm–7pm Sun 12pm–6pm **greentreestore.com**
Sustainably designed shop selling eco-friendly gifts, bath supplies, accesso-
ries and clothing for men, women, and babies.

Greenhouse Essentials 🌿🌿🌿

218 N. 7th St. (bet. Driggs Ave. & Roebling St.), Williamsburg (Bkn),
718-599-0719
Wed–Fri 12pm–8pm Sat–Sun 12pm–6pm **greenhouseholistic.com**
Shop offering yoga accessories, spiritual items, and beauty products, including handmade soaps and lotions using organic, local ingredients.

Greenjeans 🌿🌿🌿🌿

449 7th Ave. (bet. 15th & 16th Sts.), Park Slope (Bkn), 718-907-5835
Tue–Sun 12pm–7pm **greenjeansbrooklyn.com**
Handmade artisan products made in USA with sustainable, recycled,
or renewable materials.

Half Pint Citizens 🌿🌿

55 Washington St. (bet. Font & Water Sts.), DUMBO (Bkn), 718-875-4007
Mon–Fri 11am–6pm Sat–Sun 10am–6pm **halfpintcitizens.com**
Carries eco-friendly toys, gifts, and apparel for children and infants.

Huitzilli 🌿🌿

624 Metropolitan Ave. (bet. Lorimer & Leonard Sts.), Williamsburg (Bkn),
718-701-3195
Wed 11am–7pm Thu–Fri 2pm–8pm Sat–Sun 12pm–7pm **huitzilli.com**
Handmade clothing, accessories, jewelry, and bath products made from
natural ingredients and materials in Mexico.

La Tiendita 🌿🌿🌿🌿

56 E. 1st St. (1st Ave.), East Village (Man), 212-982-1633
Tue–Sat 10:30am–6pm **girlsclub.org/store**
Fair trade boutique showcasing artisan crafts from women-run indigenous
co-ops in Central America. Many items made from recycled materials. Proceeds support inner-city programs.

Metro Minis 🌿🌿🌿

821 Park Ave. (E. 75th St.), Upper East Side (Man), 212-313-9600
Seasonal hours **metrominis.com**
Shop geared toward new moms and babies; carries a wide range of natural
and organic accessories. Also provides workshops and events for local like-
minded mothers.

Mini Jake 🌿🌿

178 N. 9th St. (Bedford Ave.), Williamsburg (Bkn), 718-782-2005
Seasonal hours **minijake.com**
Eco-friendly organic toys and accessories for babies and children, including
mattresses, bedding, and clothing.

Modern Tots

53 Pearl St. (bet. Water & Plymouth Sts.), DUMBO (Bkn), 718-488-8293
Mon–Sat 11am–6pm Sun 12pm–5pm **moderntots.com**
Modern, eco-friendly furnishings, toys, accessories, and clothing for homes
with children.

Moon River Chattel

62 Grand St. (bet. Kent & Wythe Aves.), Williamsburg (Bkn), 718-388-1121
Tue–Sat 12pm–7pm Sun 12pm–5pm **moonriverchattel.com**
Home and design store with an extensive gift selection, carrying products
made from sustainable and organic materials.

Natural Heights

688 Washington Ave. (St. Marks Ave.), Prospect Heights (Bkn), 347-750-5870
Mon–Thu 12pm–7pm Fri–Sun 12pm–6pm **natural-heights.com**
Small local shop offering green household, pet, and personal care products
for the whole family; cards and gifts; small selection of gardening supplies.

Nepa Bhon'

106 MacDougal St. (Bleecker St.), Greenwich Village (Man), 212-477-8723
Daily 11am–11pm **nepabhon.com**
Handmade papyrus papers and gifts using vegetable-based dyes.

NY Artificial

223 W. 10th St (Bleecker St.), West Village (Man), 212-255-0825
Mon–Fri 2pm–8pm Sat 12pm–8pm Sun 12pm–6pm **nyartificial.com**
An alternative, eco-friendly store offering sustainable accessories, jewelry,
clothing and other items catering to both vegan and non-vegan customers.

NYA

13 8th Ave. (W. 12th St.), West Village (Man), 212-337-3400
Mon–Sat 12pm–8pm Sun 12pm–6pm **nyartificial.com**
An alternative, eco-friendly store offering sustainable accessories, jewelry,
clothing and other items catering to both vegan and non-vegan customers.

Om Sweet Home

59 Kent Ave. (N. 11th St.), Williamsburg (Bkn), 718-963-6986
Wed–Sun 12pm–6pm Sat–Sun 12pm–7pm **omsweethomenyc.com**
Eco-friendly shop offering apparel, housewares, and custom-made home
furnishings.

One Sixty Glass

160 Berry St. (bet. N. 4th & 5th Sts.), Williamsburg (Bkn), 718-486-9620
Daily 10am–6pm **onesixtyglass.com**
Glassblowing facility with a gift section offering products made from
recycled glass. All glass is hand blown on premises. Classes available.

Pickleboots

178 Lincoln Pl., Ste. A (7th Ave.), Park Slope (Bkn), 718-622-1200
Tue–Sat 11am–5pm **pickleboots.com**
Children's custom bedding and furniture resource featuring locally made
products, including an organic fabric collection and organic crib mattresses.

Scent Elate

313 W. 48th St. (bet. 8th & 9th Ave.), Clinton (Man), 212-258-3043
Mon–Wed 11am–10pm Thu–Sat 11am–12am Sun 12pm–10pm
scentelate.com
Aromatherapy shop offering healing and soothing aids, soy candles,
and a wide variety of fair trade items created by local artisans.

Showroom 64 🍃🍃

106 Greenwich Ave. (bet. 12th & 13th Sts.), West Village (Man), 212-206-8915
Mon–Sat 11am–7pm Sun 12pm–5pm **showroom64.com**
Unique eco-friendly accessories and designer apparel for babies, children and new parents.

Site 🍃

35-11 34th Ave. (35th St.), Astoria (Qns), 718-626-6030
Tue–Sun 12pm–8pm **sitedesignnyc.com**
Home gifts with some locally made, handmade, recycled, and vintage items.

Sixth Sense 🍃🍃

324 W. 49th St. (bet. 8th & 9th Aves.), Clinton (Man), 212-957-9057
217 Garfield Pl. (7th Ave.), Park Slope (Bkn), 718-623-1186
Hours vary by location **sixthsensenyc.net**
Small local shop carrying essential oils, soy candles, vegetable-based soaps, and unbleached cotton tees.

Sodafine 🍃🍃🍃🍃

119 Grand St. (Berry St.), Williamsburg (Bkn), 718-230-3060
Wed–Sat 12pm–7pm Sun 1pm–6pm **sodafine.com**
Clothing, accessories, and gifts made from organic, natural, and recycled materials; handmade items, local designers, vintage finds.

Sons + Daughters 🍃🍃

35 Avenue A (bet. 2nd & 3rd Sts.), East Village (Man), 212-253-7797
Mon–Tue 12pm–7pm Wed–Sun 10am–7pm **sonsanddaughtersinc.com**
Fair trade and organic baby toys and apparel from craftspeople and manufacturers whose products are created in ways that nurture our natural resources.

Sproutkidz 🍃

849A Union St. (7th Ave.), Park Slope (Bkn), 718-398-2280
Mon–Wed 10am–6pm Thu 10am–7pm Fri–Sun 10am–6pm **sproutkidz.net**
Children's clothing store featuring many organic infant lines.

Sustainable NYC 🍃🍃🍃🍃

147 Ave. A (9th St.), East Village (Man), 212-254-5400
Mon–Wed 12pm–8pm Thu–Sat 11am–10pm Sun 12pm–8pm
sustainable-nyc.com
Local, organic, recycled, fair trade, repurposed, and biodegradable products and gifts.

Sweet William 🍃🍃🍃

112 N. 6th St. (bet. Wythe Ave. & Berry St.), Williamsburg (Bkn), 718-218-6946
Mon–Fri 11am–7pm Sat–Sun 12pm–7pm **sweetwilliamltd.com**
Children's clothing and toy store carrying only nontoxic toys and a selection of organic clothing.

3r Living 🍃🍃🍃🍃

276 5th Ave. Ste. L (bet. 1st St. & Garfield Pl.), Park Slope (Bkn), 718-832-0951
Mon–Wed 11am–7pm Thu–Sat 11am–8pm Sun 11am–7pm **3rliving.com**
Home and lifestyle store dedicated to eco-friendly products selected with the principles of reducing waste, reusing unwanted or discarded materials, and recycling; favoring fair trade products made from organic ingredients.

TreeHouse 🍃

430 Graham Ave. (bet. Frost & Wither Sts.), Williamsburg (Bkn), 718-482-8733
Wed–Sun 1pm–8pm **treehousebrooklyn.com**
Small shop offering unique clothing, naturally dyed yarns, jewelry, accessories, and home furnishings fashioned from repurposed or recycled materials. Also offers craft classes.

Utowa 🍃

17 W. 18th St. (5th Ave.), Flatiron (Man), 212-929-4800
Mon–Sat 11am–7pm Sun 12pm–6pm **utowa.com**
Clothing and accessories made by local designers using natural and recycled fabrics.

Versani 🍃🍃🍃

152 Mercer St. (bet. Prince & Houston Sts.), Nolita (Man), 212-941-9919
227 Mulberry St. (bet. Prince & Spring Sts.), SoHo (Man), 212-431-4944
Daily 11am–8pm **versani.com**
Custom designer jewelry made locally in New York City; offers conflict-free diamonds and fair trade gems; recycles precious metals to create unique redesigned pieces for customers.

Green Tip

Traces of lead are found in some candles, decorative ceramic dishes, and crystal stemware. Be sure to read the packaging or ask about this when buying plates, bowls, and other tableware. Serve wine in lead-free glasses. Choose clean-burning candles made of pure beeswax, soy, or other vegetable-based waxes. Select ones without metal wicks, as these can contain small amounts of lead.

did you know?

A significant percentage of the world's pesticides, herbicides, and water is used in growing and processing the fibers that are made into our clothing—polluting the soil, air, and water as well as the farmers, birds, bees, insects, and other animals that come in contact with the crops.

Office and Paper Supplies

Most of us recycle our paper, try to use both sides, and read as much as we can online. But when we do need to buy paper and office supplies, what about closing the loop and buying recycled materials? By purchasing paper and paper goods with recycled content we can affect the choices that paper mills eventually make as investors in new technology and processes, thereby saving our forests and protecting our watersheds.

You'll find different levels of recycled content in paper and other supplies—from 10 to 30 percent, and sometimes up to 100 percent post-consumer waste. Look for the recycled symbol (chasing arrows), and a minimum of 30 percent post-consumer recycled content, also known as post-consumer waste. Dedicated recyclers can find three-ring binders made of recycled corrugated cardboard and pocket portfolios and dividers made from 100 percent recycled paperboard (the majority post-consumer).

As you sort through your eco-friendly options, remember also that paper products bleached without chlorine are safer all around. Making sound choices relies on understanding definitions, enforced federal standards, and accurate labeling.

Our leaf awards are based on the percentage of a store's office supplies and paper that are sustainably made and produced and/or are made from recycled or reclaimed resources.

🍃 at least 25% of items for sale meet the above criteria.
🍃🍃 at least 50% of items for sale meet the above criteria.
🍃🍃🍃 at least 75% of items for sale meet the above criteria.
🍃🍃🍃🍃 at least 90% of items for sale meet the above criteria.

JAM Paper and Envelope 🍃
516 5th Ave. (43rd St.), Midtown (Man), 212-255-4593
135 3rd Ave. (bet. 14th & 15th Sts.), Union Square (Man), 212-473-6666
Mon–Thu 8:30am–8pm Fri 8:30am–7pm Sat–Sun 10am–6pm jampaper.com
Variety of paper and envelope product lines made from recycled content. Also carries tree-free folders and wallets.

Nepa Bhon' 🍃
106 MacDougal St. (Bleecker St.), Greenwich Village (Man), 212-477-8723
Daily 11am–11pm nepabhon.com
Handmade papyrus papers using vegetable-based dyes.

Pharmacies

Pharmacies are where we go to meet health needs and sometimes to seek professional guidance. Traditionally, pharmacists mixed and dispensed medications on the orders of physicians. However, more recently, pharmacies have come to include services related to preventative care as well as to illness treatment.

When our quest is for good health, how we treat ourselves becomes paramount. Many of us consider natural remedies first, and the pharmacies listed here offer the most extensive selection of alternative medications, including homeopathic remedies, herbal tinctures, powders, medications, creams, and other holistic preparations.

A few stores are solely holistic pharmacies, while others, like some larger natural foods stores, have an extensive holistic remedy and personal care department.

In determining which pharmacies to include, we looked at the percentage of homeopathic remedies and natural remedies, and the presence of organic ingredients in these remedies. Where vitamins were concerned, we checked for plant-based (vs. synthetic), natural, organic, and/or herbal ingredients.

We also evaluated a pharmacy's stock of natural alternatives to traditional personal care products and medications (for example, cough medicines, sleep aids, cold and flu treatments, skin creams, shampoos, deodorants, makeup, and soap) and the availability of health books and books on alternative medicine. In addition, we checked whether or not the stores offered reusable bags to their customers, or if their bags were biodegradable and/or made with recycled or recyclable material and/or chlorine-free paper.

To be in the guide, at least 25 percent of a given store's pharmacy stock must include the types of products outlined above.

Avignone
281 6th Ave. (Bleecker St.), West Village (Man), 212-989-5568
Mon–Fri 8am–8pm Sat 9am–8pm Sun 10am–5pm
Full-line pharmacy carrying natural, organic skin and hair care goods; large selection of homeopathic remedies and environmentally friendly household products.

Centro Naturista
82-18 Roosevelt Ave. (82nd St.), Jackson Heights (Qns), 718-672-0790
Mon–Sat 11am–7:30pm
Pharmacy carrying Nature's Sunshine herbal supplements; juices and homeopathic remedies.

Chopin Chemists

911 Manhattan Ave. (bet. Greenpoint Ave. and Kent St.), Greenpoint (Bkn), 718-383-7822
8000 Cooper Ave. (80th St.), Ridgewood (Qns), 718-384-5900
189 Grand St. (bet. Bedford & Driggs Aves.), Williamsburg (Bkn), 718-384-5900
Hours vary by location   **chopinchemists.com**
Organic and natural homeopathic remedies, cosmetics, and baby care.

Crown Chemists, Ltd.

33-20 Ditmars Blvd. (35th St.), Astoria (Qns), 718-278-6777
Mon–Fri 8am–8pm Sat 8am–7pm   **crownchemists.com**
Organic and natural beauty products, essential oils, herbal tinctures, and natural vitamins.

Elm Health

1695 1st Ave. (E. 88th St.), Yorkville (Man), 212-348-8500
Mon–Fri 8:30am–9pm Sat–Sun 9am–9pm
Knowledgeable pharmacists who pair conventional medicine and prescriptions with natural alternatives.

Essence of Life, The

451 6th Ave. (bet. 9th & 10th Sts.), Park Slope (Bkn), 718-788-8783
By appt.   **theessenceoflife.com**
Small shop carrying a selection of homeopathic remedies, probiotics, books, and water- and air-purifying technologies.

Flower Power Herbs and Roots, Inc.

406 E. 9th St. (bet. Ave. A & 1st Ave.), East Village (Man), 212-982-6664
Daily 12pm–7pm   **flowerpower.net**
Organically grown medicinal and culinary herbs; herbal beauty and baby care products; flower essences, essential oils, books, and accessories.

Health N' Nutrition Galaxy

243 W. 231st St. (bet. Kingsbridge Ave. & Broadway), Riverdale (Brx), 718-796-7867
Mon–Sat 1pm–7pm
Selection of teas, herbal remedies, and natural vitamins.

Healthy Corner Pharmacy

116-65 Queens Blvd. (78th Ave.), Two Gardens (Qns), 718-261-6699
Mon–Thu 8:30am–8:30pm Fri 8:30am–8pm Sat 9am–6pm
healthycornershop.com
Natural pharmacy featuring aromatherapy and natural homeopathic remedies, beauty supplies, and bath and body products; conventional prescriptions also filled.

High Vibe

138 E. 3rd St. (bet. Ave. A & 1st Ave.), East Village (Man), 212-777-6645
Mon–Fri 10am–8pm Sat–Sun 12pm–7pm   **highvibe.com**
Personalized nutritional counseling, coaching, and expert information; support and supplies for juice fasts, internal cleansing, and gall and liver flushes. Creates and shares live-food recipes. Hosts informative lectures in the community.

Integral Yoga Natural Apothecary

234 W. 13th St. (bet. 7th & 8th Aves.), Greenwich Village (Man),
212-645-3051
Mon–Fri 8am–9pm Sat 8am–8:30pm Sun 9am–8pm **iynaturalfoods.com**
Natural antioxidants, flower essences, homeopathics, and minerals. The old-fashioned vitamin apothecary offers products in bottles and in bulk, as teas, tinctures, and tablets.

Live Live & Organic

261 E. 10th St. (bet. 1st Ave. & Ave. A), East Village (Man), 212-505-5504
Daily 11am–10pm **live-live.com**
Organic body care free of preservatives and solvents; organic raw foods, snacks, and superfoods; 100% whole-food vitamins, cleansing; juicers, water filters, dehydrators, vitamins; consultations and classes.

Merlin Chemists Inc.

31-64 21st St. (Broadway), Long Island City (Qns), 718-267-8900
Mon–Fri 8am–8pm Sat 9am–7pm
Natural and organic remedies, vitamins, and personal care products.

Namaskar: Bob Law's Health & Body Shop

643 Vanderbilt Ave. (Prospect Pl.), Prospect Heights (Bkn), 718-636-1967
Mon–Sat 11am–7pm Sun 2pm–4pm
Natural foods, beauty products, alternative medicine, and nutritional supplements. Specializes in Muntu's Green Drink, an energizing supplement shake.

New London Pharmacy

246 8th Ave. (23rd St.), Chelsea (Man), 800-941-0490
Mon–Fri 8:30am–8:30pm Sat 9am–8pm Sun 10am–6:30pm
Organic pharmacy offering homeopathic remedies, herbal medications, vitamins and supplements, and some personal care products; nutritionist on-site for free consultation.

Nutri Natural Life

473 46th St. (5th Ave.), Sunset Park (Bkn), 718-972-8453
Tue–Sun 1pm–7pm
Small shop selling holistic remedies, supplements, vitamins, personal care products, and organic herbs in bulk.

Olympia Chemists

23-18 31st St. (23rd Ave.), Astoria (Qns), 718-267-2766
Mon–Fri 9am–7pm Sat 9am–6pm **olympiachemists.com**
Wide range of natural and organic body care products, makeup, remedies, candles, and perfume.

Olympia Vitamins

22-42 31st St. (Ditmars Blvd.), Astoria (Qns), 718-932-1869
Daily 10am–10pm **olympiachemists.com**
Vitamins, herbal supplements, cleansing products, and a large selection of protein powders.

Organic Avenue

101 Stanton St. (Ludlow St.), Lower East Side (Man), 212-334-4593
Daily 10am–10pm **organicavenue.com**
Shop providing essential oils, hygiene products, superfoods, nutritional supplements, and health and beauty supplies.

Pharmacare

892 9th Ave. (W. 58th St.), Midtown (Man), 212-445-0932
Mon–Fri 9am–7:30pm **pharmacare.com**
Specialty pharmacy selling all natural and holistic products. Also includes a
prescription pharmacy for specialty and conventional drugs.

Pharmakolojie, Inc.

30-91 31st St. (31st Ave.), Astoria (Qns), 718-626-4600
Mon–Fri 9am–7pm Sat 10am–5pm **pharmakolojie.com**
Homeopathic remedies, natural body care products, organic baby products,
herbal teas, vitamins, and aromatherapy candles.

Sundial

3609 Boston Rd. (bet. E. 222nd & E. 223rd Sts.), Wakefield (Brx),
718-798-3962
Mon–Sat 10am–6pm **sundialherbs.com**
Specializes in traditional Ethopian herbal remedies and provisions.
Organic Caribbean and African groceries available.

Vitamin Herbal and Homeopathic Center

72-15 35th Ave. (72nd St.), Jackson Heights (Qns), 718-533-0646
Mon–Fri 10am–8pm Sat–Sun 11am–7pm **homeopathicusa.com**
Homeopathic center offering free walk-in consultations for homeopathic
remedies, medicines, vitamins, supplements, and detox programs.

Wholesome Living

113-11 Liberty Ave. (113th St.), Richmond Hill (Qns), 718-843-9430
Mon–Fri 10am–6:30pm Sat 10am–6pm Sun 12pm–4pm
Organic dry goods; natural body care; vitamins; herbal teas, tinctures,
and supplements.

Green Tips

Many grocery stores and specialty markets also have
extensive alternative pharmacy and personal care
sections. Check those listings in the "Eating In"
section of the guide for merchants that may carry
these products.

Stock your medicine cabinet with better
options, including homeopathic remedies, natural remedies, and products
made with organic ingredients. Where
vitamins are concerned, look for plant-
based (vs. synthetic), natural, organic,
and/or herbal ingredients.

Florists

Purchasing flowers may seem like a wonderful way to bring the beauty of nature into our homes or the perfect way to acknowledge our loved ones, but often flowers are not quite what they appear to be.

The truth is the flower industry is one of the heaviest users of agricultural chemicals. More than 60 percent of the fresh-cut flowers sold in the United States are imported from countries whose environmental standards are less stringent than our own.

In some cases, chemicals banned in the United States are used in other countries and find their way back here through imported agricultural goods—on all those flowers, for instance. Moreover, the packaging, vases, cards, and other accessories that accompany those flowers often end up as waste. Luckily, local, organically grown flowers in eco-friendly packaging are increasingly available, just as beautiful, and better for you and the planet. So next time you want to say it with flowers, why not choose locally and/or organically grown ones? Or you might even consider some bulbs or a live plant dressed up with reused ribbon that can later be planted in a garden or balcony pot.

To be included in the guide, at least 15 percent of a florist's total flower stock must be organically grown and/or Veriflora®-certified and, of the organic flowers stocked, at least 15 percent must be grown within five hundred miles. We also checked if the florist used eco-friendly packaging, including vases or other displays, cards, or other packaging that is biodegradable, compostable, and/or made with recycled or recyclable material, vegetable-based inks, and/or chlorine-free paper.

Of the total flower stock:

🌿 at least 15% meets the above criteria.
🌿🌿 at least 25% meets the above criteria.
🌿🌿🌿 at least 50% meets the above criteria.
🌿🌿🌿🌿 at least 75% meets the above criteria.

Gardenia Organic 🌿🌿🌿🌿
526 Hudson St. (bet. W. 10th & Charles Sts.), West Village (Man), 646-688-5753
Tue–Fri 11am–7pm Sat 11am–6pm Sun 12pm–5pm   **gardeniaorganic.com**
All-organic and Veriflora-certified flowers; fair trade and environmentally friendly gifts; carbon-neutral delivery in Manhattan via Revolution Rickshaw's bikes.

Fabric and Yarn Stores

Making your own clothing out of sustainably produced fabrics and knitting your own sweaters out of low-impact yarns may be the greenest way to dress of all. Fabric and yarn stores are beginning to carry more materials grown without the use of synthetic chemicals, dyed with natural or low-impact dyes, and processed without huge amounts of chemical input.

Although the runway red carpet just may be going green, specific standards as to what constitutes sustainability in fabrics haven't, as yet, been developed—so too with yarns. We'd like to help move things in the right direction by supporting businesses that are making an effort to carry natural fibers, so we have awarded leaves based on the following criteria:

- the percentage of fabric that is organic or natural fiber,

- the percentage of yarn that is organic or natural fiber, and

- the percentage of materials that are produced with natural or low-impact dyes.

We also looked at whether or not the store's carry-out bags or other packaging were biodegradable, compostable, and/or made with recycled or recyclable material, vegetable-based inks, and/or chlorine-free paper.

at least 25% meets the above criteria.

at least 50% meets the above criteria.

at least 75% meets the above criteria.

at least 90% meets the above criteria.

Indigo Handloom

68 Jay St., Suite 117 (Water St.), DUMBO (Bkn), 917-779-8420
Seasonal hours   indigohandloom.com
Fabrics and yarns colored with vegetable dyes and made with organic cotton, silks, and other natural materials. Hand-loomed scarves, skirts, dresses and tops also available.

Point NYC, The

37A Bedford St. (bet. Downing & Carmine Sts.), West Village (Man), 212-929-0800
Mon–Wed 12pm–8pm Thu 12pm–9pm Fri 12pm–8pm Sat 10am–6pm Sun 12pm–5pm   thepointnyc.com
Knitting cafe offering classes in knitting, crochet, dying, and spinning; large selection of alternative fibers including soy, bamboo, organic cotton, and chitin.

Purl 🌿🌿🌿

137 Sullivan St. (bet. Prince & Spring Sts.), SoHo (Man), 212-420-8796
Mon–Fri 12pm–7pm Sat–Sun 12pm–6pm **purlsoho.com**
Organic, hand-dyed, vegetable-dyed, and natural fiber yarns.

Sandy's Knit 'n' Needles 🌿

154-03B Union Tpke. (Parsons Blvd.), Flushing (Qns), 718-380-0370
Tue–Sat 10:30am–5pm **sandysknitnneedles.com**
Neighborhood yarn and fabric shop carrying hand-dyed baby bamboo
and Nori yarns.

Yarn Tree, The 🌿🌿🌿🌿

347 Bedford Ave. (S. 4th St.), Wiliamsburg (Bkn), 718-384-8030
Mon–Thu 4pm–9pm Sat–Sun 12pm–7pm **theyarntree.com**
Shop selling organic and natural yarns, natural dyes, and supplies. Also
offers a variety of classes.

Green Tip

Seven of the top fifteen pesticides used on U.S.
cotton crops are listed by the EPA as potential or
known human carcinogens, and these chemicals have
the potential to infiltrate the water, the soil, and our
bodies. In addition to organic and color-grown cotton, consumers can choose hemp, cruelty-free silk, or
recycled-plastic fleece.

- Conventional hemp plants are hardy enough to
  withstand weeds and bugs, requiring few pesticides. A strong, resilient fiber, hemp can be used
  in the same manner as cotton or wool.

- Nettle, a coarse herb that grows widely as a weed,
  is naturally moth-repellant.

- Cruelty-free silk allows wild and semi-wild
  silkworms to emerge from their cocoons before
  the silk is harvested, rather than killing them.

- Fleece is a vegan alternative to wool that can be
  made entirely from recycled plastic bottles, old
  shower curtains, and other plastics. Fleece can be
  very light, soft, and easy to wash.

Low-Impact Fabrics and Fibers

Most people think natural fibers are better for the environment than synthetic fibers. This isn't necessarily true. When considering the sustainability of fibers, it's necessary to look at the whole life cycle: from the growing or extraction, through the processing and dyeing, to the cutting and sewing of fabric to clothing. Further, the shipping from place of manufacture to point of purchase; the washing, drying, dry cleaning, and other care requirements; and ultimately the garment's disposal should be considered. Each fiber has a different impact at each stage of its life cycle.

Fabrics

Cotton. Look for fabric organically grown without pesticides or biologically produced, and colored with low-impact dyes. Selecting cotton with these characteristics will help minimize this fabric's traditionally chemically-intensive production. *Biological production* refers to how cotton fibers are purified and prepared for spinning. It is a water-based process and results in no environmental pollution. Similarly, the use of natural or vegetable-based dyes minimizes the negative impacts of the dyeing process.

Wool. Look for organic, naturally sourced, undyed wool or wool that has been dyed without the use of heavy metals.

Linen and Hemp. Ask for *dew-retted* (the means by which the fibers are extracted), organic, nonchlorine-bleached fabric.

Bamboo. A naturally antibacterial textile made from the pulp of bamboo grass. Look for unbleached fabric, since many manufacturers use extensive bleaching processes.

Polyester. Look for recycled content and recyclable options. Virgin polyester is petrochemical-based exclusively, and its production is greenhouse-gas intensive. A small but growing alternative to polyester is a hybrid of recycled polyester and cornstarch, sometimes referred to as "corn-based polyester." A growing number of items are made from this material.

Lyocell. A fabric better known by its brand name Tencel® is made from cellulose (vegetable matter), or wood pulp, typically from a mix of hardwood trees. It is noted for its durability, strength, and its eco-friendly manufacturing techniques.

Fibers

Natural. All-natural fibers are renewable and biodegradable, as long as the dyes and dye treatments are nontoxic.

Synthetic. Synthetic fibers are petroleum-based and made from a nonrenewable resource. They are not biodegradable but are readily recyclable if not blended with natural fibers.

Line dry.

Pets

What's Good for Us Is Good for Our Pets

By Phil and Randy Klein

Green thinking has always been at the base of our consciousness, so imagine the impact of the epiphany when we realized that the products we were giving our dog in no way met our "green" standards. We had never made the connection. What could be greener than to treat animals like animals—living, breathing creatures of the Earth?

In 1989, our beloved dog was diagnosed with a growing bone cancer. As a result, a new mind-set regarding animal health began to take shape in us. We started using a more natural diet for our dog and immediately saw improvements—not only in the way her skin and coat looked, but deeper changes as well. There was a vibrancy in her eyes and an energy that helped her through a very difficult surgery. Unfortunately, we made these changes too late. Years of bad food, bad medicine, and bad advice wreaked havoc on her systems—digestive, immune, physical, and mental. Why wouldn't one think that what's bad for humans can be doubly bad for domestic pets? Why wouldn't we want to give our companion animals the best in fresh, organic, natural products?

Our industry has changed dramatically over these past twenty years. Many new companies and products now exist as a direct result of pioneers like Whiskers Holistic Pet Care. We are proud to have played a major role in this change. If more and more pet "parents" are educated and reminded that the four-legged creatures of this planet teach us much more than we could ever repay, we'd do everything we could to keep the planet and their world as green as possible.

Phil Klein, a certified T-Touch practitioner and in-house consultant, along with his partner and wife, Randy Klein, have owned and operated Whiskers Holistic Pet Care since 1990 (**1800whiskers.com**).

143

Pet Care and Supplies

As with humans, natural, organic food, free from unnecessary additives, is best for pets. All too often, commercial pet food is chockfull of ingredients that may not be conducive to optimal health for dogs, cats, and other friends.

When it comes to pet care and grooming, we feel it is best to minimize the use of products containing harsh chemicals and potentially toxic treatments. Not only is your pet exposed, you and other household members are as well every time you touch, scratch, pat, or hold your animal. In fact, some pet treatments can be very harmful, so it is important to know what you are purchasing.

We have evaluated pet food purveyors based on the percentage of products sold that contain all certified organic, a mix of certified organic and natural, or all-natural ingredients.

We took a look at pet care products (such as flea/tick treatments, shampoos, and other grooming supplies) with an eye toward their content. Our listings reflect the percentage of products sold and, in the case of grooming, day/overnight care establishments, or other services, the percentage of products used that contain nontoxic, natural, and/or organic ingredients. We also asked about sanitation procedures and the presence of ventilation systems that allow for outdoor air exchange in the grooming and/or day or overnight care facilities. We also checked what cleaning supplies are used. In addition, we looked at whether or not the products the establishment carried were minimally packaged or packaged with eco-friendly materials, and whether or not the store's own carry-out bags or packaging were biodegradable or compostable and/or made with recyclable material, vegetable-based inks, and/or chlorine-free paper.

To be included in the guide, businesses must meet our minimum requirement that 25 percent of their products used or sold comply with the standards outlined above.

> at least 25% of the products meet the above criteria.
> at least 50% of the products meet the above criteria.
> at least 75% of the products meet the above criteria.
> at least 90% of the products meet the above criteria.

Types of services available:

PS Pet food and supplies   **B** Boarding or day care
G Grooming   **O** Other services as described

Animal Crackers 🍃🍃 PS

103 E. 2nd St. (1st Ave.), East Village (Man), 212-614-6786
Mon–Sat 10am–8pm Sun 10am–6pm **animalcrackersnyc.net**
Pet shop carrying mostly organic and natural food and pet care supplies;
delivery available.

Animal Pantry 🍃 PS

693 86th St. (Battery Ave.), Bay Ridge (Bkn), 718-680-2220
137-20 Cross Bay Blvd. (Pitkin Ave.), Ozone Park (Qns), 718-845-8400
Hours vary by location
Pet food and supplies for cats, dogs, birds, and fish; bath products;
some natural pet foods.

Barking Zoo, The 🍃🍃🍃 PS

172 9th Ave. (bet. 19th & 20th Sts.), Chelsea (Man), 212-255-0658
Mon–Fri 11am–8pm Sat 10am–6pm Sun 12pm–5pm **thebarkingzoo.com**
Pet supply store specializing in organic, holistic, and natural foods
and accessories.

Beasty Feast 🍃🍃 PS G

630 Hudson St. (Jane St.), West Village (Man), 212-620-7099
680 Washington St. (bet. W. 10th & Charles Sts.), West Village (Man),
212-620-4055
Hours vary by location **beastyfeast.com**
Natural foods, accessories, and sundries for cats and dogs. Delivers
throughout Manhattan with minimum order.

Brooklyn Animal Resource Coalition
(BARC Shelter) 🍃🍃🍃🍃 PS O

253 Wythe Ave. (N. 1st St.), Williamsburg (Bkn), 718-486-7489
Tue–Sat 11am–7pm **barcshelter.org**
Wide selection of natural pet supplies and food, free local delivery with
minimum order; also offers adoption services.

Brooklyn Dog House 🍃🍃🍃 G

327 Douglass St. (4th Ave.), Park Slope/Boerum Hill (Bkn), 718-222-4900
Mon–Fri 7am–10pm Sat–Sun 9am–10pm **brooklyndoghouse.com**
Boarding and day care services offered with curbside pickup available in
Park Slope, Cobble Hill, Prospect Heights, and Fort Greene; grooming with
natural shampoo available.

Buttercup's Paw-tisserie 🍃🍃🍃🍃 PS

63 5th Ave. (St. Marks Pl.), Park Slope (Bkn), 718-399-2228
Tue–Fri 11am–7:30pm Sat 10am–7pm Sun 10am–6pm **buttercupspaw.com**
Dog bakery offering freshly baked dog treats using a mix of all-natural and
organic ingredients. Also carries holistic remedies, raw diets, grain-free pet
foods, dog chews, and green pet supplies.

Capipets 🍃🍃🍃 PS G

5797 Tyndall Ave. (bet. W. 259th St. & Mosholu Ave.), Riverdale (Brx),
718-432-8091
Mon–Fri 7:30am–12:00pm 2:30pm–7:00pm Sat 9am–3pm **capipets.com**
Natural and organic pet supplies, including natural flea and tick treatments;
organic products used in grooming service; kennel-free day/overnight
care provided.

City Dog Lounge 🌿🌿 PS G O

49-02 Vernon Blvd. (49th Ave.), Long Island City (Qns), 718-707-3027
Mon–Fri 9am–8:30pm Sat 9am–7:30pm Sun 11am–7pm **citydogandcat.com**
Pet supply store offering natural pet food, supplies, and toys; carries mostly
dog supplies with some cat and bird supplies; provides grooming, dogwalk-
ing, and day care services.

Coral Aquariums Inc. 🌿🌿 PS

75-05 Roosevelt Ave. (75th St.), Jackson Heights (Qns), 718-429-3934
Mon–Fri 10am–8pm Sat 10am–7pm Sun 12pm–6pm
Some natural pet food, treats, grooming products, natural remedies,
and pet supplies.

Crazy for Animals 🌿🌿🌿🌿 PS

80-16 Cooper Ave. (80th St.), Glendale (Qns), 718-366-3310
Mon–Sat 10am–9pm Sun 11am–8pm **crazyforanimals.com**
All-organic and natural pet foods and treats, including fresh-baked pastries;
eco-friendly bedding and other products.

Creature Features 🌿🌿 PS G

21 E. 3rd St. (2nd Ave.), East Village (Man), 212-473-5992
Mon–Fri 10:30am–6:30pm Sat 10:30am–6pm Sun 12pm–6pm
Pet shop offering some organic, raw, free-range, grass-fed, and human-
grade food and treats; grooms without sedatives or muzzles, using
hypoallergenic pet care products.

Crosby Pet Center 🌿 PS G

1626 Crosby Ave. (bet. Roberts Ave. & Middletown Rd.), Throggs Neck
(Brx), 718-822-6900
Mon–Fri 9:30am–7pm Sat 9:30am–6pm Sun 10am–5pm
Some natural pet foods and pet care products; grooming service available.

D is for Doggy 🌿🌿🌿🌿 G B

156 W. 22nd St. (bet. 6th & 7th Aves.), Chelsea (Man), 212-633-0040
Mon–Fri 7:30am–9pm Sat–Sun 9am–9pm **disfordoggy.com**
Cage-free boarding, customized day care packages, and grooming with all-
natural products; high-powered ventilation system ensures fresh air circulation; uses all-natural, hypoallergenic, therapeutic shampoos.

District Dog 🌿🌿🌿🌿 PS G

142 Driggs Ave. (Russell St.), Greenpoint (Bkn), 718-290-7434
Tue–Fri 11am–8pm Sat 10:30am–8pm Sun 11am–6:30pm **districtdog.com**
Wide selection of natural and organic food and supplies for cats and dogs;
also offers grooming services using natural products, and a bakery.

Dudley's Paw 🌿🌿 PS

327 Greenwich St. (bet. Duane & Jay Sts.), Tribeca (Man), 212-966-5167
Mon–Fri 11am–7pm Sat 10am–6pm
Pet store providing some natural pet foods and supplies, including
organic fiber collars and apparel, nontoxic toys, natural treats, and
canvas dog beds.

DUMBO Pet Care 🌿🌿🌿 PS G B O

25 Jay St., #104 (bet. John & Plymouth Sts.), DUMBO (Bkn), 718-855-1363
Seasonal hours **dumbopetcare.com**
Day care, boarding, and in-home care; uses organic/holistic dog foods and
grooming products; accepts drop-offs of gently used pet accessories for
donation to NY Animal Care & Control.

East Village Pet Grooming Salon, Inc. and Doggie Day Care 🌿🌿 G B

223 Ave. B (bet. 13th & 14th Sts.), East Village (Man), 646-654-0060
Mon–Sat 10am–6pm Sun 11am–6pm
Family-run grooming and boarding business for dogs and cats utilizing all-natural shampoos and products. Features 1,000-square-foot backyard for boarders to play.

Groomerama 🌿🌿 PS G

493 6th Ave. (bet. 12th & 13th Sts.), Union Square (Man), 212-627-2899
Daily 10am–8:30pm
All-natural pet foods and supplies; grooming services also available.

It's A Dog's World 🌿🌿🌿🌿 PS G O

593 Coney Island Ave. (bet. Lewis Pl. & Matthews Ct.), Flatbush (Bkn),
718-684-5568
Mon–Fri 1pm–7pm Sat 11am–5:30pm Sun 1:30pm–5pm **nydogsworld.com**
Organic and natural dog and cat supplies; dog training and grooming also available.

Just Us Pet Supplies 🌿🌿🌿 PS G

1603 Bushwick Ave. (Stewart St.), Bushwick (Bkn), 718-452-3350
Mon–Sat 10am–7pm Sun 11am–5pm
Pet supply store with a wide selection of all-natural food and chemically sensitive care products.

La Bella Pooch 🌿🌿🌿 PS

8001 17th Ave. (80th St.), Bensonhurst (Bkn), 347-312-2856
Wed–Sat 11am–9pm Sun 1pm–9pm
Mostly organic and natural pet foods and pet care products.

Le Pet Spa 🌿🌿🌿 PS G

300 Rector Pl. (S. End Ave.), Battery Park City (Man), 212-786-9070
Mon–Thu 10:30am–7pm Fri 11am–7pm Sat 10:30am–6pm Sun 11am–5pm
lepetspanyc.com
Groomer using all natural products; pet food and treats are mostly organic and all natural.

Love Thy Pet 🌿🌿 PS

164 Union St. (bet. Henry & Hicks Sts.), Carroll Gardens (Bkn), 718-596-2399
Mon–Fri 11:30am–8pm Sat 10:30am–7pm Sun 10:30am–6pm
lovethypetbklyn.com
Pet supply store carrying some natural, organic, and raw pet foods and supplies.

Mikey's Pet Shop 🌿🌿 PS

130 E. 7th St. (Ave. A), East Village (Man), 212-477-3235
Mon–Sat 10am–9pm Sun 12pm–9pm
Some organic and all-natural pet food and supplies.

Muddy Paws 🌿🌿🌿 PS G

447 Graham Ave. (bet. Richardson & Frost Sts.), Williamsburg (Bkn),
718-349-3647
Mon–Fri 10am–9pm Sat–Sun 11am–8pm
Holistic pet boutique offering a do-it-yourself dog wash and some organic and all-natural pet products.

Must Luv Dogs 🌿🌿🌿 PS G B O

234 N. 12th St. (bet. Driggs & Union Aves.), Williamsburg (Bkn),
718-388-7091
Mon–Fri 7am–8pm Sat–Sun 10am–6pm **mustluvdogs.com**
Natural food for dogs; grooming, boarding, training, cat sitting, and in-home
pet sitting available.

Myrtle's Pets 🌿🌿 PS G B

642 Myrtle Ave. (Franklin Ave.), Bedford-Stuyvesant (Bkn), 718-783-6298
Seasonal hours
Pet supplies, grooming, and cage-free boarding services offered; uses some
organic/eco-friendly products.

Natural Pet, The 🌿🌿🌿🌿 PS

238 3rd Ave. (bet. 19th & 20th Sts.), Gramercy (Man), 212-228-4848
Mon–Fri 11am–7pm Sat 11am–6pm Sun 1pm–6pm
Wide variety of organic, all-natural pet foods, accessories, and supplies.

NYC Pet 🌿🌿 PS

241 Bedford Ave. (bet. Metropolitan Ave. & N. 4th St.), Williamsburg (Bkn),
718-387-2220
Mon–Fri 9am–8pm Sat 9am–7pm Sun 11am–6pm **nycpet.com**
All-natural food and supplies for dogs and cats offered at this location.

Pet Ark 🌿🌿 PS G

3617 Kingsbridge Ave. (bet. W. 236th & 238th Sts.), Riverdale (Brx),
718-543-7300
3450 Broadway (bet. 140th & 141st Sts.), Harlem (Man), 212-368-8200
5008 Broadway (bet. 212th & 213th Sts.), Inwood (Man), 212-544-2300
Hours vary by location
Wide selection of natural and organic pet foods and treats. Free delivery.

Pet Planet 🌿🌿 PS

166 Elizabeth St. (Kenmare Sts.), Nolita (Man), 212-941-5554
Mon–Sat 10:30am–8:30pm Sun 11:30am–7pm
Some organic and all-natural pet food products.

Petopia 🌿🌿 PS

29 Ave. A (bet. 2nd & 3rd Sts.), East Village (Man), 212-353-2863
Mon–Sat 10am–8:30pm Sun 12pm–8:30pm
Pet supply shop carrying some natural and organic brands of pet food and
pet care supplies; free delivery.

PetQua 🌿🌿🌿 PS B

2604 Broadway (bet. 98th & 99th Sts.), Upper West Side (Man), 212-865-7500
Mon–Sat 10am–8pm Sun 11am–6pm **petqua.com**
Neighborhood pet supply store providing wide range of natural and organic
pet food and products; offers boarding for birds, turtles, small mammals,
and fish.

Pets On The Run 🌿 PS

989 Manhattan Ave. (Huron St.), Greenpoint (Bkn), 718-389-0650
Daily 9am–9pm
Pet supply store offering some organic food and pet care products.

PS9 Pet Supplies 🌿🌿🌿🌿 PS

169 N. 9th St. (bet. Bedford & Driggs Aves.), Williamsburg (Bkn),
718-486-6465
Mon–Fri 12pm–8pm Sat 11am–8pm Sun 12pm–6pm **ps9pets.com**
Pet supply store specializing in products with natural and organic ingredients; also carries pet accessories.

Pup Slope 🌿🌿 PS G B

255 Flatbush Ave. (6th Ave.), Prospect Heights (Bkn), 718-783-4204
Mon–Sat 8am–8pm Sun 11am–7pm
All-natural pet foods and supplies; overnight care and grooming
services available.

Puppies 🌿🌿 PS G

32-60 86th St. (Northern Blvd.), East Elmhurst (Qns), 718-458-3967
Mon–Sat 9am–5pm
Pet supply store offering natural pet food, supplies, and toys; grooming
services using oatmeal soap are available.

Rowf 🌿🌿🌿🌿 PS

43 Hicks St. (Middagh St.), Brooklyn Heights (Bkn), 718-858-7506
Tue–Fri 11am–7pm Sat–Sun 11am–5pm **rowfny.com**
Pet supply store carrying a wide selection of natural and organic pet toys
and treats.

Tailored Pet 🌿🌿🌿 PS G B

89 Pineapple Walk (bet. Henry St. & Cadman Plz. W.), Brooklyn Heights
(Bkn), 718-875-7387
Mon–Tue, Thu–Sat 8:30am–6pm **thetailoredpet.com**
Pet supplies, grooming, and day care using all-natural products. Providing
natural products and services for 35 years.

Top Dog Shop 🌿🌿🌿 PS

169 Lincoln Pl. (7th Ave.), Park Slope (Bkn), 718-246-4600
Mon–Fri 9am–9pm Sat–Sun 9am–7pm **topdogshop.com**
Neighborhood pet shop with a focus on natural and holistic pet products;
offers delivery to Brooklyn and lower Manhattan.

Whiskers Holistic Pet Care 🌿🌿🌿🌿 PS

235 9th St. (bet. 2nd & 3rd Aves.), East Village (Man), 212-979-2532
Mon–Fri 11am–8pm Sat 11am–7pm Sun 12pm–6pm **1800whiskers.com**
Organic and all-natural pet foods, grooming products, and flea and tick
treatments; provides expert advice on the use of holistic pet treatments.

Who's Your Doggy 🌿 PS

197 Adelphi St., #1 (Willoughby Ave.), Fort Greene (Bkn), 718-522-5244
Mon–Sat 9am–7pm Sun 9am–5pm
Pet supply store carrying some organic, natural pet food and pet
care products.

Pets

Green Tip

Keep fleas away from your home and your pets with
nontoxic alternatives to traditional pesticides. They
work equally well and won't cause unnecessary harm
to people or pets.

Green Pet Care

For many people, pets make life better. Some basic "green" knowledge can help make for a happier pet, a healthier household, and a greener world.

Look for natural and organic pet food. This will not only be good for your pet's health, but buying organic products helps support good land management and sustainable practices.

Kids benefit from having a pet in the family. Certain studies have shown that children who grow up with at least two pets are more than 75 percent less likely to develop allergies later in life.

Pesticides aren't good for pets or the people who pet them. Be very cautious with pet products that include toxic pesticides. The chemicals they contain are potentially harmful to your pet, you, and especially children. But this doesn't mean you need to live in fear of fleas in your home and on your pets. There are nontoxic alternatives to traditional pesticides. They work equally well and won't cause unnecessary harm to people or pets.

Prevention is always preferable to treatment, so it is important to keep bugs in check. Ticks can carry Lyme disease, a serious and poorly understood illness that attacks the nervous system. If you live in an area where Lyme disease is a risk, be very cautious and seek sound advice on keeping ticks off you and your furry friends.

Pet waste doesn't just smell bad, it can represent a major source of bacterial pollution when rain washes it into waterways and onto beaches. ALWAYS clean up after your pet. Try to use biodegradable, nonpetroleum-based bags for this purpose. They are widely available. Put the waste in the trash. Dog waste may be put in the toilet but cat waste must not be. Water treatment systems are not able to remove all the microorganisms in cat waste.

Finally, if you are ready to add a new family member, remember that your local shelter or rescue organization is the best place to adopt.

Recycle your
newspaper.

House

Transparent Green

By David Bergman

Back in the prehistoric days of green design—say, ten years ago—the term *green design* was practically an oxymoron. If you wanted "design" and wanted to be "green," you were probably going to have to make some tough choices between the two. Material choices were few, usually came in dull shades of brown, and tended toward the rustic.

Happily, those limitations are things of the past. An eco-home no longer needs to look like one. It can look ultramodern or it can look like, well, anything. I call that "transparent green"— the green is there, but it doesn't have to hit you over the head.

My clients tend to come in two flavors: those for whom design comes first and those who put green above all. For the design buffs, I start out asking them: If we can create a green design without compromising aesthetics and without adding costs, will you do it? Phrased like that, they really can't say no.

For my clients who are already convinced, I dig a little deeper. Is their interest in saving their health, saving money (yes, a green home can save you money), or saving the planet? Or all of the above?

Point being: Green comes in many hues and opacities, ranging from "tweaks"—small changes—to reinventions of what a building is. Our expanded world of green design options creates a wide range of possibilities, whether you're a tree hugger or not. "Green" and "design" are no longer incompatible.

House

David Bergman is principal of David Bergman Architect and Fire & Water Lighting (**cyberg.com**). He is a LEED AP and also teaches sustainable design at Parsons, the New School for Design.

Building Materials and Supplies

Almost every part of home building and furnishing can be made more environmentally sound. It may take more effort to find green building materials, but they are available, and using them is worth the effort.

Green building materials save water, energy, and other natural resources. They offer better indoor air quality due to the presence of less-toxic paints and finishes. Green products include those made from recycled materials such as glass or metal, as well as sustainably harvested wood and easily replenished materials like bamboo.

Specific examples of green building materials that are more and more easily obtainable include Agboard, a wood substitute made from agricultural waste or agricultural by-products; recycled cotton (postindustrial denim) insulation; recycled rubber or plastic shingles; natural lime and clay plaster; tile made from recycled windshields or recycled bottles; recycled rubber flooring; lino-leum (made from linseed oil, pine resin, and wood flour) flooring; recycled-content carpeting; and natural (nonvinyl) wall coverings. For more options and further information, check with the **U.S. Green Building Council (USGBC)**, a nonprofit organization promoting healthy and eco-friendly building.

To determine which building material and supply centers to include in the guide, we looked at the percentage of products and materials sold by these companies that are some combination of the following four attributes: sustainably manufactured; produced with nontoxic or low-toxic materials, such as no- or low-**VOC** finishes or adhesives; made with renewable, natural, or recycled materials; and/or locally or domestically produced or manufactured. In addition, we looked at whether or not the supply centers provided any eco-friendly packaging and/or if their carry-out bags were biodegradable or compostable and/or made with recycled, recyclable and/or chlorine-free materials.

Of the products and materials sold:

at least 25% meet the above criteria.

at least 50% meet the above criteria.

at least 75% meet the above criteria.

at least 90% meet the above criteria.

Aronson's 🍃🍃🍃🍃

135 W. 17th St. (bet. 6th & 7th Aves.), Chelsea (Man), 212-243-4993
Mon–Fri 9am–6pm **aronsonsfloors.com**
Ultra-low-VOC interior paints made from mineral pigments. Hosts AIA-accredited continuing education lunchtime lectures in its showroom, open to the public.

Bettencourt Green Building Supplies 🍃🍃🍃🍃

70 N. 6th St. (bet. Wythe & Kent Aves.), Williamsburg (Bkn), 800-883-7005
Mon–Fri 9am–6pm **bettencourtwood.com**
Supply shop providing green building materials for designers, architects, contractors, and homeowners. Carries eco-friendly wall coverings, flooring, countertops, and other healthy alternatives.

Coverings Etc. 🍃🍃🍃

138 Spring St., 6th Flr. (Wooster St.), SoHo (Man), 212-625-9393
Mon–Fri 9am–6pm **coveringsetc.com**
Business committed to environmentally friendly materials and solutions for projects with sustainable bio-architecture incentives. USGBC member.

Dom NY Showroom 🍃

66 Crosby St. (bet. Spring & Broome Sts.), Soho (Man), 212-253-5969
Mon–Fri 11am–7pm Sat 12pm–6pm **valcucinena.com**
Kitchenware, appliances, and furnishings store offering energy- and water-efficient kitchen design accessories and hardware from Valcucine; other fine brand products.

Earth Built 🍃🍃🍃🍃

917-543-4064
By appt.
Certified domestic hardwoods for exterior decking and siding; flooring material from reclaimed sources.

Go Green Inc. 🍃🍃🍃🍃

485 Atlantic Ave. (bet. 3rd Ave. & Nevins St.), Boerum Hill (Bkn), 718-625-0260
Tues–Sat 12pm–7pm Sun 11am–6pm **gogreeninc.com**
Eco-friendly adhesives, caulk, nontoxic paint, cleaning products, and other green building materials. Co-op America and USGBC member.

Green Depot 🍃🍃🍃🍃

20 Rewe St. (Vandervoort Ave.), Williamsburg (Bkn), 718-782-2991
Mon–Fri 7am–6pm Sat 7am–1pm **greendepot.com**
Sustainable bamboo, cork, marmoleum, and FSC-certified wood flooring. Variety of organic and sustainable carpet options. Green cabinetry, surfaces, and countertops.

Sister's Community Hardware 🍃

900 Fulton St. (Washington Ave.), Clinton Hill (Bkn), 718-399-7023
Mon–Fri 8am–8pm Sat 10am–7pm Sun 10am–3pm
sisterscommunityhardware.com
Community hardware store carrying some low-VOC paints and finishes and other innovative eco-friendly products.

TerraMai 🍃🍃🍃🍃

217 Grant St., Ste. 803 (Elizabeth St.), Little Italy (Man), 800-220-9062
Mon–Fri 9am–5pm **terramai.com**
FSC-certified, reclaimed wood products: flooring, siding, paneling, decking, beams, lumber, and rare and unusual pieces for commercial and residential application.

House

Alternative Energy Contractors

You may be in a position to directly affect your carbon footprint and consumption of conventional energy by using alternative energy. The companies listed below specialize in alternative energy systems: design, installation, service, and/or repair. They may offer free consultation to help you decide which is the best energy alternative for you. Also, there are a number of certifying organizations and licensing boards that can help you identify qualified professionals. Check our glossary for relevant terms and what they mean.

You might also check with your local utility company for a similar consultation and alternative energy plan. Utility companies as well as city, state, and federal agencies sometimes offer help in the form of rebates and tax incentives to homeowners who qualify.

Because the work these groups do is so varied (from design to repair), they have not been leaf-awarded. However, to be included in the guide, at least 25 percent of their total annual number of projects must deal primarily with the installation, repair, servicing, or design of alternative energy systems. We also factored in how many years experience they have in providing alternative energy products and services.*

*Greenopia is not responsible for the outcome or performance of the work/service/products/ materials of any listed company or individual. When hiring a professional or tradesperson, it is up to you to verify the experience and skills of the listed practitioners. Be sure to ask about and check on the status of a contractor's state or local licenses. These businesses were selected and reviewed for residential projects only. We did not investigate, nor is the guide intended to cover, commercial contractors.

A.S.K. Construction

26-01 21st St. (27th Ave.), Astoria (Qns), 877-828-3487
By appt.   askconstruction.com
Energy efficiency installations and weatherizing based on BPI-certified Residential Energy Audit specifications. Building NYSERDA-structured improvements since 2001. Serves NYC and Nassau County, parts of Suffolk and Westchester Counties.

Akeena Solar

199 Latimer Ave. (Baron Blvd.), Travis (S.I.), 888-253-3628
By appt.   akeena.net
National company specializing in design, installation, and service of solar power systems; uses alternative fuel service vehicles. Residential and commercial projects. Serves all of New York City Area.

Alt Power

125 Maiden Ln., Ste. 307 (Water St.), Financial District (Man), 212-206-0022
By appt. **altpower.com**
Solar thermal and PV contractors offering complete system design, installation, service, and repair for both residential and commercial projects. NABCEP, NYSERDA certified. Serves all of New York City area and Tri-State Region.

City Solar

531A 6th Ave. (bet. 13th & 14th Sts.), Park Slope (Bkn), 718-768-8161
By appt. **citysolar.org**
Design services for solar facilities and wind turbines. Engineers and installs garden PV arrays. LEED AP, NYSEIA member. Serves all of New York City.

Consumers Energy Group

222 Varick Ave. (Metropolitan Ave.), Ridgewood (Bkn), 718-645-4328
Daily 24 hrs. **consumers-energy.com**
B20 biodiesel delivery for use as home heating oil. Also offers design, installation, and service of home heating systems. Serves Brooklyn and Long Island.

Duce Construction Corp.

412 W. 127th St. (Morningside Ave.), Morningside Heights (Man), 212-316-2400
Mon–Fri 8am–6pm **ducecc.com**
Energy assessments, NYSERDA-certified solar PV installation, high-end interior redesigns, and environmental consulting services. LEED AP, USGBC Member. Serves all of New York City and Tri-State Region.

Gaia Power Technologies

116 John St. (bet. Cliff & Pearl Sts.), Financial District (Man), 212-732-5507
Mon–Fri 9am–5pm **gaiapowertechnologies.com**
Pollution-free power systems with solar- and wind-compatible applications for residential and commercial buildings. NYSEIA member. Serves all of New York City and Tri-State Region.

Howell Renewable Energy Co.

75 S. Broadway, White Plains, NY 10601 646-642-0737
By appt.
Geothermal installation and BPI-certified home energy audits assessing home energy performance. Provides financial consulting on payment and incentive options for alternative energy systems. IGSHPA certified, NYSEIA member. Serves all of New York City, Westchester, Nassau.

Menocal Contracting, Inc.

2437 Bouck Ave. (Mace Ave.), Bronxdale (Brx), 718-652-1498
Mon–Fri 7:30am–5pm
Master plumber installing geothermal and solar water heating systems for residential and commercial projects. Water Furnace International, IGSHPA certified. Serves all of New York City, Westchester, and Connecticut.

Metro Fuel Oil Corp.

500 Kingsland Ave. (Greenpoint Ave.), Greenpoint (Bkn), 718-383-1400
Daily 24 hrs. **metroenergy.com**
Biodiesel home heating oil, natural gas fuel services, and wholesale products. Biodiesel blends from B5 to B20 available. NBAC BQ-9000 certified. Serves all of New York City, Long Island, and Westchester.

House

New York Solar Authority

65-59 Parsons Blvd. (bet. Jewel & 65th Aves.), Flushing (Qns), 888-479-9163
By appt. **sun4now.com**
PV solar array installation offering new clients financial incentives. NYSERDA member. Serves all of New York and New Jersey.

Plumbing Solutions, Ltd.

43-76 10th St. (44th Ave.), Long Island City (Qns), 718-786-4344
Mon–Fri 8am–5pm
Geothermal heating installation and general contractor designing or rede-signing homes for better energy efficiency. IGSHPA certified. Serves all of New York City, Nassau and Suffolk Counties.

Quixotic Systems

90 Bedford St., Ste. A (bet. Grove and Barrow Sts.), Greenwich Village (Man), 212-367-9161
By appt. **quixotic-systems.com**
Design, installation, and service in solar electric, solar thermal, radiant heat-ing, wind turbines and peak load reduction for residential and commercial projects. Serves all of New York City and Tri-State Region.

R S Covello Electric

51-20 35th St. (Gale Ave.), Long Island City (Qns), 718-786-7390
400 E. 77th St. 4B (1st Ave.), New York (Man), 212-288-0436
By appt. **rscovello.net**
Electrician and solar PV installer. Also performs BPI certified electrical and home energy audits. NYSERDA certified. Serves all of New York City, Long Island, Lower Westchester.

Schildwachter Fuel Oil

1400 Ferris Pl. (Butler Pl.), Unionport (Brx), 800-642-3646
Daily 24 hrs. **schildwachteroil.com**
Full-service retail B20 biodiesel fuel distributors providing oil burner and boiler sales, installation, and service. Delivery vehicles operate on B20 biod-iesel fuel. Serves Bronx, Manhattan, and Westchester.

Steven Thomas Heating Inc.

241 Main St. (Amboy Rd.), Tottenville (S.I.), 718-966-7419
By appt. **steventhomasheating.com**
Radiant and geothermal heating system design, installation, and service. IGSHPA certified. Serves all of New York City and Tri-State Region.

Taggart Associates

5-33 50th Ave. (bet. Veron Blvd. & 5th St.), Long Island City (Qns), 718-786-7570
Mon–Fri 8am–5pm
Geothermal system installation and service. Also educates commercial and residential clients on green HVAC solutions. IGSHPA certified. Serves all of New York City, Long Island.

Garden and Landscape Design and Services

Well-planned landscaping can conserve water, attract and protect wildlife, keep your house cooler in summer, save you money, and even feed you!

Land that is cared for naturally feels better and can actually take less maintenance in the long run. In contrast, a yard that is maintained with pesticides and other chemicals can pose a threat to your family and pets, while artificially keeping plants alive with soil-depleting chemical fertilizers.

Our list consists of garden and landscape designers, landscape architects, arborists, and garden maintenance companies and workers whose main or sole purpose is offering environmentally sound gardening and landscaping services to homeowners and other noncommercial customers.

Businesses listed may offer one or more of the following: organic gardening services, planting and maintenance of native and drought-tolerant species, use of **integrated pest-management (IPM)** techniques, designing water conservation or reclamation systems into garden plans, and/or creating wildlife habitat gardens.

To be listed, at least 25 percent of the firm's or contractor's time and/or projects in a given year must be devoted to environmentally sound landscaping and gardening practices. We also looked at how long the principal or firm had been providing sustainable landscape and gardening services. Note that some of these businesses and/or their employees may also be LEED® (Leadership in Energy and Environmental Design) accredited.

Acme Plant Stuff

917-805-5383
By appt. **acmeplant.com**
Boutique horticultural service providing design, installation, and maintenance of exterior and interior landscapes. Uses native plants, IPM, drip irrigation, solar lighting, organic fertilizers.

Balmori Associates, Inc.

820 Greenwich St., 3rd Flr. (bet. Jane & Horatio Sts.), West Village (Man), 212-431-9191
By appt. **balmori.com**
Landscape and urban designers incorporating native plants, water terracing, green roofs, and storm water management.

Council on the Environment of New York City (CENYC)

51 Chambers St., Rm. 228 (bet. Broadway & Centre St.), City Hall (Man),
212-788-7900

Mon–Fri 9am–5pm   **cenyc.org**

Open Space Greening program provides sustainable garden and landscape
design services that include rainwater harvesting, organic gardening, and
planting and pruning of native and drought-tolerant species.

Drosera

283 7th St., Ste. 2 (bet. 4th & 5th Aves.), Park Slope (Bkn), 646-244-9397

By appt.   **drosera-x.com**

Ecologically based native plant designs, grassland green roofs, woodland
gardens, wildlife-attracting landscapes, and roadside restorations. Public
projects include native plant garden in Union Square Park.

Green Sense, LLC

172 W. 79th St. (bet. Amsterdam & Columbus Aves.), Upper West Side
(Man), 212-724-5953

By appt.   **greensense.us**

Landscaping business specializing in rooftop garden design, installation, and
maintenance. Has ongoing sustainability projects, uses irrigation systems to
conserve water, and avoids exotic plants.

Greener by Design

87 Wolfs Ln., Pelham, NY 10803 914-637-9870

By appt.   **greenerdesigns.com**

Landscape design and installation firm with extensive experience in
green roofs. Designs, builds, and maintains streetscapes, roof and terrace
gardens, street trees, foundation plantings, and interior designs. Serves
all of New York City.

Horticultural Society of New York

148 W. 37th St., 13th Flr. (bet. Broadway & 7th Ave.), Clinton (Man),
212-757-0915

By appt.   **hsny.org**

Private horticultural consultations for New York City residents.

Jane Gil Horticulture, LLC

212-316-6789

By appt.

Garden design, installation, and maintenance for high-end residential and
garden projects using compost and drip irrigation. Avoids invasive plants
and pesticides.

Just Terraces

422 E. 75th St. (bet. 1st & York Aves.), Upper East Side (Man), 212-570-4830

By appt.   **justterraces.com**

Projects include terrace layout, decks, and outdoor furniture and decor
made with sustainable woods.

Lifesource Irrigation, Inc.

247 W. 30th St., 5th Flr. (bet. 7th & 8th Aves.), Chelsea (Man), 212-633-2827

By appt.   **lifesourceirrigation.com**

Design, installation, and maintenance of low-flow drip irrigation systems and
low-voltage landscape lighting; green roof projects.

Lynn Torgerson Garden Ltd.

1133 Broadway, Ste. 1606 (bet. W. 25th & W. 26th Sts.), Flatiron (Man),
212-929-8012
By appt.
Design, conceptual drawings, installations, and customized care of green
roof terraces and green walls. Floral design for events with living plants.
Teaches at Bronx Botanical Garden on sustainable practices.

Organic Gardener, The

88 Clinton Ave., Ste. 1R (Myrtle Ave.), Vinegar Hill (Bkn), 718-594-6770
By appt. **theorganicgardenernyc.com**
Landscape architect and drafter using all-organic materials in the creation of
city gardens, green roofs, terracing, and a variety of other projects.

RGR Landscape Architects & Architecture, PLLC

115 5th Ave., 3rd Flr. (bet. 18th & 19th Sts.), Flatiron (Man), 212-353-7403
By appt. **rglandscape.com**
Landscape architect using native plants and handling runoff with swales and
bio-retention basins. Sunscreens and shading devices are used to maximize
passive solar energy.

Stone and Garden

659 Vanderbilt Ave. (bet. Park Pl. & Prospect Pl.), Prospect Heights (Bkn),
917-771-9382
By appt. **stoneandgarden.net**
Permaculture-based garden installation and design specializing in natural
stone. Edible foods, water harvesting, composting systems, food forest
gardening, and herb spirals. Free on-site estimates.

Sullivan Group Design, LLC

15 W. 26th St., 12th Flr. (Broadway), Flatiron (Man), 212-352-8636
By appt. **sullivangroupdesign.com**
Green roof designer provides expertise on roof suitability and teaches
homeowner proper maintenance techniques.

House

did you know?

Green roofs can be found atop New York buildings
from the Bronx Zoo to the Rikers Island jail, on private
homes, skyscrapers, and schools. One of New York's
most famous green roofs covers 3,500 square feet on
Silvercup Studios, where *The Sopranos* and *Sex and the
City* were filmed.

Building and Design Professionals and Tradespeople

More professionals are "going green" thanks to increased consumer demand and their own awareness of the impact they can have on the planet. However, not all green building and design professionals are experienced in all areas, so check into their primary focus and field of expertise. Review their references and take a look at their portfolios. Visit their project sites, if possible.

The green home building industry is changing quickly. More products are available; more sustainable design options are being introduced. Look for professionals who are up to date and who specialize in your need, be it interior or exterior design, "green" construction, or environmental consulting. Within each of these areas there are further distinctions. You may be seeking better water use and reclamation, a chemical-free environment, a green roof, solar energy installation, use of green materials, or another eco-oriented construction project. Be very clear about what you would like before you hire someone for your job. For further information, check with the **U.S. Green Building Council (USGBC)**, a nonprofit organization promoting healthy and eco-friendly design and construction, as well as the **Leadership in Energy and Environmental Design (LEED)** certification for building professionals and projects in your area. The USBGC is one of several certifying organizations or licensing boards. Others can be found in our glossary.

The professionals listed here were chosen because of their experience in sustainable or green building design and/or construction. At least 25 percent of their annual projects must have a green, environmentally oriented approach. We also looked at the number of years they have been practicing green design or building relative to their overall number of years in business or years of experience. Because these businesses couldn't be measured against a single objective standard, we did not grant leaf awards in this category.*

Note: Some architects also offer interior and landscape design and oher services. Many firms are full-service operations that have designers, landscapers, and other service providers on staff or ones with whom they regularly work. Please see the "Architects" listing as this is generally the primary service area of such firms.

*Greenopia is not responsible for the outcome or performance of the work/service/products/materials of any listed company or individual. When hiring a professional or trade listed below, it is up to you to verify the experience and skills of the listed practitioners. Be sure to ask about and check the status of a contractor's state and local licenses. The businesses listed below are selected and reviewed for residential design and construction only. We did not investigate, nor is the guide intended to cover, contractors whose primary focus is commercial projects.

Architects

Alive Structures

21-36 44th Rd. (bet. 21st & 23rd Sts.), Long Island City (Qns), 917-743-7735
By appt. **alivestructures.com**
Interior renovation using green materials and finishes. Specializes in green roofs, green walls, landscaping using native plants, water reclamation, and sustainable irrigation.

Anderson Architects

555 W. 25th St. (bet. 10th & 11th Aves.), Chelsea (Man), 212-620-0996
By appt. **andersonarch.com**
Architecture, urban design, and interior design using eco-friendly building materials and elements for healthy, sustainable structures and spaces.

Berg Design Architects

131 Varick St., Ste. 1009 (bet. Spring & Dominick Sts.), West Village (Man), 646-486-1964
By appt. **bergdesignarchitects.com**
Architects providing modern green alternatives for upscale homes including geothermal heating, high-efficiency windows and boilers, recycled glass, concrete radiant flooring, passive solar heating, and holistic analysis.

BKSK Architects, LLP

28 W. 25th St. (bet. Broadway & Ave. of the Americas), Flatiron (Man), 212-807-9600
By appt. **bkskarch.com**
Architect designing LEED-certified buildings and green roofs, with focus on daylighting and ventilation. LEED AP, USGBC member.

Briggs Knowles Architecture & Design

4332 22nd St., Ste. 401 (bet. 43rd & 44th Aves.), Long Island City (Qns), 212-844-9060
By appt.
Architecture firm promoting energy efficiency, working with integrated PV and daylighting. International Energy Society, American Solar Energy Society, and NE Sustainable Energy Association member.

Building Studio, The

307 W. 38th St., Rm. 1701 (8th Ave.), Midtown (Man), 212-279-1507
By appt. **thebuildingstudio.com**
Architecture and interior design services. Passive solar designs, passive thermal circulation methods, and integrative design for energy efficiency. USGBC member.

Chris Benedict, R.A.

323 E. 9th St. (bet. 1st & 2nd Aves.), East Village (Man), 212-477-6016
By appt. **architectureandenergylimited.com**
Architect offering energy-efficient home rehabilitation and full-scale new construction at competitive rates. Projects are designed holistically to assure optimal building performance.

Construct Architecture Studio

66 W. Broadway, Ste. 500 (bet. Murray & Warren Sts.), Battery Park City (Man), 212-513-1007
By appt. **con-struct.com**
Architect incorporating sustainable utilitarian design to projects including solar PV, solar thermal, evacuated tubes, rainwater collection, undisturbed soil, and graywater systems. USGBC member.

David Bergman, Architect

241 Eldridge St., Ste. 3R (bet. Stanton & Houston Sts.), Lower East Side (Man), 212-475-3106
By appt. **cyberg.com**
Projects incorporate green principles in design aesthetics and functionality, promoting healthy homes and a healthy planet. Twenty-five years' experience. LEED AP, USGBC member.

Dennis Wedlick Architect LLC

85 Worth St., 4th Flr. (bet. Broadway & Church St.), Civic Center (Man), 212-625-9222
By appt. **denniswedlick.com**
Architecture firm committed to sustainable development and design, working with local suppliers, contractors, and tradespeople. Uses renewable, reusable, and biodegradable materials. Landscape designers on staff. LEED AP, USGBC member.

DNA Strategic Design

45 Main St., Ste. 1018 (bet. Front & Water Sts.), DUMBO (Bkn), 718-858-5700
By appt. **daynightafter.com**
Architecture, interior design, custom furniture, and other services with special focus on sustainable materials and energy resources. LEED AP, USGBC member.

Ellen Honingstock Architect

212-228-1585
By appt. **ehapc.com**
Architecture and interior design firm focused on energy efficiency, healthy indoor air quality, and other environmentally conscious solutions. LEED AP, USGBC member.

Eric Joseph Gering Architect, P.C.

212-751-3294
By appt.
Architect and interior designer using locally sourced materials, FSC-certified woods, and low-VOC paints and finishes.

4-pli Design

72 N. 15th St. (Wythe Ave.), Greenpoint (Bkn), 718-387-7986
By appt. **4-pli.com**
Architecture and interior design firm using reclaimed and sustainable building materials in projects.

Gleicher Design Group

54 W. 21st St., Ste. 603 (bet. 5th & 6th Aves.), Flatiron (Man), 212-462-2789
By appt. **gleicherdesign.com**
Architecture and interior design focused on indoor air quality, sustainable materials, and green energy systems. USGBC member.

Hanrahan Meyers Architects

135 W. 20th St., Ste. 300 (bet. 6th & 7th Aves.), Flatiron (Man), 212-989-6026
By appt. **hanrahanmeyers.com**
Architects specializing in custom interiors, sustainable design, and unique spatial design integrating landscape and dwelling; green roof design. LEED AP, USGBC member.

Harvey Cohn Architecture PLLC

185 Madison Ave. (E. 34th St.), Murry Hill (Man), 212-686-5226
By appt. **ecoarchitect.com**
Home design incorporating passive solar, low-toxic materials, sustainably harvested and reclaimed woods.

HJN Consulting

92 Chambers St., Penthouse (bet. Broadway & Church St.), Civic Center (Man), 646-522-0285
By appt. **hjnconsulting.com**
High-end residential projects using sustainable design and materials; environmental consulting on indoor air quality. LEED AP.

Jeffrey McKean Architect

225 Broadway, 30th Flr. (Barclay St.), Lower Manhattan (Man), 212-964-2300
By appt. **jeffreymckean.com**
Architecture incorporating storm water retention, harvesting, and reuse for irrigation; photovoltaic panels, solar-heated hot water boilers, low-VOC building materials.

Kiss + Cathcart, Architects

44 Court St., Tower C (Joralemon St.), Brooklyn Heights (Bkn), 718-237-2786
By appt. **kisscathcart.com**
Projects combining photovoltaics and green architecture since 1983, with focus on energy efficiency and conservation. LEED AP, USGBC member.

Lawrence Marek Architect

54 W. 39th St., 6th Flr. (bet. 5th Ave. & Ave. of the Americas), Murray Hill (Man), 212-594-6078
By appt. **helios-arch.com**
Architect works with nature to elevate design. Solar PV, nontoxic, and recycled material use.

Matt Gagnon Studio LLC

1013 Grand St., Ste. 20 (Morgan Ave.), South Side (Bkn), 718-384-7724
By appt. **mattstudio.com**
Architect offering green renovation, specializing in the reuse and redesign of demo materials and salvaged architectural elements. Creates interior decor objects using recycled paper and hardwoods.

Michael McDonough Architect

131 Spring St. (bet. Wooster & Greene Sts.), Greenwich Village (Man), 212-431-3723
By appt. **michaelmcdonough.com**
Projects incorporate green building and design elements, energy-efficient technologies. LEED AP, USGBC member.

Nadia Elrokhsy Design and Consulting

P.O. Box 287251, New York (Man), 646-369-7567
By appt.
Passive solar house design using natural daylighting, emphasizing building envelope, and improving indoor air quality. Serves NYC.

Paul Castrucci Architect

179 Rivington St., Ste. 1A (Attorney St.), Lower East Side (Man), 212-254-7060
By appt.
Architect focused on energy-efficient, water-conserving design and building features. Utilizes low-VOC paints and finishes, recycled aggregates and steel for interior spaces.

Prospect Architects

916 Union St., Ste. 1C (Plaza St. W.), Park Slope (Bkn), 718-783-0348
By appt. **prospectarchitecture.com**
Design, building, and construction management services with holistic, sustainable approach. BPI certified, LEED AP, USGBC member.

Resolution 4 Architecture

150 W. 28th St., Ste. 1902 (bet. 6th & Fashion Aves.), Flatiron (Man), 212-675-9266
By appt. **re4a.com**
Architect specializing in prefab homes designed for energy efficiency and powered by alternative energy. LEED AP, USGBC member.

Romero Studios

P.O. Box 737, Stuyvesant Station, New York (Man), 646-602-1319
By appt. **romerostudios.com**
Design and construction of tree houses using salvaged and reclaimed wood; garden, landscape, and interior design.

Thread Collective

117 Grattan St., Studio 205 (Porter Ave.), Bushwick (Bkn), 718-366-3988
By appt. **threadcollective.com**
Projects include consultation, small-scale renovation, and new construction, all incorporating sustainable design and building principles.

Walsh & Purdy Architects

110 Suffolk St., Ste. 1C (bet. Delancey & Rivington Sts.), Lower East Side (Man), 212-253-0200
By appt. **walshpurdy.com**
Architecture and interior design focused on the use of sustainable materials, environmentally responsible construction practices. LEED AP, USGBC member.

Builders and General Contractors

Carpistry

152 Columbus Ave., Ste. 5S (W. 67th St.), Lincoln Square (Man), 917-509-8034
By appt. **carpistry.com**
Small, high-end construction company offering green remodeling for urban clients. Specializes in indoor air quality, building material recycling and reuse.

Duce Construction Corp.

412 W. 127th St. (Morningside Ave.), Morningside Heights (Man), 212-316-2400
Mon–Fri 8am–6pm **ducecc.com**
General contracting, construction management, and environmental consulting services. Energy assessments, high-end interior redesigns, NYSERDA-certified solar PV installation. LEED AP, USGBC Member serving NYC and the Tri-State area.

FNG Home Improvements

430 Poillon Ave. (Kenwood Ave.), Blue Heron Park (S.I.), 917-416-1254
By appt.
Eco-friendly cellulose insulation installation. BPI certified.

Giancola Contracting Inc.

415 63rd St., Ste. 1 (bet. 4th & 5th Aves.), Sunset Park (Bkn), 718-439-6200
Mon–Fri 9am–5pm
Home renovations using green building materials. Energy Star–qualified
builder.

Green Street Construction

68 E. 131st St., Ste. 600 (bet. Madison & Park Ave.), Upper East Side (Man),
212-234-1027
By appt. **greenstreetinc.com**
General contractor specializing in deconstruction of reusable building components, construction waste recycling, indoor air quality management, and
on-site dust control. LEED AP, USGBC member.

Living Space Design

427 Franklin Ave. (bet. Madison & Monroe Sts.), Clinton Hills (Bkn),
718-541-1430
By appt. **buildgreennyc.com**
Building and design services using green materials; focus on energy
efficiency. Construction vehicle runs on biodiesel.

New York Design and Construction, Inc.

347-739-0033
By appt. **nydacinc.com**
Small building and design firm specializing in mold prevention systems,
installation of windows and walls; custom woodwork, masonry, and tile work.
USGBC member.

Northfield Home Performance, Inc.

160 Heberton Ave. (New St.), Port Richmond (S.I.), 718-442-7351
By appt.
General contractor improving home energy efficiency. BPI certified.

Square Indigo, Inc.

94 DeKalb Ave. (Ashland Pl.), Fort Greene (Bkn), 718-625-3086
Mon–Fri 7am–5pm
General contractor focused on large-scale commercial and residential con-
struction. Expertise in nontoxic, recycled, and alternative building materials.

Sumner Green Eco Construction

917-376-2356
By appt. **sumnergreen.com**
Construction and renovation focused on zero-energy homes and ecologically
sound projects that reduce waste, energy, and harmful chemicals.

Environmental Consultants

A.S.K. Construction

26-01 21st St. (27th Ave.), Astoria (Qns), 877-828-3487
By appt. **askconstruction.com**
Energy-efficiency installations and weatherizing based on BPI certified
Residential Energy Audit specifications. NYSERDA guidelines used; green
building materials and techniques featured. Serves NYC and Nassau County,
parts of Suffolk and Westchester Counties.

Habitat Safe Solutions

51 MacDougal St., Ste. 358 (W. Houston St.), Downtown (Man),
888-589-5562
By appt. **habitatsafesolutions.com**
Air quality and environmental testing services providing noninvasive,
nontoxic, biodegradable mold decontamination. IAQA member. Serves
Tri-State Region.

Microecologies

1829 Madison Ave. (E. 119th St.), East Harlem (Man), 212-755-3265
By appt. **microecologies.com**
Indoor environmental health consultants performing inspections, mold
remediation, and cleaning of indoor heating and ventilation systems.

Zetlin & De Chiara LLP (Stephen Del Percio, Esq.)

801 2nd Ave. (E. 43rd St.), Tudor City (Man), 212-682-6800
Mon–Fri 9am–5pm **greenbuildingsnyc.com**
Green business and construction attorney admitted to practice law in both
New York and New Jersey, with an emphasis on drafting contracts to assist
residential clients with the LEED certification process. LEED AP member.

Green Roof Designers

Alive Structures

21-36 44th Rd. (bet. 21st & 23rd Sts.), Long Island City (Qns), 917-743-7735
By appt. **alivestructures.com**
Interior renovation using green materials and finishes. Specialty in green
roofs, green walls, landscaping using native plants, water reclamation, and
sustainable irrigation.

Atoms Eco

212-614-6998
By appt. **atomseco.com**
Design and consulting services dedicated to providing urban clients
eco-friendly choices; green roof and interior design.

BKSK Architects, LLP

28 W. 25th St. (bet. Broadway & Ave. of the Americas), Flatiron (Man),
212-807-9600
By appt. **bkskarch.com**
Architect designing LEED-certified buildings and green roofs, with focus on
daylighting and ventilation. LEED AP, USGBC member.

Drosera

283 7th St., Ste. 2 (bet. 4th & 5th Aves.), Park Slope (Bkn), 646-244-9397
By appt. **drosera-x.com**
Urban conservation biologist performing botanical surveys, floristic invento-
ries, and rare plant monitoring. Serves New York City metro area.

Hanrahan Meyers Architects

135 W. 20th St., Ste. 300 (bet. 6th & 7th Aves.), Flatiron (Man), 212-989-6026
By appt. **hanrahanmeyers.com**
Architects specializing in custom interiors, sustainable design, and unique
spatial design integrating landscape and dwelling; green roof design.
LEED AP, USGBC member.

Interior Designers

Atoms Eco
212-614-6998
By appt. **atomseco.com**
Design and consulting services dedicated to providing urban clients
eco-friendly choices; green roof and interior design.

Brett Design
212-987-8270
By appt. **brettdesigninc.com**
Design and building projects utilizing sustainable building materials,
eco-friendly furniture, flooring, and décor options. USGBC member.

Darren Henault Interiors
180 Varick St., Rm. 424 (bet. King & Charlton Sts.), Greenwich Village (Man),
212-677-5699
By appt. **darrenhenault.com**
High-end interior design firm sourcing eco-friendly furniture, flooring,
carpeting, and décor items upon request.

Erika Doering Design
94 Dekalb Ave. (bet. Ashland & Rockwell Pls.), Fort Green (Bkn),
718-923-0231
By appt.
Renovation and custom furnishings created without the use of petroleum-
based materials; FSC-certified and reclaimed wood.

Interior Design Solutions
300 E. 74th St. (2nd Ave.), Upper East Side (Man), 212-628-3938
By appt. **idsny.com**
Interior design firm with focus on indoor air quality. Low-VOC finishes,
sustainably harvested woods, green kitchen cabinets. Avoids demolition
of existing structures. LEED AP, USGBC member.

Michelle Slovak
212-246-0914
By appt. **michelleslovak.com**
Interior designer using sustainably sourced and nontoxic materials.
Works with local cabinet makers and tradespeople.

Niche Design
352 11th St., Ste. 1L (bet. 5th & 6th Aves.), Park Slope (Bkn), 718-832-7274
By appt. **design-niche.com**
Full-service, high-end design and consulting. Alternative energy systems,
energy-efficient building strategies, nontoxic furnishings and décor. Helps
clients source green contractors for construction projects. LEED AP,
USGBC member.

Oskar L. Torres
47-38 11th St., Ste. 8 (47th Ave.), Long Island City (Qns), 201-420-1794
By appt. **oskartorres.com**
Interior design firm using recycled furniture, vintage tiles and fabrics,
recycled fabric pillows, low-VOC paints, cork and bamboo flooring.

House

Vital Design Ltd.

102 W. 85th St. (Columbus Ave.), Upper West Side (Man), 212-799-1540
By appt. **vitaldesignltd.com**
Interior designer employing materials crafted from natural fibers, fair trade
accessories, nontoxic paints, wall coverings, fabrics, and flooring. Works with
LEED AP contractors.

Tradespeople

Plumbing Solutions, Ltd.

43-76 10th St. (44th Ave.), Long Island City (Qns), 718-786-4344
Mon–Fri 8am–5pm
Home design and redesign for geothermal heating, Energy Star rating quali-
fication, general energy efficiency. Serves all of New York City, Long Island.

R S Covello Electric

51-20 35th St. (Gale Ave.), Long Island City (Qns), 718-786-7390
400 E. 77th St., #4B (1st Ave.), Upper East Side (Man), 212-288-0436
By appt. **rscovello.net**
Residential and commercial electricians performing BPI-certified home
energy audits. Serves all of New York City, Long Island, and Lower
Westchester.

Richmond Aluminum Supply Inc.

26 Watchogue Rd. (bet. Bradley Ave. & Treetz Pl.), Westley (S.I.)
718-698-5880
By appt. **richmondaluminum.com**
Exterior home improvement for reduction in energy use, overall energy
efficiency. BPI accredited.

Scaran Heating, Air Conditioning, and Plumbing Inc.

6767 Amboy Rd. (Richmond Valley Rd.), Richmond Valley (S.I.), 718-984-0805
By appt. **scaran.com**
Heating, cooling, and air conditioning service and replacement company,
with focus on energy- and water-efficient upgrades. BPI certified.

did you know?

The Hearst Tower in Midtown—constructed using
80 percent recycled steel—was New York City's first
LEED Gold–certified building. The forty-six-story
office building also has a roof that collects rainwater
used to irrigate plants and supplement the cooling
system.

Salvaged Architectural Elements

The purchase and reuse of recycled and salvaged goods and materials have grown more popular as the world's resources are getting depleted and landfills overflow. Unwanted items and what may have once been demolition waste products are finding new life at salvage yards and "resource malls."

You may find the perfect door, window, or clawfoot bathtub at one of the businesses listed below. By doing so, you will have taken another step on the path to a zero-waste society, a key goal of the organizations and businesses we've found.

Although salvaged materials represent the truest form of recycling, their content may or may not be "green." They may have lead paint or other toxic finishes, or they could contain formaldehyde or other toxins. For this reason, we cannot offer leaf awards in this category. Nevertheless, these businesses deserve our strong support in that they don't require the use of new materials, they keep used materials out of the landfill, and the salvaged items can be refurbished with natural, nontoxic materials or finishes. To further evaluate each business, we looked at the percentage of salvaged products that were locally sourced.

House

ABC Carpet & Home

888 Broadway (E. 19th St.), Union Square (Man), 212-473-3000
Mon–Fri 10am–8pm Sat 10am–7pm Sun 11am–6:30pm   **abchome.com**
Columns, molding, doors, door frames, and window frames salvaged from buildings in the United States and around the world.

Brownstoner's Brooklyn Flea

Lafayette Ave. (bet. Clermont & Vanderbilt Ave.), Fort Greene (Bkn),
Sunday 10am–5pm   **brooklynflea.com**
Largest outdoor market in New York City, featuring more than 200 vendors selling new, repurposed, and vintage furniture, antiques, lighting, records, clothes, jewelry, and crafts.

Build It Green! NYC

3-17 26th Ave. (4th St.), Astoria (Qns), 718-777-0132
Tue–Fri 10am–6pm Sat 10am–5pm   **bignyc.org**
Nonprofit selling salvaged and surplus building materials. All proceeds help support the Community Environmental Center's educational programs at Solar One. Donated building materials accepted.

Demolition Depot, The

216 E. 125th St. (3rd Ave.), East Harlem (Man), 212-982-5000
Mon–Sat 10am–6pm   **demolitiondepot.com**
Salvaged architectural ornamentation specializing in local mid-century pieces. Offerings include carved columns, mirrored medicine cabinets, bathroom fixtures, and more.

M. Fine Lumber

1301 Metropolitan Ave. (Gardner Ave.), Linden Hill (Bkn), 718-381-5200
Mon–Fri 8am–5pm **mfinelumber.com**
Recycled furniture-grade lumber, antique heart pine, timbers, used Douglas fir, dimensional lumber, and plywood salvaged from demolished buildings.

Moon River Chattel

62 Grand St. (bet. Kent & Wythe Aves.), Williamsburg (Bkn), 718-388-1121
Tue–Sat 12pm–7pm Sun 12pm–5pm **moonriverchattel.com**
Lighting and plumbing fixtures, doors, door hardware, and other items.

Olde Good Things

124 W. 24th St. (bet. 6th & 7th Aves.), Chelsea (Man), 212-989-8401
Mon–Sun 9am–7pm **oldegoodthings.com**
Locally sourced salvaged building materials such as lighting, wood flooring, tin ceilings, mirrors, mantels, windows, doors, doorknobs, decorative iron, and stained glass.

ReBuilders Source

461 Timpson Place (bet. E. 145th & E. 147th Sts.), Mott Haven (Brx), 718-742-1111
Mon–Sat 8am–6pm **rebuilderssource.coop**
Discount retailer of salvaged and surplus building materials, specializing in a wide range of building materials including dimensional lumber, doors, cabinetry, sinks and bathtubs, plumbing, fixtures, flooring and paint.

TerraMai

217 Grand St., Ste. 803 (Elizabeth St.), Chinatown (Man), 800-220-9062
By appt. **terramai.com**
FSC-certified reclaimed wood products offered, including flooring, siding, paneling, decking, beams, and lumber. Specializes in rare and unusual pieces.

WRITE A REVIEW

Many people begin their journey to green living by changing their home environment. You can provide a great benefit to others by sharing your insights and experiences with the professionals and tradespeople in *Greenopia*. What did you think about the options and choices you were given, or the quality of the products and services? How was your experience with these providers? Was the cost in line with what you were getting? Let us know! Write your review at **greenopia.com**.

Change your light-bulbs.

Why Build Green?

There are many reasons to build green—some personal, some planetary. Green building integrates design and construction to promote the health and well-being of the building's inhabitants as well as that of the community and the environment. **But what does green building really mean?**

- Lower water and energy bills and reduced maintenance costs.

- Better indoor air quality through the use of eco-friendly materials, paints and finishes, and mechanical systems.

- More comfortable living with smart energy design, proper insulation, and efficient heating and cooling systems.

- Conservation of natural resources and eco-systems.

So the benefits are clear. Now it's time for some specifics. What elements and materials are used in green building? **How about some concrete examples?**

- **Deconstruction**—Materials are preserved for reuse through the careful dismantling of a building. Waste is reduced, and recovered materials may be superior to replacements.

- **Passive solar design**—Structures are oriented for maximum use of sunlight, windows are placed with care, and insulation and materials that store and absorb heat reduce reliance on forced-air systems.

- **Fly ash–content concrete**—Replaces Portland cement used in concrete with what would be a waste product, thereby reducing habitat destruction, energy use, and pollution.

- **Pervious paving**—Allows water to move through to the base materials below so groundwater is recharged and storm water runoff is reduced.

- **Certified wood**—Forest Stewardship Council (FSC) certification ensures responsible forest management. Use certified wood for flooring, cabinets, moldings, veneers, and furniture.

- **Recycled-plastic lumber**—Uses grocery bags, plastic soda and milk bottles, and pallet wrap to create durable "lumber." This saves mature trees, reduces waste, and cuts maintenance.

- **Alternative insulation**—Recycled postindustrial denim is better than fiberglass on most counts and is nonirritating. Cellulose, made from postconsumer recycled newspaper with nontoxic fire and pest retardants insulates as well as fiberglass.

- **Recycled-content roofing**—Long-lasting and lightweight, this diverts material from landfills.

- **Salvaged elements**—Flooring, moldings, doors, windows, fixtures, and other building materials can be acquired from salvage yards, saving both money and resources.

- **Green or living roofs**—Plants live on top of a waterproof membrane, absorbing greenhouse gases and providing habitat.

- **High-efficiency windows**—Energy Star–labeled windows save energy and help maintain comfortable indoor air temperatures.

- **Recycled-content tile**—Recycled bottles, windshields, and post-industrial waste from gravel production go into the creation of very durable, highly attractive glass and ceramic tile.

- **Bamboo**—This rapidly renewable perennial grass can be used for cabinets, flooring, and furniture.

- **Natural fiber flooring**—Renewable and biodegradable jute, sisal, coir, sea grass, and wool can be used in lieu of vinyl and other unhealthy alternatives.

- **Recycled-content carpeting**—Some can be recycled repeatedly. Costs and colors are comparable to standard offerings, but demand for petroleum is reduced, emissions are lowered, and plastic doesn't end up in the landfill.

- **Cork flooring**—This is very durable and ultimately biodegradable. It is made from the bark of the tree, which, when harvested, does not harm the tree.

- **Linoleum flooring**—Made from linseed oil, pine resin, and wood flour, all nontoxic and biodegradable. Lasts for years and is easy to maintain.

- **Recycled-content countertops**—Crushed bottles, windshields, and stemware go into the making of terrazzo, which can be used indoors or out, and is scratch- and heat-resistant. Another alternative, Paperstone, is made from recycled paper compressed in a water-based resin. It is stain- and heat-resistant.

- **Low- or No-VOC paint**—Paint certified by Green Seal, an independent emissions standard organization, is healthier and perform as well, if not better, than traditional paint.

When it comes to outfitting your green home, you will get significant payback both monetarily and in pollution reduction when you invest in a few key areas. **What are those key investments?**

- **Energy-efficient appliances**—Look for EPA Energy Star options, to save significant energy and water costs over the life of the appliance.

- **Solar photovoltaics**—These convert sunlight into electricity and are typically in panels on the roof.

- **Water-efficient fixtures**—Use high-efficiency toilets, low-flow faucets and showerheads, and front-loading clothes washers.

House

Home

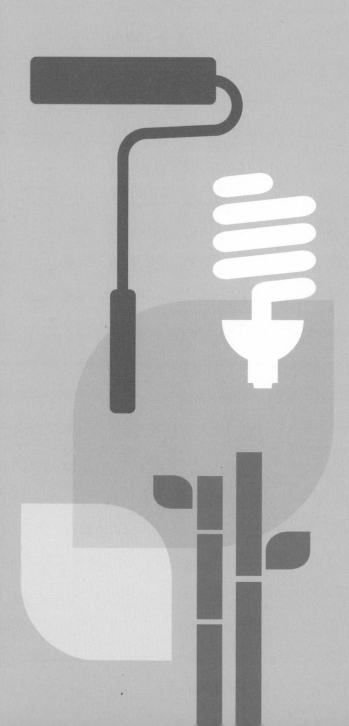

Our Collective Home

By Paulette Cole

Home is our personal healing refuge and our most intimate space, and the choices we make to create it reflect our vision in cocreating our collective home, the planet.

These are powerful times to be alive, as we witness the rapid evolution of the most innovative self-organizing movement affecting change globally, in which consumers increasingly interrogate the impact of their choices and seek assurance that this impact is sound, positive, and sustainable. This demand raises the bar on innovative design that does not compromise beauty—from furniture made with wood from responsibly managed forests or salvaged sources, to organic mattresses made with naturally tapped rubber, cruelty-free wool and organic cotton, to indigenous artistry that sustains the design DNA of our global diversity. Holistic business must now integrate well-being with beauty. Beauty and passion are tools to creatively express a commitment to nurturing the planet and its communities while actualizing home as a sacred space.

In a culture where business inherently does not take the lead in addressing complex social and environmental issues, we are witnessing an emerging shift in businesses and the corporate culture at large toward a growing realization that we can use our creativity and ingenuity and business platforms to generate real, lasting solutions in a way that provides success as well as profit. With transparency, accountability, and a commitment to guiding conscious consumerism, retailers influence a powerful shift toward effecting change. A new age is emerging, and our opportunity to manifest the necessary healing transformation for our planet and its people is becoming all the more possible and imperative.

Paulette Cole is the cofounder, CEO, and creative director of ABC Home, an experimental home design retail platform with an ongoing commitment to social responsibility, environmental stewardship, and cause-related product (**abchome.com**).

Home

Bed and Bath

The cotton in conventional bedding, bath towels, and linens requires significant chemical inputs for its growth and processing. Choose furnishings that are made from organic or sustainable fabrics or recycled materials. Begin to think about how these items are produced. Is their manufacture sustainable? Are the dyes and coatings they contain nontoxic? Your interest will spark increased supply of sustainably produced bed and bath furnishings.

And remember, you spend about a third of your life in bed, so the mattress you sleep on should be good for you. Look for mattresses, toppers, and box springs made with organic and chemical-free materials, particularly wool. Wool naturally wicks moisture away from the body, thereby creating a healthier, allergen- and mold-free environment. You may also want to consider box springs and bed frames manufactured with sustainable or **FSC-certified wood**.

Businesses that offer bed and bath furnishings are evaluated based on the percentage of products stocked that are characterized by one or more of the following:

- produced with nontoxic or low-toxic materials;
- made with renewable, natural, or recycled materials;
- sustainably manufactured; and/or
- sustainably manufactured and locally or domestically produced.

    🍃 at least 25% of the products meet the above criteria.
    🍃🍃 at least 50% of the products meet the above criteria.
    🍃🍃🍃 at least 75% of the products meet the above criteria.
    🍃🍃🍃🍃 at least 90% of the products meet the above criteria.

If the establishment sells mattresses, we evaluated the percentage of total mattress stock made with 100 percent organic and chemical-free materials.

    🍃 at least 25% of the mattresses meet the above criteria.
    🍃🍃 at least 50% of the mattresses meet the above criteria.
    🍃🍃🍃 at least 75% of the mattresses meet the above criteria.
    🍃🍃🍃🍃 at least 90% of the mattresses meet the above criteria.

ABC Carpet & Home 🍃🍃🍃🍃

888 Broadway (E. 19th St.), Union Square (Man), 212-473-3000
Mon–Fri 10am–8pm Sat 10am–7pm Sun 11am–6:30pm **abchome.com**
The ABC Home & Planet Eco-Hub carries organic mattresses, organic cotton sheets, towels, and linens using low-impact dyes. Urban-specific air purifiers available.

Hastens ✦✦✦

80 Greene St. (bet. Spring & Broome Sts.), SoHo (Man), 212-219-8022
Mon–Sat 11am–7pm Sun 12pm–6pm **hbeds.com**
Mattresses and bed frames made with all-natural materials such as
horsehair, cotton, flax, wool, and certified pine; mattress fillings made with
natural, nontoxic fire retardant properties.

Scott Jordan Furniture ✦✦✦✦

137 Varick St. (Spring St.), SoHo (Man), 212-620-4682
Mon–Wed 10am–6pm Thu 10am–8pm Fri–Sat 10am–6pm Sun 12pm–5pm
scottjordan.com
Solid wood furniture made domestically from sustainably harvested wood
and finished with plant oils and waxes. Chemical-free mattresses.

Stella ✦

138 W. Broadway (bet. Thomas & Duane Sts.), Tribeca (Man), 212-233-9610
Mon–Sat 11am–6pm
Some organic and sustainable bedding and linens, soy candles, and a house
line of down comforters.

Vivavi ✦✦✦✦

644 Manhattan Ave., 2nd Flr. (Bedford Ave.), Greenpoint (Bkn),
866-848-2840
Mon–Wed 11am–4pm Thu 11am–9pm Sat 10am–6pm **vivavi.com**
Design center and showroom featuring eco-friendly, modern-style décor
and furniture by a variety of designers. Showroom and headquarters are
powered by 100% wind energy. Member of 1% for the Planet.

Wonk ✦✦

68 Jay St., Ste. 101 (bet. Front & Water Sts.), DUMBO (Bkn), 718-596-8026
160A N. 4th St. (bet. Bedford & Driggs Aves.), Williamsburg (Bkn),
718-218-7750
Daily 12pm–7pm **wonknyc.com**
Mattresses and bedding made from eco-friendly and recycled materials.
Carries locally made furniture made of bamboo with low-VOC lacquers.

Green Tips

Replace your PVC shower curtain with a natural fiber
or nylon alternative. That plastic smell comes from the
toxic chemicals that make PVC (polyvinyl chloride). Find
a healthier option made of hemp, linen, or nylon.

Choose sheets made of organic cotton or bamboo (to
avoid pesticides) and colored with natural dyes (synthetic
dyes off-gas VOCs). Organic beds are made with wool
fibers, which act as natural repellent for mold and dust
mites, and are not treated with harmful flame-resistant
chemicals.

Fill your home with eco-friendly furniture. Many conventional pieces of furniture use formaldehyde as a binder,
are coated with toxic finishes, use synthetic fillers, and
can off-gas harmful chemicals.

Furniture, Flooring, Carpeting, and Décor

What you choose to buy for your home has a direct effect on both your personal health and the health of the planet. Many conventional pieces of furniture use formaldehyde as a binder, are coated with toxic finishes, use synthetic fillers, and can off-gas harmful chemicals. But there are a growing number of alternatives available that are both more healthful and sustainably produced.

To avoid chemicals from new materials and save money, shop at unfinished wood furniture stores and finish the items with plant-based, natural finishes. Look for wood products that have the Forest Stewardship Council (FSC) seal indicating they come from sustainably managed forests. Consider buying used furniture items, but avoid all pieces containing vinyl (PVC) and pieces that may contain lead-based paint.

Wall-to-wall carpeting may look and feel pretty, but the nylon variety is made from a chemical stew that takes a long time to fully off-gas. This can cause irritation to babies, children, and anyone who is chemically sensitive. When possible, look for all-wool carpeting with natural fiber backing made of jute or latex. Better still, choose carpeting made from 100 percent postconsumer recycled food and drink containers or other materials. Not only does its manufacture keep plastic out of landfills, it is superior to lower-grade virgin fibers on a number of counts—fewer emissions, better stain resistance, increased colorfastness.

Check into other flooring alternatives too—recycled-content tile, cork, sustainably harvested wood, real linoleum, and area rugs made with natural materials. Many companies offer alternatives to standard fibers: Jute, sisal, bamboo, and sea grass are among the most common.

The stores listed here were evaluated based on the percentage of furniture, flooring, carpeting, and/or décor sold that are sustainably manufactured; sustainably manufactured and locally or domestically produced; made with renewable, natural, or recycled materials; and contains nontoxic or low-toxic materials such as no- or low-VOC finishes, adhesives, and veneers—or some combination of these four attributes.

> at least 25% of the products meet the above criteria.
> at least 50% of the products meet the above criteria.
> at least 75% of the products meet the above criteria.
> at least 90% of the products meet the above criteria.

ABC Carpet & Home 🌿🌿🌿🌿

888 Broadway (E. 19th St.), Union Square (Man), 212-473-3000
Mon–Fri 10am–8pm Sat 10am–7pm Sun 11am–6:30pm **abchome.com**
Over 500 pieces of "Goodwood furniture" made from sustainable wood
sources; fully organic upholstery collection made from FSC-certified wood;
vintage and antique furniture. Home décor items made by local artisans;
handmade vegetable-dyed rugs and recycled, chemical-free broadloom. One
of the only places in NYC that carries LED light bulbs.

Aronson's 🌿🌿

135 W. 17th St. (bet. 6th & 7th Aves.), Chelsea (Man), 212-243-4993
Mon–Fri 9am–6pm **aronsonsfloors.com**
Sustainable cork and bamboo flooring; carpet made from natural fibers.
Hosts AIA-accredited continuing education lunchtime lectures in its show-
room, open to the public.

Aswoon 🌿🌿🌿

14 Jay St. (John St.), DUMBO (Bkn), 718-858-7006
Thu–Sat 12pm–6pm **aswoon.com**
Seating, tables, lighting, and partitions crafted with reclaimed materials.
Custom designs available.

Bazaar de La Paz 🌿🌿🌿

2662 Broadway (bet. 101st & 102nd Sts.), Upper West Side (Man),
212-662-6601
Daily 11am–8pm **bazaardelapaz.com**
Furniture handcrafted from salvaged Indonesian hardwoods and décor made
from recycled, salvaged, and sustainable materials. Member of the Fair
Trade Federation and Co-Op America.

Brave Space Design 🌿🌿🌿🌿

449 Troutman St., Studio 2A (St. Nicholas Ave.), Bushwick (Bkn),
646-831-2470
By appt. **bravespacedesign.com**
Modular and multifunctional furniture and décor made from sustainably
harvested materials.

Brooklyn Farm Table 🌿🌿🌿🌿

284 Van Brunt St. (Verona St.), Red Hook (Bkn), 917-806-6383
By appt. **brooklynfarmtable.com**
Handcrafted tables and other pieces made to order from wood found at
demolition sites in Brooklyn and other boroughs. Tung oil finished.

Carini Lang 🌿🌿🌿

335 Greenwich St. (bet. Jay & Duane Sts.), Tribeca (Man), 646-613-0497
Mon–Fri 10am–6pm **carinilang.com**
Sustainable and ecologically produced hand-woven carpets and tapestries
made with natural materials and fair trade practices.

City Joinery 🌿🌿🌿🌿

20 Jay St., Ste. 218 (Plymouth St.), DUMBO (Bkn), 718-596-6502
By appt. **cityjoinery.com**
Contemporary wood furniture made from carefully sourced domestic hardwoods. Sawdust is composted and wood scrap is burned in high-efficiency
stove for home heating.

Daniel Moyer Design & Fabrication 🍃🍃🍃🍃

221 McKibben St., GMDC #16 (bet. Bushwick Ave. & White St.),
Bushwick (Bkn), 917-301-2551
By appt. **danielmoyerdesign.com**
Furniture made exclusively of solid wood from local, small-scale, sustainable-hardwood sawyers using ancient techniques. Also designs Funkinfunction handmade skateboards and longboards made from repurposed hardwood scrap material.

EcoSystems 🍃🍃🍃🍃

140 Jackson St., Studio 3B (Graham Ave.), Williamsburg (Bkn), 718-383-6404
By appt. **ecosystemsbrand.com**
Furniture made from renewable resources, manufactured domestically, and packaged to reduce waste. Offers furniture pickup from original owner to repurpose or recycle used items.

Elucidesign 🍃🍃🍃

490 Humboldt St. (Richardson St.), Williamsburg (Bkn), 646-415-2336
By appt. **elucidesign.com**
Nontoxic, sustainable heirloom-quality furniture.

Environment Furniture 🍃🍃

876 Broadway (bet. 18th & 19th Sts.), Union Square (Man), 212-780-0051
Mon–Sat 10am–7pm Sun 11am–6pm **environment-furniture.com**
Furniture made from reclaimed, recycled, and sustainably harvested wood.

Eric Manigian Studio 🍃🍃🍃

61 Pearl St., Ste. 618 (Water St.), DUMBO (Bkn), 718-855-9097
By appt. **ericmanigian.com**
Furniture handmade from salvaged wood with oil finishes.

Fabrica 🍃

619 Vanderbilt Ave. (St. Marks Ave.), Prospect Heights (Bkn), 718-398-3831
Thu–Sun 12pm–6pm **fabricadesigns.com**
Reupholstered vintage furniture and other eco-friendly home décor.

Fire & Water 🍃🍃🍃

241 Eldridge St., Ste. 3R (Stanton St.), Lower East Side (Man), 212-475-3106
By appt. **cyberg.com/fw/fw.htm**
Sustainable lighting made with natural and recycled materials. All pieces are made from energy-efficient, recyclable, and reusable materials.

Future Perfect, The 🍃

115 N. 6th St. (Berry St.), Williamsburg (Bkn), 718-599-6278
Daily 12pm–7pm **thefutureperfect.com**
Furniture and décor items made from sustainable and reclaimed materials.

Green Depot 🍃🍃🍃🍃

20 Rewe St. (Vandervoort Ave.), Williamsburg (Bkn), 718-782-2991
Mon–Fri 7am–6pm Sat 7am–1pm **greendepot.com**
Sustainable bamboo, cork, marmoleum, and FSC certified wood flooring. Variety of organic and sustainable carpet options. Green cabinetry, surfaces, and countertops.

Hudson Furniture 🍃🍃🍃

433 W. 14th St., Ste. 2F, 2nd Flr. (Washington St.), West Village (Man),
212-645-7800
Mon–Fri 9am–6pm Sat 11am–5pm **hudsonfurnitureinc.com**
Furniture made from sustainably harvested or reclaimed wood with natural oil and wax finishes. Custom designs.

King's Road Home 🍃🍃

42 Wooster St. (bet. Broome & Grand Sts.), SoHo (Man), 212-941-5011
Mon–Sat 11am–7pm Sun 12pm–6pm **kingsroadhome.com**
Furniture fashioned from either reclaimed or FSC-certified woods.

Moon River Chattel 🍃🍃🍃

62 Grand St. (bet. Kent & Wythe Aves.), Williamsburg (Bkn), 718-388-1121
Tue–Sat 12pm–7pm Sun 12pm–5pm **moonriverchattel.com**
Home and design store carrying products made from sustainable and
organic materials including remilled flooring, lighting and plumbing fixtures,
and antique furniture.

Nicholas Furrow Design 🍃🍃

638 Leonard St. (bet. Norman & Meserole Aves.), Greenpoint (Bkn),
718-389-3147
By appt. **nicholasfurrow.net**
Custom lighting fixtures and lamps made from recycled and salvaged
materials.

NY Loft 🍃🍃

6 W. 20th St. (5th Ave.), Flatiron (Man), 212-206-7400
Mon–Fri 10am–7pm Sat 12pm–6pm **nyloft.net**
Environmentally sensitive and ergonomic contemporary furnishings. Recycled materials used where possible. Committed to sustainability through
entire design process, from product design to packaging.

Q Collection 🍃🍃🍃

915 Broadway, Ste. 1001 (E. 20th St.), Flatiron (Man), 212-529-1400
qcollection.com
Home furnishings for the whole family made with FSC-certified wood;
organic cotton batting; fabrics and textiles made with 100% biodegradable
and rapidly renewable materials.

Scott Jordan Furniture 🍃🍃🍃🍃

137 Varick St. (Spring St.), SoHo (Man), 212-620-4682
Mon–Wed 10am–6pm Thu 10am–8pm Fri–Sat 10am–6pm Sun 12pm–5pm
scottjordan.com
Solid wood furniture made in the United States from sustainably harvested
wood finished with plant oils and waxes. Chemical-free mattresses.

Shimna 🍃🍃🍃

325 Lafayette St. (bet. Bleecker & Houston Sts.), NoHo (Man), 212-529-6616
Mon–Sat 11am–7pm Sun 12pm–6pm **shimna.net**
Traditional woodworking methods using wood sustainably harvested
in Pennsylvania. Uses water-based finishes as often as possible; offers
100% natural fabrics and lead-free dyes.

Siberian Furniture 🍃🍃🍃

401 Greenwich St. (bet. Beech & Hubert Sts.), Tribeca (Man), 212-343-1514
By appt. **siberianliving.com**
Furniture made from sustainably harvested materials using traditional
woodworking techniques and chemical-free finishes.

TerraMai 🍃🍃🍃

217 Grand St., Ste. 803 (Elizabeth St.), Little Italy (Man), 800-220-9062
Mon–Fri 9am–5pm **terramai.com**
Provides FSC-certified reclaimed wood products such as flooring, siding,
paneling, decking, beams, lumber, and rare and unusual pieces for commercial and residential projects. Assist projects in earning LEED credits.

Two Jakes 🍃🍃

320 Wythe Ave. (bet. Grand & S. 1st Sts.), Williamsburg (Bkn), 718-782-7780
Tue–Sun 11am–6:30pm **twojakes.com**
Some sustainable lines of home and office furniture.

Uhuru 🍃🍃🍃🍃

160 Van Brunt St., 3rd Floor (Hamilton Ave.), Red Hook (Bkn), 718-855-6519
By appt. **uhurudesign.com**
Designs and builds furniture using reclaimed, recycled, repurposed, and
reused materials.

Vivavi 🍃🍃🍃🍃

644 Manhattan Ave., 2nd Flr. (Bedford Ave.), Greenpoint (Bkn), 866-848-2840
Mon–Wed 11am–4pm Thu 11am–9pm Sat 10am–6pm **vivavi.com**
Design center and showroom featuring eco-friendly, modern-style furniture
and furnishings by a variety of designers. Showroom and headquarters are
powered by 100% wind energy. Member of the 1% for the Planet.

Nurseries and Garden Supplies

When doing your gardening and yard work, check out the nurseries that offer organic, **VeriFlora® Certified Sustainably Grown,** and **Circle of Life-certified** options. Choose organic plants, seeds and starts, soil, potting mixes, fertilizers, and pest control products. Look for small, local retailers that tend to buy and sell plants from small, local growers.

Growers who meet specific standards may qualify for organic certification. In addition, both the VeriFlora® and Circle of Life programs address sustainability within the nursery industry. Growers that demonstrate sustainable practices that can then be documented are eligible for certification. Such practices include **integrated pest management (IPM)**, water conservation measures, habitat preservation, reduced use of plastics, and fair labor practices.

To determine which nurseries and garden centers to include in the guide, we checked into the percentage of plants sold that were grown organically and that were native to the region. In addition, we asked whether the plant starts and the planting mixes sold were organic. We also checked into the availability of nontoxic pest management solutions and eco-friendly packaging and materials—that is, biodegradable, compostable, and recycled-content options.

🍃 at least 25% of the products meet the above criteria.

🍃🍃 at least 50% of the products meet the above criteria.

🍃🍃🍃 at least 75% of the products meet the above criteria.

🍃🍃🍃🍃 at least 90% of the products meet the above criteria.

Dimitri's Garden Center 🍃

143 E. 103rd St. (Lexington Ave.), E. Harlem (Man), 212-831-4048
2413 3rd Ave. (bet. Bruckner & E. 134th St.), Mott Haven (Brx), 212-876-3996
Seasonal hours **dimitrisgardencenter.com**
Organic soils, compost, herbs, native plants, and chemical-free pest
control solutions.

Garden World 🍃

197-23 47th Ave. (Francis Lewis Blvd.), Flushing (Qns), 718-224-6789
Seasonal hours. **igardenworld.com**
Garden supply and nursery carrying some organic native plants, starts, and
soils; organic pest control; wide variety of other garden supplies and accessories. Delivery available.

Hydroponic Garden Center 🍃🍃🍃

146-49 Horace Harding Blvd. (Main St.), Flushing (Qns), 718-762-8880
Mon–Fri 10am–7pm Sat–Sun 10am–5pm **growny.com**
Hydroponic and air-growing organic garden supplies and information on
nontoxic pest control methods.

Sprout Home 🍃🍃🍃

44 Grand St. (bet. Kent & Wythe Aves.), Williamsburg (Bkn), 718-388-4440
Daily 11am–7pm **sprouthome.com**
Fresh-cut flowers grown locally without pesticides; plants, gardening
supplies, and eco-friendly home decor.

Wiesner Bros. Nursery Inc. 🍃

2402 Victory Blvd. (bet. Collfield & Crystal Aves.), Willowbrook (S.I.),
718-761-5141
Seasonal hours. **wiesnerbros.com**
Nursery and landscape design company offering organic soils, nontoxic pest
control solutions, and native plants.

Green Tip

Use organic seeds, starts, and
fertilizers in your vegetable and
herb garden.

Green Tip

Choose organic flowers to avoid contact with harmful
chemicals. More than 60 percent of the fresh-cut
flowers sold in the United States are imported from
countries whose environmental standards are less
stringent than our own. Flowers grown in some Latin
American countries, for instance, are treated with
pesticides and other chemicals that are banned in
the States.

Recycling Centers and Services

"Reduce, reuse, recycle" is still the most logical and powerful protocol for material use. Tossing goods into the recycling bin should be what we do *after* reducing our consumption and reusing existing materials.

Recycling is the law in New York City—residents, schools, institutions, and all commercial businesses must recycle. But when it comes time to recycle something, there are many avenues from which to choose. You can bring your recyclables to city-operated lots or to a variety of privately owned recycling centers. There are also recycling services that come to you, either by directly picking up your recyclables curbside or by providing boxes or envelopes for mailing in such things as toner cartridges, cell phones, and other small electronics. Follow their directions for sorting, sending, and/or setting out materials for pickup.

Gently used pet accessories can be recycled, as can baby goods. Unwanted bikes are particularly desirable, and there are several organizations that reuse them. Plastic bags can be recycled, so they shouldn't be thrown in the trash. And all those outdated consumer electronics that are piling up in the garage—recycle them!

The New York City Department of Sanitation's recycling and collection operation consists of several programs: curbside collection, containerized collection, school- night truck collections, bulk metal recycling, tire disposal, special waste sites, leaf and Christmas tree collection, and chlorofluorocarbon (CFC) evacuation. The city also operates a special NYC Compost Project, which composts the city's organic waste and offers compost education in partnership with the city's botanical gardens.

The recycling centers and services below are listed here as resources. Some offer curbside pickup of a variety of items; others are drop-off locations. Because there is no objective means of awarding leaves in this category, we have not done so.

AAA Polymer
68 Freeman St. (Franklin St.), Greenpoint (Bkn), 718-389-2498
Mon–Fri 8am–3pm
Polyethylene recycler; takes plastic bags, dry cleaning bags, and #2 and #4 plastics. Materials must be clean, with no receipts or staples.

Baby Buggy
306 W. 37th St., 8th Flr. (bet. 8th & 9th Aves.), Clinton (Man), 212-736-1777
By appt. **babybuggy.org**
Nonprofit organization providing families in need with equipment, clothing, and other products for infants and young children. Accepts donations of gently used items.

Bronx Compost Project

Bronx River Pkwy., NY Botanical Garden (Fordham Rd.), Bedford Park (Brx), 718-817-8543
Seasonal hours **nyccompost.org**
Part of the New York City Compost Project. Provides workshops on indoor and outdoor composting, drop-off locations, and discount compost bins for residents and businesses.

Brooklyn Compost Project

1000 Washington Ave., Brooklyn Botanic Garden (Crown St.), Prospect Heights (Bkn), 718-623-7290
Seasonal hours **nyccompost.org**
Part of the New York City Compost Project. Provides workshops on indoor and outdoor composting, drop-off locations, and discount compost bins for residents and businesses.

Build It Green! NYC

3-17 26th Ave. (4th St.), Astoria (Qns), 718-777-0132
Tue–Fri 10am–6pm Sat 10am–5pm **bignyc.org**
Accepts drop-offs of working and nonworking consumer electronics and building materials from New York City residents only. See website for list of accepted items.

Council on the Environment of New York City (CENYC)

51 Chambers St., Rm. 228 (bet. Broadway & Centre St.), Civic Center (Man), 212-788-7900
Mon–Fri 9am–5pm **cenyc.org**
Recycling office educates residents and building superintendents about waste prevention, recycling, and composting practices. Drop-offs and no fees. Clothing is collected weekly at Greenmarket locations on "Material Monday."

Freecycle
freecycle.org
Online local network providing individuals and nonprofits with an electronic forum to recycle unwanted items. No trades or fees, only free goods. Separated by borough.

Manhattan Compost Project

E. 7th St., Lower East Side Ecology Center Garden (bet. Aves. B & C), Lower East Side (Man), 212-477-3155
Sun 8am–6pm **nyccompost.org**
Part of the New York City Compost Project. Provides workshops on indoor and outdoor composting, drop-off locations, and discount compost bins for residents and businesses.

Neighborrow.com
neighborrow.com
Online community that facilitates local borrowing.

New York City Compost Project

346 Broadway, 10th Flr., Dept. of Sanitation (Leonard St.),
Civic Center (Man)
nyccompost.org
Main office of the New York City Compost Project, which administers the program in all five boroughs. Created in 1993 to provide compost outreach and education to residents and businesses. Each location listed here hosts a home composting demonstration site and a composting helpline, and offers a variety of compost-related workshops and classes open to the public.

NY WasteMatch

212-650-5832
wastematch.org
Free online waste brokering service helping New York businesses and residents exchange surplus and unwanted goods.

Per Scholas

1575 Bronx River Ave. (Noble Ave.), West Farms (Brx), 718-991-8400
Mon–Fri 9am–4pm **perscholas.org**
Nonprofit organization offering recycled and refurbished corporate computers to low-income children and families at low prices. Trains residents to become computer technicians.

Queens Compost Project

43-50 Main St., Queens Botanical Garden (Dahlia Ave.), Flushing (Qns), 718-539-5296
Seasonal hours **nyccompost.org**
Part of the New York City Compost Project. Provides workshops on indoor and outdoor composting, drop-off locations, and discount compost bins for residents and businesses.

Recycle-A-Bicycle

35 Pearl St. (Plymouth St.), DUMBO (Bkn), 718-858-2972
75 Ave. C (bet. 5th & 6th Sts.), East Village (Man), 212-475-1655
Mon–Sat 12pm–7pm **recycleabicycle.org**
Nonprofit environmental education and job training program for New York City youth. Repairs donated bikes and offers them to residents via earn-a-bike school programs and nonprofit retail locations.

Staten Island Compost Project

1000 Richmond Terrace, Staten Island Botanical Garden (Delafield Pl.), Randall Manor (S.I.), 718-362-1010
Seasonal hours. **nyccompost.org**
Part of the New York City Compost Project. Provides workshops on indoor and outdoor composting, drop-off locations, and discount compost bins for residents and businesses.

Wearable Collections

646-515-4387
wearablecollections.com
Clothing recycling service providing free bins and pickup service to buildings in Manhattan. Distributes discarded clothing around the world and donates proceeds to charitable organizations.

Green Tip

At home, pack your leftovers in reusable glass containers instead of disposable plastic bags or containers, which are made from ever-more-limited petroleum. Recycling helps a little but only a fraction actually gets recycled. Additionally, items that are used once then discarded will sit in land fills or blow into our waterways and cause harm.

Special Waste Disposal

The New York Department of Sanitation operates Self Help Special Waste Drop-Off Sites in every borough for the collection and recycling (or proper disposal) of a variety of hazardous materials. These programs provide safe disposal options, but the best way to keep the planet healthy is to reduce your use of toxic materials in the first place.

New York City residents may bring the following materials to the NYC Department of Sanitation Special Waste Drop-Off Sites listed below:

- all household batteries
- automotive batteries
- fluorescent and other mercury-containing lightbulbs and lamps
- mercury thermometers and thermostats
- motor oil
- paint
- tires

NYC residents can discard computers and other electronics (E-waste) that are broken or no longer wanted in the trash, but recycling these items keeps hazardous material out of the waste stream and the environment. Various manufacturers, retailers, community groups, as well as the Department of Sanitation have electronics recycling programs.

New York City Department of Sanitation Special Waste Drop-Off Sites
Bay 41st St. & Gravesend Bay (S. of Belt Pkwy.), Bensonhurst (Bkn),
605 W. 30th St. (11th Ave.), Chelsea (Man),
College Point at 30th Ave. (bet. 120th & 122nd Sts.), Flushing/College Point (Qns),
Hunts Point at Farragut St. (East River), Hunts Point (Brx),
Muldoon Ave. (West Shore Expy./NY 440), Travis (S.I.),
Last Friday of every month and every Saturday, except for last Saturday of month 10am–5pm
nyc.gov/html/nycwasteless/html/at_home/special_waste.shtml
Drop-off sites for special waste, including car batteries, household batteries, motor oil, transmission fluid, fluorescent bulbs and tubes, latex paint, mercury thermometers and thermostats, and passenger car tires.

Plastics—Know Your Numbers

The plastics industry has developed a series of markers, usually seen on the bottom of plastic containers. **Despite the confusing use of the chasing arrow symbol, these markers do NOT mean the plastic can be recycled, nor do they mean the container uses recycled plastic.** The following markers **only identify the plastic type:**

- 1—Polyethylene Terephthalate (PET or PETE)

- 2—High-Density Polyethylene (HDPE)

- 3—Polyvinyl Chloride or Vinyl (PVC or V)

- 4—Low-Density Polyethylene (LDPE)

- 5—Polypropylene (PP)

- 6—Polystyrene (PS)

- 7—Other (Polycarbonate)

Although almost everything made of plastic is marked with a recycling code, not all types can actually be recycled. Just remember:

- **Types 1** and **2** are widely accepted in container form.

- **Type 4** is sometimes accepted in bag form.

- **Types 6** and **7** (polystyrene and mixed or layered plastic, such as packaging pellets, meat trays, to-go clam-shell containers, and Nalgene bottles) have **virtually no recycling potential, and are harmful to your health and the environment.**

You should place in your bin or clear bag only those types of plastic authorized by the New York City Department of Sanitation (see pages 192-193). Besides their often limited recycling capability, there are many other reasons to limit your use of plastic. Its production poses serious health threats to the environment and humans. It breaks down but does not biodegrade, so is therefore nearly impossible to completely dispose of and very little actually gets reused. Certain types of plastic are particularly harmful: #3 (PVC or V), #5 (PP), #6 (PS), and #7 (Other). These types should be avoided. Look for alternatives and ways to reduce plastic usage overall.

Reduce, Reuse, Recycle

Recycling is critical to reducing the quantity of waste that is sent to landfills and incinerators. But waste *prevention* is what matters most—actually eliminating or reducing the quantity of trash or recyclables. Here are several ways you can help reduce your impact on the environment and save some of your own green:

Reduce Your Impact—It's Easy

- Use cloth bags or boxes for lunches instead of paper bags.
- Use washable cloth towels and napkins instead of paper towels and paper napkins.
- Stash reusable bags in your car, bike, or purse to take along when shopping.
- Use an erasable note board instead of paper notes.
- Buy products that come without boxes or excess packaging.
- Buy refillable or bulk products to reduce packaging and waste.
- Send holiday greetings electronically over the internet.
- Take advantage of public and school libraries.

Reuse or Repurpose Ordinary "Trash" Items

- Reuse large and/or padded envelopes and boxes for mailings.
- Reuse paper that has been printed on one side as scratch paper.
- Give others a chance to use or repurpose the items you no longer need. Check out **New York Stuff Exchange (nyc.gov/nycstuffexchange)** for places in your neighborhood and throughout the city where you can donate, sell, buy, rent, or repair different types of gently used goods.

Recycle What You Do Use

- Recycling is required in New York City for all residents. See "Recycling Requirements for NYC" on page 192 for information on recycling paper, plastic, glass, and other materials.

For more information on ways you can reduce, reuse, and recycle, visit **greenopia.com** or check out the NYC Department of Sanitation, Bureau of Waste Prevention, Reuse and Recycling's **NYCWasteLe$$** program at **nyc.gov/nycwasteless**.

Recycling Requirements in NYC

Recycling is the law in New York City. The requirements listed below apply to all New York City residences serviced by the Department of Sanitation and give you an easy reference to follow for what and how to recycle. If you're not serviced by NYC's Department of Sanitation, you can also log on to **earth911.org,** type in your zip code, and get all the local recycling information you need.

Paper and Cardboard

Place these items in recycling:

- white, colored, and glossy paper (staples okay)
- mail and envelopes (window envelopes okay)
- wrapping paper (remove ribbon and tape)
- smooth cardboard (remove inside/outside plastic wrappers)
- paper bags
- cardboard egg cartons and trays
- newspapers, magazines, and catalogs
- phone books, softcover books, etc. (no spiral bindings)
- corrugated cardboard (flattened boxes)

Place all paper items together in CLEAR bags, or in any bin labeled with GREEN recycling decals or marked "MIXED PAPER."

Flatten and bundle large pieces of corrugated cardboard and tie with sturdy twine, or break into small pieces to place in your recycling bin or bag.

Place these items in the trash:

- hardcover books
- napkins, paper towels, or tissues
- soiled paper cups or plates
- paper soiled with food or liquid
- paper with a lot of tape and glue
- plastic- or wax-coated paper (candy wrappers, take-out containers, etc.)
- photographic paper

Beverage Cartons, Bottles, Cans, Metal, and Foil

Place these items in recycling:

- metal cans (canned food, empty aerosol cans, dried-out paint cans, etc.)
- aluminum foil wrap and trays
- household metal (wire hangers, pots, tools, curtain rods, knives wrapped in cardboard and labeled)
- small appliances that are mostly metal, etc.
- bulk metal (metal furniture, cabinets, large appliances, etc.)
- glass bottles and jars only
- plastic bottles and jugs only

Place these items in the trash:

- any plastic items other than plastic bottles and jugs (such as deli and yogurt containers; plastic toys, cups, bags, wrap, etc.—if it's not a bottle or jug, DON'T put it in the recycling bin)
- any glass items other than glass bottles and jars (mirrors, light bulbs, ceramics, glassware, etc.)
- Styrofoam (cups, egg cartons, trays, etc.)
- batteries
- milk cartons and juice boxes (or any such cartons and aseptic packaging for drinks: ice tea, soy milk, soup, etc.)

Empty and rinse containers before recycling. Place all together in CLEAR bags, or in any bin labeled with BLUE recycling decals or marked "BOTTLES AND CANS."

REMOVE CAPS AND LIDS. Place METAL caps and lids in the recycling bin; put plastic caps and lids in the garbage.

Bulky Items

Up to six bulk items that are not reusable or recyclable (old mattresses, broken televisions, damaged sofas, etc.) can be placed at the curb on regular garbage collection days (except during weeks with a holiday or snow days).

General Information

Although the Department of Sanitation does not provide recycling or garbage bins or bags, any container can be used for recycling as long as the bag is clear and the bin is properly labeled. Use Department of Sanitation decals or mark with a permanent pen in letters at least 4 inches high. Decals are available from the city's Department of Sanitation, Bureau of Waste Management, Recycling and Reuse website (**nyc.gov/nycwasteless**) or by calling NYC Citizen Service at 311.

(Source: **nyc.gov/sanitation and nyc.gov/nycwasteless**)

Services

Greening Your Thinking

By Deirdre Imus

As a parent and children's health advocate, I believe there's nothing more important than protecting our children. That's why I have devoted my life's work to help give our children the healthy environment they deserve. If we take care of our children, we take care of ourselves, and the planet.

The Deirdre Imus Environmental Center for Pediatric Oncology at Hackensack University Medical Center, a 501(c)(3) not-for-profit corporation, represents one of the first hospital-based programs whose specific mission is to identify, control, and ultimately prevent exposures to environmental factors that may cause adult and, especially pediatric cancer, as well as other health problems with our children.

I am constantly striving to live the healthiest lifestyle possible, with a profound appreciation for how the environment, the food we eat, the air we breathe, and the products we use every day, impact our health and of course, the health of our children.

Living more healthfully, however, is not a magic bullet, but it does improve your quality of life. Healthy changes don't need to be drastic. Don't get overwhelmed thinking about "greening." Start with just one thing, whether it's getting rid of your toxic cleaning chemicals and replacing them with safe and healthy ones, or choosing a food that you or your family enjoys. For example, eating an organic apple is not just good for you, it eliminates synthetic fertilizers and pesticides from the environment. And when you buy organic, you help create a market for green products.

As our most precious resource, children deserve a clean, green, and safe environment.

Deirdre Imus, president and founder of the Deirdre Imus Environmental Center for Pediatric Oncology at Hackensack University Medical Center (**dienviro. com**); cofounder and codirector of Imus Cattle Ranch for Kids with Cancer (**imusranchfoods.com**); and author of several books, including *Green This! Volume One: Greening Your Cleaning and Growing Up Green!*

Dry and Wet Cleaners

Conventional "dry" cleaning actually involves washing clothes in a liquid chemical solvent to remove stains. In about 85 percent of dry cleaning businesses, this solvent is perchloroethylene (or perc). Perc is a dangerous chemical that harms workers, brings toxins into the home, and damages the environment. Perc has been identified as a "probable" human carcinogen by the Environmental Protection Agency (EPA).

You may have noticed certain dry cleaning establishments replacing their "perc" machines with new methods. Unfortunately, not all of the alternatives are equally healthy for you and the environment, so here's what we recommend (in order of preference):

1. Best Choice

Before taking your garment to be cleaned, decide if it could be hand washed instead. Many garments can be safely washed at home rather than professionally dry cleaned. Clothing manufacturers often put on the "dry clean only" label to play it safe. Wash these garments by hand or use your washing machine's delicate cycle.

2. Recommended Choices

If you decide the items still need to be cleaned professionally, we recommend either of the following two methods:

Wet Cleaning. This method uses pressurized liquid CO_2 in combination with water as a solvent. It is free of **volatile organic compounds (VOCs)** and poses no health and safety or environmental risks. It saves water and is energy efficient. The washer and dryer are computer-controlled, so cleaning can be tailored to the type of fabric. Sophisticated machines and trained operators ensure wet cleaning quality is equal to that of dry cleaning.

CO_2 Cleaning. This method uses pressurized liquid carbon dioxide in combination with other cleaning agents in a machine emptied of air. The liquid CO_2 can often be reused, and no new CO_2 is generated. Although the liquid CO_2 is recycled and recyclable, thereby keeping its cost low, the price of the machine itself is very high, limiting conversion to this method by existing dry cleaners.

3. Other Options

If neither of the above methods is available in your area, your next best alternative is either of the following two methods. Be advised that we only list these options because they are better than the traditional "perc" method. We still have concerns about their health and environmental effects and strongly recommend that you choose to have your clothes wet cleaned with the businesses we have listed.

Hydrocarbon Dry Cleaning. This method uses a petroleum-based solvent. This solvent is not as toxic as perc but produces significant quantities of greenhouse gases.

Silicone-Based Solvent Dry Cleaning. Cleaners call this the GreenEarth method. It replaces perc with a silicone-based solvent called siloxane, or D-5. In this system, no chemicals mix with the clothing, but the manufacture of this product requires chlorine, which, when manufactured itself, releases dioxin, a potent carcinogen.

Some dry cleaning establishments identify their cleaning methods as "environmentally friendly" or "organic." Unfortunately, this signage may be misleading, since most of these businesses are just switching to hydrocarbon or silicone-based solvents, which, as we've mentioned, have significant health and environmental risks.

We urge you to seek out cleaners from our list or ask your neighborhood cleaners (even if they still use perc) to specifically wet clean your garments. Many cleaners offer this alternative but may not use it unless you request it. In addition, be aware that not all wet cleaners use eco-friendly soaps. Choose only those that use biodegradable, nontoxic, and phosphate-free ones.

If you use a "wash and fold" service, be sure to ask what types of detergents, spot removers, fabric softeners, and dryer sheets are used. Request that they switch to biodegradable alternatives and ones that are free of artificial fragrances. Spot removers should be vegetable-based rather than chemical solvent-based.

Finally, consider how your cleaned clothing is packaged. Ask your cleaner to provide eco-friendly carry-out bags. Look for businesses that offer biodegradable, compostable packaging, and/or bags and boxes with recycled content and, when applicable, vegetable based inks and/or dyes.

Only those cleaners that meet our strict requirement of offering wet cleaning and/or liquid CO_2 cleaning exclusively qualify for a four-leaf award. Those that offer hydrocarbon/silicone-based solvent cleaning in addition to wet or liquid CO_2 cleaning qualify for a one-leaf award.

Wet and/or CO₂ Cleaners (Exclusively)

We recommend using any of the following wet and/or CO_2 cleaners before using a chemical method. Remember to ask what types of soaps they use.

Bob's Dry Cleaners

1338 Bushwick Ave. (Schaefer St.), Bushwick (Bkn), 718-455-6582
Mon–Sat 7am–7pm
Neighborhood cleaner offering dedicated wet cleaning service.

Eddie Dry Cleaner

103A Marcus Garvey Blvd. (Vernon Ave.), Bedford-Stuyvesant (Bkn),
718-574-4984
Mon–Sat 7am–7pm
Offers dedicated wet cleaning.

Green Apple Cleaners

92 Greenwich Ave. (W. 13th St.), West Village (Man), 212-206-6236
Mon–Fri 7:30am–7:30pm Sat 8:30am–5:30pm **greenapplecleaners.com**
Dedicated CO_2 cleaner. Also offers hypoallergenic wash-and-fold service, onsite environmental drape and carpet cleaning service, pickup and delivery. Reusable garment bags.

Wet or CO₂ and Hydrocarbon/Silicone-Based Solvent Cleaners

If none of the above establishments are convenient for you, have your garments wet cleaned at the following locations, which also offer hydrocarbon/silicone-based solvent methods. Remember to ask what types of soaps are used. We have not listed cleaners that provide only the hydrocarbon and/or silicone-based solvent methods because of the health hazards related to these alternatives.

B.C. Cleaners

30 E. 13th St. (bet. 5th Ave. & University Pl.), Union Square (Man),
212-727-7239
Mon–Fri 7am–7pm Sat 7am–6pm
Wet and hydrocarbon cleaning offered.

Bridgestone Cleaners

175 Court St. (bet. Bergen & Dean Sts.), Cobble Hill (Bkn), 718-643-9300
109 Front St. (bet. Washington & Adams Sts.), DUMBO (Bkn), 718-222-9958
Hours vary by location **bridgestonecleaners.com**
Dry cleaner offering wet cleaning and hydrocarbon cleaning services.

Divine Touch Organic Cleaners

41 W. 58th St. (bet. 5th & 6th Ave.), Midtown (Man), 212-980-5744
Mon–Fri 7:30am–7pm Sat 8am–6pm **organiccleanersny.com**
Hydrocarbon and wet cleaning services, providing pickup and delivery in Manhattan from 86th St. to SoHo.

Drop Spot Cleaners & Tailors

230 W. 76th St. (Broadway), Upper West Side (Man), 212-721-2480
Mon–Fri 7am–7pm Sat 8am–6pm
Hydrocarbon and wet cleaning using biodegradable cleaners, with work done on premises.

Eroika Cleaners & Tailors 🌢
205 E. 26th St. (3rd Ave.), Gramercy Park (Man), 212-213-5520
Mon–Fri 7:30am–7pm Sat 8am–5:30pm
Hydrocarbon cleaners; also provides wet cleaning services.

Fashion Town Cleaners 🌢
181 Thompson St. (bet. Bleecker & Houston Sts.), Greenwich Village (Man), 212-505-0733
Mon–Fri 7:30am–7pm Sat 8am–6:30pm
Wet and hydrocarbon dry cleaning services.

Green Cleaners 🌢
155 Nassau Ave. (bet. Newell & Diamond Sts.), Greenpoint (Bkn), 718-349-1358
445 Forest Ave. (Metropolitan Ave.), West Brighton (S.I.), 718-442-6306
Mon–Fri 7am–7pm Sat 8am–6pm
Wet and hydrocarbon cleaning.

J&J Cleaners 🌢
2306 Adam Clayton Powell Blvd. (135th St.), Central Harlem (Man), 212-862-7139
Mon 6:30am–7pm Tue–Fri 7am–6:45pm Sat 8am–6pm
Neighborhood cleaners providing hydrocarbon and wet cleaning services; tailoring.

Jo Quality Cleaners 🌢
48 7th Ave. (13th St.), Union Square (Man), 212-627-7999
Mon–Fri 7am–7pm Sat 8am–6pm
Hydrocarbon and wet cleaning services.

KB Dry Cleaners 🌢
215-05 Northern Blvd. (Bell Blvd.), Bayside (Qns), 718-224-4099
Mon–Fri 7am–7pm Sat 8am–6pm
Wet and hydrocarbon cleaning services.

Kleenofab 🌢
2103 Williamsbridge Rd. (Lydig Ave.), Pelham (Brx), 718-828-1120
Tue–Fri 7am–7pm Sat 7am–6pm
Wet cleaning and hydrocarbon dry cleaning services. Specializes in alterations and drape and gown cleaning by hand.

L&M Cleaners 🌢
105C Greene Ave. (Broadway), Bedford-Stuyvesant (Bkn), 718-453-3256
Mon–Sat 7:30am–7pm
Wet and hydrocarbon cleaning.

La Mode Dry Cleaners & Alterations 🌢
489 2nd Ave. (bet. 27th & 28th Sts.), Kips Bay (Man), 212-725-3182
Mon–Fri 7am–7pm Sat 8am–6pm
Cleaner specializing in hydrocarbon service. Also provides wet cleaning using vegetable-based spot removers and cleaners.

Lee Cleaners 🌢
187 5th Ave. (bet. Union & Berkeley Sts.), Park Slope (Bkn), 718-789-9735
Mon–Fri 7:30am–7pm Sat 8am–6pm
Wet cleaning and hydrocarbon cleaning options.

Little Day Cleaners 🍃
400 E. 64th St. (bet. 1st & York Aves.), Upper East Side (Man), 212-317-9683
Mon–Fri 7am–7pm Sat 8am–5pm
Hydrocarbon dry cleaning and traditional wet cleaning services.

Natural Cleaners 🍃
850 Manhattan Ave. (bet. Milton & Noble Sts.), Greenpoint (Bkn),
718-383-3505
Mon–Fri 7:30am–7pm Sat 8am–6:30pm
Wet cleaning using environmentally safe soaps. Also offers off-site hydrocarbon cleaning. Customers can bring back hangers for reuse.

New Modern French Cleaners 🍃
530 2nd Ave. (bet. 29th & 30th Sts.), Kips Bay (Man), 212-683-0280
Mon–Fri 7am–7pm Sat 8am–6pm
Offers hydrocarbon dry cleaning, wet cleaning, wash-and-fold services.

New York Dry Cleaners 🍃
104 W. 17th St. (6th Ave.), Union Square (Man), 212-243-0433
Mon–Fri 7am–7pm Sat 8am–5pm
Hydrocarbon dry cleaner. Also provides wet cleaning using solvent or vegetable-based cleaners. Pickup and delivery within 10-block radius.

Organic Dry Cleaners 🍃
265 1st Ave. (bet. 15th & 16th Sts.), Stuyvesant Town (Man), 212-475-0852
Mon–Fri 7am–7:30pm Sat 8am–5pm Sun 10am–6pm
Wet and hydrocarbon cleaning options. Pickup and delivery service from 6th St. to 23rd St., from 1st Ave. to Broadway.

Planet Cleaners 🍃
1351 Forest Ave. (Veltman Ave.), Westerleigh (S.I.), 718-447-7715
Mon–Sat 7am–7pm
Wet and hydrocarbon cleaning.

Plaza Cleaners 🍃
82 Montague St. (Hicks St.), Brooklyn Heights (Bkn), 718-522-2428
Mon–Fri 7am–7pm Sat 8am–6pm
Dry cleaner offering wet and hydrocarbon cleaning services.

Quality Cleaners 🍃
3029 Middletown Rd. (Hobart Ave.), Throgs Neck (Brx), 718-822-7300
Mon–Sat 7am–7:30pm
Wet cleaning and hydrocarbon dry cleaning services.

Slate NYC 🍃
96 Morton St. (Washington St.), West Village (Man), 800-573-8459
Mon–Sat 9am–7pm **slatenyc.com**
Wet and hydrocarbon cleaning services. Options for sensitive skin. Pickup service anywhere in New York City.

Spin City 🍃
180 Ave. B (11th St.), East Village (Man), 212-529-8886
Mon–Fri 7am–1am Sat–Sun 8am–1am **spincitycleaners.com**
Hydrocarbon and wet cleaning. Pickup and delivery in downtown Manhattan.

Sunny Cleaner 🌿

2040 Forest Ave. (bet. Union Ave. & Union Pkwy.), Elm Park (S.I.),
718-370-2112
Mon–Fri 7am–7pm Sat 8am–6pm
Wet and hydrocarbon cleaning service.

Turin Cleaners 🌿

609 Columbus Ave. (90th St.), Upper West Side (Man), 212-721-1166
Mon–Fri 7am–7pm Sat 8am–5pm
Neighborhood dry cleaner providing wet and hydrocarbon cleaning.
Provides same-day service and alterations.

Whitepoint Cleaners 🌿

132-07 14th Ave. (132nd St.), College Point (Qns), 718-746-5652
Tue–Fri 6:30am–6:30pm Sat 6:30am–5pm
Hydrocarbon and wet cleaning service. Uses plant-based, biodegradable
spot removers. Tailoring and tuxedo rentals available.

Tips for healthier dry cleaning:

- If you're just after that fresh-pressed look, wash
  your clothing at home and take it to the cleaners
  for ironing.

- If something you have has been dry cleaned
  conventionally, remove it from its bag and hang
  it outdoors for two days to reduce the amount of
  perc vapor you bring into your home.

- No matter which cleaners you choose, try bringing
  your own reusable garment bag to reduce your
  use of plastic, and return your unused hangers for
  recycling or reuse.

Services

WRITE A REVIEW

Tell us about your experiences with dry and wet
cleaners—the quality of the service, the value for the
price, or whether you would shop there again. Write
your review at **greenopia.com**.

Cleaning Services

The products used by housecleaning services are generally not the same as those you might find in a supermarket. They are typically stronger and more concentrated, and potentially more toxic. When hiring a cleaning company for your home or office, ask for the brand names or a list of ingredients in all products they use.

Select companies that use Green Seal™ certified products, or ask for material safety data sheets on the products they use. Workers must be trained in the proper use and application of the products and equipment. You may also want to determine if the service uses vacuum cleaners with HEPA filters and how they dispose of their wastewater.

Because professional cleaning products may be different from those found in stores, and because much depends on the proper use of even nontoxic cleaning materials, it is difficult to establish firm criteria for granting leaf awards. But the companies listed here meet a minimum requirement of using natural, nontoxic, or mostly chemical-free cleaning supplies.

At least 25 percent of the products used regularly by the following cleaning services are natural, nontoxic, and mostly chemical free or are certified by Green Seal™. Note, however, that many of the cleaning services listed below significantly out-performed this threshold requirement.

ABC Rug Cleaners, Inc.
212-938-0277, 718-444-4949
By appt.
abcrugandcarpetcare.com
Eco-safe, nontoxic, biodegradable cleaning products used on rugs, carpets, upholstery, drapery, leather, mildew, mattresses, and floors. Serves Manhattan, Brooklyn, Queens, and Bronx.

Flat Rate Carpet
888-905-7847
Daily 8am–6pm **flatratecarpet.com**
Residential, industrial, and commercial carpet cleaning service using dry, deep, and shampoo cleaning methods. Free home estimate. Emergency service available daily 24 hours. Serves all of New York City.

Go Green, Inc.
485 Atlantic Ave. (bet. 3rd & Nevins Sts.), Boerum Hill (Bkn), 718-625-0260
Tue–Sat 12pm–7pm Sun 11am–6pm **gogreeninc.com**
Environmentally friendly cleaning service. Also sells green building materials and Green Seal–certified cleaning supplies. Co-op America and USGBC member. Serves Brooklyn.

Gonsalves Cleaning and Restoration

800-657-2502

Mon–Sat 7am–7pm **gonsalvestotalcleaning.com**

Environmentally friendly carpet and upholstery cleaning using Envirodesic and Green Seal–certified products. Emergency service available 24 hours. Serves all of New York City.

Green Apple Maids

23-05 A 26th St. (51st Ave.), Long Island City (Qns), 718-626-8750

Daily 24 hrs. **greenapplemaids.com**

Cleaning service for homes and offices: wood and stone flooring, upholstery, carpets, floor stripping and waxing. Free estimates. Serves all of New York City.

Green Clean

130 7th Ave., #305 (18th St.), Chelsea (Man), 888-808-7755

Mon–Sat 8:30am–7pm **greencleannyc.com**

Green home and office cleaning service since 1993. Dry vapor steam cleaning and antiallergen service available. Serves Manhattan, Brooklyn, Queens, and Bronx.

Greenhouse Eco-Cleaning

718-303-7029

Mon–Sat 10am–6pm **greenhouseecocleaning.com**

Home, office, and postconstruction site cleaning with biodegradable, nontoxic products. Green home consulting. Serves Manhattan, Queens, Brooklyn, and Staten Island.

Maid Brigade Manhattan

212-926-9601

Mon–Sat 8:30am–5pm **maidbrigade.com**

Cleaning service using Green Seal–certified products. Vacuums certified through The Carpet and Rug Institute's Green Label program. Green Clean certified. Serves Manhattan.

Maid for You New York

38-02 34th St. (38th Ave.), Long Island City (Qns), 718-433-1499

Daily 24 hrs. **maidforyounewyork.com**

Professional green maid service, carpet cleaning. Free estimates provided. Serves all of New York City.

Maid on Call

153 W. 27th St. (bet. 6th & 7th Aves.), Flatiron (Man), 888-624-3662

Daily 24 hrs. **maidoncall.com**

Service using nontoxic, biodegradable, and environmentally friendly products. Maids on call 24 hrs. Serves all of New York City.

Ms. Green Clean

97 Arden St., Unit 6C (Broadway), Inwood (Man), 212-942-8464

By appt. **msgreenclean.com**

Maid service using nontoxic and aromatherapy products. Serves Manhattan, Bronx, Brooklyn, Queens, and metro area.

Neat Freaks Cleaning Service, Inc.

305 Hancock St. (Tompkins Ave.), Bedford-Stuyvesant (Bkn), 866-404-6328

Mon–Fri 9am–5pm Sat 9am–1pm **neatfreakscleaninginc.com**

Basic surface cleaning for residential and commercial properties, using environmentally friendly cleaning products. Serves Manhattan, Brooklyn, Bronx, and Queens.

Preferred Carpet and Upholstery Cleaning

80-06 155 Ave., #4 (80th St.), Howard Beach (Qns), 718-343-1424
Mon–Fri 8am–9am **preferredcarpetcleaning.com**
Organic and natural carpet, upholstery, floor, and rug cleaning service.
Serves all of New York City.

Pro Carpet Service

725 River Rd., Ste. 32, Edgewater, NY 07020, 201-916-1778
Mon–Fri 8am–9pm Sat 8am–8pm Sun 9am–5pm **procarpetservice.com**
Eco-friendly carpet, floor, window, upholstery, and mattress cleaning.
Offers water damage restoration. Serves Manhattan.

Pure Habitat NYC

917-529-0517
Mon–Fri 9am–6pm Sat 10am–2pm **purehabitatnyc.com**
Eco-friendly cleaning company. Educates clients on reading labels, under-
standing ingredients and standards. Co-op America member. Serves all of
New York City.

Spotless Services Inc.

45 W. 34th St., Ste. 10003 (5th Ave.), Midtown (Man), 212-273-3442
Daily 12pm–7pm **spotlessco.com**
Environmentally friendly cleaning services for homes, apartments, offices,
postconstruction sites. Serves Manhattan, Brooklyn, Bronx, and Queens.

Urban Maid Green

346 E. 15th St., Ste. 7 (1st Ave.), East Village (Man), 917-338-6102
Mon–Fri 9am–6pm Sat 10am–6pm Sun 12pm–6pm **urbanmaidgreen.com**
All-natural, nontoxic apartment and house cleaning company using Green
Seal–certified products. Serves Manhattan, Brooklyn, Queens, and Bronx.

White Glove Professional Cleaning Corp.

1304 67th St. (13th Ave.), Bay Ridge (Bkn), 347-517-4550
Daily 8:30am–5pm **whitegloveprofcleaning.com**
Residential cleaning using recycled paper towels, eco-friendly fleece
cloths, plant- and essential oil–based products. Serves Brooklyn,
Manhattan, and Queens.

Zen Home Cleaning

1123 Broadway, Ste. 700 (25th St.), Flatiron (Man), 212-462-2566
Mon-Fri 9am–5am Sat 10am–4pm **zenhomecleaning.com**
Eco-friendly, nontoxic home cleaning service with a holistic approach.
Consulting services. Serves all of New York City.

did you know?

The EPA has found that the air we breathe in our homes is
six to ten times more polluted than the air outside—and
toxic cleaning solutions bear some of the blame.

Pest Control

Pesticides are toxic and, although often considered effective against pests, can be dangerous for people and pets. Outdoors, sprayed pesticides often drift, dusting nearby gardens and yards. Indoors, pesticides remain in the air, exposing inhabitants to harmful chemicals.

Your first line of attack when it comes to pests is prevention. When that fails, look for pest control services that use nontoxic or least-toxic methods, an approach referred to as **integrated pest management, or IPM**. Despite what you might hear from mainstream providers, alternative, nontoxic pest control can be as effective as traditional methods, if not more so. Be very specific about how you want your home or garden treated.

Because we cannot truly measure the efficacy of the various alternative pest control methods, we have chosen not to assign leaf awards to these businesses. They do, however, meet our minimum requirement of promoting and using IPM techniques and offering or using nontoxic or less-toxic alternatives to traditional pest control practices to at least 25 percent of their customer base.

Alternative Pest Control, LLC

479 72nd St. (bet. 4th & 5th Aves.), Bay Ridge (Bkn), 718-444-1784
Mon–Sat 8am–6pm
Professional pest control services using nontoxic baits and IPM methods. Serves New York City metro area.

Condor Pest Control

91-08 Rockaway Beach Blvd. (Beach 91st St.), Far Rockaway (Qns), 800-734-7378
381 Gansevoort Blvd. (Vermont Ct.), Willowbrook (S.I.), 800-734-7378
Mon–Sat 10am–5pm   **condorpestcontrol.com**
Safe and discreet roach, rat, spider, termite, and insect control and extermination through IPM. Serves all five boroughs.

Ecology Exterminating

3908 Fort Hamilton Pkwy. (39th St.), Kensington (Bkn), 877-762-2437
By appt.   **ecologyexterminating.com**
IPM and plant-based, nontoxic products for extermination of bedbugs, rodents, fleas, ticks, termites, and other crawling insects. Serves all of New York City area.

Eden Environmental, Inc.

7 E. 8th St., Box 389 (5th Ave.), East Village (Man), 212-755-1480
Mon–Fri 9am–5pm   **eden-environmental.com**
Environmentally responsible pest management company using low-toxic control methods. Serves all five boroughs.

JP McHale Pest Management, Inc.

241 Bleakley Ave., Buchanan, NY 10511, 800-479-2284
By appt. **nopests.com**
Environmentally responsible IPM methods used for mosquitoes, ticks,
rodents, and other pests. Serves all five boroughs.

Magic Exterminating

59-01 Kissena Blvd. (59th Ave.), Flushing (Qns), 212-431-5009
By appt. **magicexterminating.com**
Full-service pest control and extermination company. Green Shield certified.
Serves all five boroughs.

Metro Pest Control

70-09 73rd Pl. (Edsall Ave.), Glendale (Qns), 888-770-5354
Mon–Fri 8am–5pm Sat 8am–4pm **metropestcontrol.com**
Conventional pest control with option to use less-toxic botanical pesticides
(upon request).

Pest Away Exterminating Inc.

2067 Broadway, Ste. 68 (W. 71st St.), Lincoln Center (Man), 212-721-2521
Mon–Fri 8am–6pm **pestawayinc.com**
Environmentally friendly pest control and extermination service, using
products such as boric acid powder and diatomaceous earth, and mechani-
cal methods instead of chemical methods. Products available for sale.
Serves New York City.

Pest@Rest, LLC

520 Gates Ave. (Tompkins Ave.), Bedford-Stuyvesant (Bkn), 718-309-6223
Mon–Sat 9am–5pm **pestatrest.com**
Low-impact, nontoxic methods of pest control and elimination for ants, bed-
bugs, beetles, crickets, fleas, ticks, roaches, rodents, spiders, and squirrels.
Service locations in all five boroughs.

Standard Exterminating Company

25-80 Steinway St. (28th Ave.), Astoria (Qns), 718-728-4080
Mon–Fri 8am–5pm **standardpest.com**
IPM options include mechanical control, habitat modification, and low-toxic
chemicals. Offers quality do-it-yourself instructions and materials as well as
an insect identification service. Serves New York City.

WRITE A REVIEW

We've done our best to establish how green the
providers are for the services we've identified. Now,
we would like your feedback: How was your experience? How effective was the service? Was the price
right? Was the provider on time and available when
you needed her/him? How was the customer service?
Would you recommend the same provider to a friend
or use them again? Share your findings and experiences at **greenopia.com**.

Personal Services

Wanting to "go green" and learning how is one thing; finding green service providers is another. When you need help from a specialist who is well versed in green living, you've got to do some digging.

We've uncovered some entrepreneurial service providers who can help you move along a greener path—in your home, your lifestyle, your event planning, and even in your personal career choices.

To be included, providers must have a primary focus on sustainable living. In addition, 15 percent or more of their projects or client base must be dedicated to sustainable living, and at least 15 percent of the products they use or sell in their practice need to be green or sustainable. We didn't award leaves in this category, because there aren't objective measurements across these varied services that we could reasonably apply. But we encourage you to check references and give these groundbreakers a try.

Deep Green Living

217 Grand St., Ste. 803 (bet. Elizabeth & Mott Sts.), Chinatown (Man), 212-537-3881
By appt. **deepgreenliving.com**
Lifestyle consulting service guiding and educating clients toward choices that are healthier for people and the planet.

dvGreen

787 9th Ave., Ste. 2S (52nd St.), Clinton (Man), 212-713-0013
By appt. **dvgreen.com**
Sustainable event planner and consultant with expertise in organic food, flowers, and linens; tree-free paper invitations. Donates or composts leftover food. Serves all five boroughs.

Green Irene LLC

P.O. Box 1013, New York (Man), 646-867-3007
By appt. **greenirene.com**
Green makeover program offered for home energy and water efficiency, improved indoor air quality, toxin and waste reduction. Also provides eco-party and event services. Serves all five boroughs and the Tri-State Region.

Liza Dunn, Green Consultant

345 W. 13th St., Ste. 2G (Hudson St.), West Village (Man), 917-658-7984
Mon–Fri 9am–5pm **lizadunn.com**
Home, office, commute, event, and general lifestyle sustainability consultations for busy New Yorkers.

Modern Green Living

644 Manhattan Ave., 2nd Flr. (Bedford Ave.), Greenpoint (Bkn), 866-848-2840
Mon–Wed 11am–4pm Thu 11am–9pm Sat 10am–6pm
moderngreenliving.com
Green resource guide listing eco-friendly residential developments and professionals.

Movers, Not Shakers
481 Van Brunt St., Ste. 10A (Reed St.), Red Hook (Bkn), 718-243-0221
Mon–Fri 9am–4pm **moversnotshakers.com**
Moving company offering reusable plastic bins and transport via biodiesel-powered trucks. Alternatives for plastic bubble wrap and shrink-wrap coming soon. Serves New York City area and the Eastern Seaboard.

RePlayGround!
347-546-4868
By appt. **replayground.com**
Green design studio hosting birthday parties and corporate events. Provides do-it-yourself projects and instructions demonstrating how to give discarded materials a second life. Serves all five boroughs.

Revolution Cargo Systems
454 9th Ave. (W. 35th St.), Clinton (Man), 212-239-3491
Mon–Fri 8am–6pm **revolutionrickshaws.com**
Same-day cargo delivery provides locking hardtops and transport via fossil-fuel-free rigs. Carbon neutral transportation services for events. Pedicab decoration and branding opportunities available. Serves Manhattan.

Spacialist Professional Organizing, The
212-924-4383
By appt. **thespacialist.com**
Clutter reduction, recycling, and repurposing consultation services. Creates custom-designed organizers.

Green Tip
Whether it's a birthday, baby shower, office party, or formal company event, waste does not have to be the by-product. Plan a "zero waste" event by using washable plates, cups, and cutlery; setting out recycling bins; composting food scraps and food waste; using biodegradable balloons; and printing banners on sturdy reusable material for future events or on material that can be recycled if it's a one-time event. The event planners and caterers listed here can help guide you. And be sure to ask those you work with to incorporate these practices when planning your next party or event.

Burial Services

There are more burial and cremation options than most people are aware of, many of them less polluting and more meaningful than traditional practices. With cremation, ashes can be buried, spread over a chosen area (in some cases a protected natural area that furthers conservation work), preserved in an urn, or used to create lasting ocean reefs.

Similarly, there are a variety of more sustainable options for whole-body burial. For example, one form of green burial entails preserving the body with dry ice or refrigeration and wrapping it in either a cotton or hemp shroud before placing it in the grave, in a biodegradable pine, cardboard, or wicker box, without using a concrete burial vault. (Conversely, an embalmed body goes into the ground with toxic formaldehyde and mercuric chloride in it.)

Some burial services have conservation areas where remains are buried within land that is cared for in an ecologically sound and sustainable manner. Embalmed remains are not allowed in these areas. Native vegetation, such as a memorial tree, may be planted over or near the grave in place of conventional monuments.

Many funeral services and even traditional cemeteries are also willing to accommodate a variety of end-of-life rituals, both old and new. Ask about natural alternative preservation and presentation options and other new burial service choices.

The centers listed here offer some or all of the options outlined above, and work to encourage and employ environmentally sustainable practices in the services they provide. There are, however, no consistent criteria among these types of businesses upon which to base leaf awards.

Eternal Reefs, Inc.

P.O. Box 2473, Decatur, GA 30031, 888-423-7333
Mon–Fri 8am–6pm   eternalreefs.com
Cremation memorial preserving, protecting, and enhancing the marine environment. Family and friends participate in creating the memorial reef. Nationwide services.

Green Burial Council

888-966-3330
Mon–Fri 9am–5pm PST   greenburialcouncil.org
Independent nonprofit founded to encourage ethical and environmentally sustainable death care practices. Uses the burial process as means of facilitating the acquisition, restoration, and stewardship of natural areas. Nationwide services.

Greensprings Natural Cemetery Preserve

293 Irish Hill Rd., P.O. Box 415, Newfield, NY 14867, 607-564-7577
By appt. **naturalburial.org**
Sustainable burial lots, space for cremated remains in New York's Finger Lakes region. Offers native trees and shrubs for gravesite planting.

Memorial Ecosystems, Inc.

111 W. Main St., Westminster, SC 29693, 864-647-7798
Daily 24 hrs. **memorialecosystems.com**
Conservation burials and ashes scatterings in memorial parks specifically designed to preserve and restore wildlands.

Nature's Passage

85 Shore Rd. (Braham Ave.), Amityville, NY 11701, 800-407-8917
Daily 24 hrs. **naturespassage.com**
Burial voyages in full-body caskets or sailcloth shrouds, or ashes scattering, from various seaports in the New York City and Tri-State Region.

Sea Services

P.O. Box 147, Babylon, NY 11702, 888-551-1277
Daily 8am–5pm **seaservices.com**
Burial at sea and ashes scattering services provided out of New York Harbor.

did you know?

Last year conventional death-care practices caused us to bury:

- 800,000 gallons of formaldehyde-based embalming fluid, regarded as a "known carcinogen" by the World Health Organization;

- more metal to create caskets than was used to build the Golden Gate Bridge;

- vaults using enough reinforced concrete to build a two-lane highway from San Francisco to Phoenix.

Our thanks to Joe Sehee, founder of The Green Burial Council (**greenburialcouncil.org**), for the above information.

Banking and Finance

Most people do not connect banking and finance with environmentalism, but direct links can be made through investment and lending practices. For example, an investment firm may offer ways in which potential investors can screen companies on both financial and environmental criteria. These realms are not mutually exclusive. There are companies that respect the environment and are robust financial performers.

You have the right to know if a bank's lending practices require potential clients to meet certain environmental standards or if they are directly providing funding for green projects. Dig into your financial institution's fine print. Find out what your dollars are being used for.

There are financial institutions that are making a concerted effort toward making the world greener by ensuring that, for example, their larger-scale lending practices support sustainable projects through initiatives such as the Equator Principles, or that they offer clients the option of making Socially Responsible investments (SRIs) or investments in green funds.

Furthermore, some banks now offer what is called an EEM, or energy efficient mortgage. EEMs can be used to purchase homes that are already energy efficient or to refinance ones needing energy upgrades. Monthly energy savings are factored into interest rates, making them more favorable.

Listed below are firms that meet our minimum threshold to be included by offering EEMs, "green" banking options, SRIs with an environmental focus, and/or green funds. We expect the number of banking and financial institutions providing these services to continue to grow. We will continue to seek out new ones and add them to our list.

A. Baker Woolworth, Jr., Smith Barney/Citi
345 Park Ave., 21st Flr. (E. 52nd St.), Midtown East (Man), 212-230-3624
By appt.
Designs custom portfolios for individuals using SRI and green funds.

Arline Segal, Smith Barney/Citi
450 Lexington Ave., 40th Flr. (E. 52nd St.), Murray Hill (Man), 212-692-2382
By appt.   fa.smithbarney.com/segal
Financial advisor offering customized SRI and Green Fund portfolios.

Brighter Planet Visa® Card
800-442-1521
brighterplanet.com
Visa credit card offered through Bank of America; reward points are automatically redeemed to help fund renewable energy projects.

Bruce M. Kahn, Smith Barney/Citi

345 Park Ave., 21st Flr. (E. 52nd St.), Midtown East (Man), 212-230-3588
By appt. **fa.smithbarney.com/bkahn/index.htm**
Financial advisor offering customized SRI and Green Fund portfolios.

Gary Matthews, PhD CPA/PFS AIF®, First Affirmative Financial Network

5 Penn Plaza, 23rd Flr. (W. 34th St.), New York (Man), 800-801-1219
Mon–Fri 9am–5pm **sriinvesting.com**
Specializes in socially responsible and environmentally sustainable investment, tax, and financial consulting.

GE Earth Rewards Card

866-419-4096
Mon–Fri 9am–8pm EST **myearthrewards.com**
Mastercard provided by GE Money Bank. One percent of annual net purchases are redirected into carbon offsets.

GreenPay MasterCard®

Online only **greenpay.com**
Mastercard provided by Fintura Corp. in conjunction with MetaBank.
Rewards program offsets CO_2 emissions with every purchase.

Jeffrey Scales & Associates

138 E. Market St., Ste. 201 (Beech St.), Rhinebeck, NY 12572, 845-876-1923
Mon–Fri 9am–5pm **jsafinancial.com**
Independent financial firm offering clients SRI options and personal financial planning for investments, retirement, long-term care, and wealth preservation strategies.

Kimberly Marshall, Smith Barney/Citi

345 Park Ave., 21st Flr. (E. 52nd St.), Midtown East (Man), 212-230-3522
By appt.
Financial advisor offering customized SRI and green fund portfolios.

Lily Engelhardt, Smith Barney/Citi

1 Penn Plaza, 43rd Flr. (W. 34th St.), Midtown South (Man), 212-643-5880
By appt. **fa.smithbarney.com/lilyengelhardt**
Financial planning specialist offering portfolios with SRI and Green Funds.

Louis Berger, CFA, UBS Financial Services, Inc.

200 Park Ave., Met Life Building, 11th Flr. (E. 44th St.), Murray Hill (Man), 212-490-4033
By appt.
Financial advisor customizing portfolios with SRI and Green Funds.

Marc H. Sussman, CFP, The Sussman Group

118 E. 28th St., Ste. 307 (bet. Park & Lexington Aves.), Murray Hill (Man), 800-682-0286 or 212-685-4495
Mon–Fri 9am–6pm Sat–Sun by appt. **marcsussman.com**
Socially responsible investment and planning services.

Michael H. Moskowitz, CFP, Smith Barney/Citi

345 Park Ave., 21st Flr. (E. 52nd St.), Midtown East (Man), 212-230-3652
By appt.
Financial advisor offering customized SRI and Green Fund portfolios.

Michael Reisin, Smith Barney/Citi

212-230-3419
By appt.   **fa.smithbarney.com/michaelreisin**
Financial advisor designing custom portfolios using SRI and Green Funds.

Money with a Mission/FAFN, Inc.

490 Lower Creek Rd., Ithaca, NY 14850, 800-563-8301
By appt.   **moneywithamission.com**
Provides asset management services using environmentally and socially
responsible options and comprehensive financial life planning.

New Resource Bank

405 Howard St., Ste. 110, San Francisco, CA 94105, 415-995-8100
Mon–Fri 9am–5pm PST   **newresourcebank.com**
Community-oriented, full-service bank focused on sustainable investments,
solar home equity financing, and lending to green businesses. Community
Rewards Visa check card earns cash for nonprofit organizations with
every purchase.

ReDirect Guide Visa

877-326-4326
redirectguide.com/visa
Visa card offered through ShoreBank Pacific. With every purchase
a portion of the proceeds goes to carbon offsets through Sustainable
Travel International.

Salmon Nation Visa

877-326-4326
Mon–Fri 8:30am–5:30pm PST   **salmonnation.com/growsn/snvisa.html**
Visa card offered through Shorebank Pacific supports Ecotrust's effort
to build a healthier bioregion from Alaska to California.

ShoreBank Pacific

P.O. Box 400, Ilwaco, WA 98624, 877-326-4326
Mon–Fri 8am–5pm PST   **shorebankpacific.com**
Committed to environmentally sustainable community development and
offering a variety of banking services for individuals, commercial businesses,
and nonprofits. Provides EcoIRAs, CDs, money market accounts, savings,
and checking.

Subir Grewal, CFA, UBS Financial Services, Inc.

200 Park Ave. Met Life Building, 11th Flr. (E. 44th St.), Murray Hill (Man),
212-490-4019
By appt.
Financial advisor customizing portfolios with SRI and Green Funds.

Working Assets Visa Signature Credit Card

866-438-6262
workingassets.com
Consumer credit card donating 10 cents per customer purchase to environmental and other nonprofit groups. Card issued by Bank of America.

Real Estate

It is becoming more common for real estate agents to obtain training in the features of eco-friendly properties. More agents are beginning to understand the real value of energy efficiency, healthy materials, and sustainable design and construction in the homes they sell. And more buyers are looking for these features when searching for a new home.

To meet this burgeoning need, Ecobroker.com offers online courses for brokers to earn the EcoBroker Certified® designation to accompany their real estate license. Certified EcoBrokers® are equipped with the environmental information and tools to assist their clients looking for a green property. The EcoBroker® training helps real estate professionals address the growing areas of interest in real estate, such as "green" home certification programs like Energy Star®-Qualified Homes, energy efficiency, and sustainable design.

More and more properties—to rent or buy—are being built with higher environmental standards. The homes, co-ops, and apartments we've listed are either designed and built to LEED® standards or incorporate a myriad of environmentally friendly building practices, technologies, and services to conserve energy and water, while reducing waste and the use of toxic building materials.

To be listed here, an agency or agent must meet the following minimum requirements:

- at least 25 percent of their overall sales and represented purchases must be of sustainably designed or built properties; and

- the individual agent must have received, or at least 25 percent of the organization's agents must have received, training in sustainable design and construction or be a certified EcoBroker.

We also looked at how long the agents or brokers have been dealing in "green real estate" and whether it is the primary focus of their business.

Ask one of the agents listed here about the following green properties, or see if your favorite real estate office has an agent who specializes in green, sustainably designed homes.

Archstone Clinton
515 W. 52nd St. (bet. 10th & 11th Aves.), Midtown West (Man), 212-915-3741
By appt. **archstoneapartments.com**
Studios and one- to two- bedroom units for rent. Recycled, sustainable materials and low- to no-VOC finishes utilized in construction. Auto-sensing daylight dimming system.

Brompton, The

205 E. 85th St. (3rd Ave.), Upper East Side (Man), 212-249-8505
By appt. thebromptonnyc.com
Condominium building offering 193 units, from studios to five-bedroom
and townhouse-style residences. Registered for LEED Silver certification.
Outdoor garden; indoor/outdoor children's play areas.

Corcoran Group, The (Emma Hamilton)

36 E. 12th St., 3rd Flr. (University Pl.), Greenwich Village (Man), 212-500-7034
By appt. corcoran.com/ehamilton
New York City's second Certified EcoBroker. Specializes in sales and purchases of green homes throughout Manhattan and Brooklyn; a one-stop
eco-resource for clients and colleagues.

Corcoran Group, The (Jeffrey Schleider)

636 6th Ave. (19th St.), Chelsea (Man), 212-444-7874
By appt. corcoran.com/jschleider
Certified EcoBroker representing both buyers and sellers in New York City.

Corcoran Group, The (Susan Singer)

212-444-7866
By appt. nyecospaces.com
Certified EcoBroker representing both buyers and sellers. Also assists new
homeowners with resources and directions to green their homes.

Corcoran Group, The (Susanne Steward)

490 Broadway (Broome St.), SoHo (Man), 212-941-2572
By appt. corcoran.com/sls
Certified EcoBroker representing both buyers and sellers. Provides new
homeowners resources to green their homes.

Edge, The

22 N. 6th St., S. Edge, Williamsburg (Bkn), 718-222-0211
By appt. williamsburgedge.com
Mixed-use development, with units ranging from studios to three-bedroom
residences. Furnished with energy-saving appliances; hybrid Zipcars located
on-site. Registered for LEED certification.

Epic

125 W. 31st St. (bet. 6th & 7th Aves.), Midtown (Man), 212-554-2700
Mon–Fri 10am–6pm Sat–Sun 10am–7pm theepic.com
High-rise residence constructed with sustainably harvested woods; rooftop
gardens; storm water reclamation. Green cleaning products used on premises. Units designed for water and energy efficiency, with focus on indoor
air quality.

515 Condominiums

515 5th Ave. (13th St.), Park Slope (Bkn), 718-623-0515
By appt. 5one5.com
Condominium building featuring green roof, bamboo flooring and cabinets,
recycled material countertops, and solar-powered exterior lighting. Ground-
floor retail, with 15 residences.

1400 on Fifth

1400 5th Ave. (W. 115th St.), Central Harlem (Man), 212-987-1400
By appt. 1400on5th.com
Eight-story, 129-unit building with geothermal heating and cooling system,
advanced air filtration system. Sixty percent of building constructed from
recycled and renewable resources.

Services

Greenbelt Condos
361 Manhattan Ave. (Jackson St.), Williamsburg (Bkn), 718-384-4402
By appt. **greenbeltbrooklyn.com**
LEED NC condominium project. Photovoltaic roof panels; bamboo, cork, and linseed oil–finished flooring; recycled-material countertops; energy-efficient appliances and fixtures.

Harrison, The
205 W. 76th St. (Amsterdam Ave.), Upper West Side (Man), 212-496-1000
By appt. **theharrison76.com**
Condominium featuring 123 units, studios to five-bedroom residences. Registered for LEED Silver certification. Built with sustainable materials. Focus on water conservation, energy efficiency, indoor air quality. Outdoor garden.

Helena, The
601 W. 57th St. (11th Ave.), Midtown West (Man), 212-262-6500
By appt. **thehelena.com**
Rental tower with 39 stories and 580 units featuring two-, three-, and four-bedroom residences. Powered by wind and solar power; recycles all waste heat and -water. Green roof. On-site electric vehicle charging station.

Kalahari, The
1400 5th Ave. (W. 115th St.), Central Harlem (Man), 212-348-0090
By appt. **kalahari-harlem.com**
Building features 249 two- to four-bedroom residences. Solar and wind powered, ionic and plex air filters, bamboo strip flooring, low-VOC building materials, and Energy Star appliances.

Laurel, The
400 E. 67th St. (1st Ave.), Upper East Side (Man), 212-750-5550
By appt. **laurelcondominium.com**
Condominium featuring 129 units, registered for LEED certification. Constructed using locally manufactured, recycled-content building materials.

Lucida, The
151 E. 85th St. (Lexington Ave.), Upper East Side (Man), 212-585-1510
By appt. **thelucida.com**
LEED-certified building offering 110 condominiums. Interiors designed and built with sustainably harvested wood; partial green roof irrigated with rainwater; bicycle storage.

Modern, The
343 W. 16th St. (bet. 8th & 9th Aves.), Chelsea (Man), 212-685-7777
By appt. **themodernny.com**
Building features two- to four-bedroom residences and eight boutique rental units. Geothermal heating and cooling system.

93 Nevins/453 Pacific
93 Nevins St./453 Pacific St., Boerum Hill (Bkn), 718-858-7500
By appt. **93nevins.com**
Condos feature FSC-certified wood cabinetry and flooring, no-VOC paint, low-VOC adhesives, soy-based spray foam insulation, Green Seal–certified windows, and energy-efficient subfloor heating system.

Observatory Place
2021 1st Ave. (E. 104th St.), East Harlem (Man), 212-433-2021
By appt. **observatoryplacenyc.com**
Condominium featuring 38 units ranging from studios to three-bedroom residences. Recycled-content building materials used in construction. Green power is purchased for the building; accessible roof garden; bike storage.

Octagon, The

888 Main St. N , Roosevelt Island (Man), 212-888-8692
By appt. **octagonnyc.com**
LEED Silver–certified building with units ranging from studios to three-bedrooms. Utilizes high-efficiency boilers and rooftop solar panels. Formaldehyde- and VOC-free recycled-content materials used in construction.

One Jackson Square

122 Greenwich Ave. (W. 13th St.), Greenwich Village (Man), 212-366-1110
By appt. **onejacksonsquare.com**
LEED-certified loft building features low-VOC adhesives, sealants, paints, coatings, and carpets; expansive green roof; efficient heating and cooling system. Seventy-five percent of construction waste was recycled.

Prudential Douglas Elliman (Genifer Lancaster)

90 Hudson St. (bet. Worth & Leonard Sts.), Tribeca (Man), 212-965-6046
By appt. **prudentialelliman.com**
Certified EcoBroker working with buyers, sellers, and renters interested in Manhattan's green buildings.

Riverhouse

1 Rockefeller Park (Chambers St.), Battery Park City (Man), 212-587-1200
By appt. **the-riverhouse.com**
LEED Gold–certified building using geothermal well, photovoltaic roof panels, and microturbines to supply energy. Landscaped roof gardens.

Solaire, The

20 River Terr. (Murray St.), Battery Park City (Man), 212-748-6100
By appt. **thesolaire.com**
LEED Gold–certified rental tower. In-building wastewater treatment system, natural gas central heating and cooling system, photovoltaic roof panels, Energy Star appliances, no- to low-VOC materials and paints, pesticide-free rooftop garden.

Tribeca Green

325 North End Ave. (Warren St.), Tribeca (Man), 212-693-0001
By appt. **tribecagreen.com**
Certified LEED Gold building renting 274 one- to two-bedroom units. Photovoltaic panels, microturbine utilizing waste heat for hot water. Recycles rainwater for landscape maintenance. Double-filtered air, Energy Star appliances, bike storage.

Verdesian, The

211 North End Ave. (Murray St.), Battery Park City (Man), 212-227-0222
By appt. **theverdesian.com**
Rental tower featuring photovoltaic roof panels, natural gas heating and cooling system, Energy Star appliances, FSC-certified woods, low-VOC materials and finishes, pesticide-free rooftop garden. Reclaimed water from bathrooms and kitchens supplies building's flush system.

Visionaire, The

55 Battery Pl. (bet. 1st & 2nd Pl.), Battery Park City (Man), 212-227-0222
By appt. **thevisionaire.com**
LEED Platinum–certified building. Natural gas heating and cooling system, no- to low-VOC materials and paints, rooftop garden, bamboo kitchen cabinets, FSC-certified wood flooring, and Energy Star appliances. Reclaimed water from bathrooms and kitchens used for building's flush system.

Telecommunications

No, there is nothing particular in the telecommunications industry that makes it more or less green, except how the companies choose to allocate their revenues or profits. Just as you choose where to make charitable donations, so too do phone and internet service providers. Since they all offer substantially the same services, why not support a company that puts your money to work for the environment?

Because this isn't an appropriate area in which to award leaves, we offer our list as a reference only. But we thought you might want to help support those businesses that are, in turn, helping support the planet.

The telecommunications companies listed below have chosen to donate a part of their profits or a percentage of their revenues to environmental causes. Note: Some companies identify their donations as a percentage of total revenue, others as a percentage of profit, so the actual amounts and percentages donated will vary considerably. Look carefully when comparing plans and companies.

Come From the Heart, LLC

798 Verdun St., Clarksburg, WV 26301, 888-622-0957
Mon–Fri 9am–5pm **comefromtheheart.com**
Nationwide cell phone and long distance service donating 3% of profits to environmental and nonprofit organizations.

Credo Long Distance

101 Market St., Ste. 700 , San Francisco, CA 94105, 877-762-7336
Mon–Fri 5am–8pm Sat–Sun 7am–5pm PST **credolongdistance.com**
Nationwide long distance provider donates 1% of charges to progressive nonprofit groups.

Credo Mobile

877-762-7336
Mon–Fri 5am–8pm Sat–Sun 7am–5pm PST **credomobile.com**
Nationwide cell phone service provider that donates 1% of charges to progressive nonprofit groups. Offers cell phone recycling through Collective Good.

Earth Tones

1536 Wynkoop St., Ste. 100, Denver, CO 80202, 888-327-8486
Mon–Fri 9am–5pm MST **earthtones.com**
Nationwide provider of internet access, long distance telephone, and cell phone services. Donates 100% of profits to grassroots environmental organizations. Sends regular "green alerts" to customers on environmental issues; offers cell phone recycling program.

Makana Technologies

1202 Plaza Del Monte, Santa Barbara, CA 93101, 808-283-3775
Daily 24 hrs. **makanatechnologies.com**
Nationwide provider of local and long distance phone, internet, VoIP, and
wireless services. Portion of service fee donated to the nonprofit of customer's choice.

Red Jellyfish

P.O. Box 1570, Mountain View, CA 94042, 888-222-5008
Daily 24 hrs. **redjellyfish.com**
Nationwide provider of dial-up internet access and email accounts.
Provides cell phone recycling; donates profits to a variety of
environmental organizations.

Sonopia

1560 Broadway Ste., 315 (7th St.), Manhattan (Man), 877-595-0557
Daily 24 hrs. **sonopia.com**
Provides individuals, groups, and nonprofits an opportunity to brand and
market their own mobile service to earn money. You or your organization can
earn $50 for each enrolled customer, plus 5% ongoing commission from their
phone bill.

Utilities

Some utility companies and their customers are starting to recognize that their energy choices have a direct and lasting impact
on the environment. There are clean, alternative energy choices
out there, but be careful—some are more benign than others. For
instance, many utilities consider nuclear energy a clean alternative
energy choice. Ask questions to see if your utility provider is doing
its best to minimize greenhouse gas emissions: Does it protect its
watershed lands? What about its support for solar power and other
renewables? Are rebates for energy-efficient appliances offered?
Does the company make donations to environmental organizations
and help with habitat restoration on company-owned lands?

Consolidated Edison (ConEd) offers the Power Your Way program
(poweryourway.com) to residents of New York who seek the option
of bringing alternative, clean energy into the local electrical grid.
When customers switch to green energy through this program,
ConEd continues to deliver your energy and an associated "energy
supply company" (ESCO) becomes the energy supplier. Keep in
mind, the prices and product mixes vary between the ESCOs and
are constantly evolving as new technologies emerge.

We have given a brief description of the alternative energy options
offered from each of the providers to get you started. It's up to you
to check the fine print.

Accent Energy
800-928-7775
Mon–Fri 8am–8pm Sat 9am–4pm **accentenergy.com**
Electricity sourced from either wind or a blend of wind and small hydropower delivered to the ConEd service area.

Ambit Energy
877-282-6248
Mon–Fri 8am–6pm Sat 10am–5pm **ambitenergy.com**
Certified Green Plan provides 100% of electricity from renewable resources and/or matching renewable energy credits.

Community Energy
866-946-3123
Mon–Fri 8:30am–6:30pm **NewWindEnergy.com**
Energy from new wind sources supplied to ConEd service area. Certificates sold in 100 kWh bundles with a minimum purchase required.

Consolidated Edison Solutions
888-320-8991
Mon–Fri 9am–5pm **conedsolutions.com**
Sells hydro and wind energy through its Green Power and Wind Power programs.

Energetix, Inc.
800-544-0182
Mon–Fri 8am–5pm **energetix.net**
Clean renewable energy produced from a blend of wind and certified low-impact hydropower delivered to ConEd service area.

IDT Energy, Inc.
877-887-6866
Daily 7:30am–7:30pm **idtenergy.com**
The Buy Green program delivers energy from 100% hydropower to ConEd service area customers. Variable rate plans apply to the green energy program with no fixed rate options.

Sterling Planet
877-457-2306
Mon–Fri 9am–5pm **sterlingplanet.com**
Renewable energy from a mix of wind and small hydropower delivered to ConEd service area for a fixed rate premium.

U.S. Energy Savings
888-674-7847
Mon-Fri 9am-6pm **energysavings.com**
Green Energy Option (GEOpower) delivers electricity from wind and hydro to ConEd service areas. Variable rate premiums from are applied to base kWh charges, participants must sign-up for a four- or five-year fixed price protection plan before opting into the GEOpower program.

Carbon Credits and Offsets

Although it is sometimes comforting to blame "industry" for all of our environmental ills, the fact is, each one of us contributes to the greenhouse gases (GHG) that increase global warming. The cars we drive, the flights we take, the products we buy, and the energy we use in our homes and apartments directly affect what happens to our planet. This is where "carbon offsets" come in.

The idea behind carbon offsets is to counter the effects of the carbon emissions we produce by purchasing carbon offset credits from a third party who, in turn, uses those funds to engage in projects that capture and/or reduce greenhouse gases elsewhere. The goal is not only to lessen greenhouse gas emissions, but for us to recognize and take responsibility for the things we do that may have larger, or even global consequences.

Consumers can also buy renewable energy certificates (RECs), sometimes called green tags, which verify that a certain amount of renewable electricity has been generated and fed into the power grid.

First and most important, reduce your carbon footprint by becoming more eco-efficient. Then, look to carbon offsets and RECs as a way to mitigate the effects of what's left. You can select from a variety of programs—renewable energy, reforestation/tree planting, wind farms, and energy efficiency are among the most popular.

Because this is a growing and changing field, we have not leaf-awarded these companies. However, they all provide customers with the means to calculate, and the opportunity to buy, carbon credits or offsets.

Services

Atmosclear Climate Club
P.O. Box 445, Northborough, MA 01532, 888-393-6210
Mon–Fri 9am–5pm **atmosclear.org**
Purchases VERs from renewable energy companies, reforestation programs, and landfill projects. Carbon credits certified by Environmental Resources Trust.

Better World Club
20 NW 5th Ave., Ste. 100, Portland, OR 97209, 866-238-1137
Daily 8:30am–5:30pm **betterworldclub.com**
Provides carbon offsets for auto and air travel; eco-travel services.

Bonneville Environmental Foundation
240 SW 1st Ave., Portland, OR 97204, 866-233-8247
greentagsusa.org
Sells carbon offsets as renewable energy certificates to green your business, home, event, travel, building, or ski trip.

Buy Carbon

1220 W. 6th St., Ste. 600, Cleveland, OH 44113, 216-522-8700
buycarbon.org
Calculates carbon emissions and sells offsets certified by Evolution Markets. Issues carbon credits on behalf of Clean Air Conservancy.

Carbon Fund

1320 Fenwick Ln., Ste. 206, Silver Spring, MD 20910, 240-293-2700
carbonfund.org
Low-cost carbon reductions certified by Chicago Climate Exchange and Environmental Resource Trust. Supports renewable energy, energy efficiency, and reforestation.

Clean Air-Cool Planet

100 Market St., Ste. 204, Portsmouth, NH 03801, 603-422-6464
cooldriver.org
Offers carbon offsets for auto travel through support of wind power and methane capture projects. Green-e and Native Energy certified.

Climate Trust, The

65 SW Yamhill St., Ste. 400, Portland, OR 97204, 503-238-1915
climatetrust.org
Tax-deductible contributions support projects to offset greenhouse gas emissions. Advances climate change policies and is a strong advocate for high-quality standards in the offset market as an integral part of its work.

Delta Offsets

53 W. Jackson Blvd., Ste. 230, Chicago, IL 60604, 312-554-0900 x24
deltacarbon.org
Chicago Climate Exchange–certified carbon offsets. Reviews, approves, registers, sells, and retires credits.

Driving Green

1990 W. New Haven Ave. Ste. 205, Melbourne, FL 32904, 321-409-7800
drivinggreen.com
Calculates and sells carbon offsets for your vehicle, air travel, or events. Revenues support greenhouse gas emission reduction projects managed by AgCert International.

Earth Preserver

1350 E. Flamingo Rd., Ste. 398, Las Vegas, NV 89119, 866-936-5100
Mon–Fri 9am–6pm MST   **earthpreserver.com**
As members of the Chicago Climate Exchange, they purchase carbon financial instruments (CFIs) and retire them for auto, home, flight, or life in general.

e-BlueHorizons, LLC

675 VFW Pkwy., P.O. Box 344, Chestnut Hill, MA 02467, 866-308-9213
e-bluehorizons.com
Carbon offsets are retired from the Chicago Climate Exchange; 50% of the proceeds go to the Conservation Fund for reforestation projects.

ECO2Pass, Inc.

60 S. 6th St., Ste. 2535, Minneapolis, MN 55402, 800-431-3256
eco2pass.com
Offsets carbon emissions for car, home, and travel by retiring CO_2 reduction credits from the Chicago Climate Exchange to reduce global warming.

Green Mountain Energy Company

P.O. Box 689008, Austin, TX 78768, 800-810-7300
Mon–Sat 9am–5pm EST **greenmountainenergy.com**
Retail provider of cleaner energy and carbon offset solutions for individuals and businesses.

LiveNeutral

2601 Mission St., Ste. 401, San Francisco, CA 94110, 415-695-2355
liveneutral.org
Carbon emissions calculator and offsets provided in collaboration with Chicago Climate Exchange. Provides education and outreach on climate change issues and methods to reduce your carbon footprint.

Native Energy

937 Ferry Rd., P.O. Box 539, Charlotte, VT 05445, 800-924-6826
nativeenergy.com
Carbon offset fees used to build wind power on Native American lands, farms, and school districts. Carbon credits certified by Green-e.

Prairie Tree Project

7703 Ralston Rd., Arvada, CO 80002, 800-715-8753
prairietreeproject.com
Provides strategies to become carbon neutral. Calculates your carbon footprint and sells Green-e certified offsets to fund tree plantings on the Colorado prairie.

Renewable Choice Energy

2500 55th St., Ste. 201, Boulder, CO 80301, 877-810-8670
Mon–Fri 9am–6pm MST **renewablechoice.com**
Green-e-certified carbon offsets for home, travel, and auto emissions; promotes the development of clean energy alternatives to fossil fuels.

Save Green Earth

800-715-8753
savegreenearth.com
Calculates carbon footprint from home electricity usage and fuel for transportation. Sells carbon offsets to fund environmental education programs for children, reforestation projects, and technology investments.

Sky Energy

2131 Woodruff Rd., Ste. 2100, Greenville, SC 29607, 866-759-3637
sky-energy.com
Sells Green-e-certified carbon offsets and renewable energy credits.

Standard Carbon

15600 NE. 173rd St., Woodinville, WA 98072
Contact via email/website only **standardcarbon.com**
Carbon credits certified by the Chicago Climate Exchange. Provides green business consulting services and environmental investment opportunities through the purchase of reforestation and renewable energy offsets.

Sustainable Travel International

P.O. Box 1313, Boulder, CO 80306, 720-273-2975
Mon–Fri 8am–5pm MST **sustainabletravelinternational.org**
Sells offsets to travelers and invests in renewable energy and reforestation projects.

Terra Pass Inc.

568 Howard St., 5th Flr., San Francisco, CA 94105, 877-210-9581
terrapass.com
Carbon credits supported by wind energy projects, farm sequestration, and landfill gas capture.

3 Phases Renewable

2100 Sepulveda Blvd., Ste. 37, Manhattan Beach, CA 90266, 310-939-1283
Mon–Fri 8am–5pm PST **3phases.com**
Sells renewable energy credits certified by Green-e to individuals and businesses.

3Degrees

6 Funston Ave., San Francisco, CA 94129, 866-476-9378
Mon–Fri 8am–5pm PST **3degreesinc.com**
Verified carbon offsets and certified renewable energy certificates assist customers in reducing their carbon footprint.

U.S. Energy Savings

888-674-7847
Mon–Fri 9am–6pm **energysavings.com**
Green Energy Option (GEOgas) offsets your household's natural gas-related carbon emissions by contributing to local carbon offset projects. Participants must commit to a four- or five-year price protection plan before opting into the GEOgas program.

Green Tips

Be an eco-tourist. Eco-tourism offers opportunities to explore the world without leaving a heavy footprint. Many agencies now offer eco-tours (we list travel agencies in our guide that offer many options). If you're booking a tour from a traditional agency, find out what percentage of your trip's cost goes to supporting local community efforts and what percentage goes to the tour operator (often, local communities get nothing and rely on tips or purchases from tourists).

Buy local and really reduce your carbon emissions! The average piece of produce travels 1,500 miles to get to a grocery store.

(Source: Leopold Center for Sustainable Agriculture, **sustainabletable.org/issues/ buylocal**)

Going Carbon Neutral

Lots of things are going "carbon neutral" these days, but what does that really mean? Carbon offsetting is the process by which global warming gases emitted by a certain activity are calculated and then effectively offset by removing or preventing an equal amount elsewhere. These offsets usually involve renewable energy projects like wind or solar power, reforestation projects, or energy efficiency programs. These can take place next door or on the other side of the world, but the goal is that they reduce the net amount of greenhouse gases released into the atmosphere.

The list of carbon-neutral events, companies, and products is growing fast. Music tours, films, colleges, books (yes, *Greenopia*), entire companies, and huge events like the Winter Olympics and the Super Bowl have all gone carbon neutral. But it's also something we can each do with our own actions.

Carbon offsets are most often purchased by individuals for air travel, driving, and electricity use. There are a growing number of services that will help you calculate your emissions, whether it's on a case-by-case basis (like air travel), or over time (like commuting or home energy use for the year). If the thing you want to offset is more complex (like an event, film, or product), there are independent companies able to calculate the associated environmental footprint.

Customers who want to buy renewable energy also have the option of purchasing renewable energy certificates (RECs). Each one of these tradable commodities verifies that one megawatt hour of renewably generated electricity has been fed into the grid. This electricity is not being sent directly to your house, but rather being put into the power grid as a whole, increasing the overall percentage of power from green sources.

It should be noted that there is a certain amount of contention around carbon offsets. Since there is no official regulation in this market, it is important that companies selling offsets have a reliable way of verifying their actions. The lack of regulation has led to accusations of fraudulent offsets and other shady dealings. For this and other reasons, it is often suggested that people not lean too heavily on carbon offsets, but rather reduce emissions as much as possible first.

Trans-
portation

The Greener Way to Get There

By Paul Steely White

For New Yorkers, green transportation is as simple as can be. Because our city is so dense, the average outing is less than two miles, meaning that most trips are walkable or bikeable. Heck, 80 percent of us don't even own a car. So it's not surprising that the average New Yorker's carbon footprint is a third of that of the average American.

We have the nation's best public transport system, one that gets greener every year. The MTA has a new sustainability initiative that could power subways on electricity drawn from wind; every new bus the City buys is a hybrid; and our entire cab fleet will be hybrid by 2012.

There are more than three hundred miles of bike lanes and greenways around New York City, and going nonmotorized is now a more social choice than ever before. In the past I was often the only bike commuter on the road, but now I find myself at red lights next to other riders, striking up conversations, giving directions, or helping out with a flat tire. This conviviality makes riding more fun, and it also makes it much safer.

The ways that you commute say a lot, and the best way to make green transportation more viable is simply to do it. Every time you choose to walk or bike, you're contributing to the walkability and bikeability of the city, and sending a message that this is how New Yorkers get around. This message is coming through loud and clear, and there's a modal shift away from driving and toward wider sidewalks, bike lanes, bus lanes, greenways, and public spaces.

Transportation

Paul Steely White is the executive director of Transportation Alternatives (**transalt.org**) and an avid New York City bike commuter.

Public Transportation

That train ticket, transit pass, or bus transfer may not look like much, but it is one of the most potent weapons you can use to combat global warming and climate change. Research has demonstrated that when compared to other household actions that limit carbon dioxide, taking public transportation can be more than ten times greater in reducing this greenhouse gas.

If one solo commuter of a household switches from daily driving to using public transportation, he or she can reduce the household carbon footprint by 10 percent. If one household's driver gives up that second car and switches to public transit, a household can reduce its carbon emissions up to 30 percent. And, not only is it the right thing to do, it reduces that commute-related stress by letting someone else do the driving.

We have listed contact numbers and web addresses for local public transportation services. Get in touch with the organizations listed below, and they will set you up with bus and train schedules and let you know the closest pickup spot to your home or office so you can be on your way.

Amtrak
400 W. 31st St. Penn Station (8th Ave.), Clinton (Man), 800-872-7245
Daily 24 hrs. **amtrak.com**
Northeastern service runs five lines from Penn Station running on hybrid electric/diesel engines with regenerative braking technology.

Downtown Connection
120 Broadway Ste., 3340 (Cedar St.), Financial District (Man), 212-566-6700
Daily 10am–final run 7:30pm **downtownny.com/gettingaround**
Free bus service provided by the Downtown Alliance of New York. Buses operate on ultralow-sulfur diesel fuel with particulate exhaust filters along a 32-stop horseshoe in Downtown Manhattan. Route map on website.

Hampton Jitney
395 County Rd., #39A (David White Ln.), Southhampton, NY 11968
212-362-8400
Seasonal schedule **hamptonjitney.com**
Biodiesel-fueled bus fleet offering both charter and standard service between Brooklyn, New York City, and the Hamptons since 1974. Refer to website for schedule, reservations, and Northeast Region destinations.

Long Island Rail Road
93-02 Stutphin Blvd., Jamaica Station (bet 94th & Archer Ave.), Jamaica Bay (Qns), 718-217-5477
Daily 24 hrs. **mta.info/lirr**
Over 80% of trains run on direct current electricity converters covering 700 miles of track on 11 branches from Penn Station through Brooklyn and Queens, Nassau and Suffolk Counties, and Montauk at the tip of Long Island.

Metro North

347 Madison Ave. (44th St.), Madison Square (Man), 800-638-7646
Daily 24 hrs.   **mta.info/mnr**
Provides 100% ultralow-sulfur B5 biodiesel train service that connects
Manhattan and the Bronx with neighboring Fairfield and New Haven CT,
Westchester, Putnam, Dutchess, Rockland, and Orange Counties.

New York Airport Service

212-875-8200
Daily 24 hrs.   **nyairportservice.com**
Frequent bus service to and between JFK and LaGuardia Airports; departs
from Manhattan at Penn Station, Port Authority, and Grand Central locations.

New York City Transit Authority

718-330-1234
Daily 24 hrs.   **mta.info/nyct**
New York City's bus and subway system operates with a combination of
biodiesel, CNG, and hybrid engines that serve all five boroughs.

New York Water Taxi

499 Van Brunt St. (Van Dyke St.), Red Hook (Bkn), 212-742-1969
Seasonal schedule   **nywatertaxi.com**
Hop-on/hop-off service at 15 stops departing from South Street Seaport at
Pier 17 to Brooklyn, Manhattan, and Long Island City destinations. Fleet uses
100% CFL and new-generation fluorescent lighting.

Olympia Trails Newark Liberty Express

877-863-9275
Daily 24 hrs.   **coachusa.com/olympia/ss.newarkairport.asp**
Bus service departing every 15 to 30 minutes from Grand Central, Bryant Park,
and Port Authority locations on express routes to Newark Liberty Airport.

Port Authority of New York and New Jersey, The

212-435-7777
Daily 24 hrs.   **panynj.gov**
Electric PATH trains operate between NJ stations and three Manhattan
stops, traveling LED-lit tunnels throughout the system. New GreenPass Plan
for enrolled EZ Pass users gives off-peak discounts for prequalified vehicles
getting 45mpg or greater. Enroll through registration office.

Staten Island Ferry

4 South St., Whitehall Terminal, Battery Park City (Man), 718-727-2508
1 Bay St., St. George Terminal, St. George (S.I.), 718-727-2508
Daily 24 hrs.   **siferry.com**
Free public ferry traveling 50+ relays daily between Whitehall Terminal in
Manhattan and the LEED-certified St. George Terminal on Staten Island.

Staten Island Railway

347 Madison Ave. 44th St.), Madison Square (Man), 718-876-8261
Daily 24 hrs.   **mta.info/nyct/sir/sirinfo.htm**
Railway makes 23 stops that run the length of Staten Island. Composed of
recycled R44 NYC subway cars on an electrified third-rail system.

Statue Cruises

NYC Pier 3 (In Battery Pk.), Battery Park (Man), 877-523-9849
Daily, from 8:30am.   **statuecruises.com**
National State Park tours to Ellis and Liberty Islands. Daily ferries from
Battery Park, New York City, and Liberty State Park, NJ. Low-VOC paints
and eco-friendly cleaners are used in facilities and vessels; Respect Our
Planet principles in effect since January 2008.

Taxicabs, Pedicabs, and Limousine Services

When the subway isn't an option or the bus isn't headed your way, you may want to flag down a taxi or hop in a pedicab. A hybrid taxi or a huffing-and-puffing pedi-pusher will curb a bit of carbon while getting you where you want to go.

So, the next time you hail a cab, look for a "green" one and then sit back and enjoy the ride. Or support your local pedicabbie by buying a fine outside ride. Many are members of the **New York City Pedicab Owners' Association (NYC PDA)**. And about that limo: Whether you are headed for the airport or the prom, not only should there be room for your crew, it should be rollin' on the latest in eco-friendly fuels.

We have not leaf-awarded this category, as this service sector is one where new types of services and companies are emerging, and existing taxicab and limousine services are beginning to retire their low-mileage, high-emissions models and integrate hybrid vehicles into their available offerings. However, the companies listed have at least 25 percent of their fleet running on an alternative fuel, a hybrid system, or human power.

Bicy Taxi NYC

73 Morton St. (Hudson St.), West Village (Man), 646-549-0616
Daily 10am–10pm **BicyTaxi.com**
Pedal-power transportation services in all five boroughs. Zero-emission mobile advertising. Member of NYCPOA.

Bike Central Park

Columbus Cir., Merchants' Gate (bet. E. 59th St. & Broadway), Midtown West (Man), 917-371-6267
Seasonal hours **bikecentralpark.com**
Guided pedicab and bike tours, plus bike rentals in Central Park from two separate locations just south of Central Park West. Online reservations preferred. Member of NYCPOA.

Hybrid Limousine

145 W. 24th St. (bet. 7th and 8th Aves.), Chelsea (Man), 800-822-8767
Daily 24 hrs. **hybridlimousine.com**
Contracted providers of chauffeured, CO_2-reducing hybrid vehicle service for corporate travelers since 2006. Uses hybrid Toyota Camrys and Lexus RX 400h's. Serves the New York City Metro Area, Long Island, Westchester, NJ, and CT.

Limo Green

163 Amsterdam Ave., #156 (W. 67th St.), Lincoln Square (Man), 888-546-0476
Daily 24 hrs. **limogreen.net**
Fleet of luxury natural gas vehicles providing energy efficient executive travel; nontoxic, chemical-free cleaning products used to clean vehicles. Serves Tri-State Region.

Manhattan Rickshaw Company

212-604-4729

Seasonal hrs. **manhattanrickshaw.com**

Insured pedicabs, trained drivers, and safe equipment provided all hours in Manhattan and by arrangement in outer boroughs since 1995. Extensive recycling program for parts, batteries, and materials. Owner is president of NYCPOA.

Mr. Rickshaw

617 W. 29th St. (11th Ave.), (Man), 212-736-1950

Seasonal hrs. **mrrickshaw.com**

A fleet of 40 pedal-powered rickshaws in Manhattan and Brooklyn. Uses biodegradable degreaser for rickshaw maintenance; recycles all aluminum, steel, and bike parts. Member of NYCPOA.

NYC Green Car

100 Perry St. (bet. Hudson & Bleecker Sts.), Greenwich Village (Man), 800-809-2073

Daily 24 hrs. **nycgreencar.com**

Hybrid fleet of Toyota Camry and Lexus vehicles for corporate car service; text message reservation/schedule updates; NY *Times* four-page digest on recycled paper in each limo. Donates 10% of profits to tree planting charities. Serves Tri-State Region.

Ozo Car

866-696-5966

Daily 24 hrs. **ozocar.com**

A fleet of over 100 Toyota and Lexus hybrid vehicles servicing the Tri-State Region since 2002. Wireless high-speed internet and A/C power strip are provided for passenger use in every vehicle.

Revolution Rickshaws

454 9th Ave. (W. 35th St.), New York (Man), 212-239-3491

Seasonal hrs. **revolutionrickshaws.com**

A fleet of 17 three-passenger cycle rickshaws in Manhattan. Offers taxi-style runs, group shuttles, and transport for weddings and corporate events. Member of NYCPOA.

did you know?

Research has demonstrated that when compared to other household actions that limit carbon dioxide, taking public transportation can be more than ten times greater in reducing this greenhouse gas. It takes one solo commuter of a household to switch his or her daily driving to using public transportation and he or she can reduce the household carbon footprint by 10 percent. If one household's driver gives up that second car and switches to public transit, a household can reduce its carbon emissions up to 30 percent.

Bikes, Scooters, and Other Transportation

Let's talk about some lean, green, drivin' machines. Bicycles. Yep. It's time to cut the number of wheels we're moving around on from four to two. We have identified businesses that rent bikes by the day or by the week, in any number of styles—road bikes, mountain bikes, even tandems and beach cruisers.

Although we encourage everyone to take time for a joy ride as often as possible, we have listed only bike shops that rent by the day or longer, rather than the hourly recreational vendors you may find around town. Our goal is to provide you with options to fill an occasional or temporary need, or a way to try a bike before you buy. When you're ready to purchase your own set of wheels, many of these businesses also sell new and used bicycles.

For those requiring a motor to make their wheels move, we've identified some scooter, Segway, and other transportation shops. Check the rules of the road before putting the pedal to the metal when you choose these options.

We have not leaf-awarded this category because bikes are intrinsically eco-friendly, as are these other transportation options, relatively speaking. Note that many of the companies listed here even go the extra mile by recycling parts, donating used bikes, and promoting bike riding or other non-car alternatives as primary modes of transportation.

Bike and Roll

Pier 84, 557 12th Ave. (W. 43rd St.), Clinton (Man), 886-736-82224
Battery Park, Pier A Battery Pl. (West St.), Financial District (MAN), 866-736-8224
10 S. St., Battery Maritime Pl. Bldg., Slip 7 (43rd St.), Goerner's Island National Park (Man), 866-736-8224
Fri–Sun 10am–close **bikeandroll.com**
Mountain, road, hybrid, comfort, tandem and children's bikes rented by the hour, day, or multiday. Baby seats, tag-alongs, and wagons available. Free helmet and lock included with rental. Reservations encouraged.

Bike Central Park

221 W. 58th St. (bet. Broadway & 7th Ave.), Columbus Cir. (Man), 917-371-6267
Seasonal hours. **bikecentralpark.com**
Hybrid and mountain bike rentals by the day, hour, and week. Helmet, lock, and light included with rental. Donates bikes and parts to Time's Up! and Freegans. Central Park bike tours available. Reserve online.

Champion Bicycles

896 Amsterdam Ave. (bet. 103rd & 104th Sts.), Upper West Side (Man),
212-662-2690
Mon–Fri 10am–7pm Sat–Sun 10:30am–6pm   **championbikes.com**
Hybrid and mountain bikes rented by the hour or day. Helmet and lock offered for extra fee.

Chelsea Bicycles

130 W. 26th St. (bet. 6th & 7th Aves.), Chelsea (Man), 212-727-7278
Mon–Sat 10am–8pm Sun 11am–7pm   **chelseabicycles.net**
Hybrid, road, and mountain bikes rented by the hour, day, week, or month.
Offers pedal options; helmet provided for extra fee. Donates old parts to
resellers at end of life.

City Bicycles

315 W. 38th St. (bet. 8th & 9th Aves.), Clinton (Man), 212-563-3373
Mon–Fri 9am–6:30pm Sat 10am–5pm   **citybicycles.net**
Hybrid and road bike rentals by the hour or day; special Fri–Mon rental
packages available. Free helmet with rental; lock available for extra fee. No
reservation needed.

Eddie's Bicycle Shop

490 Amsterdam Ave. (bet. 83rd & 84th Sts.), Upper West Side (Man),
212-580-2011
Sun–Fri 9am–7pm
Hybrid and mountain bikes for hourly and daily rental with no reservations
required. Helmet and lock available for extra fee.

Enoch's Bike Shop

480 10th Ave. (W. 37th St.), Hudson Yards (Man), 212-582-0620
Seasonal hrs.
Hybrid, mountain, and comfort bikes rented by the hour or day; helmet and
lock available for a flat fee.

Larry & Jeff's Bicycles Plus NYC

1400 3rd Ave. (bet. E. 79th & 80th Sts.), Upper East Side (Man),
212-794-2929
Daily 10am–6:30pm   **bicyclesnyc.com**
Hybrid and road bikes available for hourly or up to five-day rentals. Helmet
for extra fee. Walk-ins welcome, reservations taken.

Liberty Bicycles

846 9th Ave. (bet. W. 55th & 56th Sts.), Clinton (Man), 212-757-2418
Seasonal hours. **libertybikesny.com**
Mountain, hybrid, tandem, and road bikes for rent by the hour or day; discount offered for long-term rentals. Free helmet provided and lock for a flat
fee; baby seats available. Walk-ins welcome; one-day advance reservation
for road bikes.

Manhattan Velo

141 E. 17th St. (bet. 3rd Ave. & Irving Pl.), Union Square 212-253-6788
Daily 10am–7pm   **manhattanvelo.com**
Hybrid, mountain, tandem, and children's bikes for rent. Helmet and lock
rented per day. Three-day advance reservation best for kids' bikes and five
days for road bikes. Donates all reusable parts to Recycle-A-Bicycle's education program.

Master Bike Shop

225 W. 77th St. (bet. Broadway & Amsterdam), Upper West Side (Man), 212-580-2355

Mon–Fri 10:30am–7pm Sat–Sun 10am–6pm **masterbikeshop.com**

Hybrid, road, mountain, and children's bikes rented by the hour, day or weekend (winter only). Helmet and locks extra, baby seats free, pedal options available, no reservation required.

Metro Bicycles

360 W. 47th St. (bet. 8th & 9th Aves.), Clinton (Man), 212-581-4500
332 E. 14th St. (bet. 1st & 2nd Aves.), Lower East Side (Man), 212-228-4344
1 Hudson Sq. (bet. Varick & Watts Sts.), SoHo (Man), 212-334-8000
1311 Lexington Ave. (E. 88th St.), Upper East Side (Man), 212-427-4450
546 6th Ave. (W. 15th St.), West Village (Man), 212-255-5100

Hours vary by location **metrobicycles.com**

Hybrid and road bikes for daily and hourly rental; free helmet included. Call ahead for road bikes to specify size. Reservations and walk-ins welcome.

New York Motor Cycle

222-02 Jamaica Ave. (222nd St.), Bronxdale (Brx), 800-527-2727

Tue–Fri 9am–8pm Mon, Sat 9am–6pm **bigapplesegway.com**

Dealer offering Segway and T3 Motion PETs with full service.

NYC Velo

64 2nd Ave. (bet. E. 3rd & 4th Sts.), East Village 212-253-7771

Mon–Fri 11am–8pm Sat 11am–7pm Sun 11am–6pm **nycvelo.com**

Hybrid, mountain, beach cruiser, and road bikes available for hourly, daily, or multiday rental. Helmet rented per day. The shop donates parts to Recycle-A-Bicycle and Freegans, recycles metals, and sends old tubes to a recycled messenger-bag maker in Seattle.

NYCe Wheels

1603 York Ave. (84th St.), Yorkville (Man), 212-737-3078

Daily 11am–7pm **nycewheels.com**

Dealership specializing in electric scooters, electric bikes and trikes, folding bikes, and electric bicycle motor kits.

On The Move

400 7th Ave. (bet. 12th & 13th Sts.), Park Slope (Bkn), 718-768-4998

Seasonal hours.

Hybrid and road bikes for rental by the hour or day; helmet available for extra fee.

Peak Bicycle Pro Shop

42-42 235th St. (43rd Ave.), Douglaston (Qns), 718-225-5119

Seasonal hours. **peakmtnbike.com**

Comfort, mountain, and road bikes for hourly or daily rental; clipless pedals available; free helmet provided. Sponsors legal-trail mountain bike ride (6½- mile single-track loop) at 9:30am sharp on Sundays in Cunningham Park.

Pedal Pusher Bike Shop

1306 2nd Ave. (E. 69th St.), Upper East Side (Man), 212-288-5592

Mon, Wed, Fri–Sun 10am–6pm Thu 10am–8pm **pedalpusherbikeshop.com**

Hybrid, road, and mountain bikes for hourly, daily, or multiday rentals. Helmets and locks available for extra fee; child seats and pedal trailers for kids. Reservations required for groups of eight or more.

Recycle-A-Bicycle

35 Pearl St. (Clement St.), DUMBO (Bkn), 718-858-2972
75 Ave. C (bet. E. 5th & 6th Sts.), East Village (Man), 212-475-1655
Mon–Sat 12pm–7pm **recycleabicycle.org**
Customers can volunteer to fix bikes and learn on the job or just rent cruisers, comforts, and tandems by the hour, day, or week. Free helmet and lock provided.

Spokesman Cycles

49-04 Vernon Blvd. (Hunter's Point Ave.), Long Island City (Qns), 718-433-0450
Daily 10am–7pm **spokesmancycles.com**
Hybrid, road, mountain, comfort, tandem, and children's bikes for rental by the hour, day, or week. Helmets, baby seats, and child trailers available for extra fee. Make reservations up to two weeks in advance.

Toga! Bike Shop

1153 1st Ave. (E. 63rd St.), Upper East Side (Man), 212-759-0002
110 W. End Ave. (W. 64th St.), Upper West Side (Man), 212-799-9625
Seasonal hours. **togabikes.com**
Hybrids and road bikes available for hourly, daily, or weekly rental from shop serving NYC since 1967. Helmet available for extra fee.

Green Tips

Riding a bike is already a healthy and planet-friendly mode of transportation. So what more can you do? Use biodegradable, nontoxic cleansers and lubricants for routine cleaning and maintenance; recycle worn tubes and tires instead of throwing them in the trash bin; use rechargeable batteries in headlights and taillights; purchase sustainably produced cycle clothing and gear; and fuel up on organic locally produced food.

Can't find a place to securely park your bike? The New York City Department of Transportation (NYC DOT) runs a CityRacks program. Anyone can obtain a bicycle rack—on a particular street, in your neighborhood, near a commercial district—by requesting the installation of one from NYC DOT. Call 212-442-7687 or visit **nyc.gov/html/dot/html/bicyclists/bikerack.shtml**.

Car Rentals and Rideshare Services

Do you have friends or family coming to town who need a set of wheels? Want to test drive a hybrid or biodiesel car? Ready to go car-free except once in a while? Then check out these car rental and rideshare options. They are adding some gas-sipping and climate-conscious vehicles to their fleets.

We have not leaf-awarded this category, because we have found that rental companies generally offer either alternative fuel vehicles exclusively (which we are all for) or, as with the large mainstream rental companies, are making an effort to supply some hybrids and alternative fuel vehicles (which we also want to recognize).

For those ready for a substitute for individual car ownership, we have listed a number of rideshare and carpool resources. For rental companies, those that offer alternative transportation options or cars running on alternative fuels (biodiesel, hybrid, CNG, and flex fuel) meet our criteria for inclusion.

Enterprise Rent-A-Car

800-736-8222
Daily 24 hrs. **enterprise.com**
Hybrids or E85 models can be booked by phone; also provides a carbon offset option through TerraPass when reserving online, by phone, or at time of pickup. Operates 28 locations in New York City area.

Go Loco

Daily 24 hrs. **goloco.org**
Rideshare service that builds travel networks and offsets public transportation burden with local carpooling. Email alerts are sent when friends or groups travel to your chosen destinations. Travel costs can be split online for a 10% fee.

Hertz

800-654-3131
Daily 24 hrs. **hertz.com**
Rental vehicles at 16 locations in New York City area, including all major airports. Specify "Green Collection" to reserve hybrids and high-mileage cars online or with phone reservations.

Ride Amigos

Daily 24 hrs. **rideamigos.com**
Free local rideshare network linking individuals in text message groups organized by location and direction of travel. Web-based carbon calculator tracks emission savings and cost calculator estimates taxi fare-splitting.

Vehicle Manufacturers, Dealerships, and Maintenance

One of the most effective ways to start slowing global climate change is by driving less, and, when you do drive, by using a fuel-efficient, low-polluting vehicle.

The average new car is responsible for about two metric tons of carbon emissions each year. That means, if you're like many households and have a second car, your average annual emissions is up to 3.7 metric tons—and that doesn't even take into account the production of car or maintenance items.

So when it's time to clean up your corner of the sky, why not buy a high-mileage vehicle or one that runs on compressed natural gas or biodiesel? Even electric cars are no longer out of the question. In fact, one of the most exciting areas of alternative energy use is the new crop of eco-friendly vehicles. After a century of reliance on gas-powered cars and trucks, there is a growing number of dealers dedicated to providing you with low-emission, fuel-efficient alternatives to yesterday's gas guzzler.

Check out the diverse group below. We've found some green car brokers who can hook you up with biofuel or compressed natural gas vehicles. We have also identified a number of car manufacturers with some super fuel-efficient and hybrid models. Not all dealerships, however, carry all of a manufacturer's hybrid or fuel-efficient models, and fewer still might actually have them on the lot. So, of the manufacturers we have included, only those individual locations that have eco-friendly models on the lot, available for test driving, are listed. If you don't see a make or model listed here that is available to try out, check the manufacturer's Web site for a dealership near you that carries it.

Hybrids can be a hot ticket to great MPG, but not always. Be sure to check out the most fuel-efficient vehicle in its class (SUV, sedan, etc.) on **fueleconomy.gov** before making a decision. For simplicity, we have chosen to list only new vehicles that achieve 30+ miles per gallon in city driving (as of February 2008). Look to **greenopia.com** for updates on new makes and models that meet our criteria as they actually become available (not just promised).

The listed businesses are included as a resource for you. We have not leaf-awarded this category, but if we've listed it, we are impressed. If you are looking for a way to create a major change in your own energy consumption, this is a key place to start.

Manufacturers and Dealerships

Chrysler
gemcar.com
Manufacturer of GEM neighborhood electric vehicles.

Ford
ford.com
Manufactures the Escape hybrid SUV.

Ford—Major World Ford Lincoln Mercury
50-30 Northern Blvd. (bet. 50th St. & Newton Rd.), Long Island City (Qns),
800-672-0881
Mon–Thu 9am–9pm Fri 9am–7pm Sat 10am–7pm Sun 12pm–6pm   major-
worldfordlincolnmercury.dealerconnection.com
Dealer offering Ford Escape hybrids.

Ford—Manhattan Automobile Company
787 11th Ave. (bet. W. 54th & 55th Sts.), Midtown West (Man), 212-974-1010
Mon–Fri 9am–8pm Sat 9am–6pm **manhattanauto.com**
Dealer offering Ford Escape and hybrids on the lot.

General Motors
livegreengoyellow.com
Manufactures E85 FlexFuel vehicles.

Honda
honda.com
Manufactures Civic and Accord hybrids, Civic CNG, and the fuel-efficient Fit.

Honda—Potamkin Honda
706 11th Ave. (bet. 50th & 51st Sts.), Midtown West (Man), 212-974-1010
Mon–Fri 9am–8pm Sat 10am–6pm Sun 12pm–5pm **potamkinhonda.com**
Dealer offering Honda Civic hybrids and Honda GX natural gas vehicles. Also
offers the Phill home refueling appliance and provides aid in processing Phill
NY State tax incentives.

Mazda
mazda.com
Manufacturer of the Tribute hybrid SUV.

Mercury
mercuryvehicles.com
Manufacturer of the Mariner hybrid SUV.

Mercury—Manhattan Automobile Company
787 11th Ave. (bet. W. 54th & 55th Sts.), Midtown West (Man), 212-974-1010
Mon–Fri 9am–8pm Sat 9am–6pm **manhattanauto.com**
Dealer offering Mercury Mariner hybrids on the lot.

Mini
miniusa.com
Manufactures the small fuel-efficient Mini Cooper vehicles made in England.

Mini—Mini of Manhattan
555 W 57th St. (11th Ave.), Midtown West (Man), 212-586-6464
Mon–Thu 9am–7pm Fri 9am–6pm Sat 10am–5pm
Local dealership offering a full selection of Mini's. Call or visit website for
specials and to schedule a test drive.

Nissan

nissanusa.com
Manufacturer of the Altima hybrid.

Nissan—Nissan of Manhattan

646 11th Ave. (47th St.), Clinton (Man), 212-459-1500
Mon–Thu 9am–8pm Fri 9am–7pm Sat 9am–6pm Sun 12pm–5pm
nissanofmanhattan.net
Dealer offering Nissan Altima hybrids.

Smart

smartusa.com
Manufactures the compact and fuel-efficient smart fortwo models. Visit
website to reserve a car.

Smart—Smart Center Manhattan

536 W. 41st St. (11th Ave.), Clinton (Man), 212-629-1639
Mon–Wed 9am–6pm Thu 9am–8pm Fri 9am–6pm Sun 9am–5pm
smartcentermanhattan.com
Smart dealer offering test drives of space-efficient Smart Cars.

Tango

commutercars.com
Manufacturer of electric vehicles.

Tesla Motors

teslamotors.com
Manufacturer and distributor of a high performance electric vehicle. Sign up
online for 2009 wait list for new purchase.

Toyota

toyota.com
Manufactures the Prius and Camry hybrids and the fuel-efficient Yaris and
Corolla.

Toyota—Fordham Toyota

236 W. Fordham Rd. (bet. Landing Rd. & Cedar Ave.), University Heights
(Brx), 212-690-8000
Mon–Thu 9am–9pm Fri–Sat 9am–7pm Sun 12pm–5pm **fordhamtoyota.com**
Dealer offering Prius, Camry, and Highlander hybrids on the lot.

Toyota—Queensboro Toyota

62-10 Northern Blvd. (62nd St.), Woodside (Qns), 718-355-8600
Mon–Thu 9am–9pm Fri 9am–7pm Sat 10am–7pm Sun 12pm–6pm
queensborotoyota.com
Dealer offering Prius, Camry, and Highlander hybrids on the lot. Also sells
pre-owned hybrids when available.

Zap

zapworld.com
Manufacturer of neighborhood electric vehicles.

Zenn

zenncars.com
Manufacturer of neighborhood electric vehicles.

Diagnostics, Maintenance, and Repair

Bay Diagnostic

1717 Gravesend Neck Rd. (17th St.), Gravesend (Bkn), 718-615-0705
Mon–Fri 8am–5:30pm Sat 7:30am–1pm **baydiagnostic.com**
Diagnostics, repair, and maintenance for Toyota Prius hybrids, OEM natural gas vehicles, and ethanol-system vehicles. Conducts CNG vehicle certifications for key card, leak, and service inspection requirements.

Clean Vehicle Systems

1168 Castelton Ave. (bet. Roe & Elizabeth Sts.), Port Richmond (S.I.), 718-447-3038
Mon–Fri 8am–5pm
Diagnostics, repair, and maintenance for natural gas vehicles. Also conducts inspections and offers verifications for NGV certifications.

Re-Action Auto

12-30 Clintonville St. (12th Rd.), Whitestone (Qns), 718-767-3113
Mon–Fri 6:30am–6pm Sat 6:30am–1pm
Full diagnostic service and repair of all hybrid, NGV, fleet service vehicles, and previously converted biodiesel engines; additional capacity to perform NGV inspections for key card certification.

Greener Roadside Service

There is one national auto club that is environmentally friendly. This club offers the standard 24/7 emergency roadside assistance, trip planning, and maps, but also supports mass transit funding, the Clean Air Act, and higher fuel economy standards. Its name: Better World Club. Not only does Better World Club have a unique policy agenda, it offers bicycle roadside assistance, carbon offsets, discounts on hybrid car rentals and eco-travel. For more information, go to **betterworldclub.com.**

If you don't already belong to Better World Club, do some research on your current auto club to make sure they don't use membership funds to lobby against mass transit projects, bike paths, or increasing mileage standards in automobiles.

Fueling Stations

New York will always be a subway city and a place of other public transportation options. The number of bike riders is on the upswing, and there are, and will always be, countless pedestrians. But maybe somewhere in the mix a desire for alternative fuels and alternative fuel vehicles exists, in which case, you will need to know where to fill up.

To get you started, we have listed the most readily available compressed natural gas (CNG) and biodiesel facilities in the NYC area. These stations may require membership cards for access, or company-specific credit cards for payment. NYC Fire Department regulations require a "driver's certificate" before fueling at CNG facilities. Certificates can be obtained after completing a free twenty-minute training program offered through ConEd.

If you're traveling, check out the U.S. Department of Energy's alternative fuel locator at **eere.energy.gov/afdc/fuels/stations.html** or **biodiesel.org** for a list of alternative fueling stations outside the NYC area. (Be sure to call ahead for hours before hitting the road.)

This is not a leaf-awarded category, but if you have an alternative fuel vehicle, these stations and resources offer the kind of fuel, supplies, and services you need.

Clean Energy Fuels—BP LaGuardia Airport Gas Station
Parking Lot 7, Bldg. 37 (Grand Central Pkwy., Marine Air Term. exit,), Flushing (Qns), 718-803-1418
Daily 24 hrs.   **cleanenergyfuels.com/stations/newyork.html**
CNG station requiring certified key card issued by Clean Energy Fuels. Cash and all major credit cards are accepted upon presenting the Clean Energy Card. To open key card account, call 718-685-2912 or check website.

Con Edison CNG Fueling Stations
The following list of CNG stations require a certified key card issued by Con Edison. All payments are made through a Con Edison fueling card. For more information, or to open an account, contact the Fueling Stations Administrator at 718-204-4048, or contact the station manager at the individual station listed below.

Bronx—Van Nest Service Center
1615 Bronxdale Ave. (bet. Van Nest & Pierce Aves.), Van Nest (Brx), 718-904-4763
Mon–Fri 7am–6pm

Manhattan—E. 16th St. Service Center
700 E. 16th St. (Ave. C), Stuyvesant Town (Man), 212-460-6747
Daily 24 hrs.

Manhattan—W. 29th St. Service Center
W. 29th St. (12th Ave.), Chelsea (Man), 212-643-3059
Daily 24 hrs.

Queens—College Point Service Center
124-15 31st Ave. (College Point Blvd.), Flushing (Qns), 718-321-4815
Daily 24 hrs.

National Grid (formerly Key Span) CNG Fueling Stations
The following CNG stations require a certified key card issued by National Grid. All payment is made through the card account. For more information, or to open an account, contact the station manager or visit **nationalgrid.com**, click on "Keyspan Customers" and enter "CNG fueling stations" in the search box.

Brooklyn—Canarsie Service Station
8424 Ditmas Ave. (Branton St.), Canarsie (Bkn), 718-270-5866
Daily 24 hrs.

Brooklyn—Greenpoint Energy Station
287 Maspeth Ave. (bet. Varick & Vandervoort Aves.), Greenpoint (Bkn)
Daily 24 hrs.

Brooklyn—Marine Park Service Station
2900 Flatbush Ave. (NYC Dept. of Trans.), Marine Park (Bkn)
Daily 24 hrs.

Brooklyn—Prospect Heights Mobil Service Station
195 Flatbush Ave. (bet. Dean & Pacific Sts.), Prospect Heights (Bkn)
Daily 24 hrs.

Queens—Jamaica (JFK) Service Station
John F. Kennedy International Airport, Jamaica (Qns), 718-963-5495
Daily 24 hrs.

Queens—Springfield Service Station
127-11 Farmers Blvd. (175th St.), Queens (Qns), 718-963-5495
Daily 7am–11pm

Staten Island—Staten Island Service Station
200 Gulf Ave. (Western Ave. S), Bloomfield (S.I.), 718-982-7354
Daily 7am–11pm

Tri-State Biodiesel
36 E. 23rd St., 9th Flr. (bet. Park & Madison Aves.), Flatiron (Man), 646-432-5759
By appt. only   **tristatebiodiesel.com**
New York City–based company making B5 to B100 biodiesel blended from recycled cooking oil collected from over 1,500 local restaurants. The biodiesel is available to a members-only buyers club that meets weekly in Red Hook, Brooklyn. Membership is free.

Drive
less.

New Yorkers Get Around

New Yorkers are known for embracing public and alternative transportation. Cars aren't the first transportation choice for many New Yorkers, and this tendency has served the city well, given its vast population. Using subways, buses, bikes, and feet keeps the city's per capita carbon footprint significantly lower than it would otherwise be. All indications are that it will continue to decline as more and more New Yorkers get on their bikes, take the A train, step on a hybrid bus, or put on their walking shoes.

Mass Transit

A great way to get around New York City is on its extensive public transportation network (the MTA). Subway trains and buses operate 24/7, and rides are just $2. Passengers can choose to pay by the ride or purchase value-added unlimited MetroCards that provide access to both subways and buses.

Subways transport 7 million people a day. That translates into approximately 700,000 fewer cars on the streets of NYC every day. It also means 400 million fewer pounds of soot, carbon monoxide, hydrocarbons, and other toxic substances are released into NYC's air each year. NYC Transit's Storm Water Management Program uses a recycled graywater collection system to clean the subway cars. This is nonindustrial wastewater generated from sources such as residential dishwashing, laundry machines, and bathwater.

Buses are going hybrid, with 550 already in the fleet and many more slated for entry. Buses are also wheelchair accessible and air-assist-designed so that those with physical impairments can board more easily.

Taxicabs

Taxis in New York set a national standard. As announced by Mayor Michael R. Bloomberg and the Taxi and Limousine Commission (TLC), NYC will have "a fully hybrid fleet by 2012—the largest, cleanest fleet of taxis on the planet." New York's extensive fleet of regulated yellow taxicabs, many of which are already hybrid electric-gas vehicles, can be hailed by anyone on any street corner 24 hours a day (especially in Manhattan).

Liveries and Black Cars

In February 2008, Mayor Bloomberg announced that all TLC black cars would be required to go green, necessitating the conversion to hybrid vehicles. Through legislation requiring heightened fuel-efficiency standards, emissions from black cars will be cut in half.

Walking

New York City is a great walking city—whether one is strolling to sightsee or just trying to get from point A to point B in a short time. Streets are wide, unobstructed, and usually designed on a straight-line grid system. Curb corners have been remodeled to accommodate those who are wheelchair bound. In addition, major events, attractions, restaurants, and businesses are often within easy access of each other.

Bicycling

NYC has expanded its dedicated bike lanes. Besides paths in the parks, the city has set aside more miles of safer, dedicated bike lanes on city streets as part of a long-term bicycle plan started in 2006. With more than eighty miles of lanes installed to date, New York City's eighteen-hundred-mile bike-lane goal is on track for completion by 2030.

(Sources: **mta.info** and **nyc.gov**)

Transportation

Information provided by NYC & Company, the official marketing and tourism organization for the City of New York, dedicated to maximizing travel and tourism opportunities throughout the five boroughs, building economic prosperity, and spreading the positive image of New York City worldwide.

Travel

A Green-Eyed View of NYC

By Wendy Brawer

With just a bit of forethought, you can get to the City's green-est places in a sustainable way. Of the 120,000 tourists that arrive in NYC every day, many expect to explore the splendors of the Green Apple, staying in green accommodations and maximizing every moment. Joining them are increasing numbers of New Yorkers opting to vacation at home, sparing the carbon to trace organic roots beneath the City grid.

I've been seeing and sharing a green-eyed view of NYC since 1992, even giving Green Apple Tours to showcase our progress. NYC offers great diversity, mobility, and waterborne adventures alongside intensely authentic cultural experiences, all just an economical MetroPass away.

Or, grab a bicycle and connect with 111 miles of on-street lanes. Pedal along the Hudson River Greenway through Battery Park City's green developments, native plants, and site-specific artworks, connecting south to the labyrinth toward harbor views and Staten Island's Ferry (free voyage, green terminals, 24/7!).

Refill your water bottle, unfold your canvas shopping bag, and head over to the totally fresh scene at Union Square Greenmarket. Pick up a Green Apple Map there, then head to the vibrant cultural mash-up of the East Village community's Garden District. Pedicabs, the Roosevelt Island Tram, and great walking through four hundred villages await you. You'll build up an appetite saving all that fossil fuel and have enough money left over for an organic meal on the town!

Travel

The first to use the "Green Apple" as the NYC eco-moniker in 1991, Wendy Brawer is founding director of the fifty-country Green Map movement (**greenmap.org**), creator of NYC's own **greenapplemap.org**, and an everyday cyclist.

Travel Services

We live in a world in which travel has become increasingly essential and complex. We, as travelers, are faced with a myriad of choices—the form of transport, the type of accommodation, and the planning of an itinerary.

Eco-tourism offers some exciting new opportunities to experience the world without leaving a heavy footprint. Work with an agency or service that specializes in that kind of travel if you'd like to see faraway places in an environmentally friendly way. *Bon voyage!*

This is a changing area, so this category has not yet been leaf-awarded. However, to be listed here, businesses must be very familiar with, focus primarily on, and actively promote eco-travel.

Better World Club Travel Service
866-238-1137
Daily 8:30am–5:30pm   **betterworldclub.com**
Auto club and insurance company offering online database of eco-friendly hotels, eco-tourism packages, and travel agent consultation. Nationwide service. Discounts for members.

Common Circle Expeditions
3848 SE Division St., Ste. 364, Portland, OR 97202, 503-239-8426
Daily 24 hrs.   **commoncircle.com**
Bicycle tours in Oregon and Hawaii with a focus on organic farming, permaculture, green building, and sustainability. Food provided is mostly organic, locally sourced, and vegan. Book online.

Earth Routes
207-326-8635
Mon–Sat 9am–6pm   **earthroutes.net**
Nationwide green travel planning service with a focus on transportation.

Ecoclub.com (International Ecotourism Club)
Mon–Fri 24 hrs.   ecoclub.com
Online network promoting eco-conscious tourism worldwide.

Ecotravel.com
Daily 24 hrs.   **ecotravel.com**
Online magazine, community, and directory with eco-tourism information and resources. International service.

Ela Brasil Tours
14 Burlington Dr., Norwalk, CT 06851, 203-840-9010
Online or phone   **elabrasil.com**
Responsible travel company offering sustainable tourism trips to Brazil.

Escape Adventures
8221 W. Charleston Blvd., Ste. 101, Las Vegas, NV 89117, 800-596-2953
Daily 24 hrs.   **escapeadventures.com**
Specializes in eco-friendly cycling and multisport adventure travel in Northwest America, Belize, and Hawaii.

G.A.P Adventures

364 6th Ave. (Waverly Pl.), Greenwich Village (Man), 212-228-6655
Mon–Fri 10am–6pm Sat 10am–5pm **gapadventures.com**
Specializes in worldwide, small-group outdoor adventure travel with a commitment to sustainable eco-tourism practices.

Global Exchange Reality Tours

800-497-1994
Daily 9am–5pm PST **globalexchange.org/tours**
Socially responsible, community-oriented, education- and service-based travel to more than 30 countries.

Good Travel Company, The

Mon–Fri 9am–6pm **goodtravelcompany.com**
International travel company booking eco-friendly vacations, hotels, and transportation that support local people and culture. Provides carbon offsets.

Green Earth Travel, LLC

7 Froude Cir. (MacArthur), Cabin John, MD 20818, 888-246-8343
Daily 9am–5:30pm **greenearthtravel.com**
Specializes in eco-friendly, vegetarian, and sustainable international travel. Offers package trips, adventure travel, cooking tours, and more.

Green Tortoise

494 Broadway Ave., San Francisco, CA 94133, 800-867-8647
Mon–Fri 9am–7pm Sat 12pm–6pm PST **greentortoise.com**
Eco-friendly tours in Mexico, Belize, Guatemala, and U.S. national parks.

Hidden Treasure Tours

509 Lincoln Blvd., Long Beach, NY 11561, 877-761-7276
Daily 24 hrs. **hiddentreasuretours.com**
International eco-tours, eco-trekking workshops, volunteer vacations and sustainable travel customized to clients' needs. Donates to the Chandra Gurung Conservation Trust.

Lonely Planet

150 Linden St., Oakland, CA 94607, 800-275-8555
lonelyplanet.com
Advocates responsible travel and donates to aid projects, human rights organizations, and environmental programs. International service.

Responsible Travel

6 Old Stein, 3rd Flr., Brighton, UK 44, (0)1273 600030
Mon–Fri 9am–5pm **responsibletravel.com**
Holiday travel directory with an emphasis on benefiting local livelihood and minimizing environmental impact. Book online.

Solikai

310-455-6900
Mon–Fri 9am–6pm PST **solikai.com**
Adventure sports destination club using low-impact, sustainable housing around the globe. Membership includes full use of surfing, biking, skiing, and snowboarding equipment.

Sustainable Travel International

P.O. Box 1313, Boulder, CO 80306, 720-273-2975
Mon-Fri 8am-5pm MST **sustainabletravelinternational.org**
Promotes eco-tourism, sustainable development, and green travel products and provides a directory of environmentally friendly vacations. National and international travel.

Hotels and Lodging

Whether you are planning a family vacation, welcoming family or friends into town, or going away on business, the hotel you choose matters. Next time, when selecting a hotel, take into account factors that will affect your personal health and the health of the planet.

We have evaluated hotels in a number of key areas, all of which directly impact both the hotel guest and/or the environment. Some of the hotels listed below have an official environmental policy to which they aspire to adhere. Others are making a concerted effort to be better planetary citizens. Our criteria is extensive and includes the following areas:

- Extent of recycling program.

- Efficient resource management including energy, water, and waste systems.

- Good ventilation and fresh air exchange for healthy indoor air.

- Use of nontoxic or low-toxic maintenance and cleaning products and practices.

- Environmentally sound purchasing practices.

- "Green" landscaping.

- Sustainable restaurant and food services.

- Eco-friendly building materials.

- Beds, bedding, towels, and other linens made of organic and/or natural fibers; mattresses made of mostly organic, chemical-free, and/or natural materials.

Hotels performed at an overall average of:

at least 25% in each of the above areas.
at least 50% in each of the above areas.
at least 75% in each of the above areas.
at least 90% in each of the above areas.

Average room price:

$	$175 or less	$$$	$251–$325
$$	$176–$250	$$$$	$326 and up

Benjamin Hotel, The $$$$
125 E. 50th St. (bet. Lexington & 3rd Aves.), Murray Hill (Man), 212-715-2500
Daily 24 hrs. **thebenjamin.com**
Luxury hotel with organic or all-natural fiber bedding and linens, Energy Star–rated appliances, and water efficiency fixtures in all rooms. Airport transportation offered to guests in hybrid limos. ECOTEL-rated.

East Village Bed and Coffee 🍃🍃🍃 $

110 Ave. C (bet. E. 7th & 8th Sts.), East Village (Man), 917-816-0071
By appt. **bedandcoffee.com**
Eco-friendly B&B with 10 energy-efficient rooms, bamboo fiber bedding, and
recycling bins; direct trade coffee served; bicycles available for guests' use.
Owner also runs a seasonal organic community garden.

1871 House 🍃 $$$$

212-756-8823
By appt. **1871house.com**
Suites and studios in a historic brownstone with energy- and water-efficient
fittings. Rooms cleaned using chemical-free, biodegradable products. Recycling program.

Greenpoint Lodge 🍃🍃🍃 $

95 Norman Ave. (bet. Manhattan Ave. & Leonard St.), Greenpoint (Bkn),
917-385-2416
Daily 9am–10pm **greenpointlodge.com**
B&B garden apartment that can sleep one to four. Organic linens and towels; uses nontoxic cleaning supplies, CFLs, and green power from ConEd;
serves organic fair trade coffee, milk, and sugar. Stocks other eco-friendly
accessories from the Green Tree General Store downstairs.

Muse Hotel, The 🍃 $$$$

130 W. 46th St. (bet. 6th & 7th Aves.), Midtown (Man), 212-485-2400
Daily 24 hrs. **themusehotel.com**
Pet-friendly boutique hotel providing in-room recycling bins and organic or
all-natural fiber bedding and linens. Rooms painted with low- to no-VOC
paint and equipped with energy- and water-efficient devices. Chemical-free
and biodegradable cleaning products are used.

Park Slope Bed and Breakfast 🍃🍃 $$

718-965-2355
By appt. **bbparkslope.com**
B&B with Energy Star–rated appliances, recycling, and a linen reuse pro-
gram. Serves organic breakfasts.

70 Park Avenue Hotel 🍃🍃 $$$$

70 Park Ave. (E. 38th St.), Murray Hill (Man), 212-973-2400
Daily 24 hrs. 70parkave.com
Luxury hotel with in-room recycling as well as water- and energy-efficiency
programs. Restaurant offers certified organic produce when available, wild-
caught seafood, and fair trade coffee. Uses chemical-free cleaning products.

Sugar Hill Harlem Inn 🍃🍃🍃 $

212-234-5432
Daily 24 hrs. **sugarhillharleminn.com**
B&B with organic fiber bedding and linens. Uses chemical-free, biodegradable cleaners. Solar panels provide half of the energy for the inn. Organic
local food ingredients used to prepare mostly vegan cuisine; food waste is
composted on-site.

West Eleventh Townhouse 🍃🍃 $$

278 W. 11th St. (bet. Bleecker & W. 4th Sts.), Greenwich Village (Man),
212-675-7897
By appt. **west-eleventh.com**
Apartment-style accommodations equipped with water- and energy-efficient
devices. Recycling and linen reuse program.

Travel

Day-Tripping the Great Green NYC Way

For visitors and residents alike, New York City has many great ways to experience its eco-friendly urban environment. As one of the greenest big cities in the United States, New York has more than six thousand acres of woodland parks—an impressive amount of green space that doesn't even include the miles of canopied city sidewalks, pocket parks, wetlands, and leafy waterfront promenades. Together, these green spaces account for more than twenty-eight thousand acres, or 14 percent of the city's total area.

New York is also home to a surprising range of green recreational activities—many of them free—in all five boroughs. These activities celebrate nature and promote health while leaving little impact on the environment.

There are more than seventeen hundred parks, playgrounds, and recreational facilities in the city's five boroughs and about fourteen miles of sandy beaches (**nyc.gov/parks**), from Orchard Beach in the Bronx and Brighton Beach in Brooklyn to Rockaway Beach in Queens and South Beach on Staten Island. There are also fifty-four public pools—the newest is the Olympic-sized pool in Flushing Meadows–Corona Park, Queens. The Hudson River is cleaner than it's been in more than a century. Modern-day explorers will find free canoe lessons in Brooklyn on the Gowanus Canal, in Red Hook, and in DUMBO (**gowanuscanal.org**). Kayak rides can be had on Manhattan's west shoreline (free twenty-minute ride, **downtownboathouse.org/links.html**).

Walking is the easiest way to see the city and be environmentally thoughtful. There are scores of walking tours for those wishing to explore iconic or "secret" places in each borough. Choose from well-planned, self-led audio tours or sign up with licensed companies with knowledgeable specialists. Study horticulture with Urban Park Rangers (free, **nyc.gov/parks**), relax on vehicle-free Governor's Island (free, **govisland.com**), take in views from the elevated High Line set to open fall 2008 (**thehighline.org**), or stroll Stuyvesant Cove Park (212-673-7507, **stuyvesantcove.org**).

If you opt to bike the city, try one of the many rental or purchase options listed here, including Recycle-A-Bicycle (**recycleabicycle. org**), a nonprofit group where kids repair and refurbish bikes otherwise destined for the trash heap. Skaters can try the Central Park Skate Patrol (**skatepatrol.org**, 212-439-1234), offering free weekend tutorials for inline skaters at various skill levels, and Blades Board and Skate (**blades.com**, 888-552-5233) for snowboarding and skating instruction, servicing, sales and rentals.

Another low-impact, eco-friendly summertime activity is to step outdoors for a night on the town. You can watch film, opera, dance, and theater out of doors—and all for free. Rooftop Films (**rooftopfilms.com**) showcases underground independent movies on Brooklyn rooftops. HBO Bryant Park Summer Film Festival (**bryantpark.org/calendar/film-festival.php**) features classics every Monday in Midtown Manhattan. The Metropolitan Opera House brings performances to citywide parks (**metoperafamily.org**), and Lincoln Center Out-of-Doors (**lincolncenter.org**) presents hundreds of events annually on its plaza.

Go to **nycvisit.com** for more information on living it up in a green way in NYC.

Travel

Being
Involved

Cast Your Vote for Wildlife

By John Calvelli

People think of New York City as a jungle of concrete, not trees, yet there are still a surprising number of green spaces within our city limits. These vary from diminutive city parks dotted with a few shade trees, to the Bronx's Pelham Bay Park, which at three thousand acres is not only the largest park in New York, but also a key stopover for migratory birds. Stewardship of these last "wild" places is the responsibility of every New Yorker.

At the Wildlife Conservation Society (WCS), one of the world's largest global conservation organizations, I'm proud to say that the notion "think globally, act locally" is something we practice every day. At the five city zoos that WCS manages, the Bronx Zoo, New York Aquarium, Central Park Zoo, Queens Zoo, and Prospect Park Zoo, we inspire four million visitors annually to care about nature around the world.

Being green is also about personal responsibility, which is why WCS opened the city's largest composting toilet facility at our Bronx Zoo headquarters in 2007. In addition, our historic one-hundred-year-old Lion House has been transformed into a Madagascar exhibit that earned a LEED (Leadership in Energy and Environmental Design) Gold certification—New York's first green landmark building.

As the world enters a period of tremendous environmental challenge brought on by climate change, species loss, and habitat conversion, we need advocates and champions for green ideas more than ever. Remember that wildlife can't vote and trees don't lobby Congress. They need your voice.

John Calvelli is the senior vice president of public affairs for the Bronx Zoo-based Wildlife Conservation Society, which runs the world's largest network of urban zoos and conservation programs in sixty countries (**wcs.org**).

Being Involved

Environmental Organizations

It's easy to be overwhelmed by the sheer number of environmental problems that plague our planet, but the organizations listed below are making a real difference. They inform and motivate, promote environmental awareness in different areas, and provide opportunities to get involved. Engaging with any one of these groups is a great way to learn about the problems your own community faces and to help find and implement the solutions to solve those problems.

All organizations in this section promote environmental preservation, conservation, and education, or habitat management. They offer direct, local community involvement through classes and/or environmental work programs. None operate on a for-profit basis.

Alley Pond Environmental Center
228-06 Northern Blvd. (228th St.), Douglaston (Qns), 718-229-4000
Mon–Sat 9am–4:30pm Sun 9:30pm–3:30pm (Sep–Jun) **alleypond.com**
Private, nonprofit corporation dedicated to establishing awareness, understanding, and appreciation of the environment and the responsibility of preserving the environment in an urban setting.

American Geographical Society of New York
120 Wall St., Ste. 100 (bet. Front St. & E. River Piers), Wall Street (Man), 212-422-5456
Mon–Fri 9am–5pm **amergeog.org**
Business, professional, and scholarly worlds are linked in the creation and application of geographical knowledge and techniques to address economic, social, and environmental problems. Internship opportunities available.

Astoria Residents Recycling Our Wastes
P.O. Box 9060, Astoria (Qns), 718-595-2829
arrowonline.org
A community organization addressing local environmental problems in Western Queens through long- and short-term hands-on projects. Volunteer opportunities available.

Bayside Anglers Group Ltd.
46-35 Oceania St., Marie Curie Middle School, M.S.158 (bet. 46th Rd. & 47th Ave.), Bayside (Qns), 347-804-6525
baysideanglers.com
Organization promotes safe, effective, and environmentally sound recreational fishing practices through community outreach events. Volunteer opportunities available.

Blacksmith Institute

2014 5th Ave. (bet. 124th & 125th Sts.), Harlem (Man), 646-742-0200
blacksmithinstitute.org
Organization developing and implementing solutions for pollution-related problems in the developing world; works cooperatively with partnerships to provide support to local champions while striving to solve pollution-related problems.

Bronx River Alliance

1 Bronx River Pkwy. (Birchall Ave.), Van Nest (Brx), 718-430-4665
Mon–Fri 9am–5pm **bronxriver.org**
Works to protect, improve, and restore the Bronx River corridor and greenway.

Buckminster Fuller Institute

181 N. 11th St., Ste. 402 (bet. Driggs & Bedford Aves.), Williamsburg (Bkn), 718-290-9280
Mon–Fri 9am–5pm **bfi.org**
Serves as a catalyst for the design and implementation of breakthrough strategies for achieving a sustainable future. Volunteer opportunities available.

Cloud Forest Conservation Alliance

119 W. 82nd St. (Columbus Ave.), Upper West Side (Man), 212-362-9391
Hours vary by project **cloudforests.org**
Tropical cloud- and rain-forest preservation efforts include reforestation, research, and creating public awareness on issues related to the world's diminishing tropical forests. Volunteer opportunities available.

Council on the Environment of New York City

51 Chambers St., Rm. 228 (bet. Broadway & Centre St.), Civic Center (Man), 212-788-7900
Mon–Fri 9am–5pm **cenyc.org**
Privately funded citizen group that promotes environmental awareness among New Yorkers and solutions to environmental problems. Programs cover environmental education, Greenmarkets, open space greening, and recycling outreach and education.

Earth Celebrations

638 E. 6th St. (bet. Aves. B & C), Lower East Side (Man), 212-777-7969
earthcelebrations.com
Programs dedicated to fostering ecological awareness through the arts; includes educational art and ecology workshops for youth and adults, exhibitions, and more. Volunteer opportunities available.

Earth Day New York

201 E. 42nd St., Ste. 3200 (3rd Ave.), Murray Hill (Man), 212-922-0048
By appt. **earthdayny.org**
Organization promoting environmental awareness through school involve-ment in the Earth Day Education Program, educating policymakers through conferences and publications, and involving the general public in annual Earth Day events.

Earth Share of New York

305 7th Ave., 15th Flr. (bet. W. 27th & 28th Sts.), Chelsea (Man), 212-822-9567
Mon–Fri 9:30am–5:30pm **earthshareny.org**
Network of nearly 60 environmental organizations that engage individuals and organizations in creating and promoting healthy, safe, and sustainable communities.

East New York Farms!

613 New Lots Ave. (bet. Schenck Ave. & Hendrix St.), East New York (Bkn),
718-649-7979

Mon–Fri 9am–5pm **eastnewyorkfarms.org**

Organization that directs a youth internship program, supports community
gardeners to grow food for local consumption, and runs a farmers' market
featuring locally grown produce. Volunteer opportunities available.

EcoAgents

318 E. 70th St. (2nd Ave.), Upper East Side (Man), 212-879-5630

Mon–Fri 11am–8pm **ecoagents.org**

Programs connect and unite Amazon tribes, while working to preserve the
local ecology through tribal education regarding the rights to protect their
land and people.

Emerging Green Builders of NY

Alexander Hamilton U.S. Custom House, 1 Bowling Green, Ste. 419 (Canyon
of Heroes), Battery Park (Man), 212-514-9380

Mon–Fri 9am–5:30pm **egbny.com**

Coalition of students and young professionals promoting the integration of
future leaders into the green building movement. Hosts seminars, promotes
social events, and arranges green building tours in NYC. USGBC affiliated.
Volunteer opportunities available.

Environmental Defense Fund

257 Park Ave. S (bet. 20th & 21st Sts.), Gramercy (Man), 800-684-3322

By appt. **edf.org**

Online activist membership and legal advocacy organization shaping public
policy by advancing science and nonpartisan leadership to benefit the planet
and people.

Farm Sanctuary

1123 Broadway, Ste. 912 (bet. W. 25th & 26th Sts.), Midtown South (Man),
farmsanctuary.org

National nonprofit animal protection organization that works to expose
and stop cruel practices of the "food animal" industry. Shelters in New York
and California care for hundreds of rescued animals. Volunteer and internship opportunities available.

FoodChange

39 Broadway, 10th Flr. (bet. Morris St. & Exchange Pl.), Financial District
(Man), 212-894-8094

Mon–Fri 9am–5pm **foodchange.org**

Organization focused on improving lives through nutrition, education, and
financial empowerment. Provides emergency meals to New York City's
hungry children and adults. Volunteer opportunities available.

For a Better Bronx

199 Lincoln Ave., Ste. 214 (E. 138th St.), Mott Haven (Brx), 718-292-4344

Mon–Fri 12pm–6pm

Nonprofit environmental justice organization serving low-income communities in the Bronx. Work focuses on issues of pollution, local health issues, and
strengthening and expanding their community garden services.

Friends of Hudson River Park

311 W. 43rd St., Ste. 300 (8th Ave.), Clinton (Man), 212-757-0981

Mon–Fri 9am–5pm **fohrp.org**

Volunteers work to secure the completion and care of the Hudson
River Park.

Gaia Institute, The

440 City Island Ave. (bet. Bowne & Ditmars Sts.), City Island (Brx),
gaiainstituteny.org
Nonprofit research and educational institute involved in watershed and wetlands restoration, storm water runoff reduction, green roof installation, and
waste-into-resources technologies. Volunteer opportunities available.

Green Apple Map

220A E. 4th St. (bet. Aves. A & B), East Village (Man), 212-674-1637
By appt. **greenapplemap.org**
Printed and online maps charting NYC's diverse environment and sustainable living opportunities. Check out the global Green Map System program
at greenmap.org.

Green Worker Cooperatives

1231 Lafayette Ave., 4th Flr., Box 23 (bet. Barretto & Barry Sts.), Hunts Point
(Brx), 718-617-7807
Mon–Sat 10am–6pm **greenworker.coop**
South Bronx–based organization dedicated to incubating worker-owned and
environmentally friendly cooperatives in the South Bronx.

Greenbelt Conservancy, The

200 Nevada Ave. (off Rockland Ave.), Richmond (S.I.), 718-667-2165
sigreenbelt.org
Volunteer opportunities available to help promote environmental education
and preserve woodlands, hiking trails, and public access to green spaces in
Staten Island.

GreenHomeNYC

P.O. Box 1052, JAF Building, New York (Man)
greenhomenyc.org
Online green building resource connecting building owners with local green
building service and material providers. Provides monthly forums and annual
tour of green buildings. See website for events.

GreenThumb

49 Chambers St., Rm. 1020 (bet. Broadway & Centre St.), Civic Center (Man),
212-788-8070
Mon–Fri 9am–5pm **greenthumbnyc.org**
Green Thumb's aim is to foster civic participation and encourage neighborhood revitalization while preserving open space. Provides materials,
technical assistance, and support to neighborhood volunteers who manage
community gardens.

Horticultural Society of New York

148 W. 37th St., 13th Flr. (bet. Broadway and 7th Ave.), Clinton (Man),
212-757-0915
Mon–Fri 10am–6pm **hsny.org**
Organization enhancing NYC's environmental and cultural life by providing library resources, art exhibitions, horticultural education, vocational,
and therapeutic outreach programs in schools, prisons, and underserved
NYC neighborhoods.

Inform

5 Hanover Sq. (Pearl St.), Financial District (Man), 212-361-2400
Mon–Fri 9am–5pm **informinc.org**
A video- and web- focused outreach organization that fuels policy change by
empowering and educating businesses, government, and citizens on issues
of sustainability.

Being Involved

Just Food

208 E. 51st St., 4th Flr. (3rd Ave.), Turtle Bay (Man), 212-645-9880
Mon–Fri 9am–6pm **justfood.org**
Nonprofit organization fostering environmental stewardship and new marketing and food-growing opportunities that address the needs of regional
family farmers and New York City urban gardeners and neighborhoods.

La Familia Verde

2158 Mapes Ave. (bet. E. 181st & 182nd Sts.), East Tremont (Brx),
Hours vary by event **lafamiliaverde.org**
A coalition of community gardens in the Crotona, East Tremont, and West
Farms neighborhoods in the Bronx, with a mission to sustain the environ-
ment and culture through education, community service, and horticulture.

Metropolitan Waterfront Alliance

457 Madison Ave. (bet. 50th & 51st Sts.), Midtown (Man), 212-935-9831
Mon–Fri 9am–5pm **waterwire.net**
A coalition of over 300 organizations, companies, utilities, union locals, and
public agencies determined to transform New York and New Jersey Harbor
and Waterways to make them clean and accessible.

Natural Resources Defense Council

40 W. 20th St. (bet. 5th & 6th Aves.), Flatiron (Man), 212-727-2700
By appt. **nrdc.org**
National headquarters for an advocacy organization using law, science, and
support from members and online activists. Defends wilderness and wildlife
and promotes clean air, clean water, and a healthy environment.

Nature Conservancy of New York, The

322 8th Ave., 16th Flr. (E. 26th St.), Chelsea (Man), 212-997-1880
nature.org~/volunteer
Lectures, guided nature preserve research, and stewardship volunteer opportunities deepen conservation efforts at work in New York, the United
States, and over 30 countries.

Neighborhood Open Space Coalition, The

232 E. 11th St. (bet. 2nd & 3rd Aves.), East Village (Man), 646-458-1627
treebranch.net
Advocacy, research, education, and planning dedicated to expanding and
enhancing New York City area parks and open spaces. Volunteer opportunities available.

New York City Audubon Society

71 W. 23rd St., Ste. 1523 (bet. 5th & 6th Aves.), Flatiron (Man), 212-691-7483
Mon–Fri 9:30am–5:30pm **nycaudubon.org**
Society dedicated to the protection of birds, other wildlife, and their habi-
tats through advocacy and education. Volunteer opportunities available.

New York Parks & Conservation Association

731 Lexington Ave., 17th Flr. (bet. 58th & 59th Sts.), Midtown (Man),
212-617-2771
npca.org/northeast
Association working to protect and enhance America's national parks for
present and future generations. Volunteer opportunities available.

New York Public Interest Research Group

9 Murray St, 3rd Flr. (bet. Broadway & Church St.), Tribeca (Man),
212-349-6460
nypirg.org
Nonpartisan nonprofit group established to affect policy reforms while training students and other New Yorkers to become advocates.

New York Restoration Project

254 W. 31st St., 10th Flr. (bet. 7th & 8th Aves.), Midtown (Man),
212-333-2552 212-333-2552
Mon–Fri 9am–6pm **nyrp.org**
Organization that restores, develops, and revitalizes underserved parks, community gardens, and other open spaces in New York City. Founded by Bette Midler. Volunteer opportunities available.

New York Sun Works

1841 Broadway, Ste. 200 (W. 60th St.), Lincoln Square (Man), 212-757-7560
Mon–Fri 9am–5pm **nysunworks.org**
Environmental engineering nonprofit concerned with promoting and designing sustainable, ecologically responsible, urban agriculture systems.

NY/NJ Baykeeper

52 W. Front St. (bet. Beers & Main Sts.), Keyport, NJ 07735, 732-888-9870
nynjbaykeeper.org
Volunteer opportunities available to help protect, preserve, and restore the ecological integrity and productivity of the Hudson-Raritan Estuary.

Open Space Institute

1350 Broadway, Ste. 201 (W. 36th St.), Midtown South (Man), 212-290-8200
Mon–Fri 9:30am–5:30pm **osiny.org**
Institute's mission is to protect scenic, natural, and historic landscapes to ensure public enjoyment, conserve habitats, and sustain community character. Internship opportunities available.

Rainforest Alliance

665 Broadway, Ste. 500 (Bond St.), NoHo (Man), 212-677-1900
By appt. **rainforest-alliance.org**
Advocates of sustainability and environmental preservation working with citizens and businesses to bring sustainable products to market. Lecture series open to New York members.

Rainforest Relief

122 W. 27th St. (6th Ave.), New York (Man), 917-543-4064
By appt. **rainforestrelief.org**
Advocacy and educational organization that shifts building practices and purchasing policy away from the use of virgin wood and ancient-growth forests by offering proven, lasting alternatives.

River Project, The

Pier 40 at West St., 2nd Flr. (W. Houston St.), West Village (Man),
212-233-3030
Mon–Fri 9am–5pm **riverproject.org**
Marine science field station working to protect and restore the ecosystem of the Hudson River estuary through scientific research, hands-on environmental education, and urban habitat improvement.

Being Involved

Rocking The Boat

60 E. 174th St. (bet. Townsend & Walton Aves.), Mt. Eden (Brx),
718-466-5799
rockingtheboat.org
Traditional wooden boatbuilding and on-water education for high school
youth. Programs operate during the fall and spring academic semesters and
the summer.

Shorewalkers

P.O. Box 20748, Cathedral Stn., New York (Man), 212-330-7686
Hours vary by event **shorewalkers.org**
Advocacy for green shorelines through volunteer-led waterway walks and
trail building. "The Great Saunter" each May: one-day, 32-mile walk around
Manhattan's rim. Volunteer opportunities available.

Sierra Club NYC Group

116 John St., Ste. 3100 (bet. Pearl & Cliff Sts.), Wall Street (Man),
212-791-3600
Mon–Fri 9am–5pm **newyorksierraclub.org/nyc**
Group works to promote alternative energy, protect air quality, rivers
and coastal areas, and encourage smart growth and public transportation
options. Volunteer opportunities available.

Sixth Street Community Center

638 E. 6th St. (bet. Aves. A & B), Lower East Side (Man), 212-677-1863
Mon–Fri 10am–10pm **sixthstreetcenter.org**
Nonprofit organization focused on issues related to food, health, and the
environment. Programs educate youth in sustainable agriculture, health,
and nutrition.

Solar One

2420 FDR Dr., Service Rd. East (23rd St. at Stuyvesant Cove), Kips Bay (Man),
212-505-6050
By appt. **solar1.org**
Green energy arts and education center run entirely on solar power to intro-
duce New Yorkers to a "Net Zero" lifestyle. Hosts educational programs to
advance community understanding of alternative energy.

Sustainable South Bronx

890 Garrison Ave., #24 (Tiffany St.), Hunts Point (Brx), 718-617-4668
Mon–Fri 9am–5pm **ssbx.org**
Organization promoting environmental justice through economically sustainable projects within the community. Addresses land-use, energy, transportation, water, and waste policy in the South Bronx.

Terreform

180 Varick St., Ste. 930 (King St.), West Village (Man), 212-627-9120
Mon–Fri 9am–5pm **terreform.org**
Organization working to find urban ecological planning solutions: urban self-
sufficiency infrastructures, performative material technologies, and smart
mobility vehicles.

Time's Up!

73 Morton St. (bet. Hudson & Greenwich Sts.), West Village (Man),
212-802-8222
Seasonal hours **times-up.org**
Volunteer-run nonprofit using educational outreach and community activities
to promote a less toxic, more sustainable New York City through promoting
bicycle use.

Transportation Alternatives
127 W. 26th St., Ste. 1002 (6th Ave.), Chelsea (Man), 212-629-8080
Mon–Fri 9am–5pm **transalt.org**
Education and advocacy encourage and increase nonpolluting, quiet, city-friendly travel through improvement in five areas: bicycling, walking and traffic calming, car-free parks, safe streets, and sensible transportation.

U.S. Green Building Council
Alexander Hamilton U.S. Custom House, 1 Bowling Green, Ste. 419 (Canyon of Heroes), Battery Park (Man), 212-514-9380
Mon–Fri 9am–5:30pm **usgbcny.org**
Mission aims to transform the way buildings are designed, built, and operated to create environmentally responsible, profitable, and healthy living and working spaces. Volunteer opportunities available.

United Nations Environment Programme
2 UN Plaza, Rm. DC2-803 (bet. 1st & 2nd Aves.), Tudor City (Man), 212-963-8210
Mon–Fri 9am–5pm **nyo.unep.org**
Organization promoting the wise use and sustainable development of the global environment. Works with national and international government and nongovernment organizations. Internship opportunities available.

United Puerto Rican Organization of Sunset Park
166A 22nd St. (bet. 3rd & 4th Aves.), Sunset Park (Bkn), 718-492-9307
Mon–Fri 10am–6pm **uprose.org**
Latino community-based organization organizes, advocates, and develops intergenerational indigenous leadership through activism. Primary efforts focus on environmental, social, and economic justice.

West Harlem Environmental Action, Inc.
271 W.125th St. (bet. 126th & St. Nicholas Ave.), Harlem (Man), 212-961-1000
Mon–Fri 9am–5pm **weact.org**
Nonprofit environmental justice organization dedicated to building resident power to improve environmental health, protection, and policy in communities of color.

Wetlands Activism Collective
P.O. Box 344, New York (Man), 775-871-7473
wetlands-preserve.org
Volunteer-run organization campaigning for earth, human, and animal liberation through protest, direct action, street theater, political advocacy, and public education. Volunteer and internship opportunities available.

Wildlife Conservation Society
2300 Southern Blvd. (bet. Garden & 182nd Sts.), East Tremont (Brx), 718-220-5100
Mon–Fri 9am–5pm **wcs.org**
Global conservation organization saving wildlife and lands through international management of urban wildlife parks, including the Bronx Zoo.

Being Involved

Environmental Education

If you want to study something in the environmental arena in depth, there are a growing number of opportunities for further education. You'll find opportunities in traditional and nontraditional settings. We think you'll be amazed at the choices that are now available—for adults and children alike. There are schools that offer environmental studies programs and ones that incorporate sustainable living and real-world environmental issues into their curriculum. If you're looking to get a taste of something new, we've even included a number of local culinary or cooking schools that offer classes on sustainable cooking and incorporate organic foods into their programs.

If you don't find what you are looking for here, many of the environmental organizations we've listed in the previous section also offer a variety of educational workshops or other learning options.

All of the institutions and organizations listed below provide ongoing environmental education, and many also provide community outreach. Some offer advanced degrees in environmental fields. Others are geared specifically to educate and inspire adults and/or children to become good stewards of the Earth. Be sure to check the organizations' websites regularly to see when classes are offered. Programs are listed based on their primary educational focus and who they serve.

Accredited Degree Programs

Adelphi University—Manhattan Center
75 Varick St., 2nd Flr. (bet. Canal & Watts Sts.), West Village (Man), 212-965-8340
Mon–Fri 9am–4pm **adelphi.edu/manhattan**
BA and MS in Environmental Studies at Garden City location. Master's program is divided into Global Human Environment and Global Physical Environment concentrations or integrated Environmental Education degree.

Bard Graduate Center for Studies in the Decorative Arts, Design, and Culture
18 W. 86th St. (bet. Central Park W. & Columbus Ave.), Upper West Side (Man), 212-501-3000
Mon–Fri 9am–5pm **bard.edu/bgc**
MA degrees in garden history and landscapes, with additional opportunities in landscape architecture, horticulture, planning, environmental conservation, historic preservation, and public garden administration.

Barnard College

3009 Broadway (bet. 116th & 120th Sts.), Upper West Side (Man), 212-854-5262

Mon–Fri 9am–5pm **barnard.columbia.edu**

Women's liberal arts college offering programs in Environmental Science, Policy, and Biology. Campus sustainability policy aims to reduce CO_2 emissions 30% by 2017.

Clarkson University

8 Clarkson Ave., Potsdam, NY 13699, 315-268-6400

clarkson.edu

Majors are offered in Environmental Engineering, Health Science, and Science and Policy, as well as Master's and doctoral degrees in Environmental Science and Engineering.

Columbia University

2960 Broadway (W. 116th St.), Morningside Heights (Man), 212-854-1754

Mon–Fri 9am–5pm **columbia.edu**

Wide variety of environmental Bachelor's, Master's, and Ph.D. programs. Many eco-oriented concentrations, centers, institutes, and initiatives. One of the city's 2030 Challenge Partners, committed to reducing emissions 30% by 2017.

CUNY (City University of New York)— Bronx Community College

University Ave. (181st St.), University Heights (Brx), 718-289-5100

Mon–Fri 8am–4pm **bcc.cuny.edu**

Offers AAS Environmental Technology and AS Earth Sciences; both degree programs provide an EPA field study. School is home to the CUNY-wide Center for Sustainable Energy (see listing in General Interest–Adults).

CUNY—Brooklyn College

2900 Bedford Ave. (Campus Rd.), Flatbush (Bkn), 718-951-5000

Mon–Fri 9am–5pm **brooklyn.cuny.edu**

BA in Environmental Studies, BS and MS in Environmental Geology. Aquatic Resource and Environmental Assessment Center (AREAC) on campus.

CUNY—City College of New York

160 Convent Ave. (135th St.), Morningside Heights (Man), 212-650-7000

Mon–Fri 9am–5pm **ccny.cuny.edu**

BS in Environmental and Earth System Science, and BE in Earth System Science and Environmental Engineering. CUNY Sustainability Project represents the school's commitment to reduce emissions 30% by 2017.

CUNY—College of Staten Island

2800 Victory Blvd. (Richmond Ave.), Willow Brook (S.I.), 718-982-2000

Mon–Fri 9am–5pm **csi.cuny.edu**

Graduate program offered in Environmental Science with weather, Fresh Kills Landfill, and other research opportunities available.

CUNY—Hunter College

695 Park Ave., Rm. E1502 (bet. E. 68th St. & Lexington Ave.), Lenox Hill (Man), 212-772-4000

Mon–Fri 9am–5pm **hunter.cuny.edu**

BA in Environmental Studies. Hosts the Climate and Sustainability Lecture Series, providing eight weeks of free programming open to the public. Home to CUNY Institute for Sustainable Cities.

Being Involved

CUNY—LaGuardia Community College, Design Business Center

45-50 30th St. (bet. Thompson & 47th Aves.), Long Island City (Qns),
718-663-8403 **lagc.cuny.edu**
Mon–Fri 9am–4pm
Courses include Sustainable Design, Intro to PV, and Marketing Green
Designs; offered to the professional design community and students.

CUNY—Medgar Evers College

1650 Bedford Ave. (Crown St.), Crown Heights (Bkn), 718-270-4900
Mon–Fri 9am–5pm **mec.cuny.edu**
BS in Environmental Science offered through the Atmospheric/Ocean and
Environmental Science Research Program, a collaboration with the NASA
Goddard Institute for Space Studies. Program includes high school students.

CUNY—Queens College

65-30 Kissena Blvd. (Horace Harding Expy.), Flushing (Qns), 718-997-5000
qc.cuny.edu
BA and BS in Environmental Science; School of Earth and Environmental
Sciences offers an undergraduate degree in Environmental Studies.

Manhattan College

4513 Manhattan College Pkwy., Rm. 8 (Waldo Ave.), Fieldston (Brx),
718-862-8000
Mon–Fri 9am–5pm **manhattan.edu**
Undergraduate and graduate programs in Environmental Engineering.

New School, The

79 5th Ave., 5th Flr. (16th St.), Union Square (Man),
newschool.edu/environmentalstudies
BA and BS in Environmental Studies, with an emphasis on urban ecosystems,
sustainable design, and public policy.

New York Institute of Technology

1855 Broadway (W. 61st St.), Lincoln Square (Man), 212-261-1500
Mon–Fri 9am–5pm **nyit.edu**
Graduate school offers degrees in Environmental Technology and Energy
Management.

New York, State University of

State University Plz., 353 Broadway, Albany, NY 12246, 800-342-3811
Mon–Fri 8:30am–4:30pm **suny.edu**
Associate's, Bachelor's, and Master's degrees in Environmental Studies,
Environmental and Forest Biology, Environmental Science, Environmental
Design, Environmental Biology, Environmental and Natural Resource Conser-
vation, Environmental Analysis, and Environmental Geochemical Science.

New York University

60 W. 4th St. (Washington Sq. S), Greenwich Village (Man), 212-998-4500
nyu.edu
Environmental Studies Program offers opportunities in environmental
science, values, policy, and law. Sustainability program awards grants for
environmental projects and enlists a task force to ensure progress toward
greening the campus.

Pace University

1 Pace Plz. (Nassau St.), Civic Center (Man), 800-874-PACE
pace.edu
Undergraduate and graduate degrees in Environmental Studies and
Environmental Science.

Polytechnic University

6 Metro Tech Ctr. (Jay St.), Downtown Brooklyn (Bkn), 718-260-3600
Mon–Fri 9am–5pm **poly.edu**
Certificate and MS degree in Environmental Behavior studies and BS in Sustainable Urban Environments.

Pratt Institute

200 Willoughby Ave. (bet. Hall St. & Classon Ave.), Clinton Hill (Bkn), 718-636-3600
144 W. 14th St. (6th Ave.), West Village (Man), 718-636-3600
Mon–Fri 9am–5pm **pratt.edu**
Undergraduate and graduate liberal studies school with specific emphasis on art, design, and architecture. Committed to a sustainability mission on both academic and administrative sides of the Institute.

Rochester, University of

601 Elmwood Ave., Rochester, NY 14627, 585-275-2121
Mon–Fri 9am–5pm **rochester.edu**
Private undergraduate and graduate university with the Department of Earth and Environmental Sciences offering multiple degrees.

St. John's University

8000 Utopia Pkwy., Jamaica (Qns), 888-9STJOHNS
stjohns.edu
Catholic University offering BA and BS in Environmental Studies.

Wells College

170 Main St., Aurora, NY 13026, 315-364-3266
Mon–Fri 8:30am–4:30pm **wells.edu**
Liberal arts and sciences for undergraduates. Environmental Studies Department partners with a number of environmental organizations in New York City for student internships and is steadily working to "green" the campus.

Accredited K–12 Programs

Academy for Conservation and the Environment

6565 Flatlands Ave. (Ralph Ave.), Canarsie (Bkn), 718-935-3442
Mon–Fri 8am–4pm
Sustainability-focused program for grades 9–12. Inaugural class (Fall '08) will engage in scientific research and environmentally oriented community service projects.

Academy for Environmental Leadership

400 Irving Ave. (bet. Woodbine St. & Putnam Ave.), Ridgewood (Bkn), 718-935-3339
Mon–Fri 8am–4pm **aelnyc.org**
Small learning community developing grades 9–12 into environmental leaders with a curriculum based on science, mathematics, and technology.

Bard High School Early College

525 E. Houston St. (FDR St.), Lower East Side (Man), 212-995-8479
Mon–Fri 8am–5pm **bard.edu/bhsec**
Partnership between Bard College and the NYC Department of Education providing high school students both a diploma and an AA degree in four years; courses available in environmental studies; school clubs include the Environmentalist Conservationist Organization of BHSEC.

Being Involved

Brooklyn Academy of Science and the Environment

883 Classon Ave., Prospect Heights Educational Campus (Union St.),
Prospect Lefferts Gardens (Bkn), 718-230-6363
An active learning community addressing the needs of young people, grades
9–12; BASE study includes environmental science and justice, urban ecology,
and scientific research.

Brooklyn New School PS 146, The

610 Henry St. (3rd Pl.), Carroll Gardens (Bkn), 718-923-4750
thebrooklynnewschool.org
Pre-K through fifth-grade Magnet School for Applied Learning. Children
study the city, the environment, history, and culture though hands-on,
project-based curriculum.

Brooklyn School for Collaborative Studies

718-923-4750
bcs448.org
Grades 6–12. High school program offers Earth Science, Living Environment
and Environmental Independent Study curriculum. Middle school teaches a
two-month intensive study of the history, use, and cleanup of the Gowanas
Canal.

Buckminster Fuller Institute

181 N. 11th St., Ste. 402 (bet. Driggs & Bedford Aves.), Williamsburg (Bkn),
718-290-9280
bfi.org
Organization that showcases design and implementation of a sustainable
future; offers the annual Design Science Lab and Buckminster Fuller
Challenge for ages 13 and up.

Calhoun School, The

433 West End Ave. (81st St.), Upper West Side (Man), 212-497-6500
Mon–Fri 9am–3:15pm   **calhoun.org**
Private school for children, age three through 12th grade; first educational
institution in NYC to build an eco-friendly green roof.

Cloud Institute for Sustainability Education, The

307 7th Ave., Ste. 1201 (bet. W. 27th & W. 28th Sts.), Chelsea (Man),
212-645-9930
Mon–Fri 9am–5pm   **cloudinstitute.org**
Academic programs in sustainability designed for grades K–12. Consultants
to colleges, universities, and nonacademic organizations; offices built using
salvaged woods.

Earth School, The

600 E. 6th St. (Ave. B), East Village (Man), 212-477-1735
Mon–Fri 8am–3pm   **theearthschool.org**
Public elementary school for pre K–6th grade students offering an arts rich
curriculum dedicated to fostering responsible stewardship of the Earth's
resources and eco-literacy.

Food and Finance High School

525 W. 50th St., Rm. 166 (bet. 10th and 11th Aves.), Clinton (Man),
212-586-2943
Mon–Fri 8:30am–3pm
A program for grades 9–12, with emphasis on culinary arts and a focus on
organic, local, and sustainably raised produce and meats. Students give
organic food demonstrations at the Union Square Farmers' Market.

Friends Seminary

222 E. 16th St. (3rd Ave.), East Village (Man), 212-979-5030
friendsseminary.org
K–12th grade private school founded in 1786 on Quaker practices and educational standards; heavy emphasis on community service for all grade levels.

Gateway School for Environmental Research and Technology at Adlai E. Stevenson High School

1980 Lafayette Ave., Adlai E. Stevenson Educational Campus, Rm. 399 (Pugsley Ave.), Soundview (Brx), 718-824-9327
gateway.cuny.edu
Small school located on the Stevenson High School campus, with a focus on environmental and social justice issues; hands-on experimentation and field trips.

Green School: An Academy for Environmental Careers

223 Graham Ave., 3rd Flr. (Maujer St.), Williamsburg (Bkn), 718-599-1207
Mon–Fri 8:30am–5pm **greenschoolnyc.org**
Environmentally themed curriculum and activities for grades 9–12. Promotes internships in ecological and community renewal, with an emphasis on community involvement and real world learning projects.

High School for Environmental Studies

444 W. 56th St. (9th Ave.), Clinton (Man), 212-262-8113
envirostudies.org
Environmentally infused courses and hands-on programs incorporating the rich diversity of NYC. Offers both environmental seminars and core environmental courses.

Little Red School House and Elisabeth Irwin High School

272 6th Ave. (Bleecker St.), West Village (Man), 212-477-5316
lrei.org
K–12 school providing classes covering social and political environmental issues, organic food, and Greenmarkets; offers wide range of service projects focusing on sustainability; laptops charged with solar power.

Tottenville High School

100 Luten Av. (Amboy Rd.), Princes Bay (S.I.), 718-356-2220
Mon–Fri 8:30am–3pm **tottenvillehs.org**
High school offering courses emphasizing performing and visual arts; advanced placement courses include Environmental Science; school team participates in the NY State Envirothon and Golden Apple Awards.

Urban Assembly School for the Urban Environment

70 Tompkins Ave. (Martin Luther King Pl.), Bedford-Stuyvesant (Bkn), 718-599-0371
Mon–Fri 9am–4pm **urbanassembly.org/uasue.html**
Small public school preparing grades 6–12 for college. Teaches "think global, act local" methods that affect change in the Urban Environment.

General Interest—Adults

Alley Pond Environmental Center

228-06 Northern Blvd. (228th St.), Douglaston (Qns), 718-229-4000
Mon–Sat 9am–4:30pm Sun 9:30pm–3:30pm **alleypond.com**
Private nonprofit corporation dedicated to establishing an awareness of the environment and its preservation in an urban setting; offers lessons in ecology and life sciences for students from pre-kindergarten through high school and beyond.

Auto-Free New York

1 Washington Sq. Village, #5D, Greenwich Village (Man), 212-475-3394
auto-free.org
Advocates for better public transit, fewer cars, and more space for people in NYC; offers monthly mass transit education meetings.

Bike New York

891 Amsterdam Ave. (W. 103rd St.), Upper West Side (Man), 212-932-2453
bikenewyork.org
Promotes bicycling and bicycle safety through events and education. Its Bicycle Education program offers free classes for adults and children.

Brooklyn Botanic Garden

900 Washington Ave. (Eastern Pkwy.), Prospect Heights (Bkn), 718-623-7200
Tue–Fri 8am–6pm Sat–Sun 10am–6pm   **bbg.org**
Fifty-two-acre living museum hosting annual events to celebrate seasonal plants, fruits, and vegetables. Urban composting project, volunteer "Garden Guide" training, and a hands-on vegetable garden for kids and families.

Brooklyn Center for the Urban Environment

168 7th St. (3rd Ave.), Gowanus (Bkn), 718-788-8500
Mon–Fri 9am–5pm   **bcue.org**
The Center offers hands-on family programs ranging from composting to DIY projects using recycled materials.

Center for Sustainable Energy at Bronx Community College

W. 181st St. & University Ave., Bldg. GML-102 , University Heights (Brx), 718-289-5332
Mon–Fri 9am–5pm   **csebcc.org**
The Center promotes renewable and energy-efficient technologies in urban communities. Academic and continuing education classes in solar PV installation, alternative vehicle technologies, and sustainable energy options are offered to students and public.

Cornell University Cooperative Extension, New York City

16 E. 34th St., 8th Flr. (5th Ave.), Murray Hill (Man), 212-340-2900
Mon–Fri 9am–5pm   **nyc.cce.cornell.edu/environment**
Environmental and science education, community improvement and sustainability, and professional development learning opportunities for teens, young adults, and adults through its Urban Environment Program.

Earth Celebrations

638 E. 6th St. (bet. Aves. B & C), Lower East Side (Man), 212-777-7969
earthcelebrations.com
Ecological awareness through art. Youth and adult art and ecology workshops, exhibitions, advocacy campaigns. School, garden, and community center partnerships. Offers students high school and college credits.

Emerging Green Builders of NY

1 Bowling Green, Ste. 419 (State St.), Battery Park (Man), 212-514-9380
Mon–Fri 9am–5:30pm   **egbny.com**
USGBC-affiliated coalition of New York students and young professionals promoting future leaders in the green building movement. Hosts green building seminars, tours, and social events in New York City. Volunteer opportunities available.

Five Borough Bicycle Club

891 Amsterdam Ave. (103rd St.), Manhattan Valley (Man), 212-932-2300 x115
Hours vary by event **5bbc.org**
Free year-round educational and recreational group rides in New York
City; offers ride leadership training for adults and extended trips outside
of the city.

Gateway National Recreation Area

718-354-4500
Sunrise to sunset **nps.gov/gate**
Conservation and educational programs for adults and children in five
parks, including the sustainably designed visitor center at Jamaica Bay
Wildlife Refuge.

Get Fresh

370 5th Ave. (5th St.), Park Slope (Bkn), 718-360-8469
Mon–Fri 11am–9pm Sat–Sun 11am–7pm **getfreshnyc.com**
Adult organic cooking classes focused on health and nutrition as well as food
sources and sustainability; cooking classes for kids (ages 3–18) educating on
healthy eating; gardening series on growing your own food, composting,
and planting herbs, vegetables, and urban fruit trees.

Green Depot

20 Rewe St. (Vandervoort Ave.), Williamsburg (Bkn), 718-782-2991
Mon–Fri 7am–6pm Sat 7am–1pm **greendepot.com**
Green Depot provides LEED tutoring and educational courses on indoor air
quality, environmental building, and green remodeling for building professionals and interested individuals.

Green Edge Collaborative

434A 9th St., Ste. 2, Brooklyn (Bkn)
greenedgennyc.org
Online platform gathering NYC residents to support sustainable dining
practices. Organizes monthly eco-eatery tours, local supper club potlucks,
composting, and other seasonal workshops year-round.

Greenpeace USA

153 Roebling St. (bet. Hope St. & Metropolitan Ave.), Williamsburg (Bkn),
718-486-6715
By appt. **greenpeace.org/usa**
Organization using nonviolent confrontation to expose global environmental problems and offer solutions. The Northeast campaigns focus on wind
power initiatives and putting an end to clear cutting.

Horticultural Society of New York

148 W. 37th St., 13th Flr. (bet. Broadway and 7th Ave.), Clinton (Man),
212-757-0915
Mon–Fri 10am–6pm **hsny.org**
The society enhances NYC's environmental and cultural life through horticultural outreach programs in schools, prisons, and underserved neighborhoods; extensive library with garden and art exhibitions.

Lower East Side Ecology Center

P.O. Box 20488, Lower East Side (Man), 212-477-4022
Hours vary by event **lesecologycenter.org**
Center offers recycling and composting programs, develops local stewardship of NYC's open spaces, and provides environmental education classes
for the community.

Being Involved

Municipal Art Society of New York

457 Madison Ave. (bet. E. 50th & E. 51st Sts.), Midtown (Man), 212-935-3960
Mon–Sat 10am–6pm **mas.org**
An 1890s organization focused on livable cities; "Preservation and Sustainability" theme in museum exhibits; classes, lectures, and tours are open to the public.

Natural Gourmet Institute

48 W. 21st St., 2nd Flr. (bet. 5th & 6th Aves.), Flatiron (Man), 212-645-5170
Mon–Fri 9am–10pm Sat–Sun 9am–6pm **naturalgourmetschool.com**
Chef training and public classes in health-supportive culinary arts and theory using local, organic, and sustainably produced ingredients whenever possible; public classes are available to the entire family.

New York Aquarium

602 Surf Ave. (W. 8th St.), Coney Island (Bkn), 718-220-5100
Daily 10am–4:30pm **nyaquarium.com**
Demonstrations and education programs for all ages, with 8,000 animals from marine and freshwater habitats.

New York Audubon Society

71 W. 23rd St., Ste. 1523 (6th Ave.), Flatiron (Man), 212-691-7483
Hours vary by event **nycaudubon.org/home**
Partnership with New York City schools to teach students about environmental conservation.

New York Botanical Garden

200th St. (Kazimiroff Blvd.), Bedford Park (Brx), 718-817-8777
Tue–Sun 10am–6pm **nybg.org**
Children's Gardens to Graduate Studies have living collections and topics including green roofing and "Gardening In a Changing Climate." This 250-acre living classroom features over 1 million plants representing all seven continents.

New York Hall of Science

47-01 111th St., Flushing Meadows-Corona Park (47th Ave.), Flushing (Qns), 718-669-0005
Seasonal hours **nyscience.org**
More than 400 hands-on exhibits for toddlers and adults. Educational programs for school-age visitors; recycling of rubber tires and graywater practiced.

New York Harbor School

400 Irving Ave., 4th Flr. (Woodbine Ave.), Bushwick (Bkn), 718-381-7100 x5101
Mon–Fri 8am–4pm **newyorkharborschool.org**
Program focused on estuaries, maritime industry, and riverine ecology training. High school relocates to a new eco-efficient facility on Governor's Island in the '09–10 school year.

New York Restoration Project

254 W. 31st St., 10th Flr. (bet. 7th & 8th Aves.), Flatiron (Man), 212-333-2552
Mon–Fri 9am–6pm **nyrp.org**
The project restores, develops, and revitalizes underserved parks, community gardens, and open spaces in New York City. Gardening education and volunteer opportunities available.

New York Sun Works

1841 Broadway, Ste. 200 (W. 60th St.), Lincoln Square (Man), 212-757-7560
Hours vary by event **nysunworks.org**
Free public classes on The Science Barge, a sustainable urban farm and educational facility demonstrating renewable energy and supporting sustainable urban food production.

Queens Botanical Garden

43-50 Main St. (bet. Dahlia & Elder Aves.), Flushing (Qns), 718-886-3800
Tues–Fri 8am–6pm Sat–Sun 8am–7pm **queensbotanical.org**
Sustainable gardens and culture, LEED-certified buildings, and the Queens Composting Project are hallmarks of this outdoor museum's environmental stewardship mission; offers Live Green tours and workshops.

River Project, The

Pier 40 at West St., 2nd Flr. (W. Houston St.), West Village (Man), 212-233-3030
Seasonal hours **riverproject.org**
Marine science field station protects and restores the ecosystem of the Hudson River estuary through scientific research, hands-on environmental education, and urban habitat improvement.

Shorewalkers

P.O. Box 20748, Cathedral Station, New York (Man), 212-330-7686
Hours by event **shorewalkers.org**
Volunteer-led waterway walks, trail building, lectures and small public talks given to build awareness on ecological, natural, and cultural aspects of NYC's coastal environments. Volunteer opportunities available.

Sixth Street Community Center

638 E. 6th St. (bet. Aves. A & B), Lower East Side (Man), 212-677-1863
Mon–Fri 10am–10pm **sixthstreetcenter.org**
Nonprofit focused on issues related to food, health, and the environment. Features The Organic Soul Cafe.

Solar One

2420 FDR Dr., Service Rd. E (E. 25th St.), Gramercy (Man), 212-505-6050
Mon–Fri 9am–5pm **solar1.org**
Classes ranging in length from two to three sessions, to 10 weeks on topics dealing with energy and green design.

Staten Island Botanical Garden

1000 Richmond Ter. (Delafield Pl.), Livingston (S.I.), 718-273-8200
Daily 8am–dusk **sibg.org**
A 20-acre wetlands restoration project, children's discovery classroom, Chinese scholar's garden, and composting classes are some of the education opportunities available to visitors.

Staten Island Museum

75 Stuyvesant Pl. (Wall St.), St. George (S.I.), 718-727-1135
Mon–Fri 1pm–5pm Sat 10am–5pm Sun 12pm–5pm
statenislandmuseum.org
Weekend ecology walks, April NatureFest, and daily natural science talks and classes for school children. By 2010, all 500,000 insect specimens will move to two geothermal LEED Silver–certified Landmark buildings now under construction.

Being Involved

U.S. Green Building Council
Alexander Hamilton U.S. Custom House, 1 Bowling Green, Ste. 419
(Canyon of Heroes), Battery Park (Man), 212-514-9380
Mon–Fri 9am–5pm **usgbcny.org**
Certification in and public workshops on LEED building standards and rating
system. Forums, master classes, and bimonthly introductions to teaching
and integrating sustainable design.

Wildman Steve Brill Foraging Tours
914-835-2153
Seasonal hours **wildmanstevebrill.com**
Teaches throughout the greater New York City area on topics such as edible
and medicinal wild plants, nature, science, ecology, history, folklore, and conservation. Call at least 24 hours in advance to reserve a tour spot

General Interest— Youth and Young Adults

Alley Pond Environmental Center
228-06 Northern Blvd. (228th St.), Douglaston (Qns), 718-229-4000
Mon–Sat 9am–4:30pm Sun 9:30pm–3:30pm **alleypond.com**
Private nonprofit corporation dedicated to establishing an awareness of the
environment and its preservation in an urban setting; offers lessons in ecology and life sciences for students from prekindergarten through high school
and beyond.

Bike New York
891 Amsterdam Ave. (W. 103rd St.), Upper West Side (Man), 212-932-2453
Hours vary by event **bikenewyork.org**
Promotes bicycling and bicycle safety through events and education. Its
Bicycle Education program offers free classes for adults and children.

Bronx Zoo
2300 Southern Blvd. (Bronx Park S.), E. Tremont (Brx), 718-220-5100
Daily 10am–4:30pm **bronxzoo.org**
The LEED-Gold Madagascar! exhibit opening in Summer '08 showcases
green construction and education; also offers cell phone recycling bins, the
FSC-wooded Tiger Mountain, and an Eco-Restroom with graywater garden.

Brooklyn Botanic Garden
900 Washington Ave. (Eastern Pkwy.), Prospect Heights (Bkn), 718-623-7200
Tue–Fri 8am–6pm Sat–Sun 10am–6pm **bbg.org**
Fifty-two-acre living museum hosting annual events to celebrate seasonal
plants, fruits, and vegetables. Urban composting project, volunteer "Garden
Guide" training, and a hands-on vegetable garden for kids and families.

Brooklyn Center for the Urban Environment
168 7th St. (3rd Ave.), Gowanus (Bkn), 718-788-8500
Mon–Fri 9am–5pm **bcue.org**
The Center offers hands-on family programs ranging from composting to
DIY projects using recycled materials.

Brooklyn Children's Museum
145 Brooklyn Ave. (St. Marks Ave.), Crown Heights (Bkn), 718-735-4400
Wed–Fri 1pm–6pm Sat–Sun 11am–6pm (schl. yr.) **brooklynkids.org**
LEED-certified, Vinoly-designed "green museum" reopened in Spring 2008;
retains its 1899 mission with interactive learning adventures through hands-
on exhibitions; now powered with solar PV and geothermal wells.

Central Park Zoo

830 5th Ave. (in Central Park at E. 64th St.), Central Park East (Man), 718-220-5100

Daily 10am–4:30pm **nyzoosandaquarium.com/cpz**

Rain forest, Antarctic, and barnyard education with green-themed zookeeper chats and tours offered; K–12, adult, and professional programs.

Christodora

1 E. 53rd St., Ste. 1401 (5th Ave.), Midtown (Man), 212-371-5225

christodora.org

Organization offering environmental education and leadership training to motivated New York City public school students. Wilderness programs take the students to the Manice Education Center in the Berkshire Mountains of Massachusetts on weekends and during school vacations.

Cornell University Cooperative Extension, New York City

16 E. 34th St., 8th Flr. (5th Ave.), Murray Hill (Man), 212-340-2900

Mon–Fri 9am–5pm **nyc.cce.cornell.edu/environment**

Environmental and science education, community improvement and sustainability, and professional development learning opportunities for teens, young adults, and adults through its Urban Environment Program.

Council on the Environment of New York City

51 Chambers St., Rm. 228 (bet. Broadway and Centre St.), Wall Street (Man), 212-788-7900

Mon–Fri 9am–5pm **cenyc.org**

The environmental program works with students grades 6–12 to learn about specific environmental issues and motivates students to organize and participate in environmental improvement projects in their neighborhoods, schools, and homes.

Earth Celebrations

638 E. 6th St. (bet. Aves. B & C), Lower East Side (Man), 212-777-7969

Hours vary by event **earthcelebrations.com**

Ecological awareness through art. Youth and adult art and ecology workshops, exhibitions, advocacy campaigns. School, garden, and community center partnerships. Offers students high school and college credits.

Gateway National Recreation Area

718-354-4500

Sunrise to sunset **nps.gov/gate**

Conservation and educational programs for adults and children in five parks, including the sustainably designed visitor center at Jamaica Bay Wildlife Refuge.

Get Fresh

370 5th Ave. (5th St.), Park Slope (Bkn), 718-360-8469

Mon–Fri 11am–9pm Sat–Sun 11am–7pm **getfreshnyc.com**

Adult organic cooking classes focused on health and nutrition as well as food sources and sustainability; cooking classes for kids (ages 3–18) educating on healthy eating; gardening series on growing your own food, composting, and planting herbs, vegetables, and urban fruit trees.

Greenbelt Conservancy Environmental Education Department, The

200 Nevada Ave. (Rockland Ave.), Todt Hill (S.I.), 718-667-7475
Hours vary by event **sigreenbelt.org/about/edcenter/edcenter.htm**
A federal landmark educational resource augmenting science curricula for school students. Children engage in hands-on learning about local habitats, wildlife, and natural history. Summer camp sessions, studio art classes, hikes, and school vacation programs. Special programming available for senior adults, educators, and the general public.

Habana Works

757 Fulton St. (S. Portland Ave.), Fort Greene (Bkn), 718-858-9500
Mon, Wed–Sun 12pm–12am **ecoeatery.com**
Free weekend workshops on ecology and recycling for kids; monthly workshops on sustainable energy.

Magnolia Tree Earth Center

677 Lafayette Ave. (bet. Marcy & Tompkins Aves.), Bedford-Stuyvesant (Bkn), 718-387-2116
Mon–Fri 9am–6pm Sat 10am–8pm **magnoliatreeearthcenter.org**
Training for the young adult Tree Corps. Hosts the local CSA in its Hattie Carthan Garden; stages the annual Garden Horizons career conference for middle schoolers.

New York Hall of Science

47-01 111th St., Flushing Meadows-Corona Park (47th Ave.), Flushing (Qns), 718-669-0005
Seasonal hours **nyscience.org**
More than 400 hands-on exhibits for toddlers and adults. Educational programs for school-age visitors; recycling of rubber tires and graywater practiced.

Prospect Park Zoo

450 Flatbush Ave. (in Prospect Park), Prospect Park East (Bkn), 718-220-5100
Daily 10am–4:30pm **prospectparkzoo.com**
Kids can see alpaca haircuts at the Fleece Festival, with guided tours and green-themed zookeeper chats; also offers professional, adult, and K–12 programs.

Queens Botanical Garden

43-50 Main St. (bet. Dahlia & Elders Aves.), Flushing (Qns), 718-886-3800
Tues–Fri 8am–6pm Sat–Sun 8am–7pm **queensbotanical.org**
Sustainable gardens and culture, LEED–certified buildings, and the Queens Composting Project are hallmarks of this outdoor museum's environmental stewardship mission; offers Live Green tours and workshops.

Queens Zoo

53-51 111th St. (bet. 53rd & 54th Aves.), Corona (Qns), 718-220-5100
Daily 10am–4:30pm **nyzoosandaquarium.com/qz**
Guided tours, zookeeper habitat chats from buffalo plains to pudu savannas, and adult and K–12 programs are offered.

Recycle-A-Bicycle

35 Pearl St. (Plymouth St.), DUMBO (Bkn), 718-858-2972
Mon–Sat 12pm–7pm **recycleabicycle.org**
Nonprofit environmental education and job training program for New York City youth. Repairs and reintroduces donated bicycles to the community through earn-a-bike programs in schools and sales from its nonprofit retail locations.

Roots & Shoots New York City

675 3rd Ave., Ste. 315, Murray Hill (Man.), 646-289-5009 **rootsandshoots.org**
Youth-driven network where young people and adults come together to
share ideas and implement community service projects that connect global
environmental issues with local initiatives.

Staten Island Botanical Garden

100 Richmond Ter. (Delafield Pl.), Livingston (S.I.), 718-273-8200
Daily 8am–dusk   **sibg.org**
A 20-acre wetlands restoration project, childrem's discovery classroom,
Chinese scholar's garden, and composting classes are some of the educa-
tional opportunities available to visitors.

Staten Island Children's Museum

1000 Richmond Ter. (Snug Harbor Cultural Center), St. George (S.I.),
718-273-2060
Tue–Sun 12pm–5pm **statenislandkids.org**
Kids K–12 get hands-on experience to build critical thinking about eco-issues
facing their generation. Exhibits include green building, solar panels, rainwater turbines, and skylight wind scoops.

Staten Island Museum

75 Stuyvesant Pl. (Wall St.), St. George (S.I.), 718-727-1135
Mon–Fri 1pm–5pm Sat 10am–5pm Sun 12pm–5pm
statenislandmuseum.org
Weekend ecology walks, April NatureFest, and daily natural science talks
and classes for school children. By 2010, all 500,000 insect specimens will
move to two geothermal LEED Silver–certified landmark buildings now
under construction.

Staten Island Zoo

614 Broadway (Clarence T. Barrett Park), West Brighton (S.I.), 718-442-3100
Daily 10am–4:45pm **statenislandzoo.org**
Zoofari Summer Camp, Radical Rainforest, the Touring Zoo van, and Breakfast with Beasts are key programs with eco-components; features organically
managed grounds and professional seminars.

WRITE A REVIEW

So many great organizations are providing a means
for activism, learning, and involvement in environmental issues. What are your experiences with these
groups? Have you checked out any of the classes and
workshops? If so, how would you rate them? Have
you volunteered with any of these organizations?
What was your experience? On **greenopia.com**, you
can share your thoughts and also list some of your
favorite groups or organizations for others to see.

Being Involved

References

Now that you have a guide to help you find the most environmentally friendly businesses and resources around New York City, we've included some additional information to help you expand your knowledge, invite your further study, and simply help you make the most out of Greenopia.

First, we have included a section highlighting a number of books that we really like—and we think you will, too, whether you're looking for a great cookbook, a book to help you design and build that green home you have been dreaming about, or if you're just looking to read about the environment and our changing world. All of our books have been reviewed by Greenopia staff and many were written by our local expert advisors in New York, Los Angeles, and San Francisco (where Greenopia is also available).

In addition, you'll find our own "Greenopia Glossary" filled with terms we have used and **highlighted** throughout the guide— and more. Some will be familiar; others will be ones just starting to gain currency in the green world. Also, when you are ready to turn your attention to making your work life greener, you will want to check out the tips we've provided in "Greening Your Workplace or Business: Ten Steps You Can Take to Improve Sustainability" on page 284. You can start today to make your job or your business more eco-friendly.

And to help you locate our listings, we have included a regional map showing the areas of the city we researched. The alphabetical and borough/category indexes will help you find a business near you. We encourage you to flip to these indexes often—dog-ear your favorite pages—and support all of the businesses, services, and organizations we've researched and presented here for you.

Greenopia®

For more information about Greenopia, visit **greenopia.com** where you'll find more news, features, and practical tips for living green. We invite you to join our online community where you can write a review about any of the businesses you find here, share your experiences, and tell us what's happening in your own community.

References

Books We Recommend

Eating Out/Eating In

The Candle Café Cookbook: More Than 150 Enlightened Recipes from New York's Renowned Vegetarian Restaurant
Joy Pierson and Bart Potenza, with Barbara Scott-Goodman

Vegan food from the top-rated New York restaurant. Includes tips on cooking beans and grains.

Everyday Greens: Home Cooking from Greens, the Celebrated Vegetarian Restaurant
Annie Somerville

Innovative vegetarian cooking. Title refers to Zen concept of every-day mindfulness. Recipes vary in complexity; all are inspired by readily available fresh and sometimes unusual ingredients.

Grub: Ideas for an Urban Organic Kitchen
Anna Lappé and Bryant Terry

Promotes benefits of sustainable eating. Provides how-tos for creating an affordable organic kitchen. Includes dozens of delec-table recipes.

Hollywood Dish: More Than 150 Delicious, Healthy Recipes from Hollywood's Chef to the Stars
Akasha Richmond

Healthy and chic food with recipes and stories from an A-list Hollywood chef.

The Santa Monica Farmer's Market Cookbook: Seasonal Foods, Simple Recipes and Stories from the Market and Farm
Amelia Saltsman

The author shares her knowledge of and enthusiasm for the Santa Monica market. Recipes are delicious and accessible.

Your Organic Kitchen: The Essential Guide to Selecting and Cooking Organic Foods
Jesse Ziff Cool

Easy-to-prepare, delicious, healthy recipes listed by season. Clear format. Includes main dishes, side dishes, and desserts.

Goods

Stuff: The Secret Lives of Everyday Things (New Report, No. 4)
John C. Ryan and Alan Thein Durning

Documents a day in the life of the average North American consumer and unravels the hidden costs of everything around us. Traces the environmental impact of consumer decisions.

Sustainable Fashion and Textiles: Design Journeys
Kate Fletcher

An in-depth look into sustainable fashion and textile products, systems, and materials. Discusses resource issues, waste, and implications for users and makers of fashion.

Pets

The Holistic Animal Handbook: A Guidebook to Nutrition, Health, and Communication

Kate Solisti-Mattelon and Patrice Mattelon

Detailed information and tools for offering whole-being care to your companion animals. Focuses on dogs, cats, and horses.

House

Green Building & Remodeling for Dummies

Eric Corey Freed

Step-by-step guide to Earth-friendly construction. Shows how to build responsibly, reduce waste, save money, and preserve the environment.

The Passive Solar House: The Complete Guide to Heating and Cooling Your Home

James Kachadorian

Proven techniques for building homes that heat and cool themselves using readily available materials and methods.

Prescriptions for a Healthy House: A Practical Guide for Architects, Builders, and Homeowners

Paula Baker-Laporte, Erica Elliot, and John Banta

Shows how to create interior spaces that promote physical health and well-being. Addresses every aspect of the construction process.

Women in Green: Voices of Sustainable Design

Kira Gould and Lance Hosey

Implications for design industry of women's support of environmental causes. Encompasses viewpoints from architects, designers, consultants, policymakers, educators, and students.

Home

Green This! Volume 1: Greening Your Cleaning

Deirdre Imus

Insights, advice, and practical solutions for less-toxic cleaning.

Green Living: The E Magazine Handbook for Living Lightly on the Earth

By the Editors of E/The Environmental Magazine

Practical tips for living a healthier, more eco-friendly life. Smart food choices, natural health care, socially responsible investing, healthy home care. Chapter-by-chapter resource list.

Naturally Clean: The Seventh Generation Guide to Safe and Healthy, Non-Toxic Cleaning

Jeffrey Hollender, Geoff Davis, and Meika Hollender

Useful information on chemicals and cleaners to avoid. Good resource section.

Travel

Code Green: Experiences of a Lifetime

Kerry Lorimer

Travel publisher Lonely Planet's first eco-tourism guide. Offers practical tips for socially and environmentally responsible travelers, including how to immerse oneself in a culture and make a positive economic impact at the same time.

Fragile Earth: Views of a Changing World

Collins UK Staff (ed.)

Stunning photographs of the dramatic changes affecting today's world. Features satellite imaging and outstanding cartography.

Being Involved

The Big Green Apple:
Your Guide to Eco-Friendly Living in New York City

Ben Jervey

Specific actions and simple ways residents and visitors alike can make a difference. Explains why addressing environmental problems is important and how lifestyle choices can lower one's impact.

The Consumer's Guide to Effective Environmental Choices:
Practical Advice from the Union of Concerned Scientists

Michael Brower and Warren Leon

A guide to living responsibly. Outlines choices consumers can make to reduce their environmental impact. Includes priority actions in transportation, food, and household operations.

An Inconvenient Truth: The Planetary Emergency of Global Warming and What We Can Do About It

Al Gore

Eloquently outlines the necessity for immediate action to reduce global warming.

The Lazy Environmentalist:
Your Guide to Easy, Stylish, Green Living

Josh Dorfman

Convenient and important actions to take in every aspect of life, from clothing selection to furniture choice. Identifies specific brands that are good for the planet.

Stop Global Warming: The Solution Is You! An Activist's Guide

Laurie David

Provides inspiration for global warming activists. Raises public awareness. Invites action. Lots of resource listings.

Worldchanging: A User's Guide for the 21st Century

Alex Steffen (ed.)

A compendium of the latest and most innovative solutions, ideas, and inventions for building a sustainable, livable, prosperous future.

Go to the library.

Greening Your Workplace or Business

Ten Steps to Improve Sustainability

If you'd like to make a difference by greening your own business (large or small) or your work environment, here are some easy steps you can take or share with your employer:

1 Assess and Plan—If you aren't measuring resource consumption, you won't know what improvement will look like. Pick one thing—paper, fuel, electricity—and measure what you're consuming over time and what it costs. Could you save gas by not idling while making deliveries? Develop some simple actions for reduction and test the results.

2 Involve and Reward Your Employees or Customers—Invite your coworkers, even your customers, to weigh in, look around, and brainstorm together.

3 Focus on Energy Efficiency—Even if you've already changed all your light bulbs to CFLs, try turning off all your lights during the day and walking through your workplace to see where you can eliminate artificial lighting without compromising effectiveness or safety. Set your thermostats more efficiently to reduce your heating or cooling bills and save energy. You may also be able to purchase green power directly from your current electric company for only a small but worthwhile premium.

4 Look at Your Inputs—Whether you're a manufacturing company, a service provider, or you telecommute from a home office, you have to consume resources in order to produce your product or provide a service. Make the switch from using throwaway or non-recyclable materials to reusable, recyclable, or even postconsumer recycled materials.

5 Don't Forget the *Before and After*—Your company's environmental impact starts *before* your products are made and continues *after* they are in your customers' hands. Take a look at how you source your products, and what happens to your product packaging once products are purchased and after customers are finished. Source your supplies and raw materials locally to reduce their shipping impact. And remember that using environmentally friendly, or most importantly, minimal or no packaging saves valuable resources and keeps trash out of landfills.

6 Reduce Waste—As a restaurant or an event planner, could you use recyclable or compostable containers for take-out or for the events you organize? Even though some cities are already moving to ban their use, take the lead by replacing your polystyrene containers or disposable plates with biodegradable or compostable ones.

7 **Communicate with Your Customers**—When you improve some-thing that impacts the environment or your customers' health, tell them about it—make sure they know what you did, how you did it, and what difference it makes to them and to the planet. Your suc-cesses are examples for your customers and your employees, who, in turn, can inspire others to do the same.

8 **Help Your Customers Do Their Part**—Your customers want to help, too. If you're a dry cleaner, make it easy for or reward your customers when they bring back plastic bags and wire hangers for recycling or reuse—or, better yet, arrange for reusable alternatives for your regular customers.

9 **Keep Big Changes in Mind**—From time to time, you'll have the opportunity to make big decisions that can have even bigger impacts. Locate close to public transit. When it's time to replace equipment, recycle or donate the old and purchase new Energy Star or other energy-efficient models.

10 **Take One Step, Then Take Another**—A journey starts with a single step, but it doesn't end there! Make the sustainability review process a continuous part of your business, your workday, and even your personal strategy. Periodically fine-tune your plan and adjust as your business grows or needs change. You'll make a big difference.

Remember, each action, big or small, can spark a chain of events that will impact our planet and your company's bottom line for the better.

Brand Neutral   OPPORTUNITY green

Information provided by Opportunity Green and Brand Neutral. Founded by Karen Solomon and Mike Flynn, Opportunity Green offers conferences, salons, and retreats for businesses and individuals to explore ways to implement social, environ-mental, and economic sustainability (**opportunitygreen.com**). Brand Neutral advises companies on eco-efficiency and eco-branding (**brandneutral.com**).

References

Greenopia Glossary

Alternative energy

Energy from sources that do not deplete natural resources (such as solar, wind, biomass, or geothermal).

Alternative fuels

Vehicle fuels that are nonpetroleum-based, including biodiesel, ethanol, electricity, and hydrogen.

Biodiesel

An alternative fuel derived from biological sources, biodiesel usually comes from recycled or virgin vegetable oils. Biodiesel is cleaner for the air than petrol-diesel and releases less carbon monoxide, aromatic hydrocarbons, and particulate matter (soot).

Biodynamic farming

Begun about seventy years ago, biodynamic farming uses basic organic practices but adds special plant, animal, and mineral preparations to the soil and follows the rhythm of the sun, moon, planets, and stars to create a self-supporting farming eco-system.

Building Performance Institute (BPI)

A multi-stakeholder group offering national training, certification, and quality control for building-performance contractors. **bpi.org**.

Carbon footprint

The effect of actions and lifestyle as measured in units of carbon dioxide. Key contributors include transportation (air and car), and electricity use. Other factors include diet (the average grocery store item travels fifteen hundred miles before it reaches the shopper) and clothing (cotton grown in Turkey, sewn in China, sold in the United States). For more information on offsetting your carbon footprint, see page 225.

Carbon offsetting

Mitigating the carbon dioxide emitted by a certain activity is called carbon offsetting, whereby an equal amount of global warming pollution is removed or prevented. Common ways of offsetting carbon dioxide are tree planting, renewable energy projects, and methane gas capture.

Carbon trading

A system in which carbon credits can be exchanged in the open market to achieve economical limits on carbon dioxide pollution. Carbon trading is one way that countries can meet the reductions called for by the Kyoto Protocol.

Circle of Life Certification

Circle of Life promotes sustainable growing practices designed to bring quality plants in biodegradable pots to home gardeners. **circleoflifeplants.com**.

Community-supported agriculture (CSA)

CSAs let consumers buy a share in a local farm operation. Members or "shareholders" of the farm typically pay in advance to cover farming costs. In return, they receive shares of the farm's produce throughout the growing season. By direct sales to community members, growers receive better prices for their crops and a steadier income.

Direct trade

Though not a formal certification, *direct trade* is a term used when coffee roasters buy beans directly from farmers. Boutique roasters and coffee shops create these direct relationships to improve farmer profits and to gain better control of crop quality and farming methods. (*See also* Fair trade, below.)

EcoBroker

EcoBroker Certification is awarded to licensed real estate professionals who have completed EcoBroker International's continuing education curriculum in energy efficiency, green marketing, and other green home attributes. **ecobroker.com**.

Electronic waste (E-waste)

Any broken or unwanted electrical or electronic appliance. This includes computers, entertainment electronics, mobile phones, handheld devices, and other items. Many components of such equipment are toxic, and exposure to the heavy metals they contain can be hazardous.

Equator Principles

A financial industry benchmark for determining, assessing, and managing social and environmental risk in project financing. **equator-principles.com**.

Ethanol

An alcohol fuel made from starchy feedstocks such as corn and sugarcane.

Fair trade

Fair trade certification seeks to help farmers in the developing world get a fair price for their crops. It also helps to maintain humane working conditions, agricultural traditions, and ecological diversity. Fair trade certification can also have significant environmental benefits. (See page 43 for more information on fair trade.)

Farmers' market

Often held outdoors, farmers' markets bring together growers and craftspeople to sell their products directly to the public. There are many farmers' markets in New York City, including those under the Greenmarket program with its rigorous "grow your own" policy.

Forest Stewardship Council (FSC)

An international third-party certifier promoting responsible forest management. The FSC Certification label marks products like wood and paper that come from certified forests and tree plantations. **www.fsc.org**.

Formaldehyde

A known human carcinogen that is found in many products, from nail polish to plywood.

Genetic engineering (GE) and genetically modified organisms (GMOs)

Unlike traditional plant breeding, genetic engineering manipulates the genes and DNA of plants and animals to create new life forms, or genetically modified organisms (GMOs). This creates the risk of new and unpredictable health and environmental impacts.

Geothermal

A system that draws on the temperatures found below the Earth's surface to generate energy or heat.

Graywater

Any water that has been used in the home, except water from toilets, is called graywater. Dish, shower, sink, and laundry water comprise 50 to 80 percent of residential "waste" water. This may be reused for other purposes, especially landscape irrigation, and results in significantly lower fresh water use.

Green Seal™ Certification

Ensures that a product or service meets rigorous, science-based environmental standards set by Green Seal, a nonprofit organization. **greenseal.org**.

Greenmarket

Greenmarket is a network of New York City farmers' markets whose policies, with a few exceptions, ensure that its farmers sell only produce they have grown themselves. **cenyc.org/greenmarket**.

Indoor Air Quality Association (IAQA)

The Indoor Air Quality Association (IAQA) is a nonprofit, multi-disciplined organization, dedicated to promoting the exchange of indoor environmental information, through education and research, for the safety and well-being of the general public. **iaqa.org**.

Integrated pest management (IPM)

A pest management strategy that seeks to control pests through nonchemical and low-toxicity methods. This can include using traps to monitor pests, introducing beneficial insects, and applying pesticides so they pose a minimal hazard.

International Ground Source Heat Pump Association (IGSHPA)

A nonprofit association promoting the design, development, and installation of geothermal energy systems. Offers training and accreditation to ground source heat pump installers (look for "Accredited Installers") and other certification programs. **igshpa.okstate.edu**.

Leadership in Energy and Environmental Design (LEED)

The LEED Green Building Rating System is the U.S. Green Building Council's national benchmark for the design, construction, and operation of high-performance green buildings. The U.S. Green Building Council also offers a LEED-accreditation exam for building professionals who have demonstrated a thorough understanding of green building practices and principles. **usgbc.org/leed**.

Material safety data sheet (MSDS)

A material safety data sheet is designed to provide both workers and emergency personnel with the proper procedures for handling or working with a particular substance. MSDS's include information such as physical data (melting point, boiling point, flash point etc.), toxicity, health effects, first aid, reactivity, storage, disposal, protective equipment, and spill/leak procedures.

National Biodiesel Accreditation Commission (NBAC)

The nonprofit body that develops and upholds the BQ-9000 standard, the basic certification for biodiesel producers. **bq-9000.org/nbac**.

New York City Pedicab Owners' Association (NYCPOA)

A not-for-profit trade association that acts on behalf of responsible pedicab owners citywide. **nycpedicabassociation.org**.

New York Solar Energy Industries Association (NYSEIA)

A nonprofit membership and trade association of solar thermal and solar PV installers. **nyseia.org**.

New York State Energy Research and Development Authority (NYSERDA)

A public-benefit corporation that provides certification for solar photovoltaic installers. **nyserda.org**.

North American Board of Certified Energy Practitioners (NABCEP)

A nonprofit agency offering national credentialing and certification of renewable energy professionals. **nabcep.org**.

Organic certification

Organic certification means that a grower or food processor has demonstrated to an organic certification agency that only acceptable organic methods have been used. Farmers need to respond to site-specific conditions by integrating cultural, biological, and mechanical practices that foster the cycling of resources, promote ecological balance, and conserve biodiversity. Certified organic farms and organic processors have been inspected and must keep extensive records to document their compliance with organic rules. (See "Organic Standards for Food" on page 44 for more info.)

Parabens

A family of preservatives commonly used in cosmetics and foods.

Passive solar

The process of using or capturing energy from the sun to heat spaces, water, or pools, or for other heating purposes.

Photovoltaic (PV)

A solar power technology that uses solar cells to convert light from the sun into electricity.

Polyvinyl chloride (PVC)

PVC is commonly used for plastic pipes and outdoor furniture. It is seldom, if ever, recyclable. PVC plastics often contain phthalates, toxic chemicals that make plastics soft and flexible, and a by-product of its manufacture is dioxin.

Post-consumer waste (PCW) and Post-consumer recycled content

Post-consumer waste (PCW) is paper that has been used by the end consumer and then collected for recycling from various recycling programs. This is the best paper to buy as it uses and creates demand for paper that would normally end up in the landfill. No trees are cut down for making this paper.

The actual percentage of the recycled and post-consumer recycled content is important to note when buying paper, e.g. 50% recycled 20% PCW, means 50% comes from virgin wood, 30% is pre-consumer recycled and 20% is post-consumer recycled.

Processed-chlorine free (PCF)

Recycled paper in which the recycled content is unbleached or bleached without chlorine derivatives.

Rainforest Alliance

A private nonprofit organization that promotes sustainable agriculture, responsible forestry, and eco-tourism through its certification and labeling system. For more on Rainforest Alliance certification, see page 43. **rainforest-alliance.org**.

Recovered material/fiber

Paper materials that have been separated, diverted, or removed from the solid waste stream for the purpose of use, reuse, or recycling.

Renewable energy certificate (REC)

Also known as renewable energy credits, these tradable commodities certify that one megawatt hour of electricity has been generated renewably and fed into the power grid.

Socially responsible investing/investments (SRI)

An approach to investing that seeks to maximize financial returns as well as social and environmental benefits.

Totally chlorine free (TCF)

Virgin paper produced without chlorine or chlorine derivatives.

U.S. Green Building Council (USGBC)

A nonprofit membership organization made up of leaders from diverse sectors of the building industry. The USGBC administers the LEED building standard, and its goal is to promote buildings that are environmentally responsible and healthy for occupants. **usgbc.org**.

VeriFlora® Certification

A sustainability certification program for fresh-cut flowers and potted plants. **veriflora.org**.

Volatile organic compounds (VOCs)

VOCs are emitted as gases from certain solids or liquids. VOCs include a variety of chemicals, some of which may have short- and long-term adverse health effects. VOCs are especially hazardous indoors, where concentrations may be up to ten times higher than outdoors. New carpet, paint, and interior finishes are common sources of VOCs in the home. Look for a products labeled "low-VOC," "no-VOC," or "zero-VOC."

The Five Boroughs

These maps show the areas we researched and the relative placement of neighborhoods where you can find the businesses listed in the guide. These maps are not drawn to scale and are included for reference only.

Inwood

George Washington Brg

9A

Washington Heights

Harlem River

Central Harlem

Henry Hudson Pky

Broadway

Morningside Heights

Manhattan Valley

East Harlem

Triborough Brg

Randalls-Wards Island

Upper West Side

Yorkville

Hudson River

Upper East Side

Lincoln Square

Fdr Dr

Lenox Hill

Lincoln Tunl

Clinton

Sutton Place

Roosevelt Island

Midtown

Murray Hill

Midtown South

Turtle Bay

Chelsea

Tudor City

11th Ave

Flatiron

Gramercy

I-495

West Village

Stuyvesant Town

9A

Union Square

Holland Tunl

Greenwich Village

East Village

Fdr Dr

NoHo

SoHo

Lower East Side

Tribeca

Little Italy

Battery Park City

Civic Center

Chinatown

Manhattan Brg

East River

Financial District

Brooklyn Brg

Brooklyn Battery Tunl

Governors Island

Manhattan

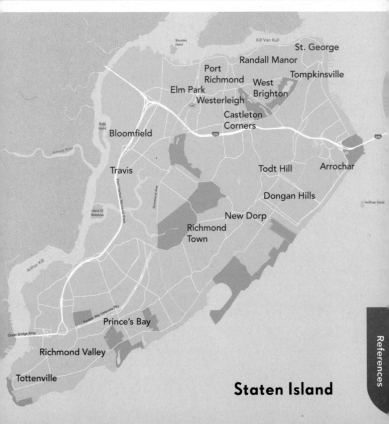

The Bronx

Fieldston
Riverdale
Wakefield
Norwood
Williamsbridge
Bedford Park
Fordham
University
Heights
Pelham
Gardens
Morris
Heights
Mount Hope
Pelham Parkway
East Tremont
Pelham Bay
City
Island
Mount Eden
West
Van Nest
High Bridge
Farms
Eastchester Bay
Concourse
Concourse
Village
Soundview
Melrose
Throgs Neck
Mott Haven
Hunts Point

East River

Rikers Island

Randalls
Wards Island

Jerome Ave
Henry Hudson Pky
Bronx And Pelham Pky E
Grand Concourse
Cross Bronx Expy
Cross Bronx Expy
Bruckner Expy
Hutchinson River Pky
Harlem River
Triborough Bridge

St. George
Randall Manor
Port
Richmond
Tompkinsville
Elm Park
West
Brighton
Westerleigh
Castleton
Corners
Bloomfield
Todt Hill
Arrochar
Travis
Dongan Hills
New Dorp
Richmond
Town
Prince's Bay
Richmond Valley
Tottenville

Shooters
Island
Kill Van Kull
Prahs
Island
Island Of
Meadows
Arthur Kill
Outer Bridge Xing
Korean War Veterans Pky
Hoffman
Island

References

Staten Island

Brooklyn/Queens

Mill Creek

kensack River

Hudson River

Steinway

278

Astoria Grand Central Pky

Ravenswood

Jac
He

Woodside

Long Island City Elr

495 Queens Blvd

Sunnyside

Greenpoint

Brooklyn-Queens Expy 278

East River

South Side

Manhattan Brg Williamsburg East
Williamsburg Ridgewood

Brooklyn Brg DUMBO Williamsburg

Vinegar Hill

Brooklyn Battery Tunl Brooklyn
Heights Bushwick

Governors
Island Downtown Clinton Hill

278 Fort Greene Bedford Stuyvesant

Cobble Hill Boerum
Hill

Carroll
Gardens Prospect Heights

Park Slope Crown Heights

Red Hook Brownsville

Gowanus East Ne

Upper New York Bay Prospect Lefferts
Gardens

Brooklyn-Queens Expy Windsor
Terrace Prospect
Park South

East Flatbush

Ditmas Park Canarsie

Flatbush Ave

Flatlands

Sunset Park

Beth Pky Kensington Flatbush

4th Ave Borough Park

Bay Ridge Mill Basin

Marine
Park

278 Bensonhurst

Gravesend

Sheepshead
Bay Beth Pky Flatbush Ave

Lower New York Bay

Hoffman Island Coney
Island Brighton
Beach

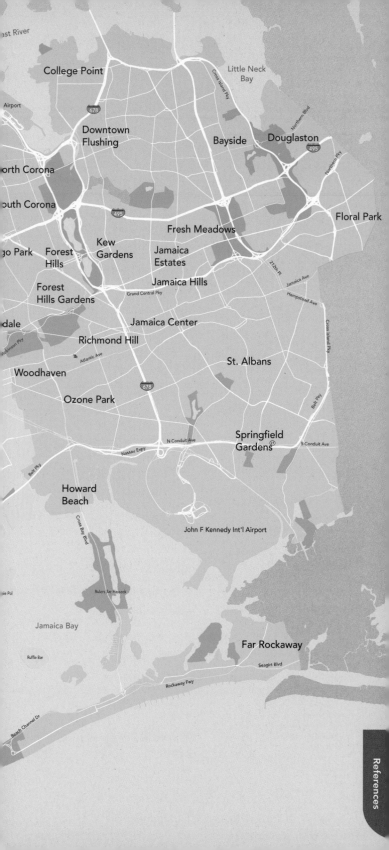

Borough/Category Index

Bronx

Alternative Energy Contractors

Menocal Contracting, Inc., 157
Schildwachter Fuel Oil, 158

Auto Sales and Services

(see Vehicle Manufacturers, Dealerships, and Maintenance)

Bikes, Scooters, and Other Alternatives

New York Motor Cycle, 234

Cafés

(see Restaurants and Cafés)

Cleaning Services

Gonsalves Cleaning and Restoration, 203

Day Spas

WellSpring Holistic Health Center & Day Spa, 115

Dealerships, Auto

(see Vehicle Manufacturers, Dealerships, and Maintenance)

Dry and Wet Cleaners

Kleenofab, 199
Quality Cleaners, 200

Environmental Education

Bronx Zoo, 274
Center for Sustainable Energy at Bronx Community College, 270
CUNY—Bronx Community College, 265
Gateway School for Environmental Research and Technology @ Stevenson, 269
Manhattan College, 266
New York Botanical Garden, 272

Environmental Organizations

Bronx River Alliance, 257
For A Better Bronx, 258
Gaia Institute, The, 259
Green Worker Cooperatives, 259
La Familia Verde, 260
Rocking The Boat, 262
Sustainable South Bronx, 262
Wildlife Conservation Society, 263

Fueling Stations

Con Edison—Van Nest Service Center, 241

Garden Supplies

Dimitri's Garden Center, 185

Greenmarkets, Farmers' Markets, and CSAs

Bissel Gardens Farmers' Market, 75
Bronx Borough Hall Greenmarket, 72
City Island CSA, 80
Harvest Home Forest Avenue Market, 76
Harvest Home Jacobi Market, 76
Harvest Home Morris Park Market, 76
Harvest Home Mt. Eden Avenue Market, 77
Harvest Home Sunday Market, 77
Healthy Kids CSA, 82
Hunts Point Farmers' Market, 77
La Familia Verde Farmers' Market, 77
Lincoln Hospital Greenmarket, 73
New York Botanical Garden Farmers' Market, 78
Northeast Bronx Farmers' Market, 78
Norwood CSA, 83
Poe Park Greenmarket, 74
Riverdale CSA, 83
Sister's Hill Farm CSA, 84
South Bronx Community Garden Market, The, 78
South Bronx CSA, 84
Taqwa Community Farm Stand, 78
United Tremont CSA, 85
Van Cortlandt Village CSA, 85

Grocery Stores

(see also Specialty Markets)

Good 'N Natural, 55
Healthy Life Nutritional Center, 56
Probiotics, 60
Riverdale Health Food Store, 61
South Bronx Food Cooperative, 61
Sundial, 62
Vegan's Delight, LLC, 63

Hair and Nail Salons

Aria Hair, 107
Pure Salon, 109

Juice Bars

H.I.M. Ital Restaurant & Juice Bar, 36
Probiotics, 38

Nurseries and Garden Supplies

Dimitri's Garden Center, 185

Manhattan

Alphabetical Index